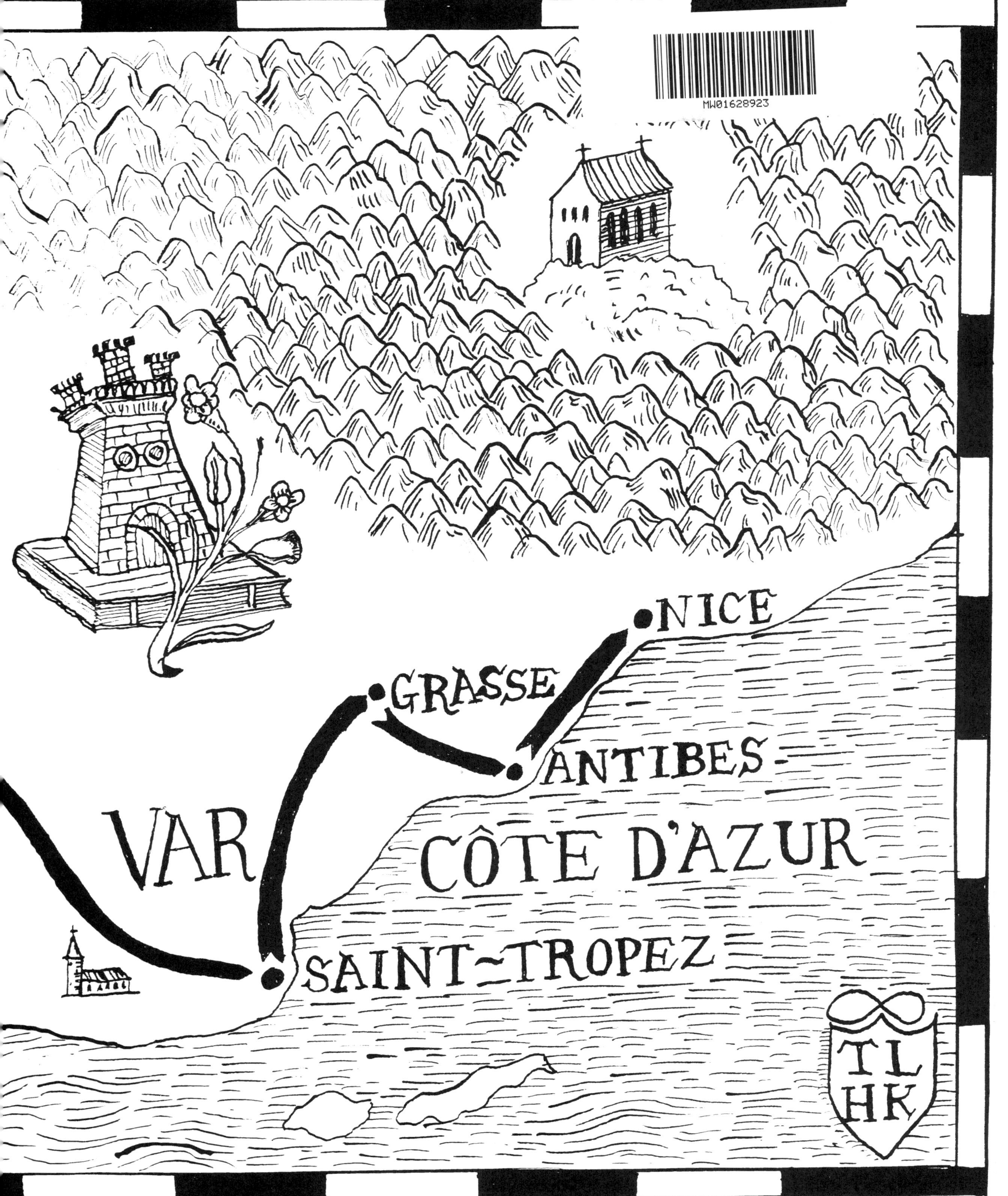
MW01628923
NICE
GRASSE
ANTIBES
VAR
CÔTE D'AZUR
SAINT-TROPEZ
TL
HK

GRAND TOUR PROVENCE

HANNES KRAUSE
TIM LABENDA

THE RENAISSANCE OF REFINED TRAVEL

ILLUSTRATIONENS BY
JOSEPH DUPRÉ

teNeues

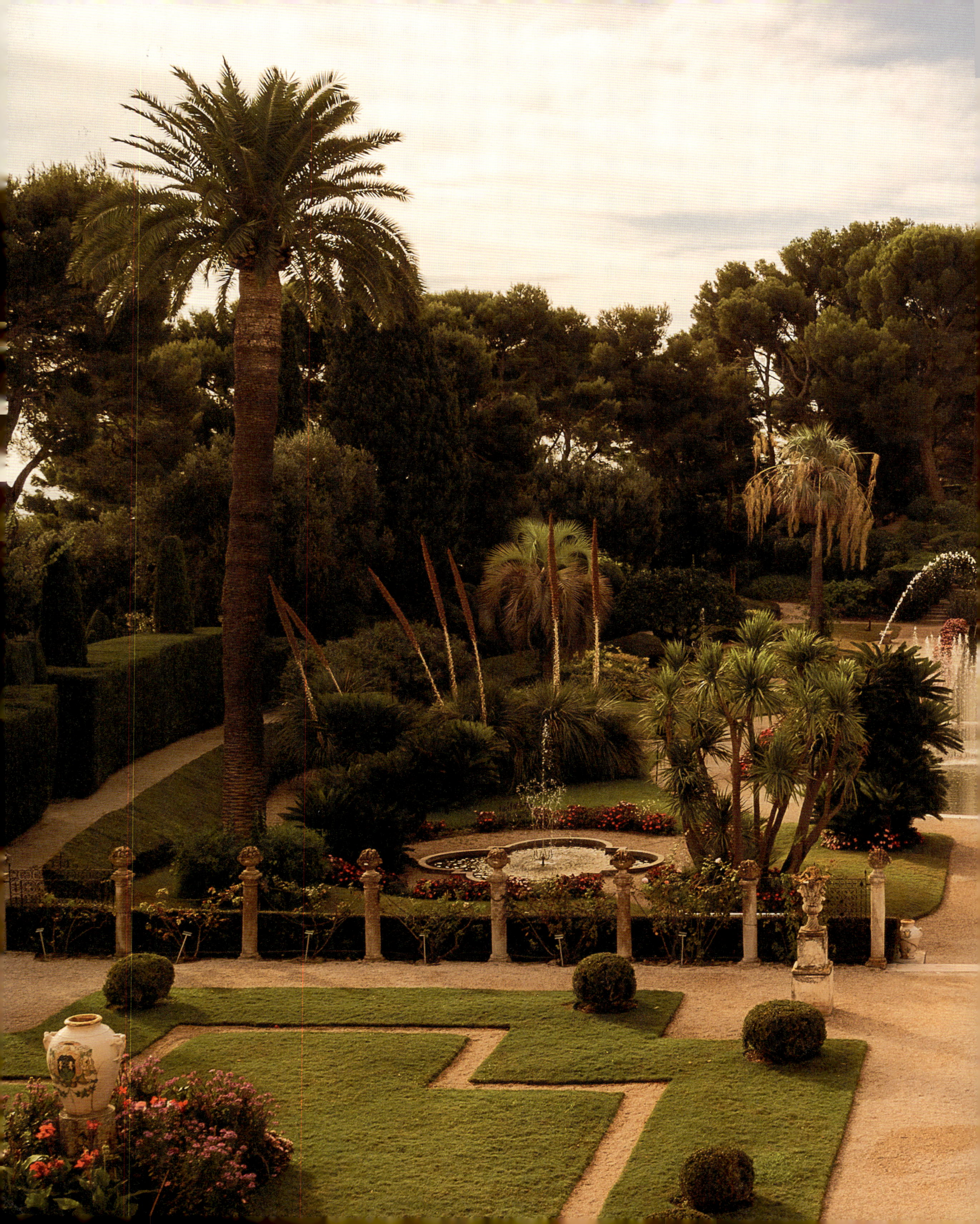

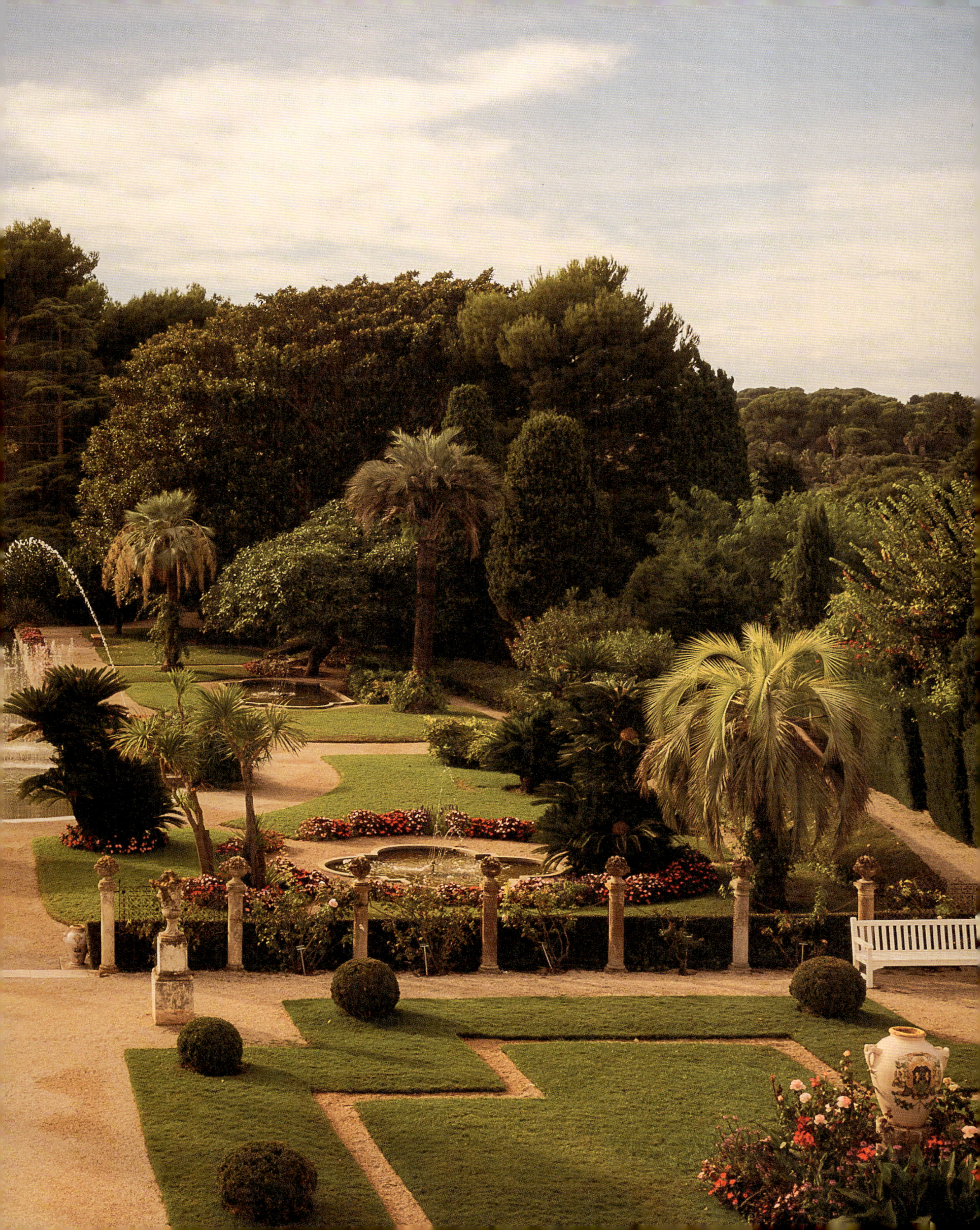

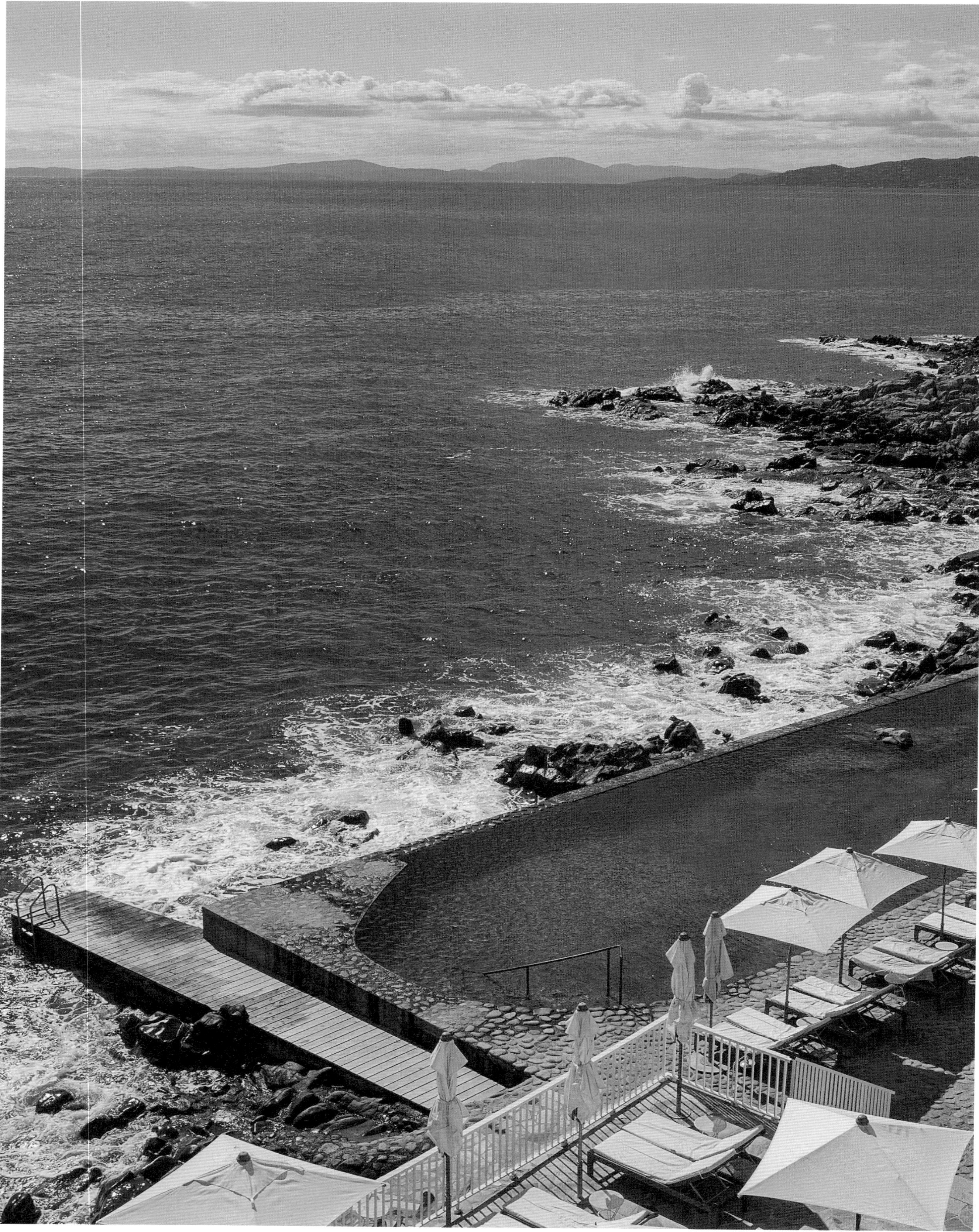

CONTENTS

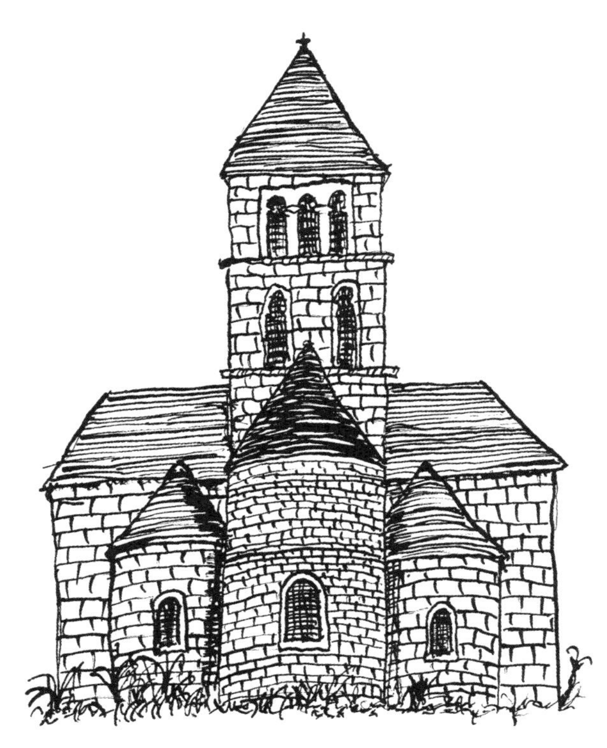

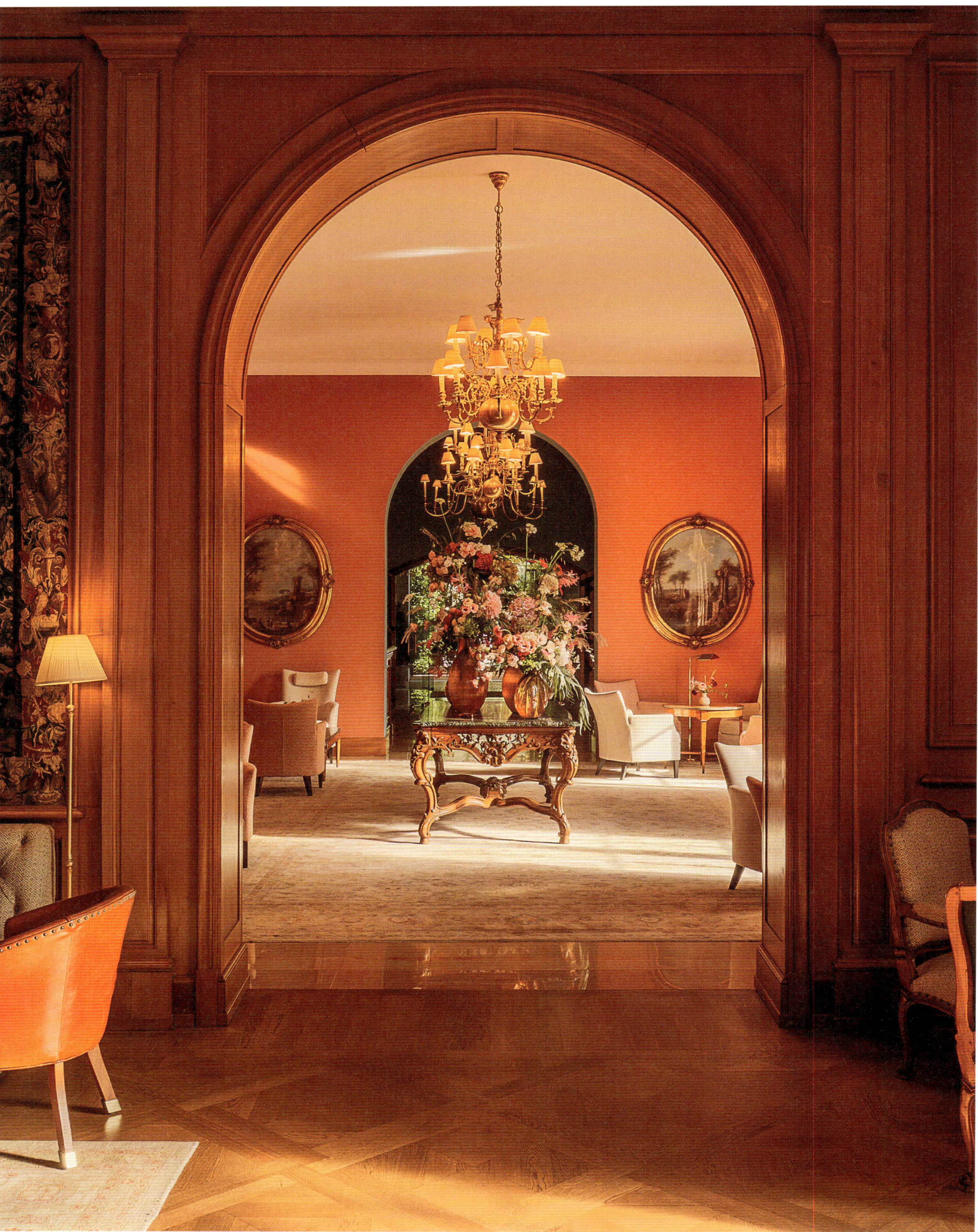

FOREWORD

Tim and I have always shared a passion for beautiful things—interior design, fashion, cuisine, art, and craftsmanship. These aren't just interests; they're our calling, and they've shaped our travels around the world for years. For a long time, we've dreamed of capturing these experiences in a book—to inspire others and share our deeply personal perspective on travel, countries, and cultures. That's how the idea for the Grand Tour was born: a modern take on a historic tradition.

In the seventeenth century, the Grand Tour was a key part of a classical upbringing. Young aristocrats were expected to broaden their horizons by observing the manners and customs of other countries and immersing themselves in Europe's cultural riches. With our Grand Tour, we're breathing new life into this old idea and giving it a thoroughly modern twist. No tutor, no carriage, no teenage noblemen—just a culture-hungry couple and their poodle, travelling by road and rail. What we've kept, however, is the spirit of the original: a quest for beauty, cultural depth, traditional craftsmanship, and the soul of the places we visit. Our Grand Tour is a vibrant mix of hotels, gardens, galleries, workshops, and restaurants—places that move us, that stay with us. This book isn't a travel guide in the usual sense, but rather our personal travel journal—a glimpse through our eyes, captured by Tim's photographs and my words. It's a record of the magic, beauty, and essence that make places and countries what they are. This time, we're off to the south of France—a classic Grand Tour destination even in centuries past. From Italy, we'll make our way along the Côte d'Azur, falling particularly for Nice and Saint-Tropez, before venturing inland to explore Var, Bouches-du-Rhône, and finally Vaucluse. Defining where Provence begins and the Côte d'Azur ends is tricky enough on a map. Once you're there, it becomes an impossible puzzle. The south of France is more varied than almost anywhere else in Europe—its landscapes, culture, cuisine, and aesthetics are dazzling in their diversity. We want to take it all in on our Tour de France: hotel design from classic luxury to cutting-edge concept; glimpses into the hidden arts of perfumers, pâtissiers, and chefs; art, interiors, and architecture spanning from avant-garde to Impressionism; and Provence itself, suspended somewhere between Europe and California.

Contrasting, refined, effortlessly exquisite—the south of France awaits, as insouciant as it is beautiful. And so, our Grand Tour begins.

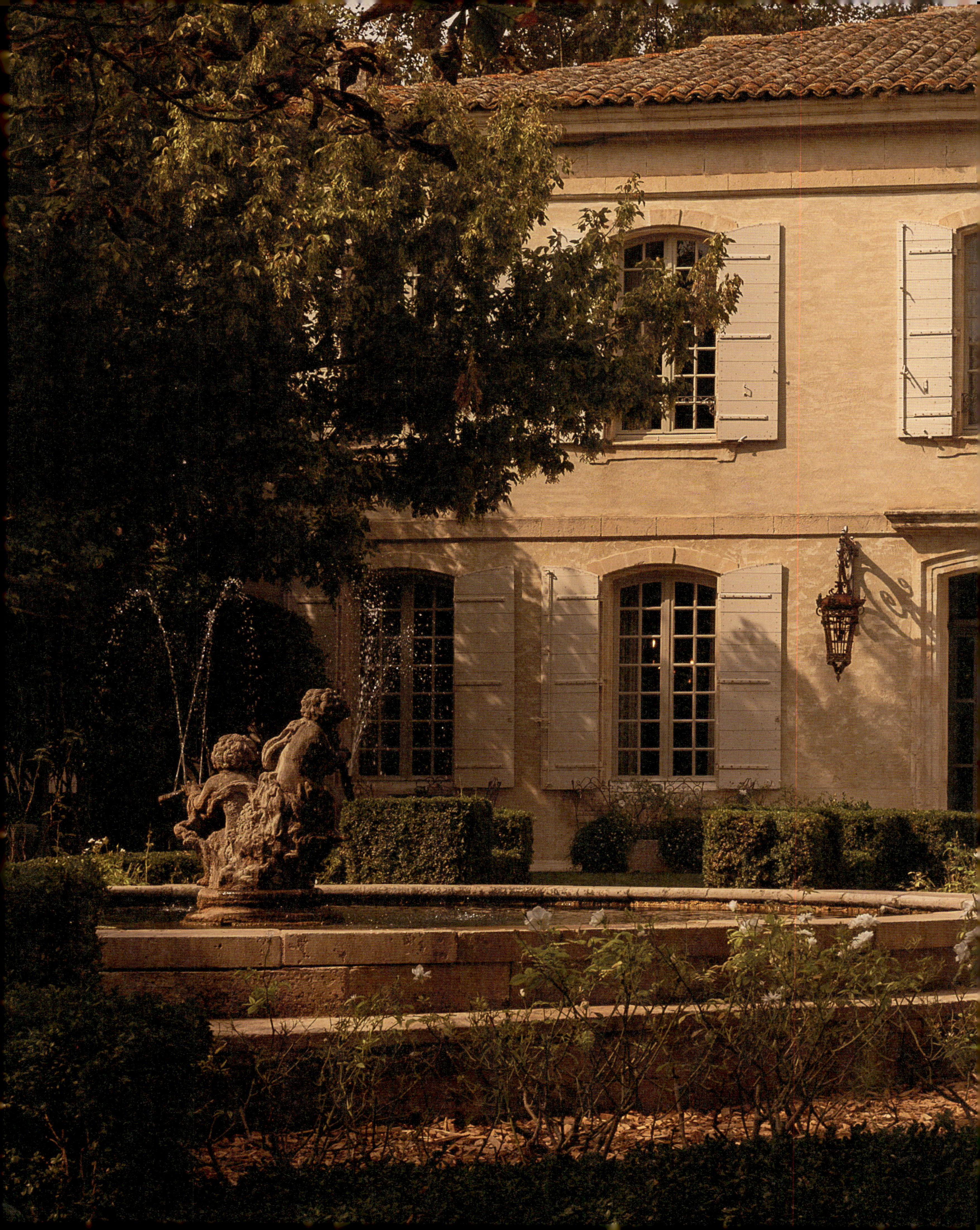

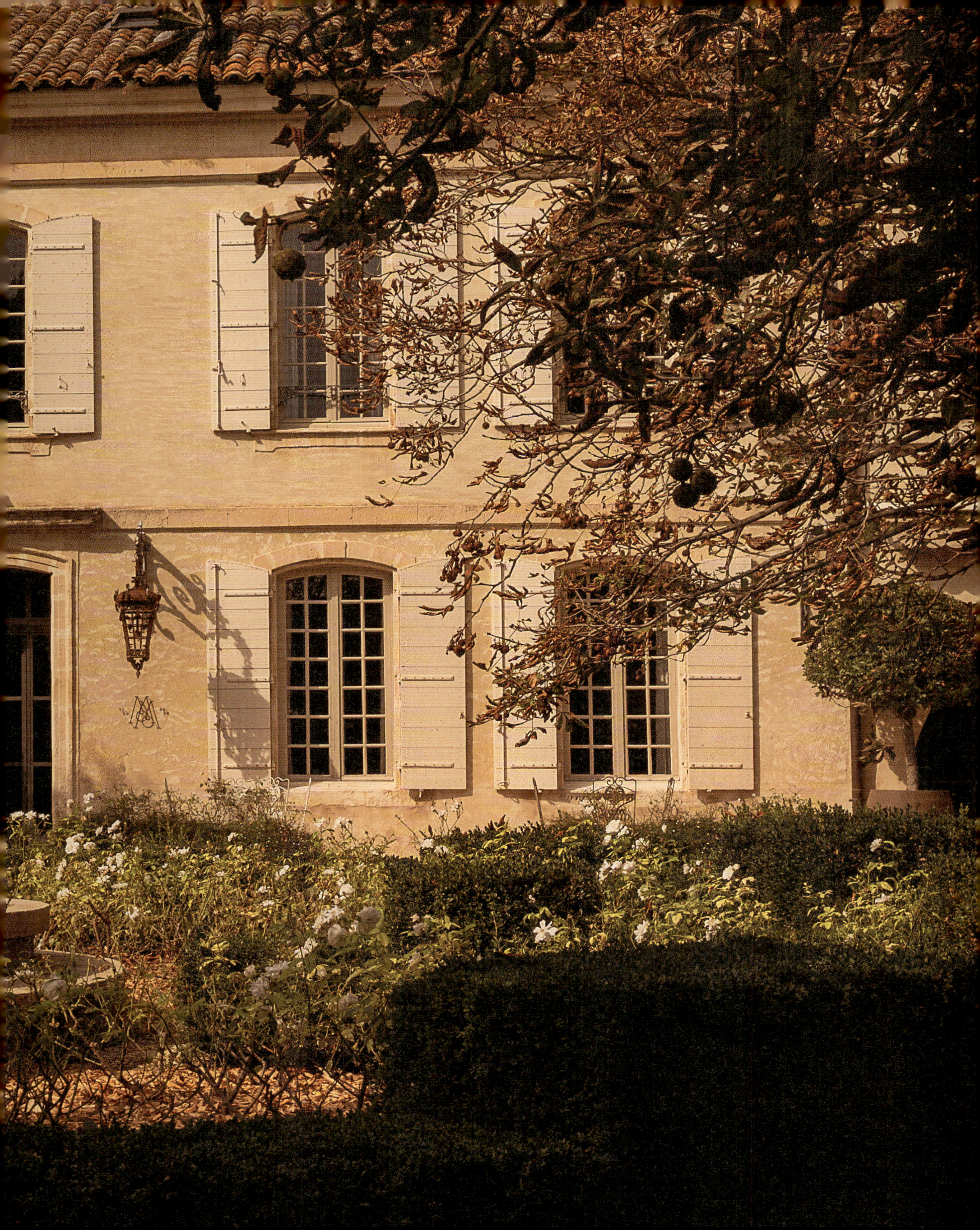

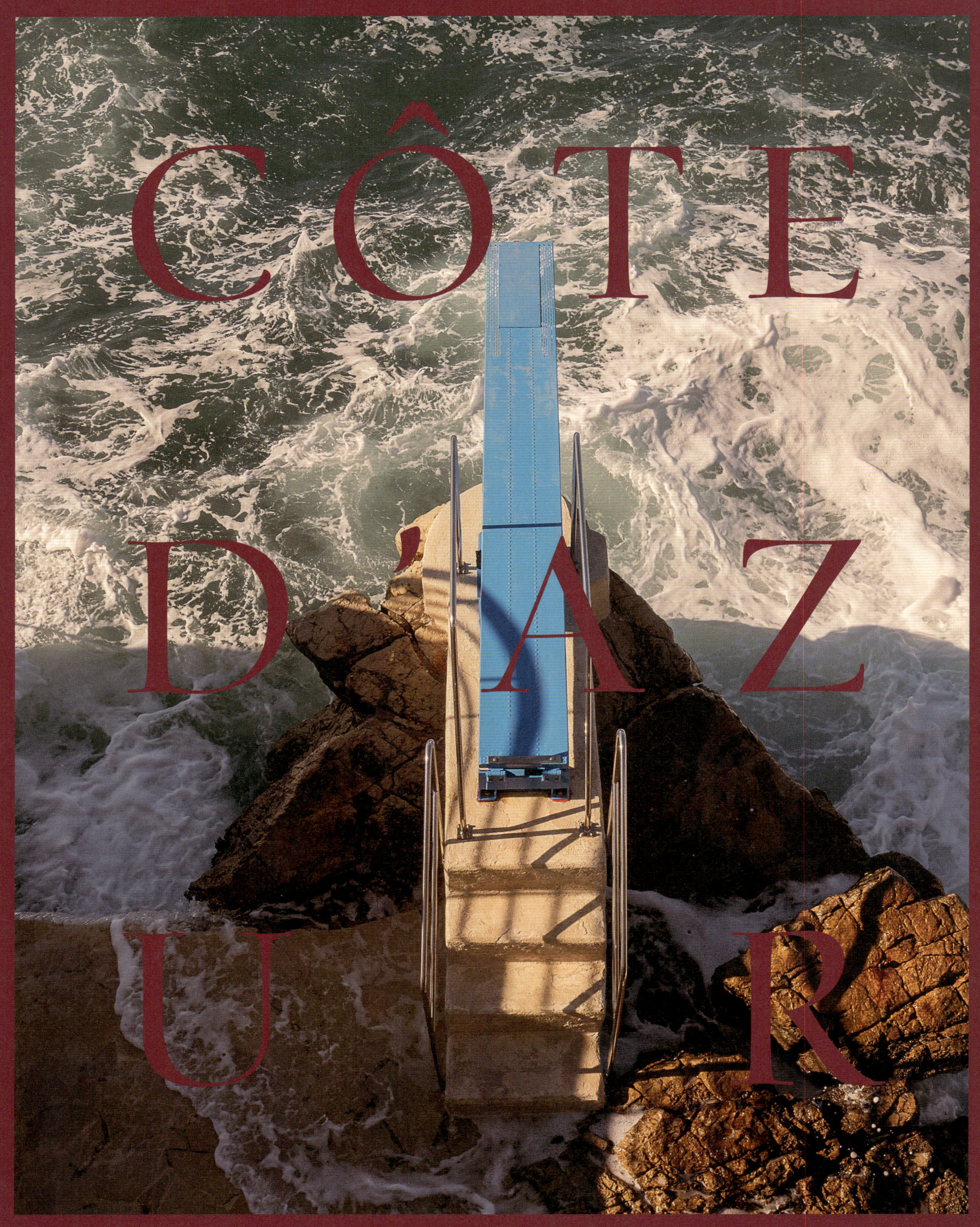
CÔTE
D'AZ
UR

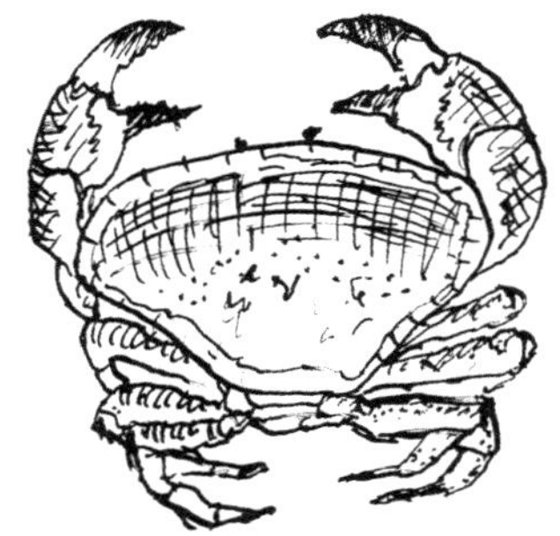

We approach the south of France from the coast, leaving Italy behind and beginning our Grand Tour along the Côte d'Azur. The road snakes along the shoreline, each curve revealing fresh impressions—and confirming every cliché. There's the sea, bluer than blue, never seen it like that, lending the region its name and rightly so. And there's the unmistakable presence of wealth, gleaming as brazenly as the sunlight on the water.

In the coastal towns draped along the shore like a Cartier necklace, grand villas and tightly packed apartment blocks vie fiercely for the best view—of the azure sea, the rugged cliffs, or the white-sand beaches. Yes, there's luxury, jet-set glamour, and perhaps a touch of superficiality—all as much a part of the Côte d'Azur as the Cannes Film Festival. But that's not the whole story. Artists and writers have drawn inspiration from this coast of endless blue, created masterpieces, left traces, or simply sought escape. Architects have let brutalism and modernism ring out against the backdrop of Belle Époque splendor, while nature itself has staged a spectacular show of one bay framed by tropical palms, the next by red rock outcroppings and the atmosphere of a steppe. The places along our route—from Cap Ferrat to Saint-Tropez—capture all of these facets, including a detour to what may be the most sensual artisan's town in the world. Our Grand Tour begins on the Côte d'Azur: the coast of blue, yes—but also of breathtaking contrasts.

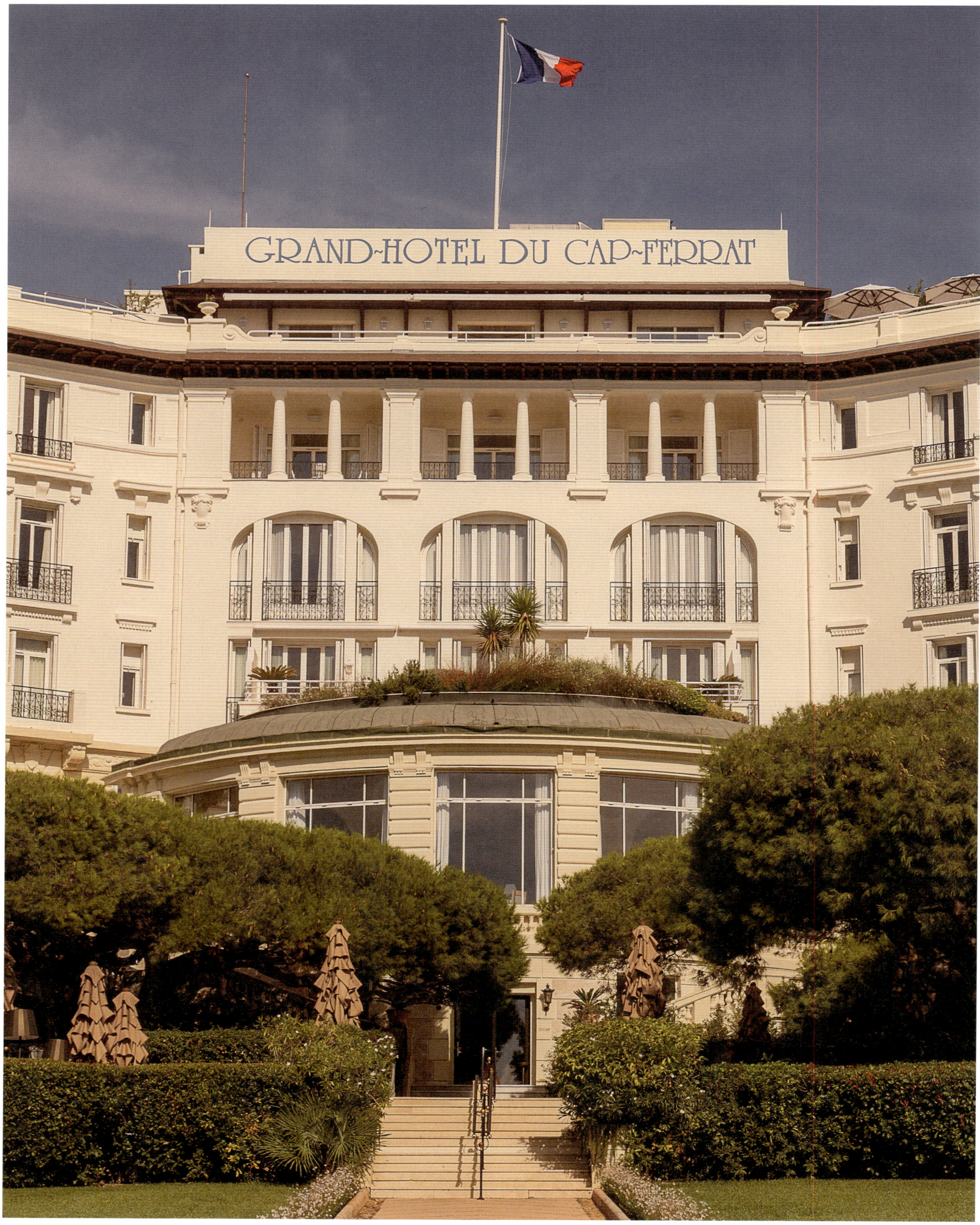
GRAND-HOTEL DU CAP-FERRAT

GRAND-HÔTEL DU CAP-FERRAT

CÔTE D'AZUR

END OF THE WORLD

Monaco lies ahead. Skyscrapers rise shoulder to shoulder, making the most of every square meter in this compact city-state. The road carries us on past this artificial enclave, toward Nice. Soon, Cap Ferrat appears on the horizon, like a ship almost completely encircled by the sea, its crown of palms and villas catching the sun. At the tip of the peninsula, we reach our destination: the Grand-Hôtel du Cap-Ferrat—a true icon, and the perfect starting point for our Grand Tour de France. Bright white, majestic, and serene, the hotel sits enthroned at the end of the cape, nestled in a lush green fringe of pines, perched directly above the cliffs of the Côte d'Azur. Since its founding in the early twentieth century, it has been a discreet and elegant retreat for aristocrats, Cannes celebrities, and the international jet set. It's now part of the Four Seasons family, guaranteeing not only world-class service but also adding a distinctive warmth and hospitality. The charming and energetic manager, Benjamin, leads us beneath the pines to the south gate of the estate, where a glass funicular awaits. We glide on it gently down the steep cliffs, the sea stretching out before us, the cape's lighthouse to our right. Our James Bond moment takes us to Club Dauphin, the hotel's beach club, with a large pool, white parasols, and spacious cabanas. Here is maximum privacy—tucked into the cliffs of the French Riviera.

Our long day in this sprawling oasis draws to a close on the balcony of our suite, truffle-infused cocktail in hand, the gentle flashing of the lighthouse casting its rhythmic glow. The world could end here at Cap Ferrat, and all

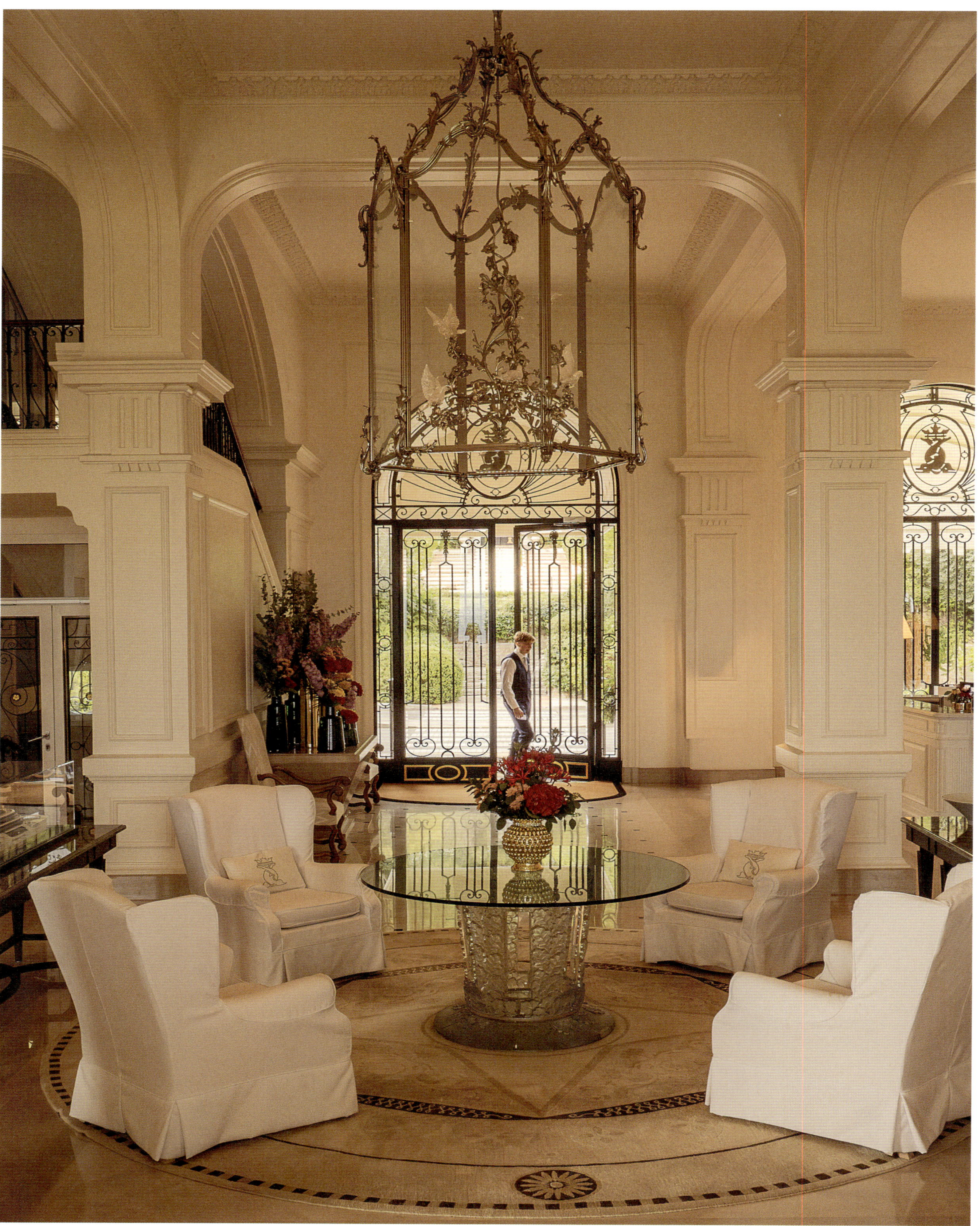

would be well. But with the rest of the Côte d'Azur's pearls in mind, we set aside the notion, which we admit would be slightly unfair.

The foyer of the Grand-Hôtel du Cap-Ferrat in the hotel's characteristic color scheme: creamy plaster elements and displays of silver-plated metal with aqua accents. The sea as well as the carpet of pine trees that surround the hotel is omnipresent, indoors and outdoors alike.

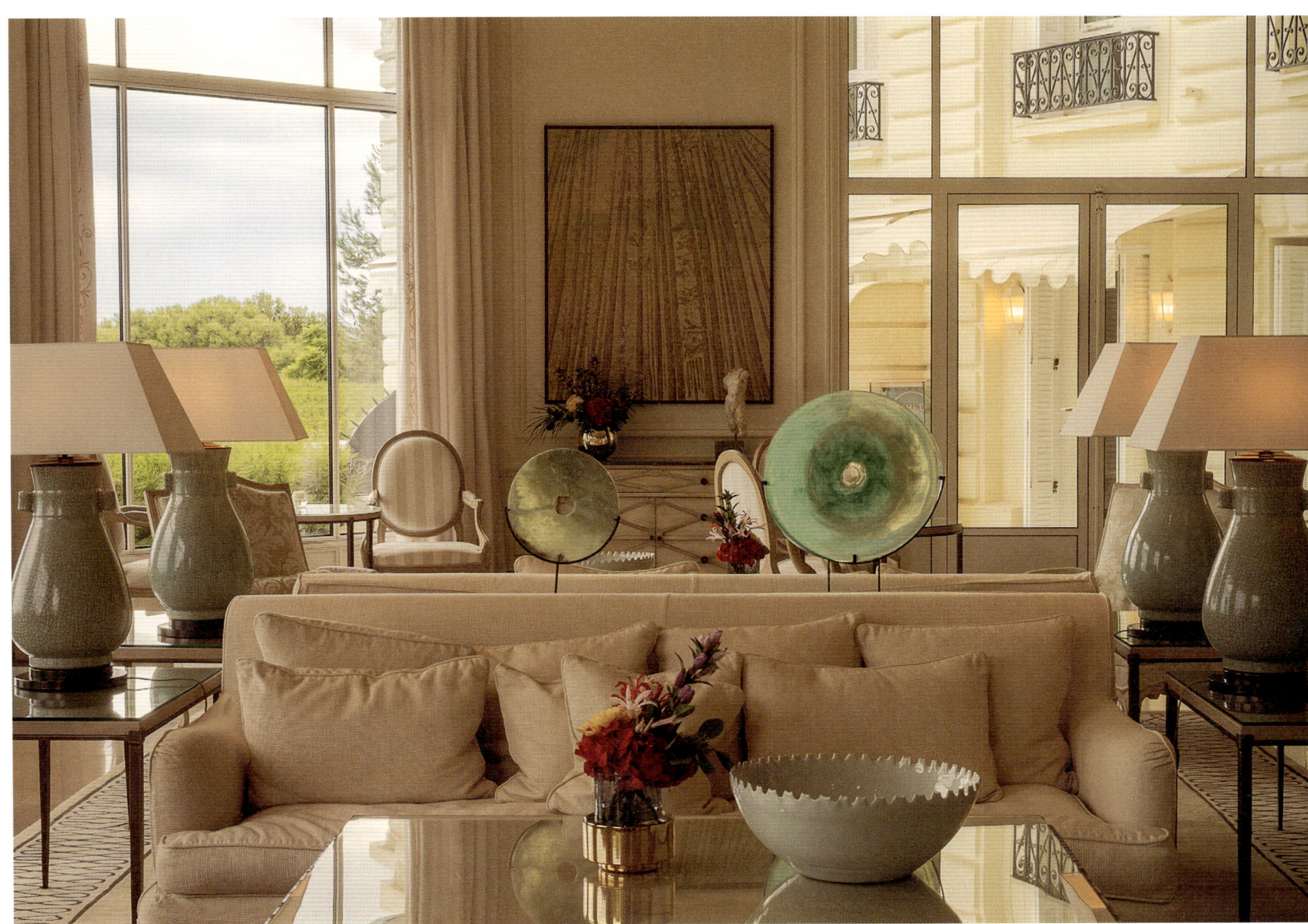

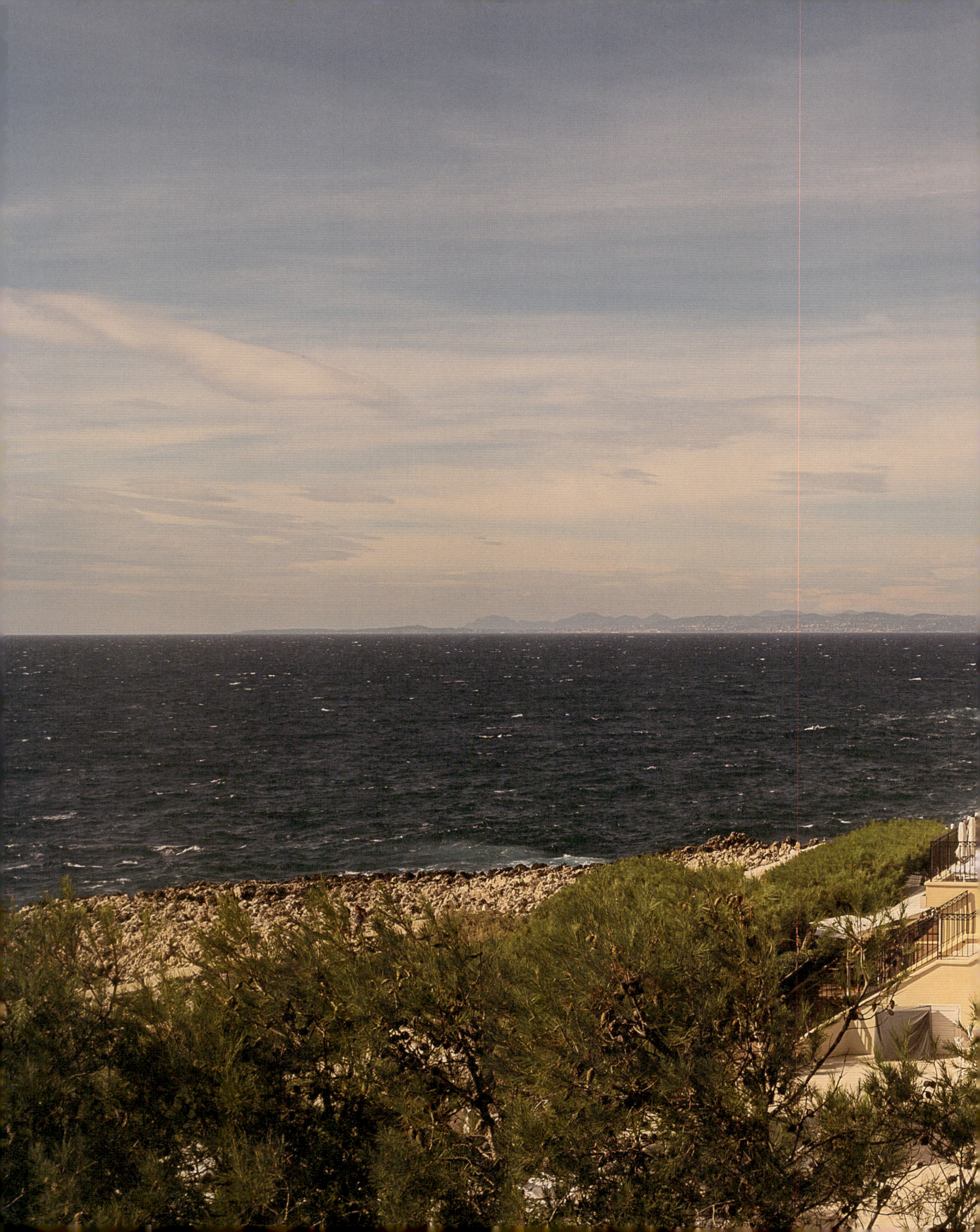

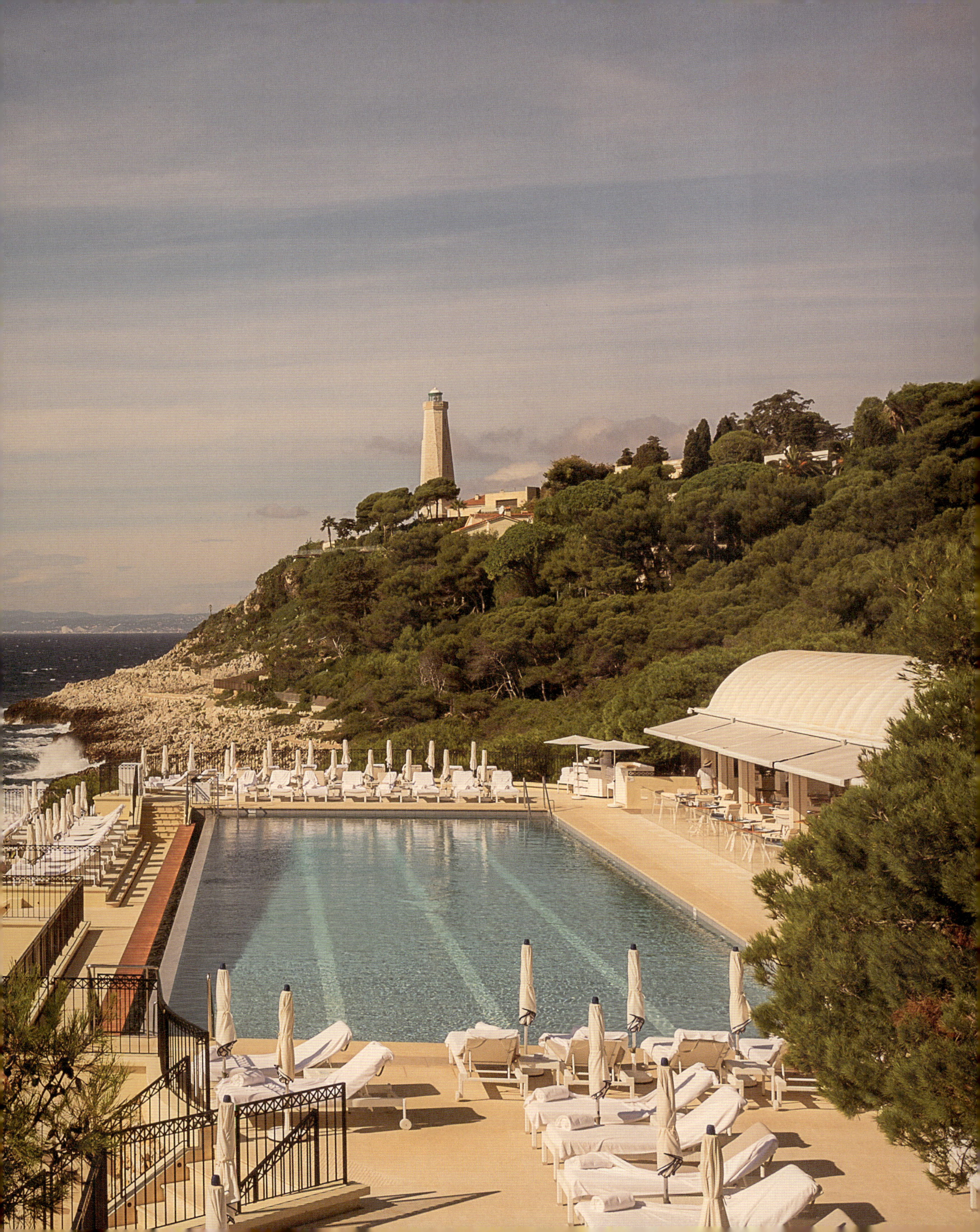

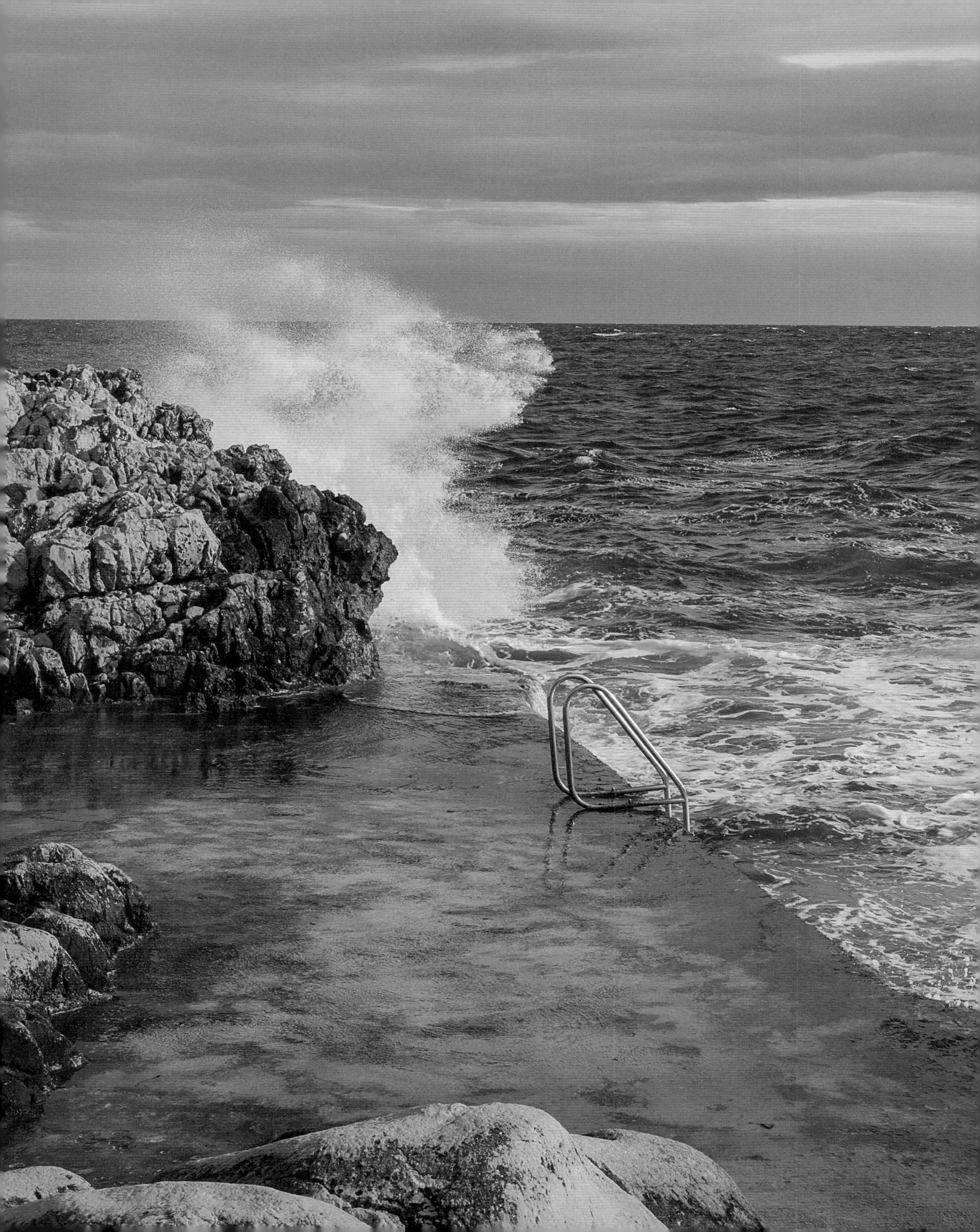

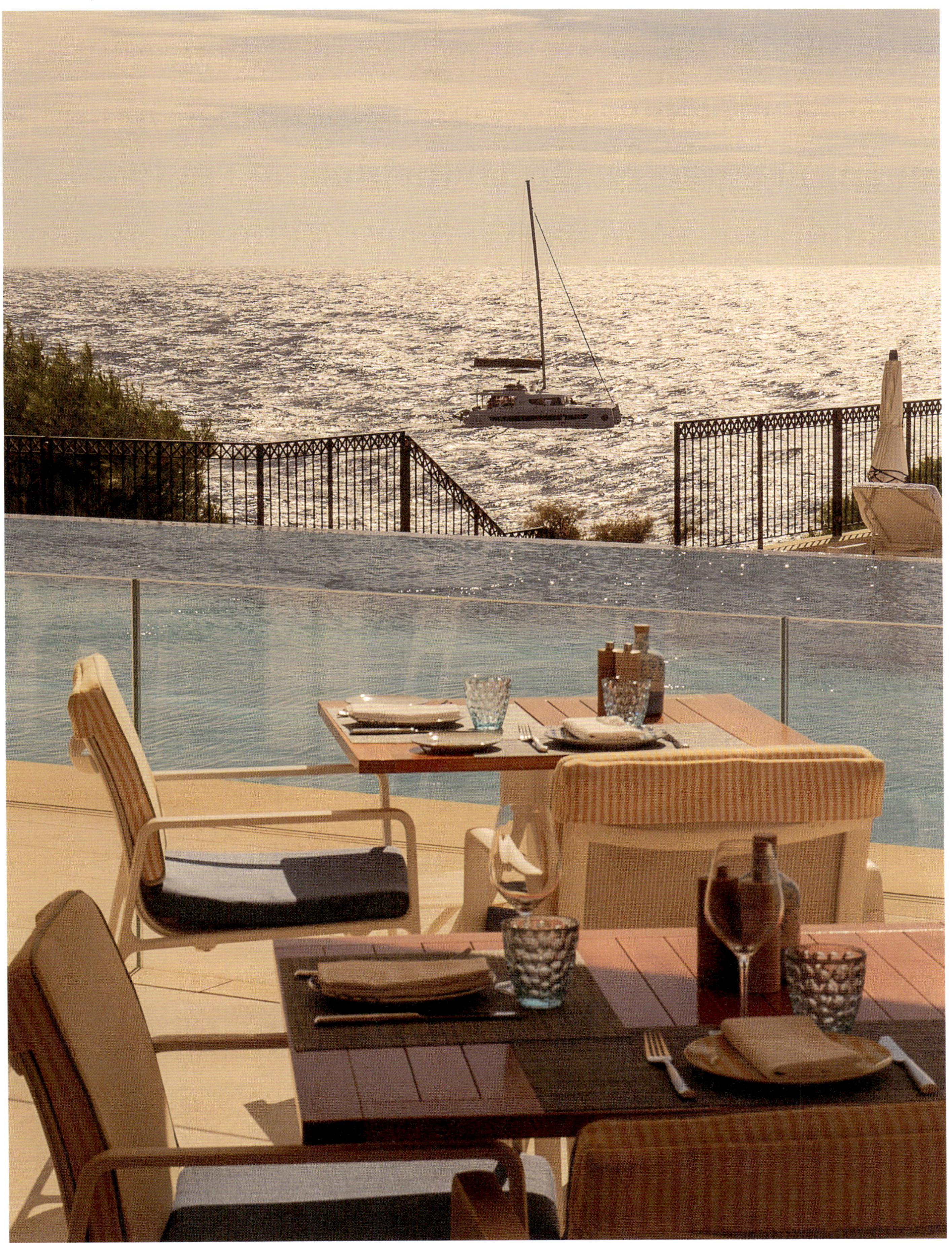

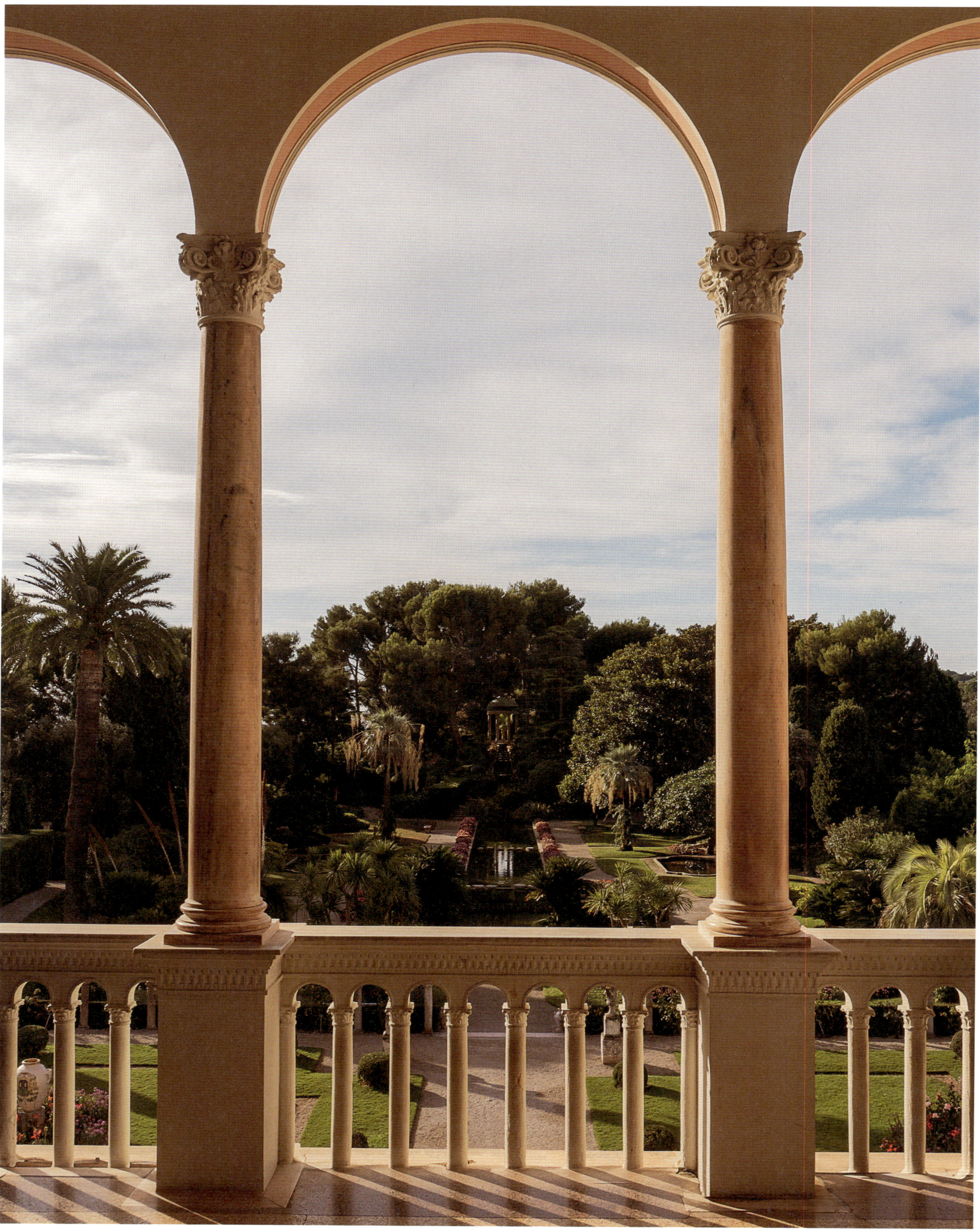

VILLA & JARDINS EPHRUSSI DE ROTHSCHILD

CÔTE D'AZUR

QUEEN OF VILLAS

After *œufs cocotte*, a green omelet, and other delicacies from the Grand-Hôtel's refined breakfast hall, we're primed for another dose of beauty. We stay on Cap Ferrat and stroll only twenty minutes before an unassuming path delivers us to a majestic black iron gate. Sometime before the day's horde of visitors arrives, the gate swings open. Beyond it lies Villa Ephrussi de Rothschild—the queen of villas—ringed by expansive gardens. Built in the early twentieth century for Béatrice de Rothschild, famed collector and devotee of all things exquisite, the pale-pink mansion looks almost restrained from afar.

Step by step, though, it discloses a wealth of detail, poised somewhere between a Gothic château and a Medici Renaissance masterpiece. We cross the square entrance hall in awe—airy, colonnaded, with open balconies above and a vast baldachino that feels like borrowed sky. For a heartbeat we think we've been spirited to Florence; then the first parlor opens, and we're immersed in pure Belle Époque splendor: gold-framed frescoes, mirrors upon mirrors, music boxes upon music boxes, room after room, each flooded with warm light and gazing out toward garden and sea. A spiral stair framed by Gothic windows carries us up a level.

There we lose ourselves among Meissen porcelain, lustrous Chinese fabrics, and Renaissance paintings until we stumble onto the broad balcony. Below, Aphrodite presides over her pavilion; at that moment, the fountains begin, sending fine jets arcing between jasmine hedges. It feels like Versailles—until

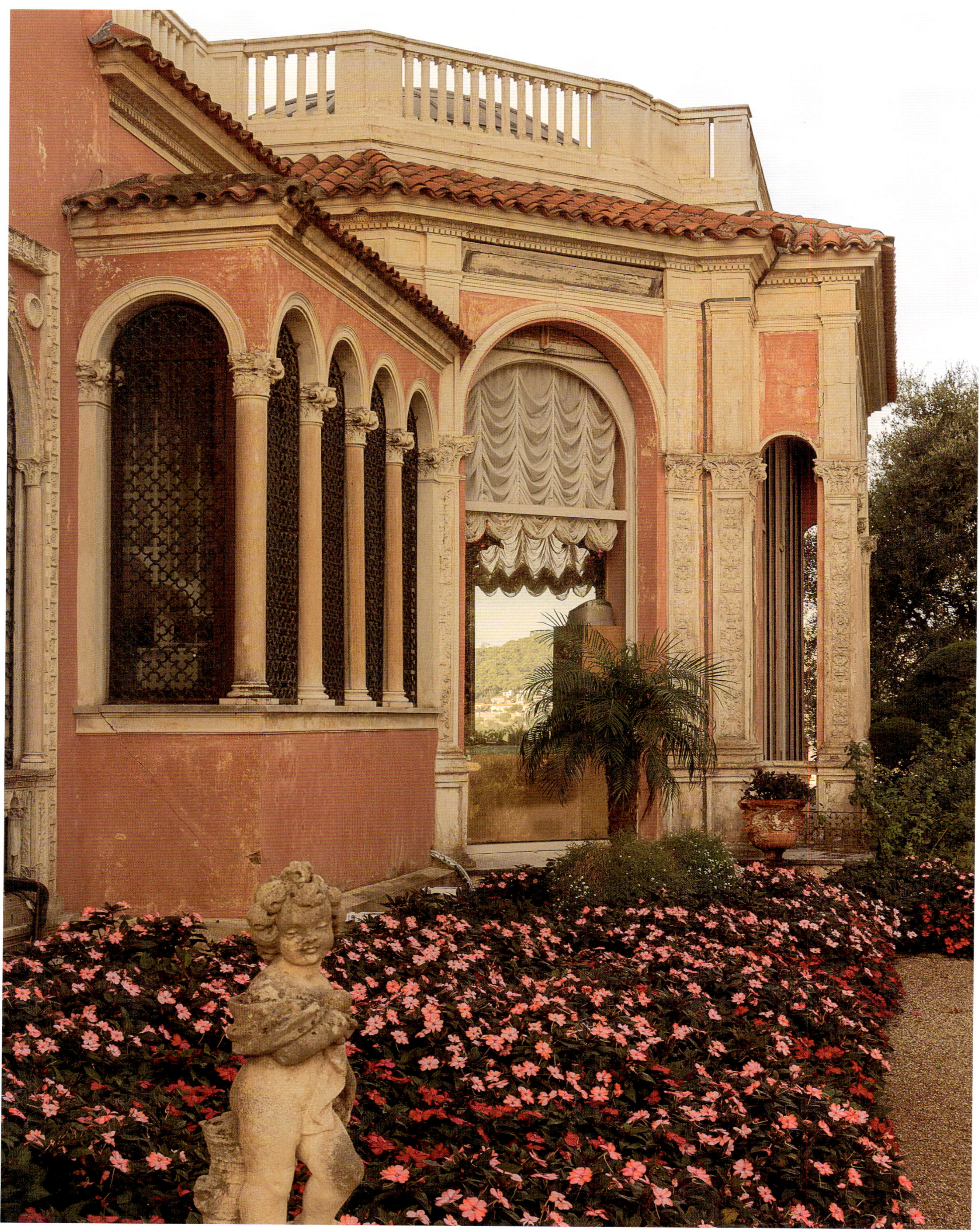

the palm trees remind us we're still on the Riviera. Not a hint of kitsch intrudes. Villa Ephrussi de Rothschild fuses eras and styles with effortless grace, celebrating a passion for beauty like nowhere else.

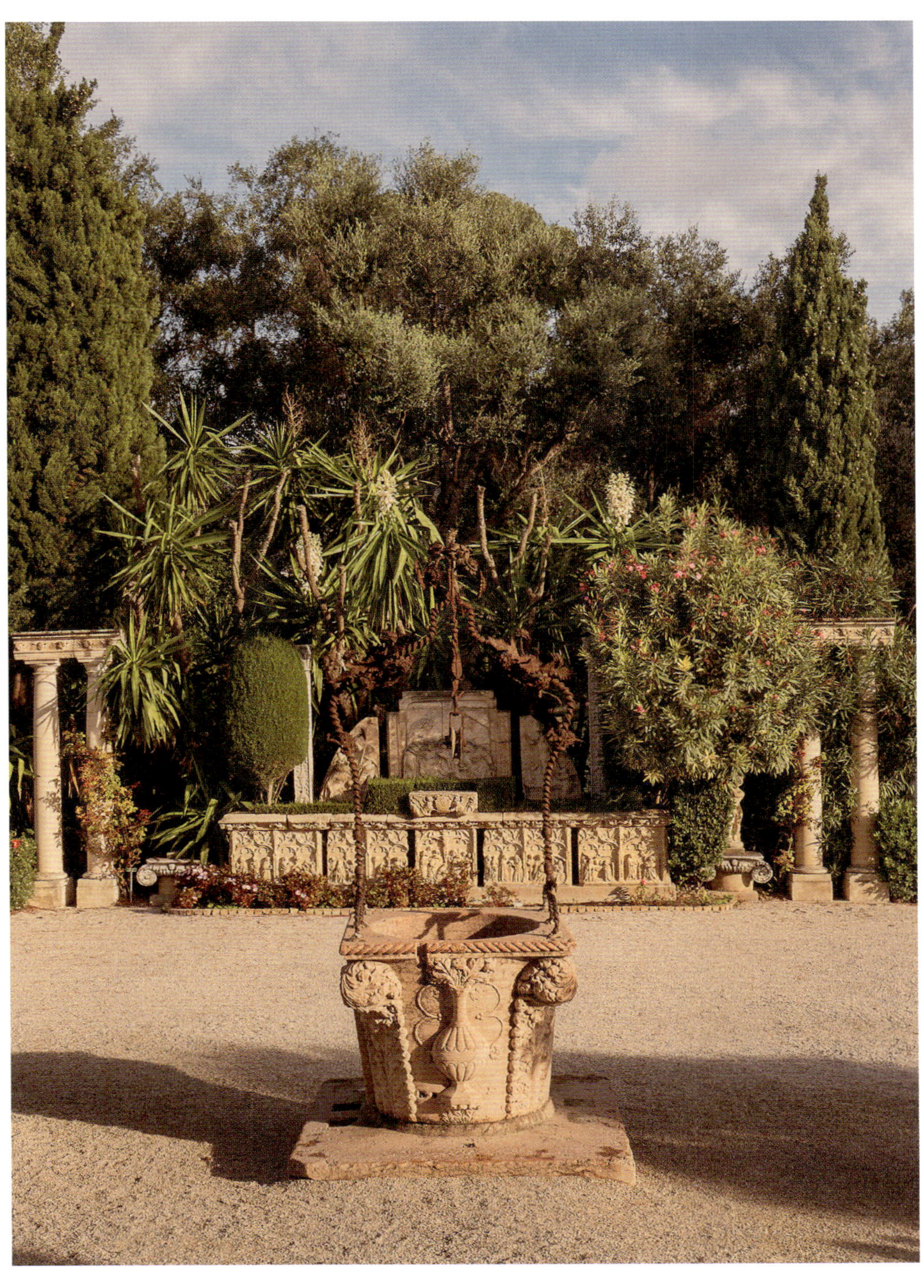

Villa Ephrussi de Rothschild is a melting pot of beauty from every epoch, and as such, the villa is an optimal representation of its builder, Beatrice—a Medici diva and Belle Époque starlet hybrid.

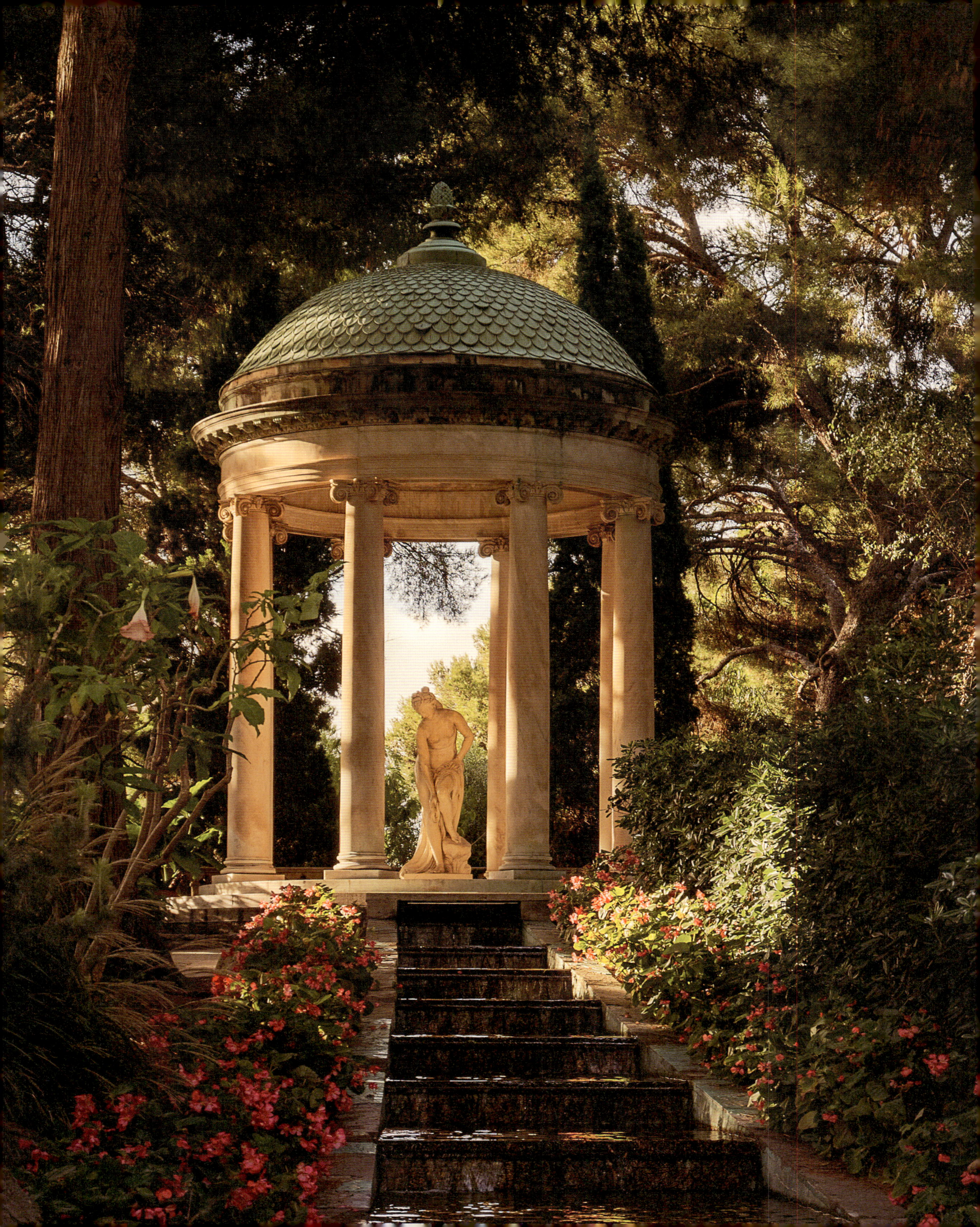

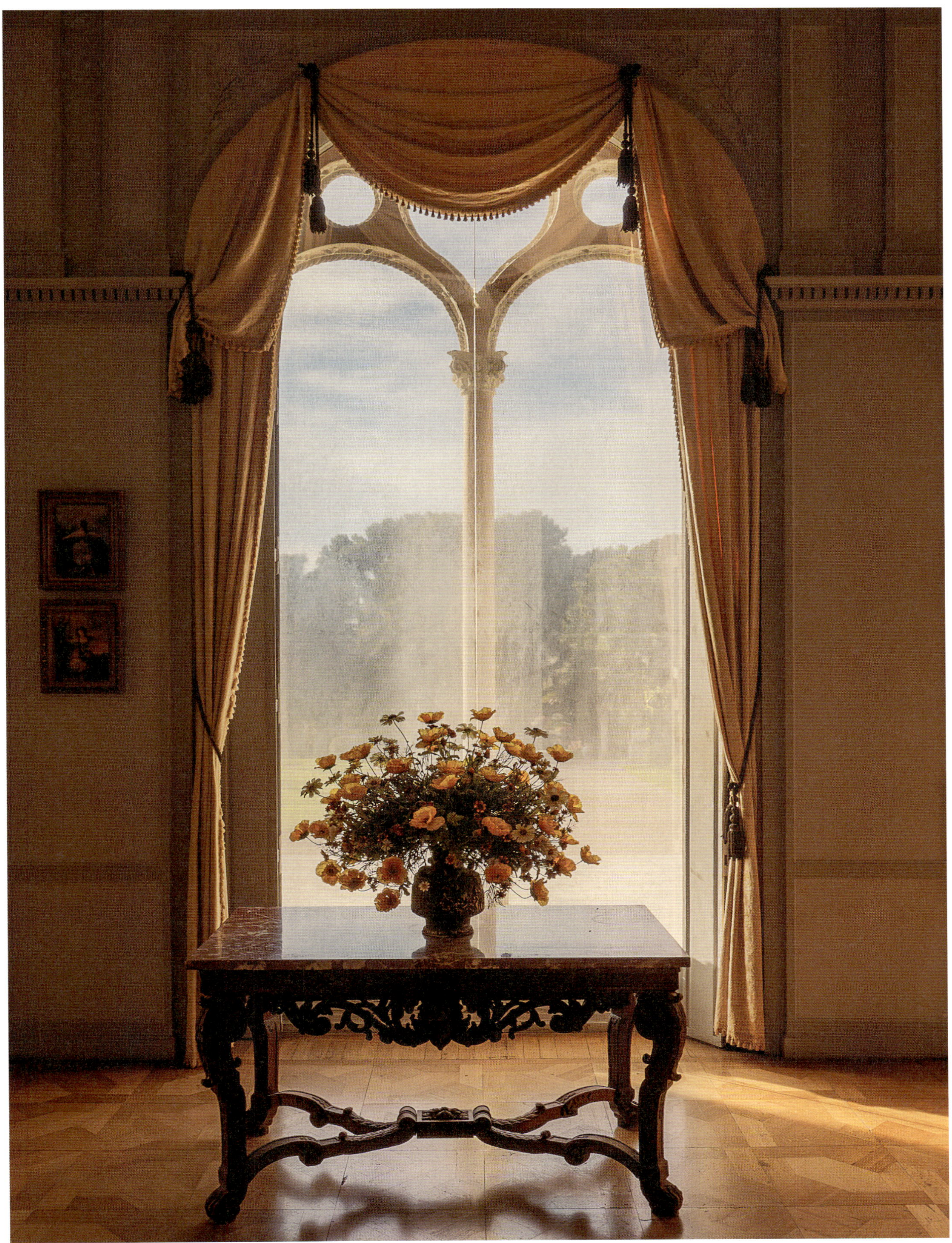

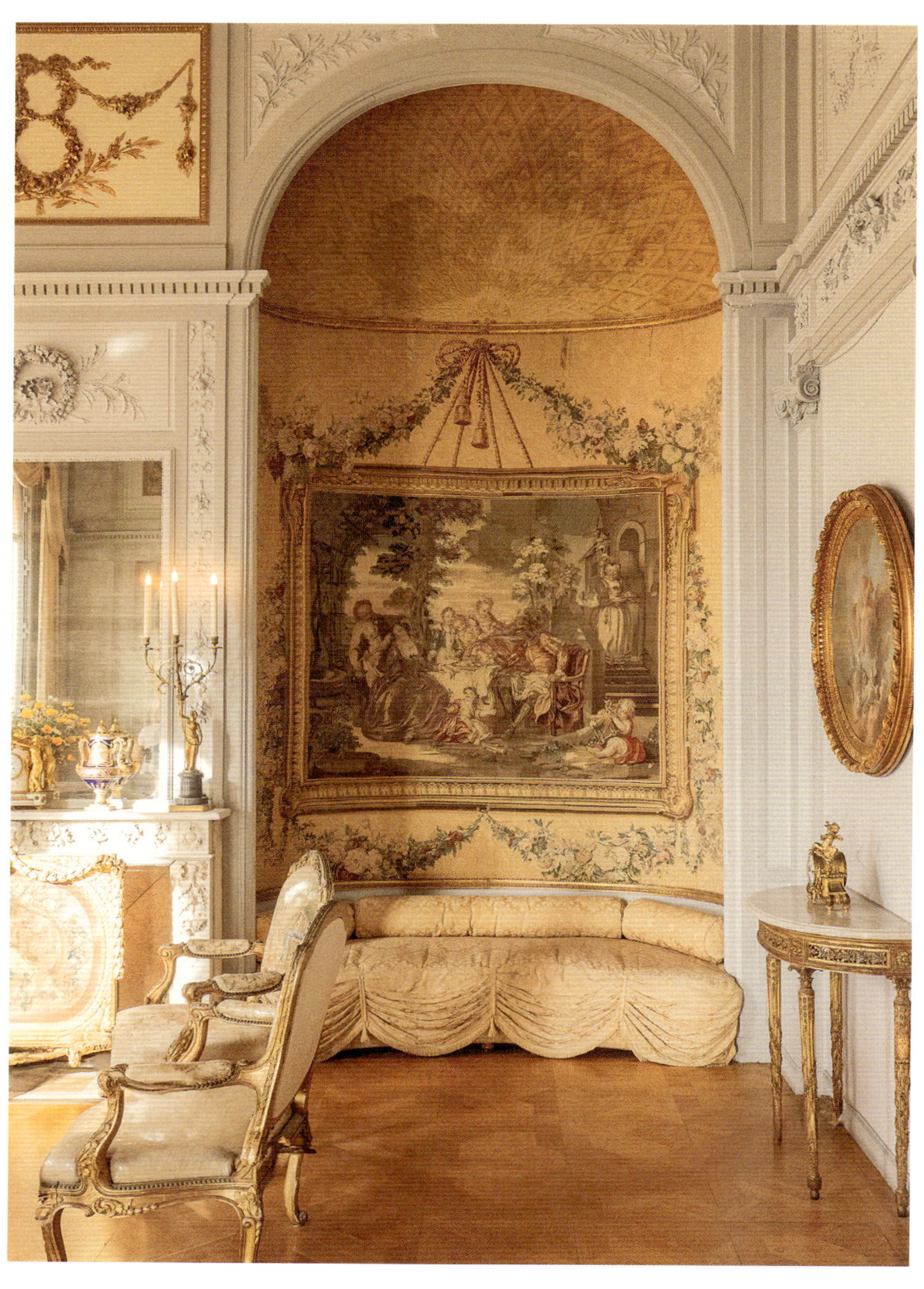

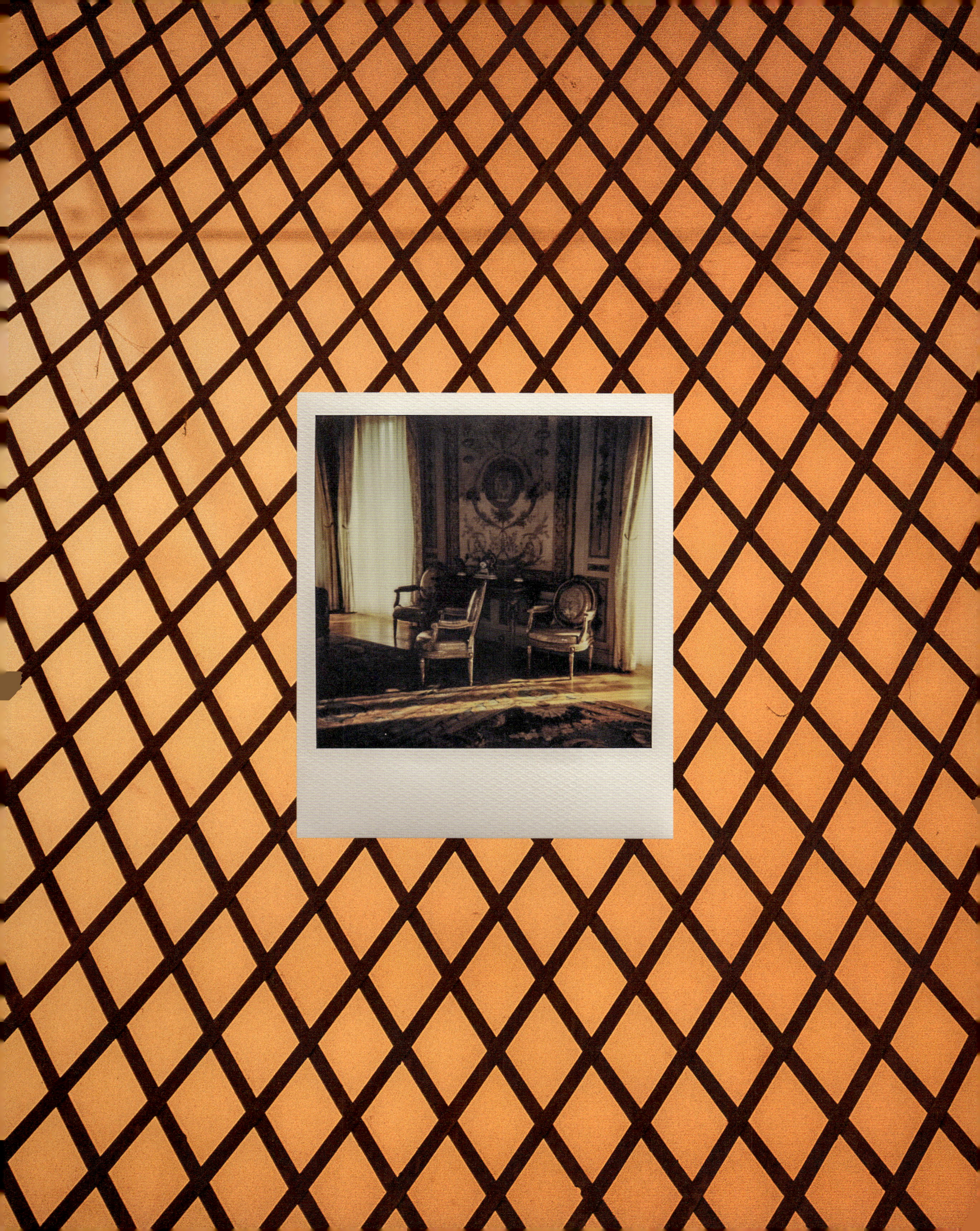

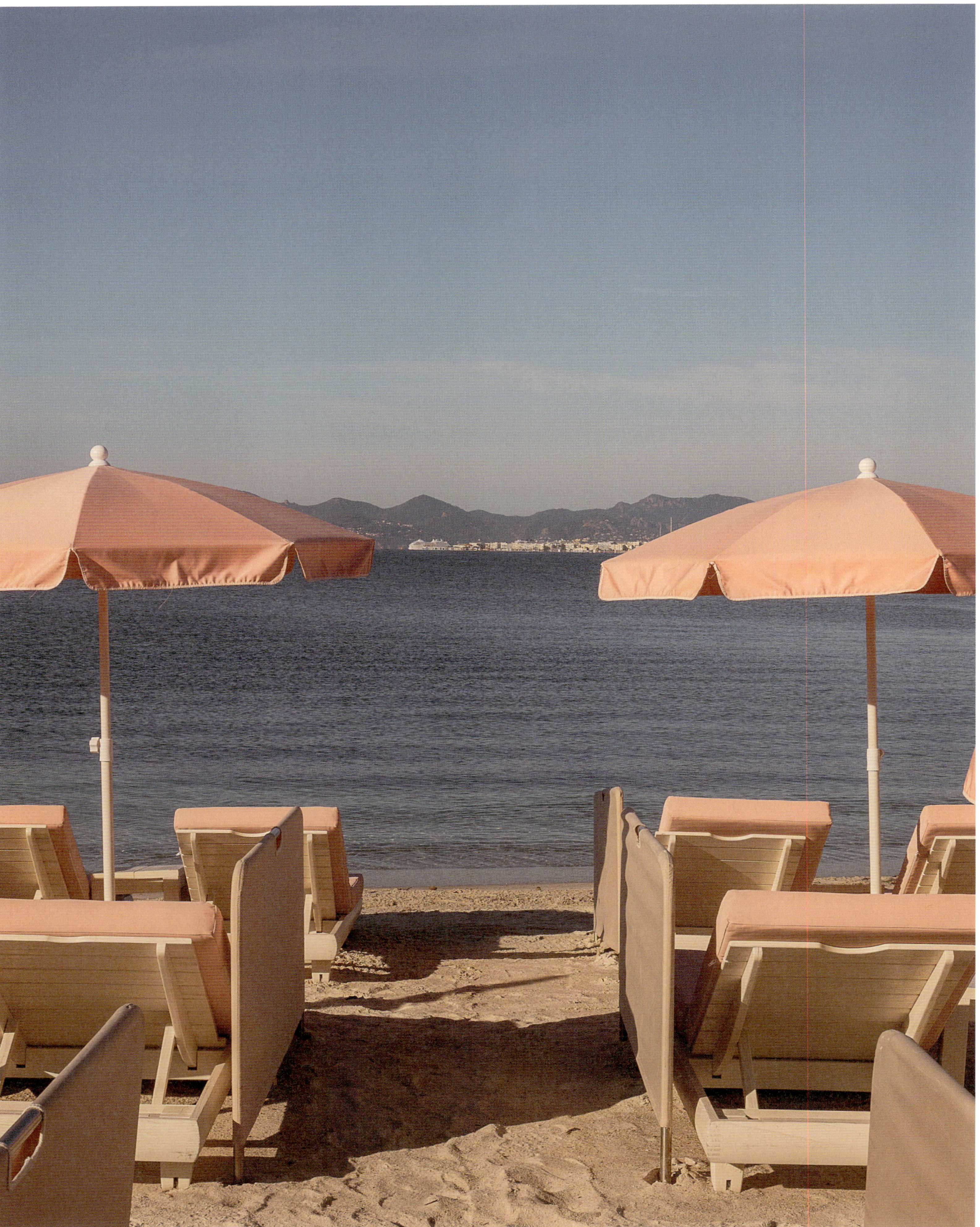

CAP D'ANTIBES BEACH HOTEL

CÔTE D'AZUR

SPLASH OF ROSÉ

We leave the cape, still under the spell of all the beauty gathered at this tip of the peninsula, and follow the long coastal road southwest. A sea of sails and leviathan yachts announces our arrival in Antibes, the next stop on our journey. Just off the road skirting the Golfe-Juan, we spot a long, low-slung white bungalow with a crooked, timeworn olive tree next to it. The Cap d'Antibes Beach Hotel is worlds away from the Belle Époque splendor of Cap Ferrat—and yet somehow it feels just as perfectly at home on the Côte d'Azur. Minimalist bungalows, interlocking rich-brown teak railings, glass cubes, and clean sans serif numbers marking the 30 rooms—everything here channels the spirit of the 1960s, the decade when the Riviera truly came into its own. As the charming Alicia shows us to our room, the uncompromising aesthetic flows seamlessly along rough stone floors, white-painted wood panels, and a glass wall facing directly onto the beach create a feeling almost like stepping into a private cabana. The Cap d'Antibes is a beach hotel through and through—with a generous splash of rosé. The hotel's signature hue is everywhere from the pink marble in the bathroom to the rose umbrellas, sun loungers, and towels that line the beach club.

We order frozen margaritas at the round bar, lit by dim ball lights, as even the sky blushes pink. The hotel never gives in on its vision: radically consistent, relentlessly on theme, perfectly in the zeitgeist. It's like we might see Lana Del Rey or Sabrina Carpenter appear on the balcony any moment, enchanting us with their siren songs. After sunset, we drift from the bar to Baba, the

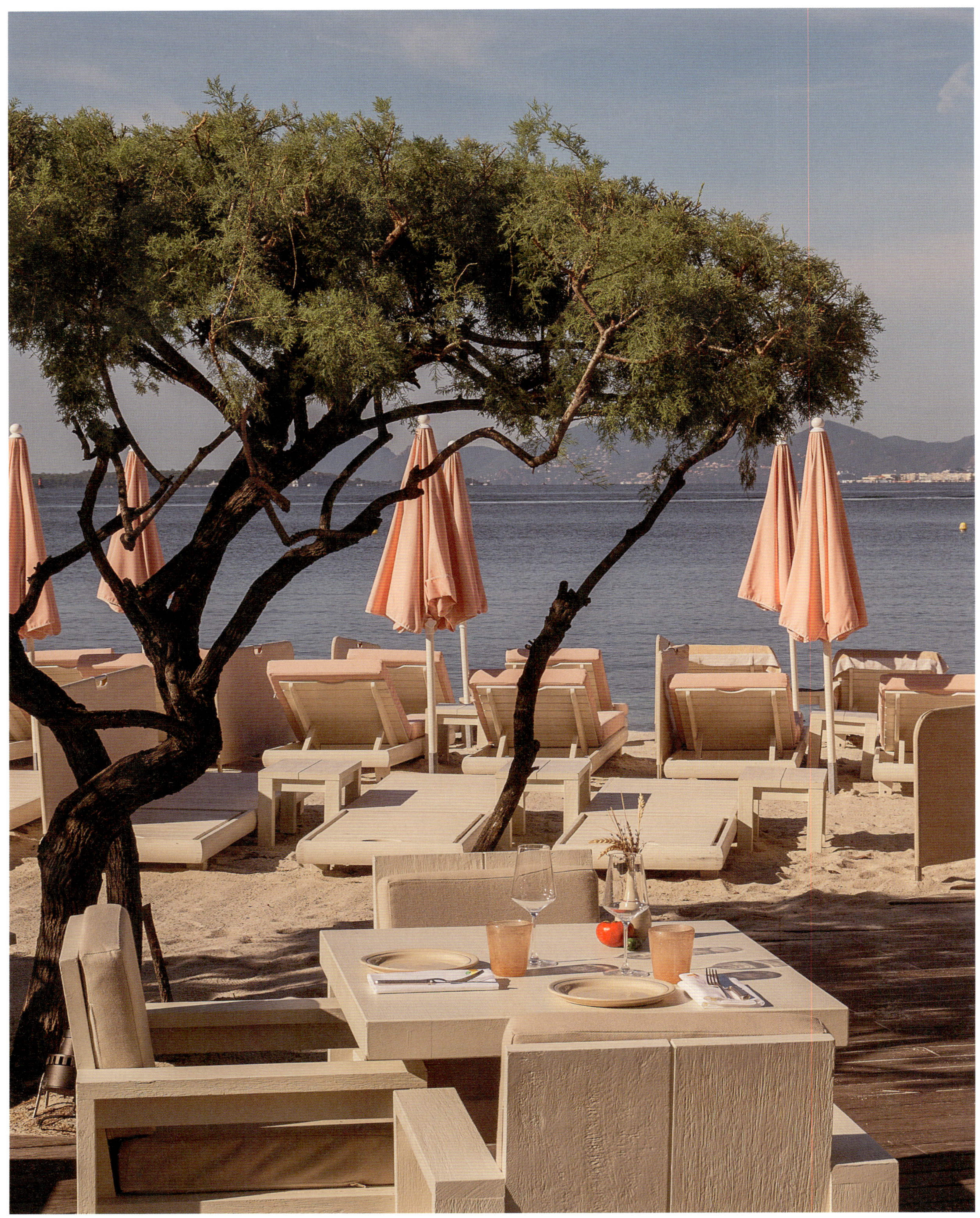

beachside restaurant where scoring a table is just as tricky as at Les Pêcheurs, where the hotel operates its Michelin-starred kitchen. The fare at Baba is a culinary dialogue between Levantine and French traditions. Blissful, full, and drifting on a gentle blend of margarita and rosé, we collapse into bed. The color of roses fades to darkness, and only a green light flashes in the harbor—a preview of the next stop on our tour, just a few meters away.

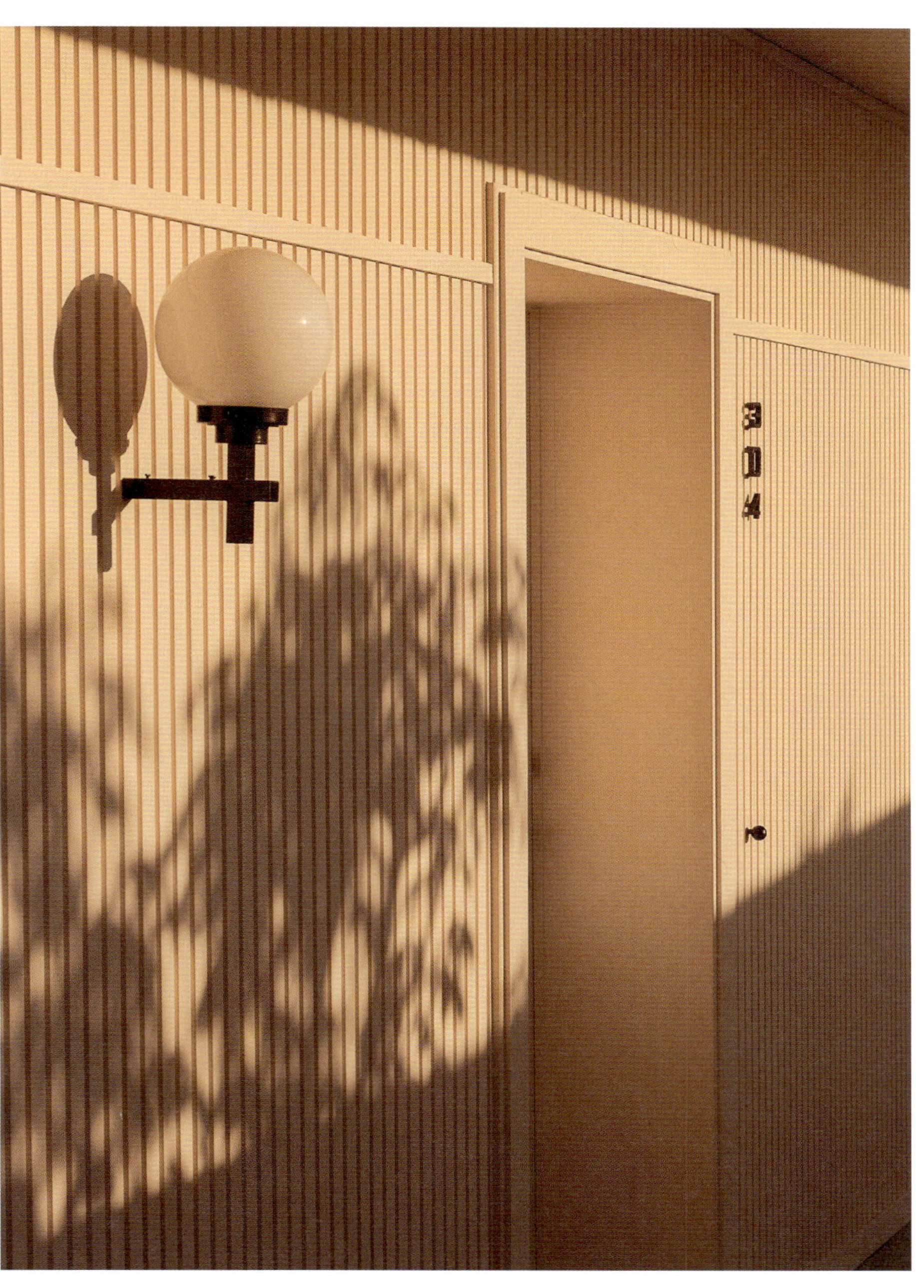

The Cap d'Antibes Beach Hotel is an unabashed homage to the sixties, through and through: from the sans-serif numerals next to glowing orb lights that identify the rooms in the bungalow complex, down to the Barbie-pink in which everything from the bathrooms to the parasols is rendered.

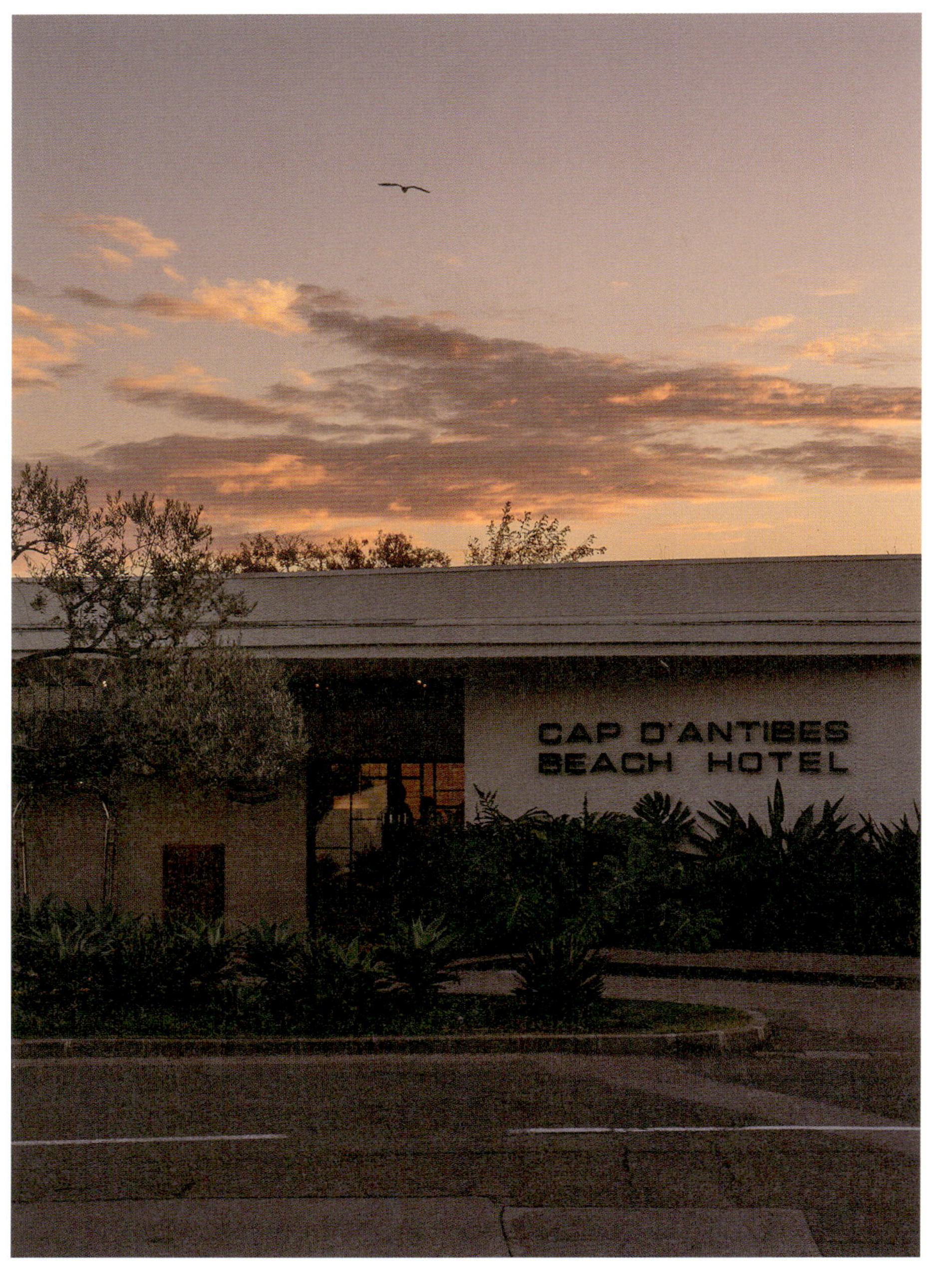
CAP D'ANTIBES
BEACH HOTEL

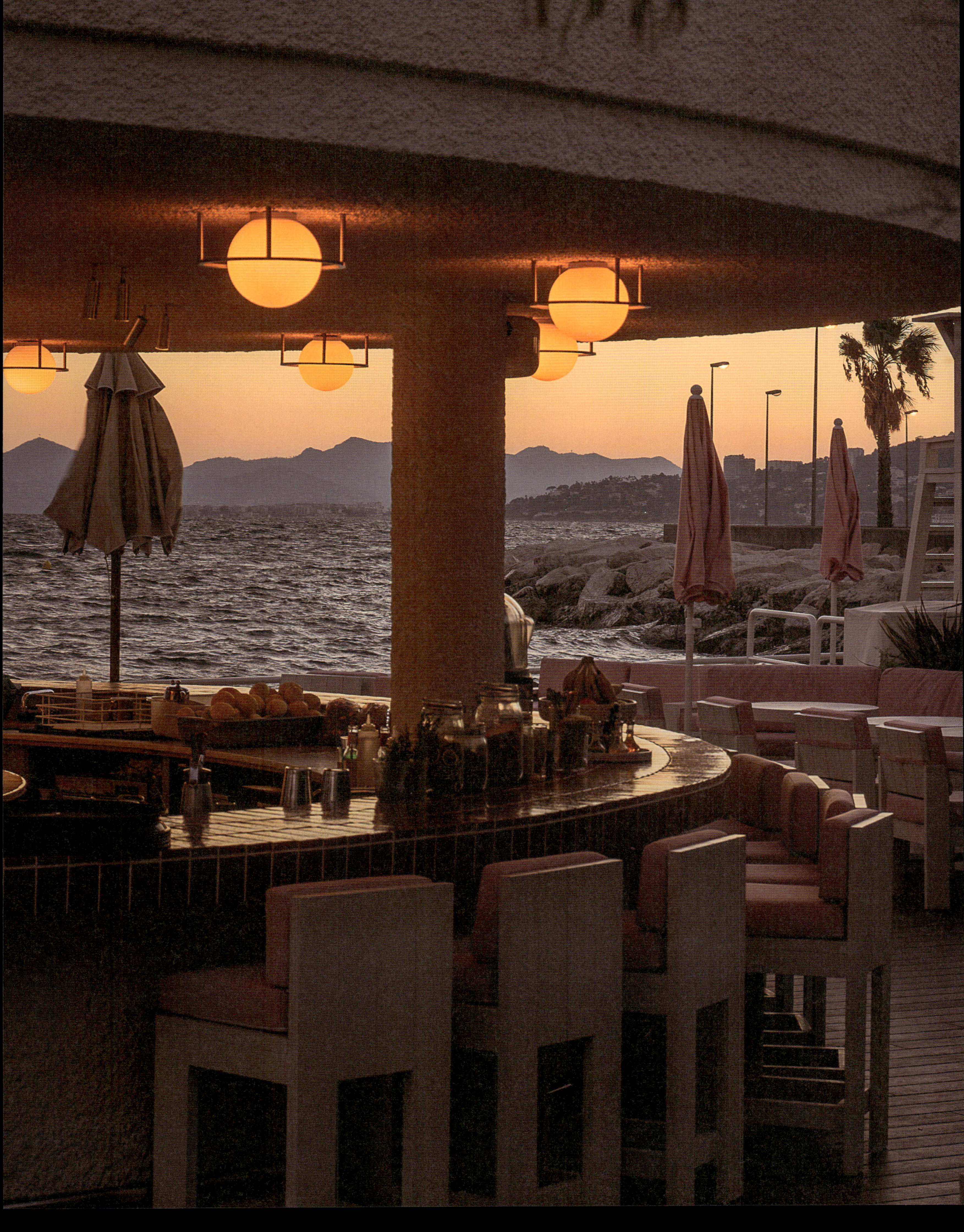

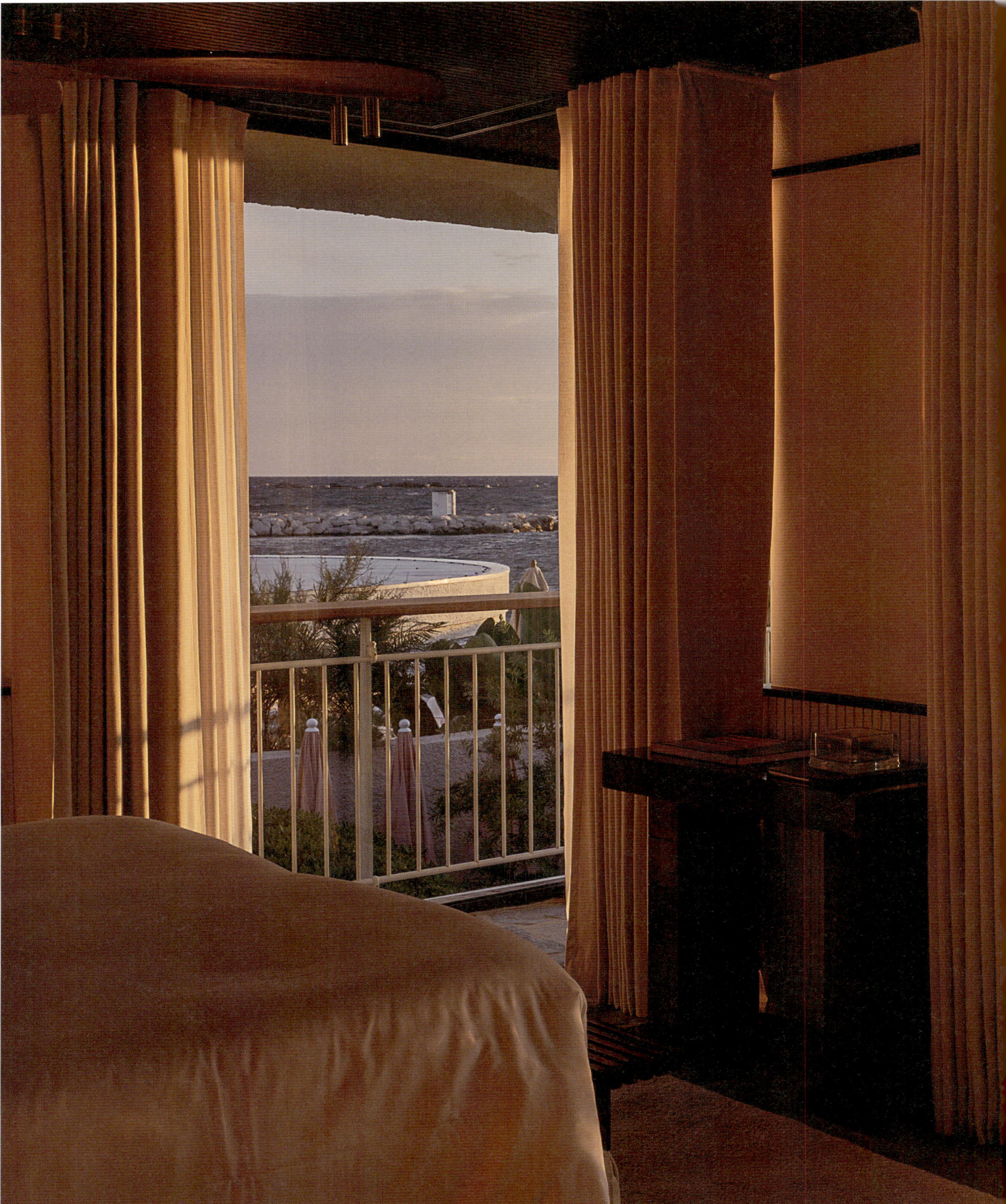

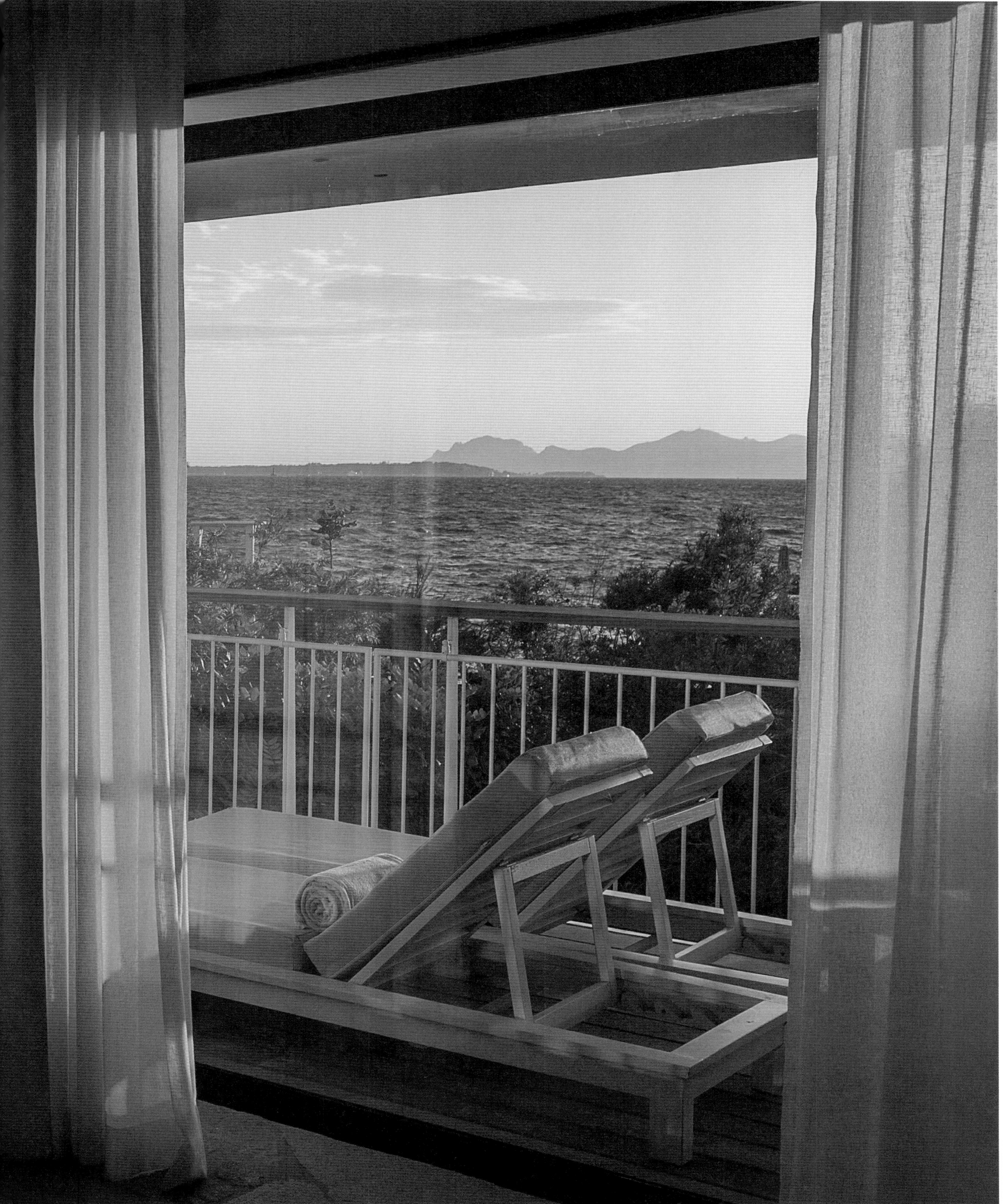

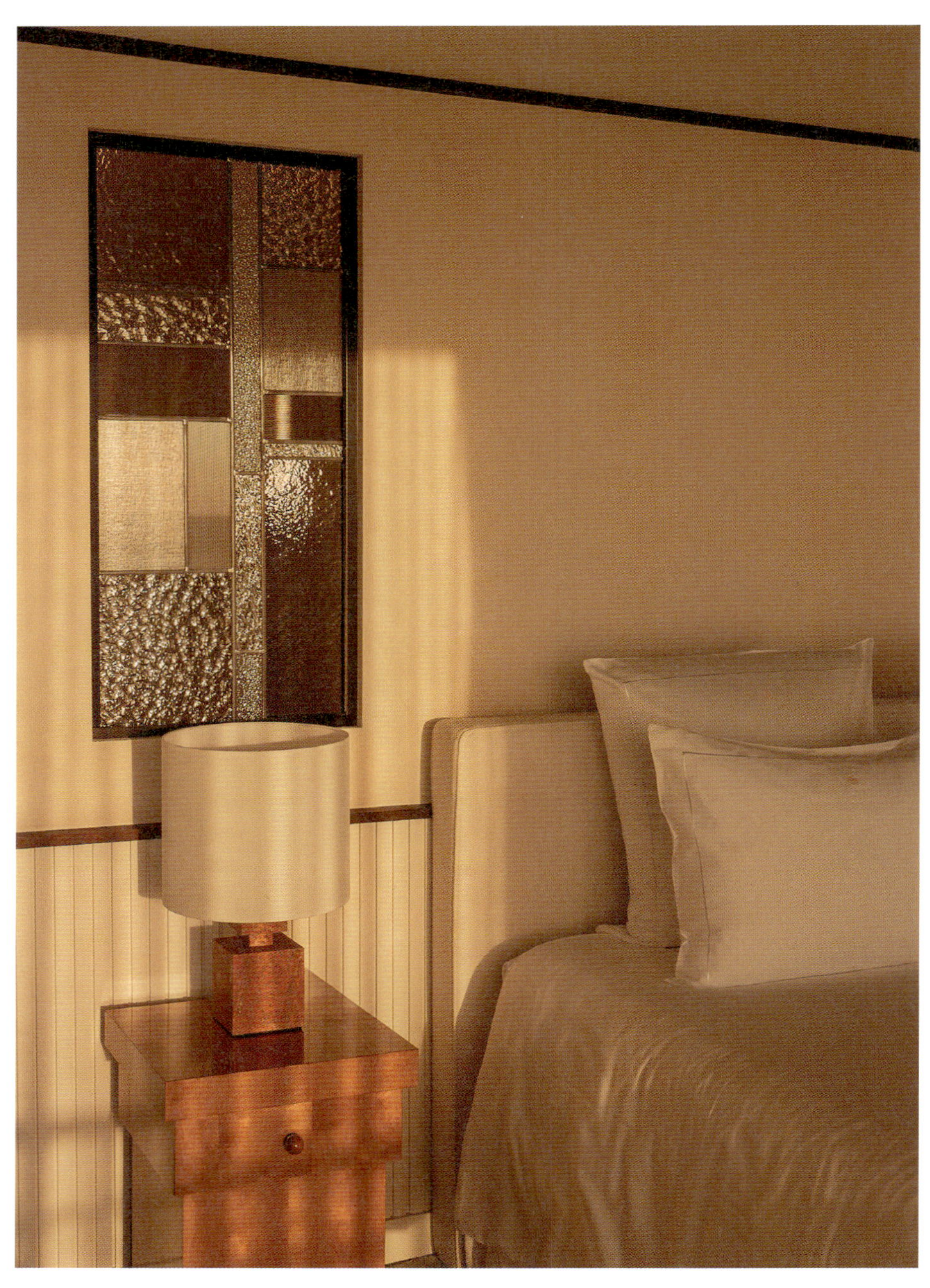

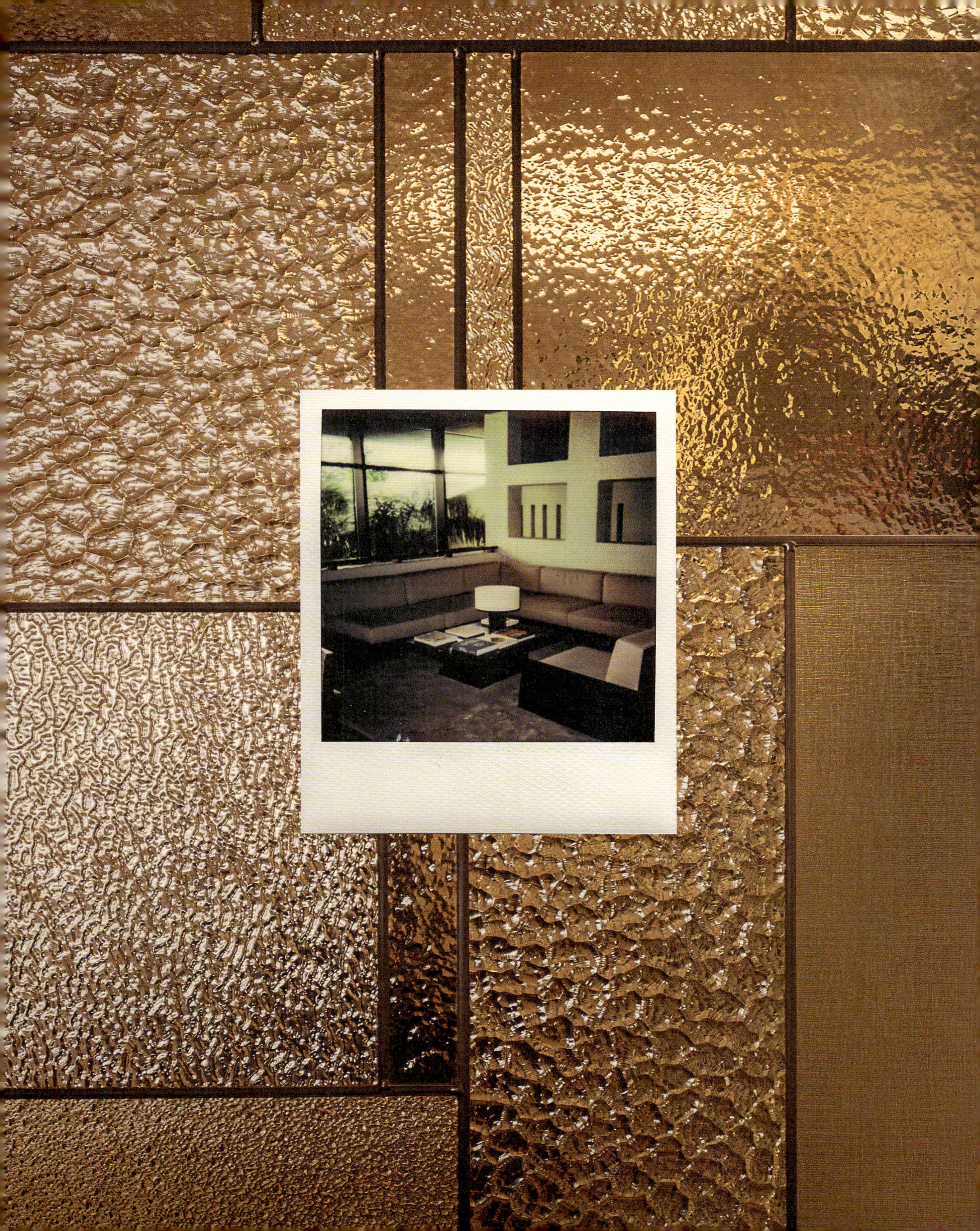

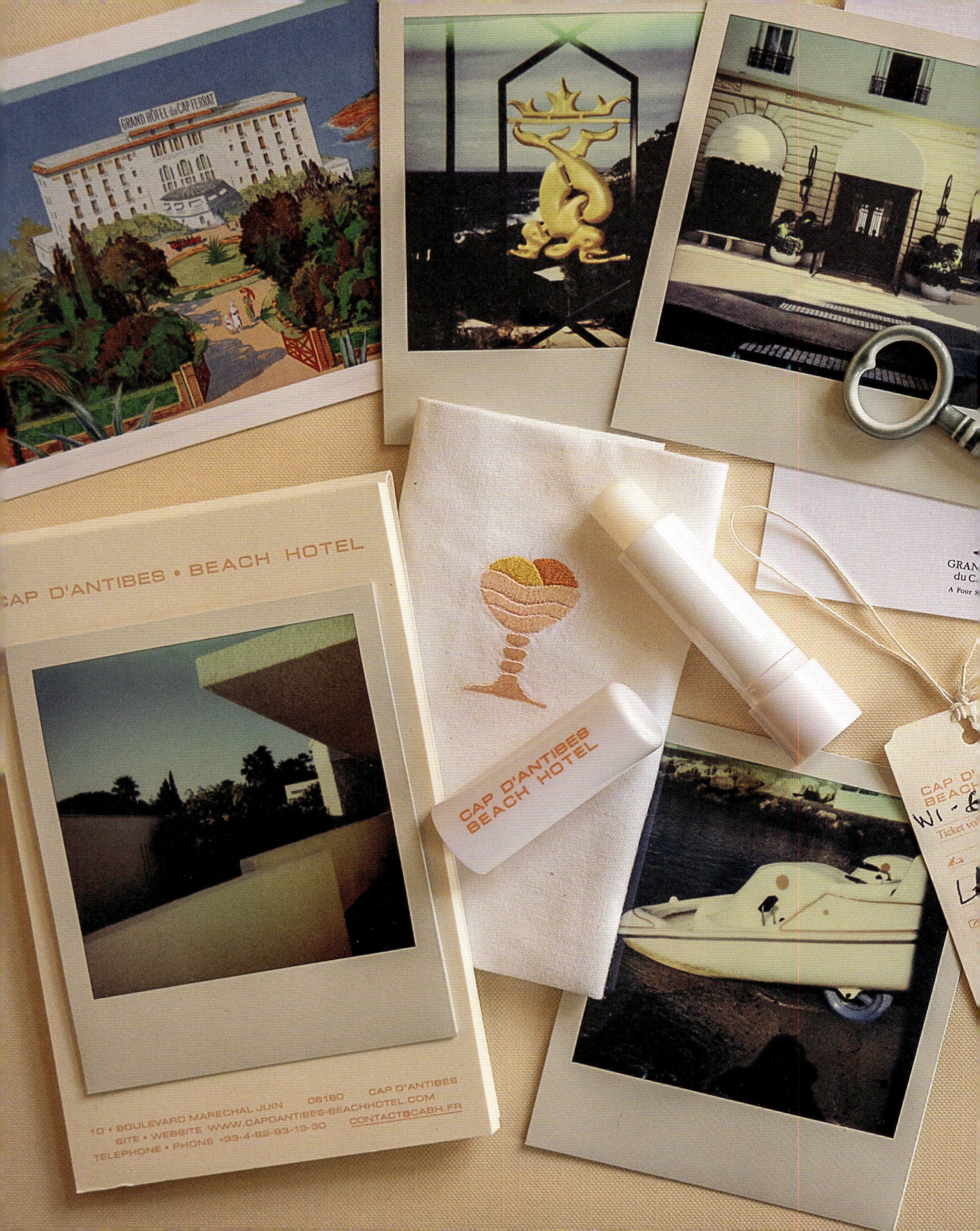
GRAND HOTEL du CAP FERRAT
CAP D'ANTIBES • BEACH HOTEL
10 • BOULEVARD MARECHAL JUIN 06160 CAP D'ANTIBES
SITE • WEBSITE WWW.CAPDANTIBES-BEACHHOTEL.COM
TELEPHONE • PHONE +33-4-92-93-13-30 CONTACT@CABH.FR
CAP D'ANTIBES
BEACH HOTEL

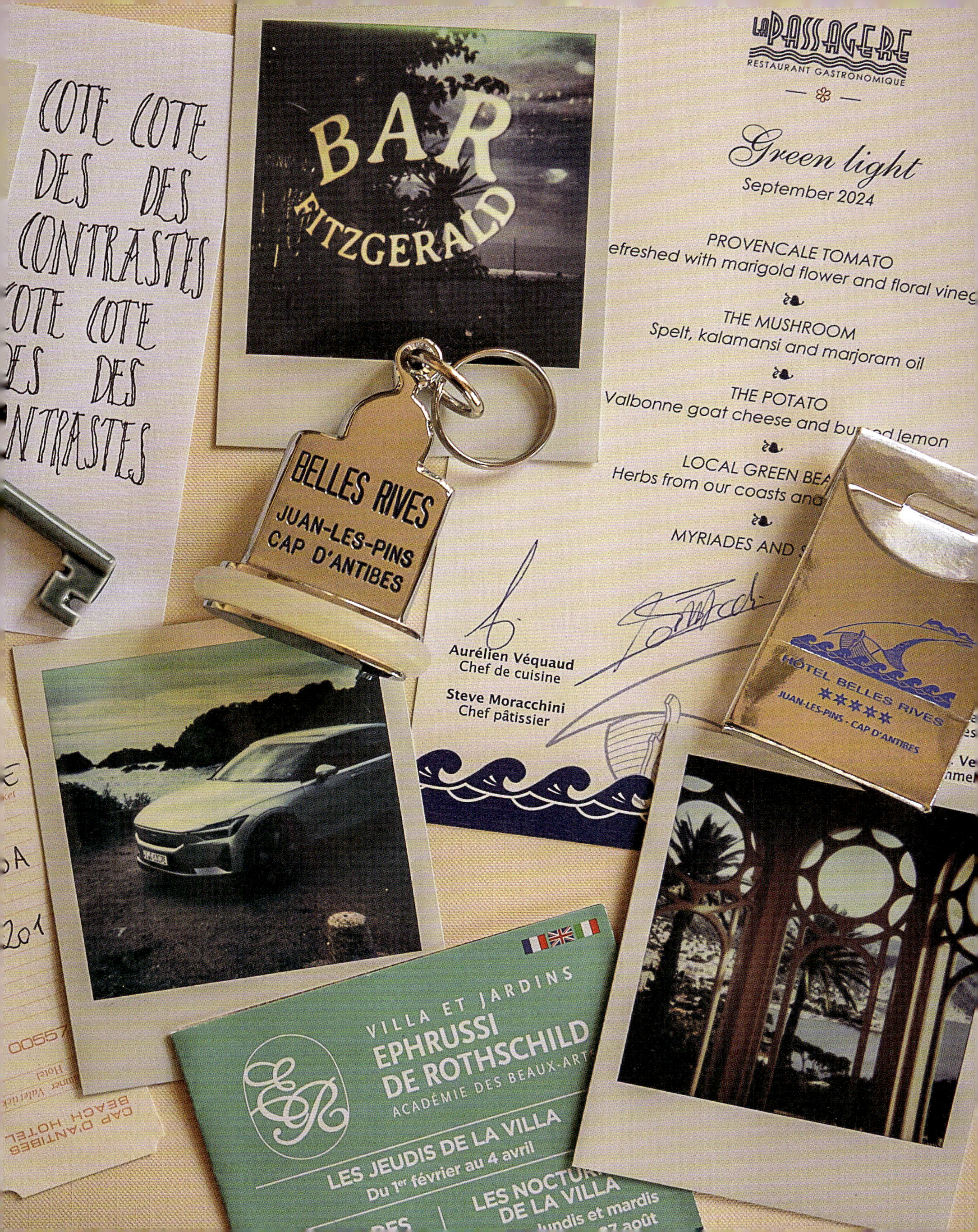
COTE COTE
DES DES
CONTRASTES
BAR
FITZGERALD
LA PASSAGERE
RESTAURANT GASTRONOMIQUE
Green light
September 2024
PROVENCALE TOMATO
THE MUSHROOM
Spelt, kalamansi and marjoram oil
THE POTATO
LOCAL GREEN BEA
MYRIADES AND S
BELLES RIVES
JUAN-LES-PINS
CAP D'ANTIBES
Aurélien Véquaud
Chef de cuisine
Steve Moracchini
Chef pâtissier
HÔTEL BELLES RIVES
JUAN-LES-PINS - CAP D'ANTIBES
VILLA ET JARDINS
EPHRUSSI
DE ROTHSCHILD
ACADÉMIE DES BEAUX-ARTS
LES JEUDIS DE LA VILLA
Du 1er février au 4 avril
LES NOCTUR
DE LA VILLA
CAP D'ANTIBES
BEACH HOTEL

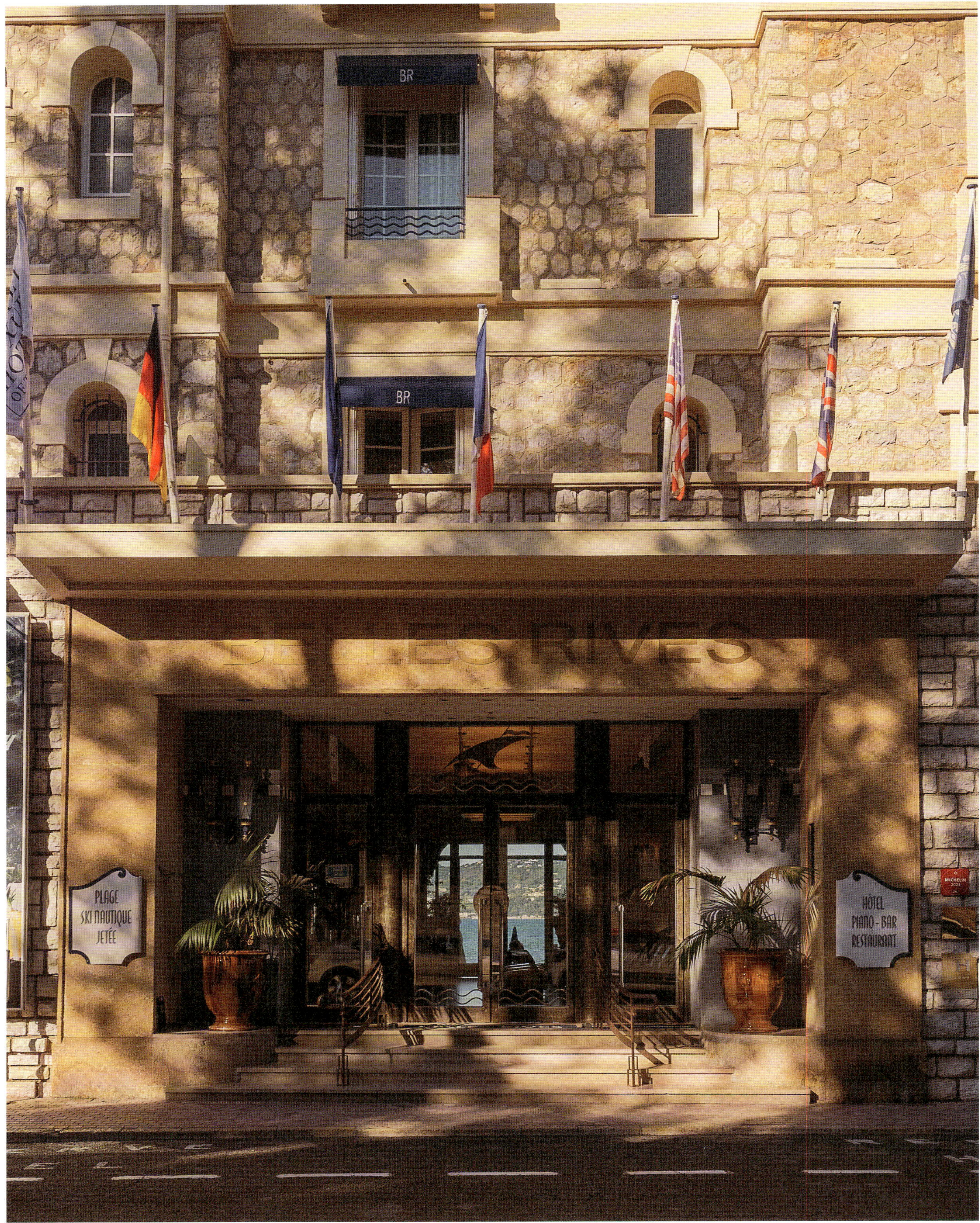
BR
BR
BELLES RIVES
PLAGE
SKI NAUTIQUE
JETÉE
HÔTEL
PIANO - BAR
RESTAURANT

BELLES RIVES

CÔTE D'AZUR

GREEN LIGHT

The next morning, we continue on our tour of contrasts. We leave the car where it is and walk just a few meters down the coastal road. Blue flags by a brick villa, the color of vanilla, flank the entrance to the Belles Rives—gateway to a world of Art Deco elegance, the legendary Jazz Age, and the storied past of F. Scott Fitzgerald, who stayed here with his wife, Zelda, during their tour of the Côte d'Azur in 1926. Here Fitzgerald finished *The Great Gatsby*, worked on *Tender Is the Night*, and quarreled infamously with Zelda, something his jazz soirées with Picasso or Hemingway didn't necessarily get in the way of. It was shortly after their stay that Hôtel Belles Rives was founded, and it's been in the same family ever since, the Fitzgeralds' spirit lingering in every fiber. We cross a delicate mosaic floor to the open Art Deco lift with the hotel's emblem of a golden ship. It carries us to the third floor and our Zelda Suite: small, refined, wrapped in nautical-themed Hermès wallpaper, and granting our first view of the blue-and-white parasols at the beach club. But the palm-lined terrace draws us out again, with promising cocktails and jazz drifting over from the bar. We watch other guests lounging dreamily on blue chaises longues with views of the sea, on candy-colored paddle boats and water skis, or sipping champagne at the waterside restaurant. The doors of La Passagère—the hotel's Michelin-starred restaurant—open at sunset. Crowning our day will be a six-course dinner ending in a breathtaking dessert symphony complete with an absinthe fountain brought to our table. From our suite, we can just make out the shimmer of Cannes in the distance, and still the green light from the harbor casts its glow across the room—a quiet echo of Gatsby's longing for Daisy, and a reminder of what's drawn creatives, eccentrics, and lovers of beauty from around the world to the Belles Rives all these years. The Belles Rives resists comparison with other hotels. Suspended somewhere in the golden glow of the 1920s and as charismatic as its former resident, it offers a tangible sense of history, a perfect day at the sea—or both.

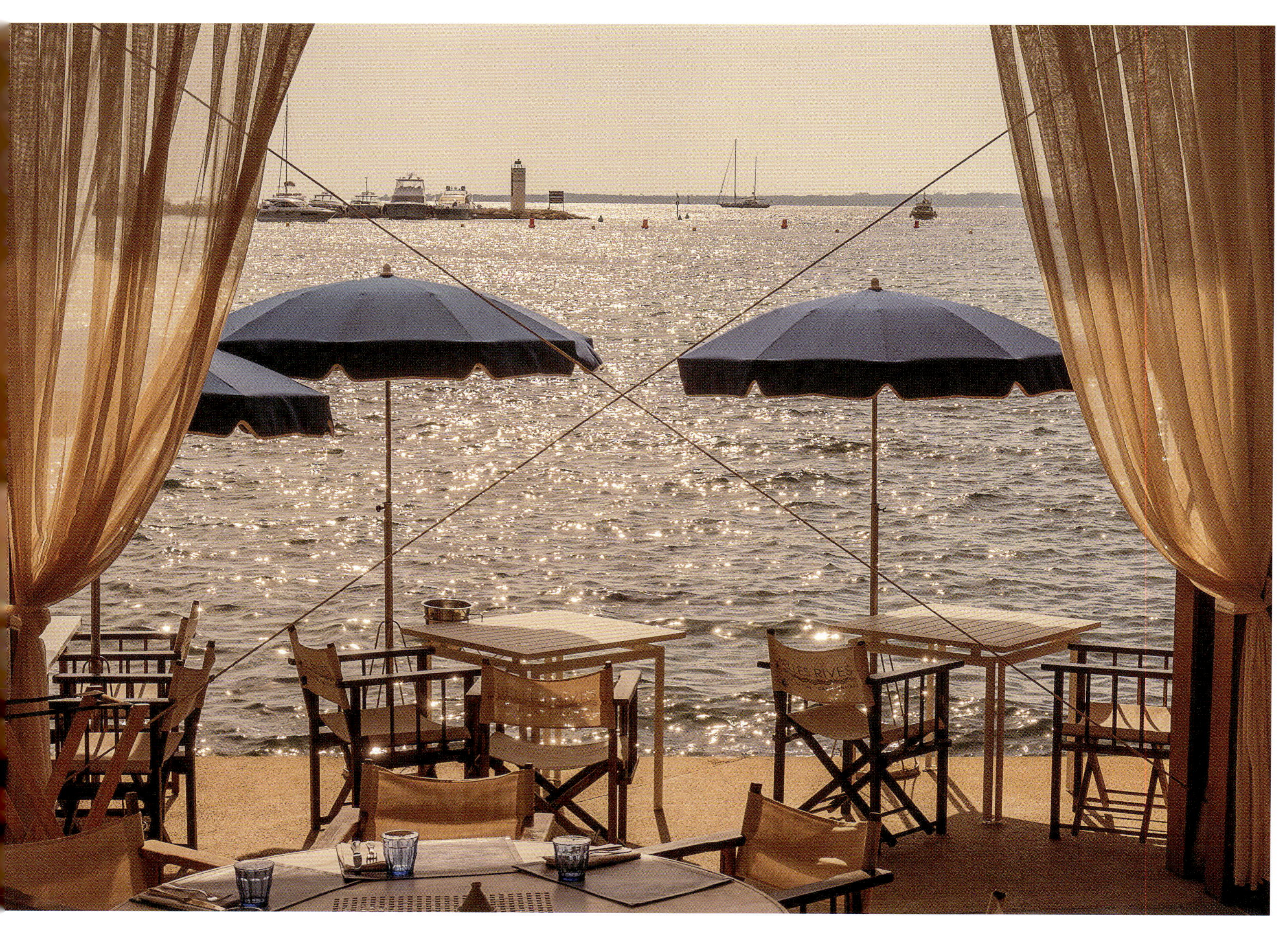

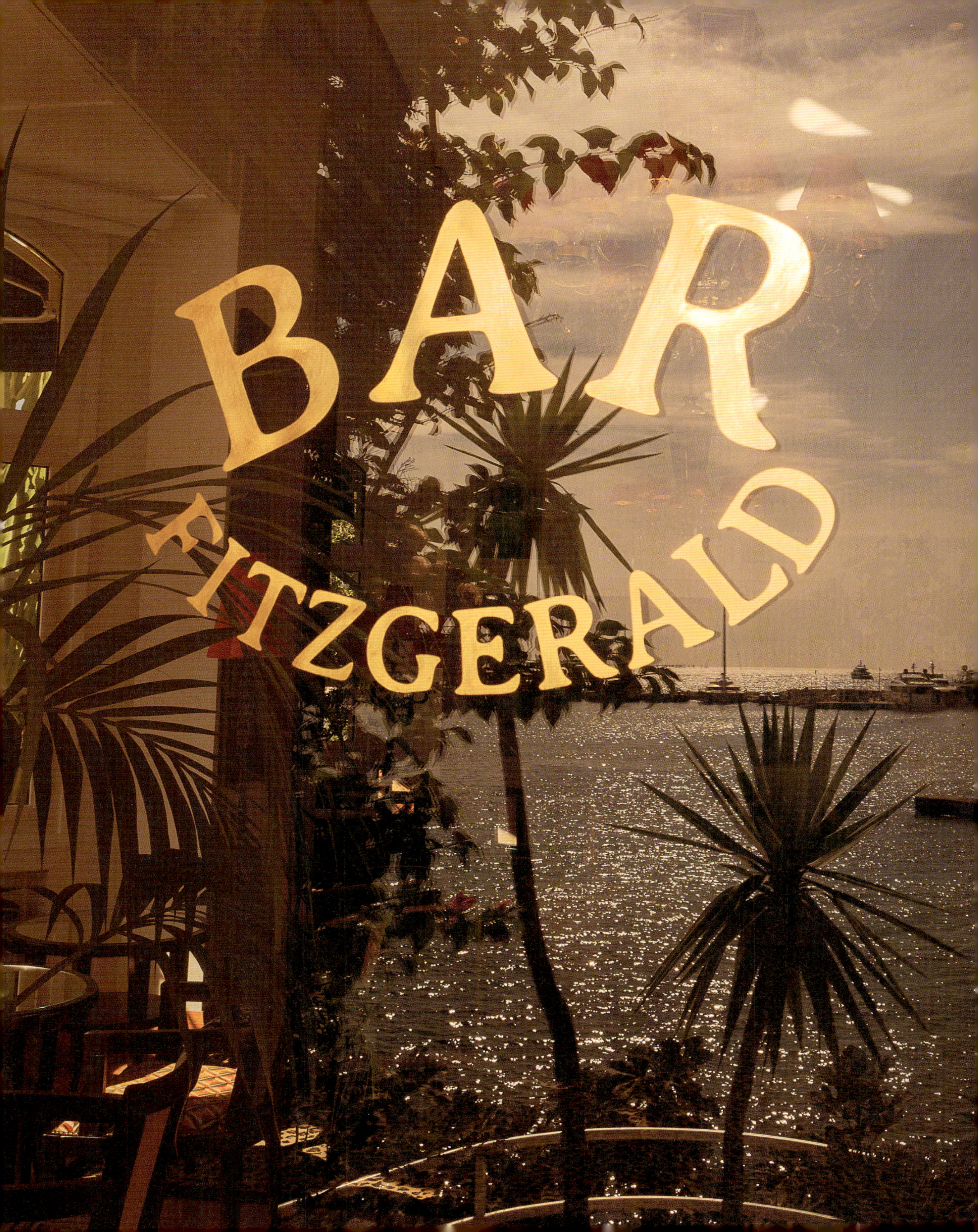
BAR
FITZGERALD

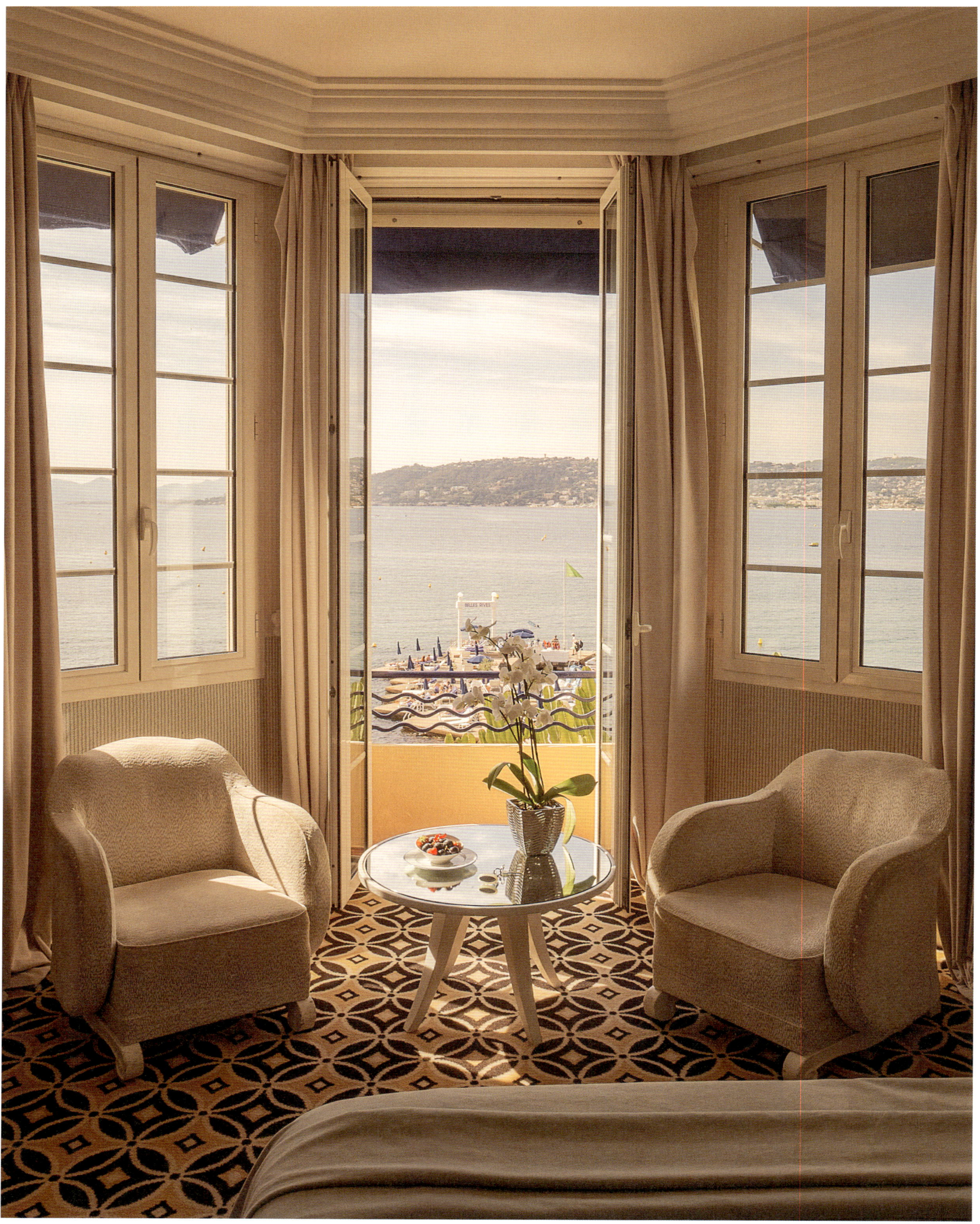
BELLES RIVES

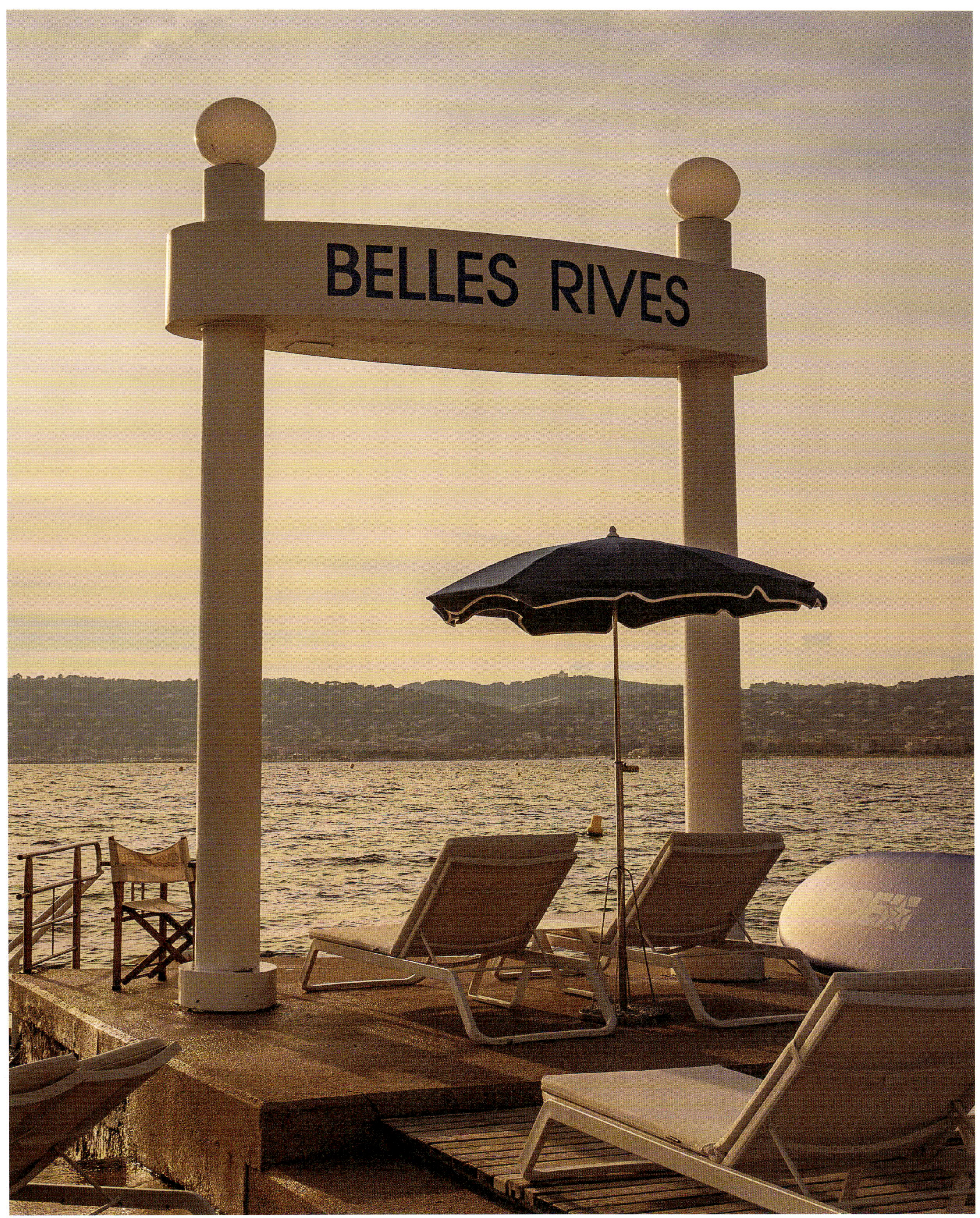
BELLES RIVES

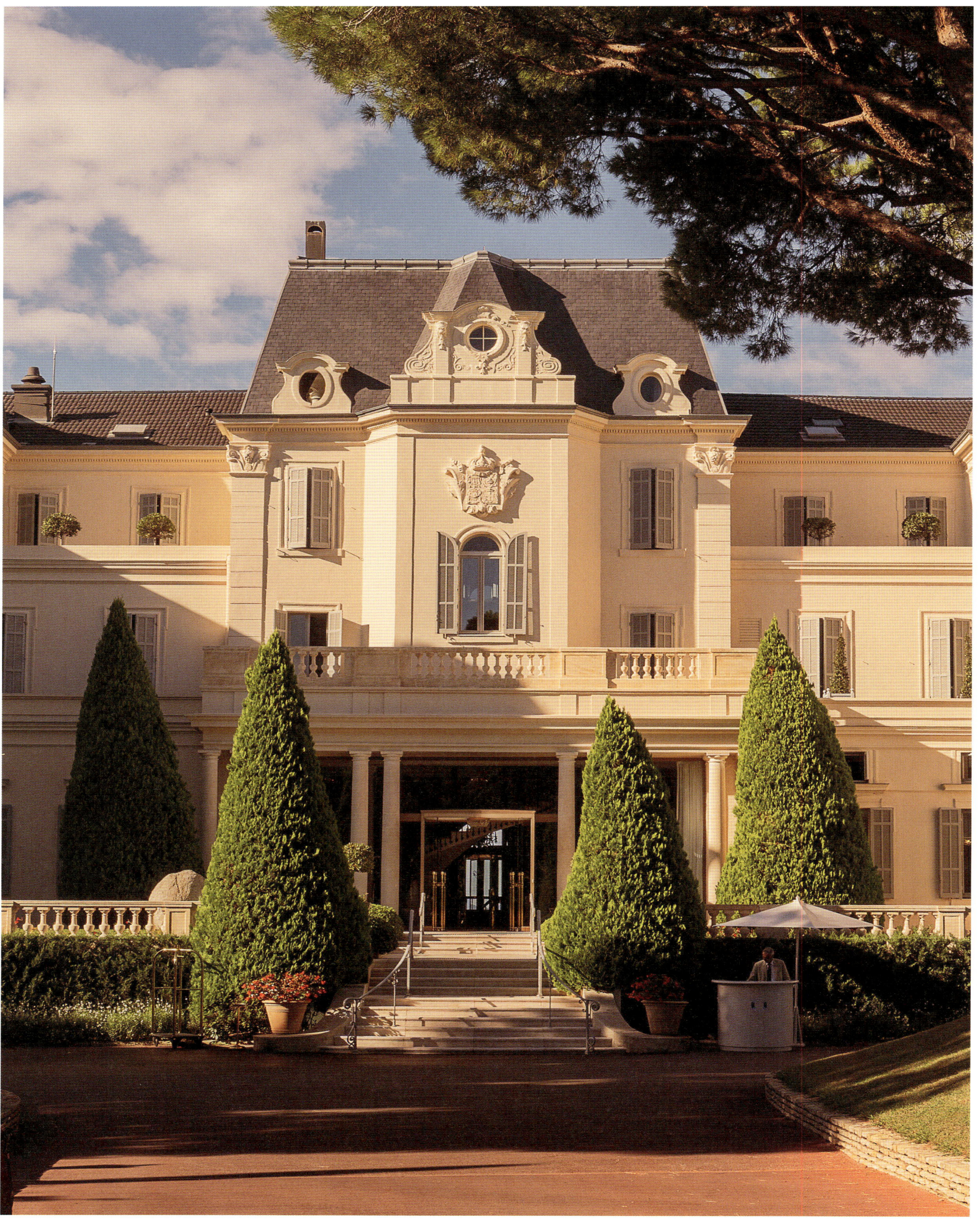

HÔTEL DU CAP-EDEN-ROC

CÔTE D'AZUR

DRESSCODE

For days, our gaze has kept drifting back to that regal white villa perched at the very tip of Cap d'Antibes. *Aujourd'hui*, its doors—anything but ordinary—swing wide to admit us to the Riviera's ultimate jewel: the Hôtel du Cap-Eden-Roc. Libraries could be filled with its lore of music and film icons, politicians and artists, Kennedys and Kardashians, and the annual amfAR gala that brings them all together. The château-like villa welcomes us with a light-filled foyer flanked by a wrought-iron *ascenseur* and a spiral staircase. Passing through the burled-wood revolving door on the west side, we reach the true heart of the estate: a magnificent promenade to the sea—over 500 meters long, generously wide, and offering an uninterrupted view of a rough sea and the Eden-Roc. Our pace naturally slows, because what is called for at the Hôtel du Cap is to *promenade*. There's probably a directive about this somewhere in the hotel's extensive *règlement intérieur*, drafted to safeguard the place's almost mystical luxe. At the end of the promenade, high waves crash against rugged cliffs, where an organically curving pool has been blasted out of the rock. And so the quintessential Riviera dilemma arises: spend the day right here; settle in next door at Le Grill; retreat to a cabana on the cliffs; surrender to the house's Dior spa—or play some tennis? Choices, choices.

Michel, the doorman, heart and soul of the house for more than forty years, decides for us. With warm charm, he swings open the doors to the restaurant. Mid-forkful of *moules-frites* and the champagne fizzing, we suddenly notice that, apart from a handful of other diners, there's no one else in sight.

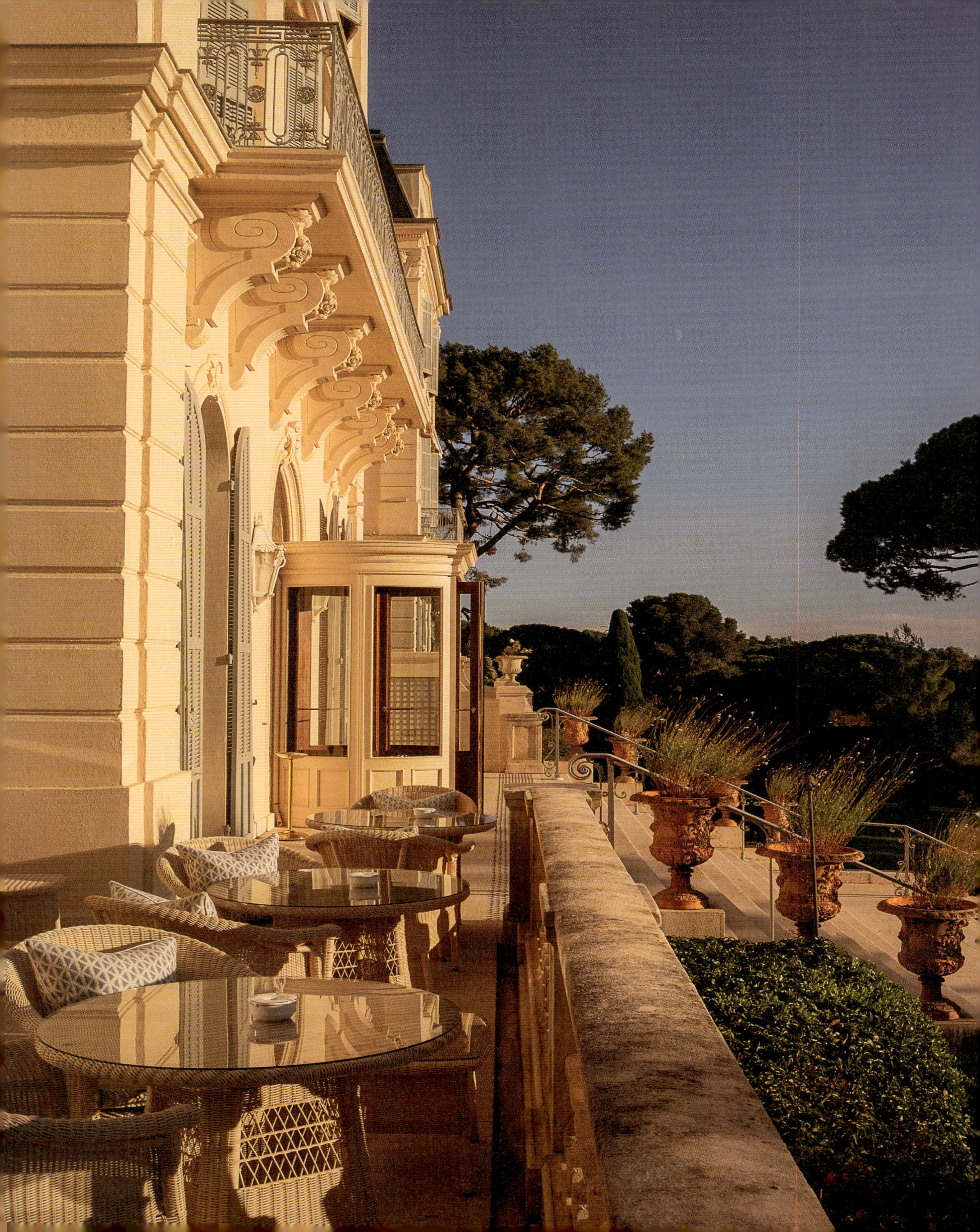

This is part of the property's quiet sleight of hand: the feeling of ultimate privacy, a château all to yourself, even when the hotel is fully booked.

Not until sunset does the true scene materialize. The promenade becomes flooded with silk chiffon dresses and razor-sharp suits; sequins glitter in the glow of the lanterns. Glamour is the rule. We sprint off to change—after all, in this bijou location, the dress code is sacrosanct. Maintain it at all costs.

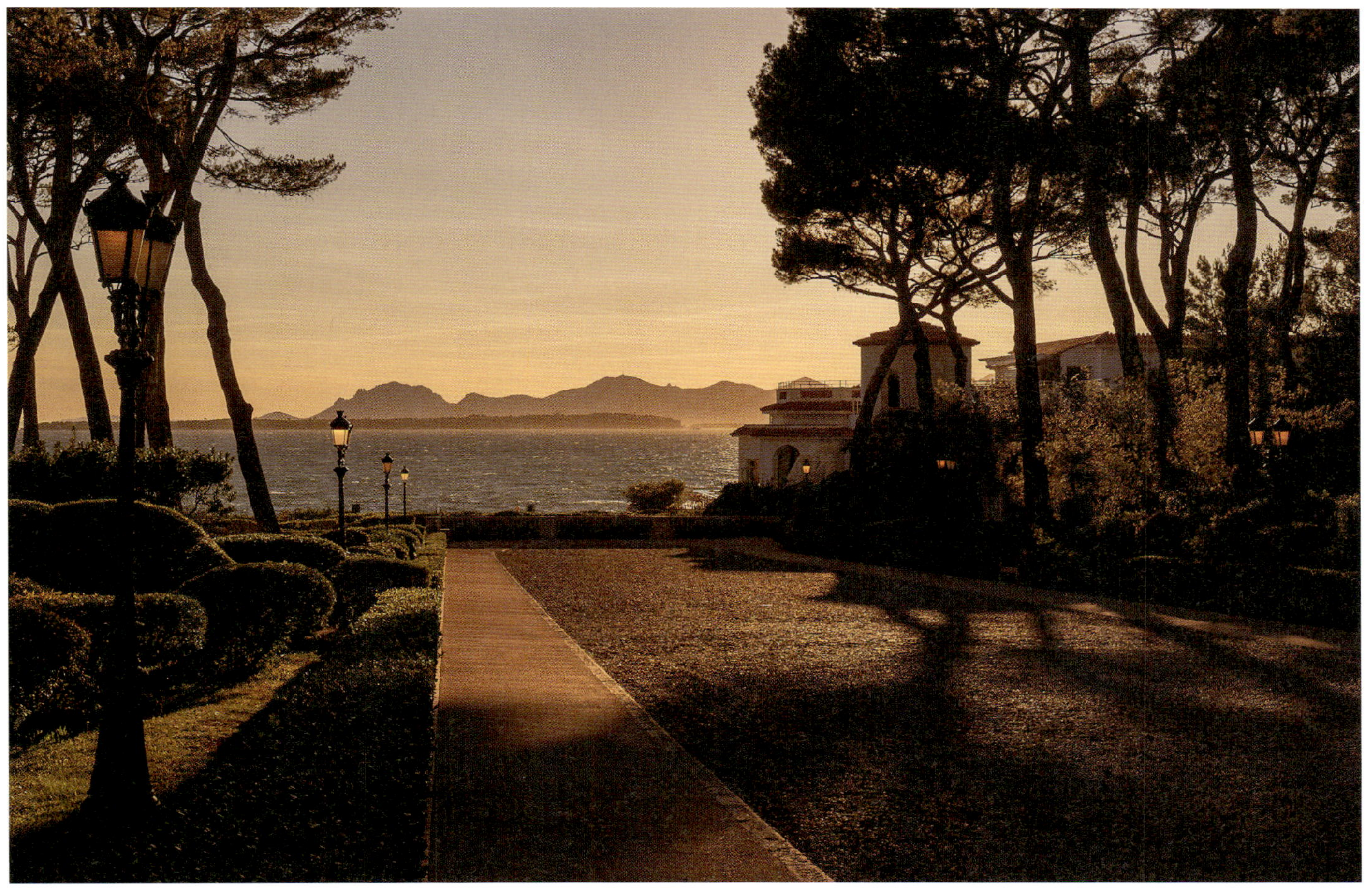

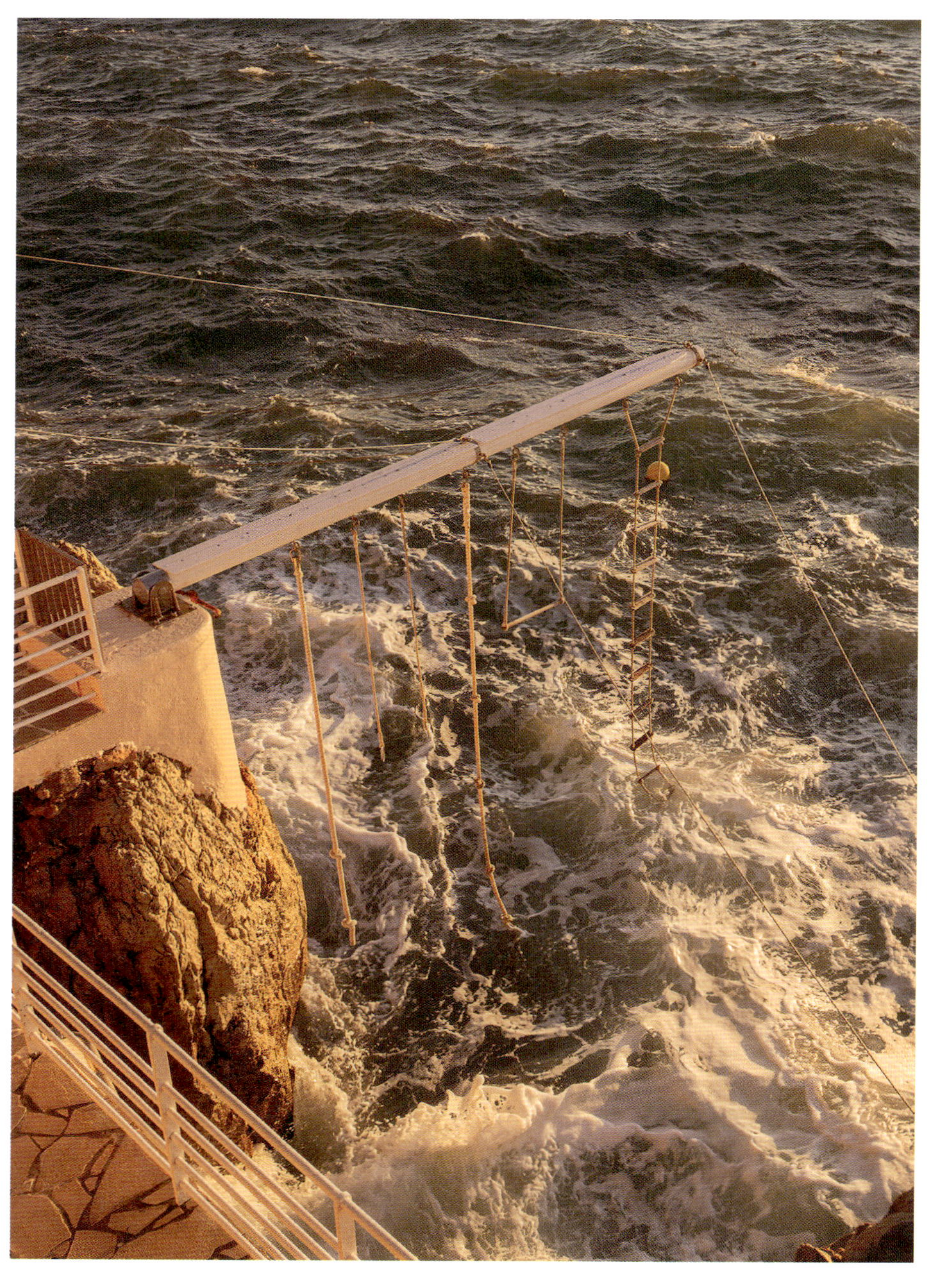

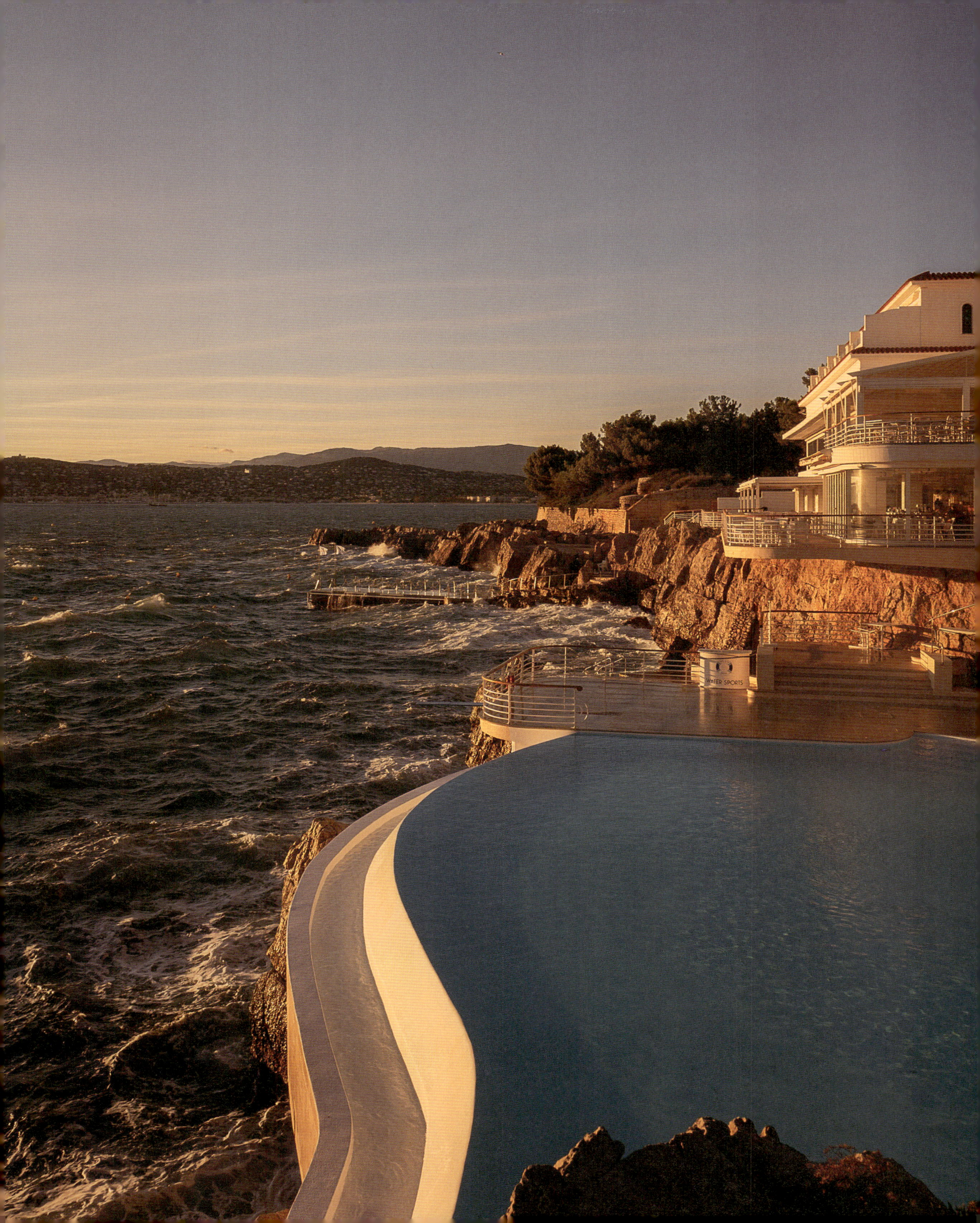
WATER SPORTS

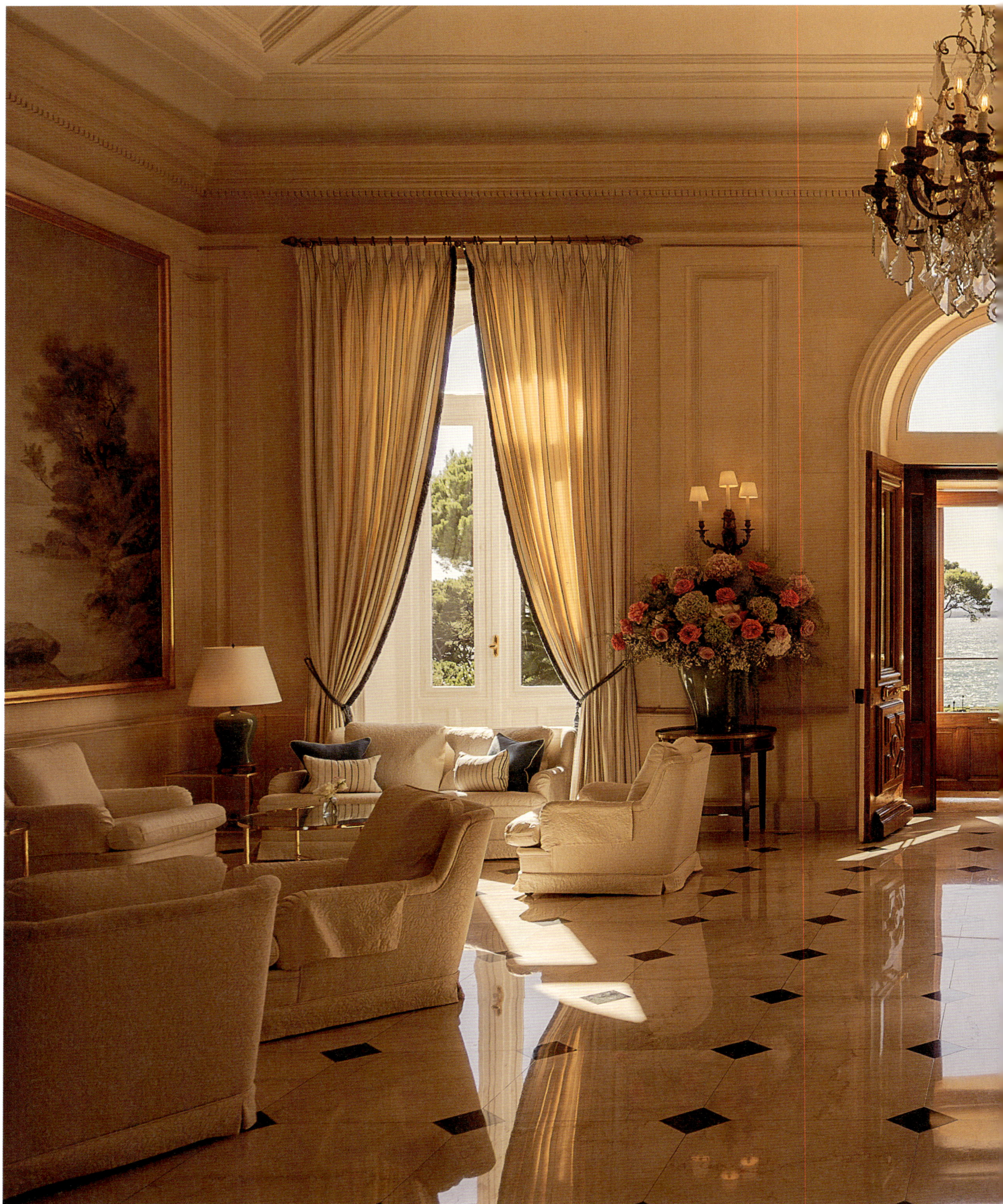

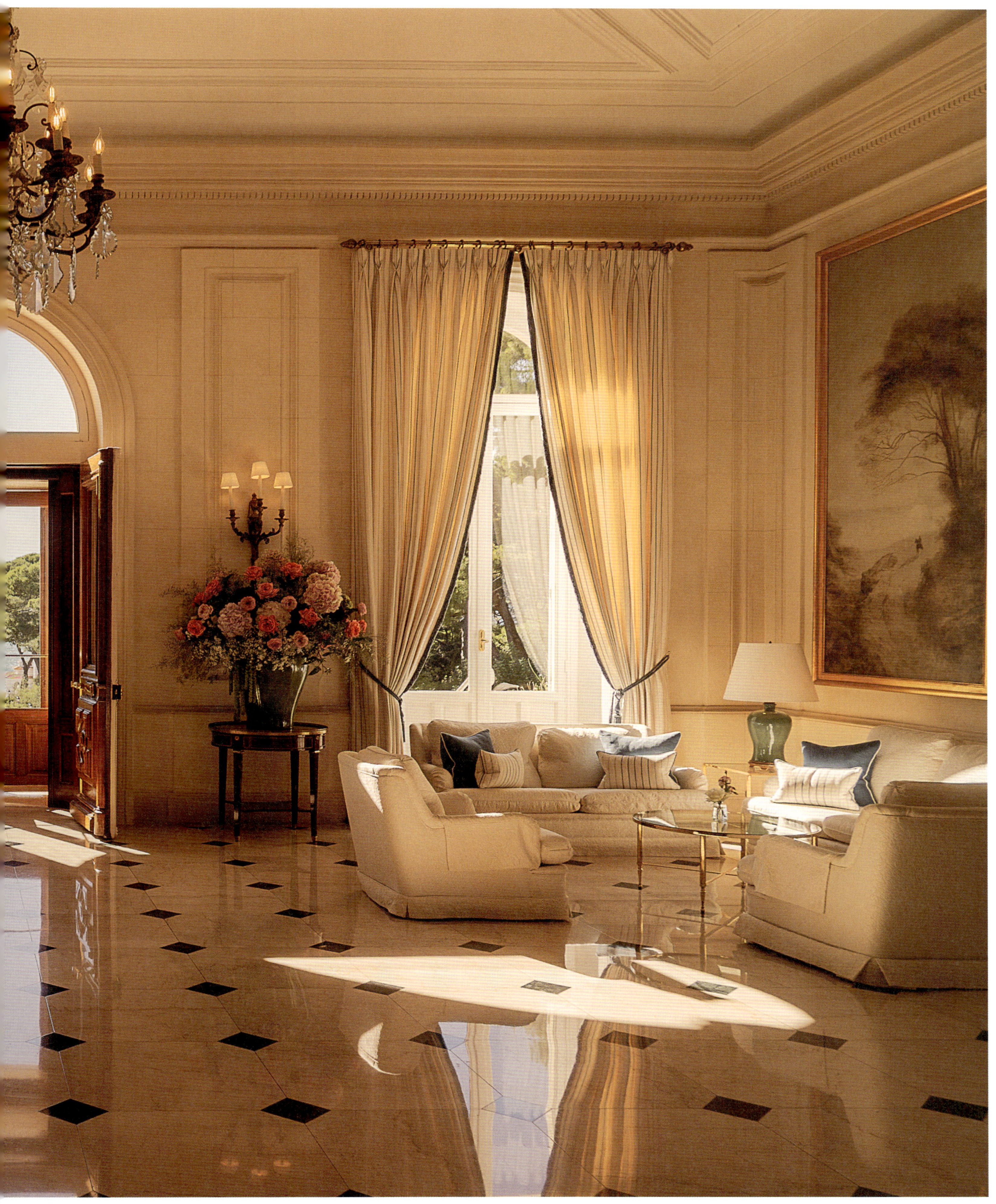

The rooms at the Hôtel du Cap-Eden-Roc are classy, on par with the compound overall: warm linden green, Empire furniture, mirrored boudoirs, and fat bouquets of flowers. Access to the rooms—it goes without saying—is by the classic room key, rather than a key card.

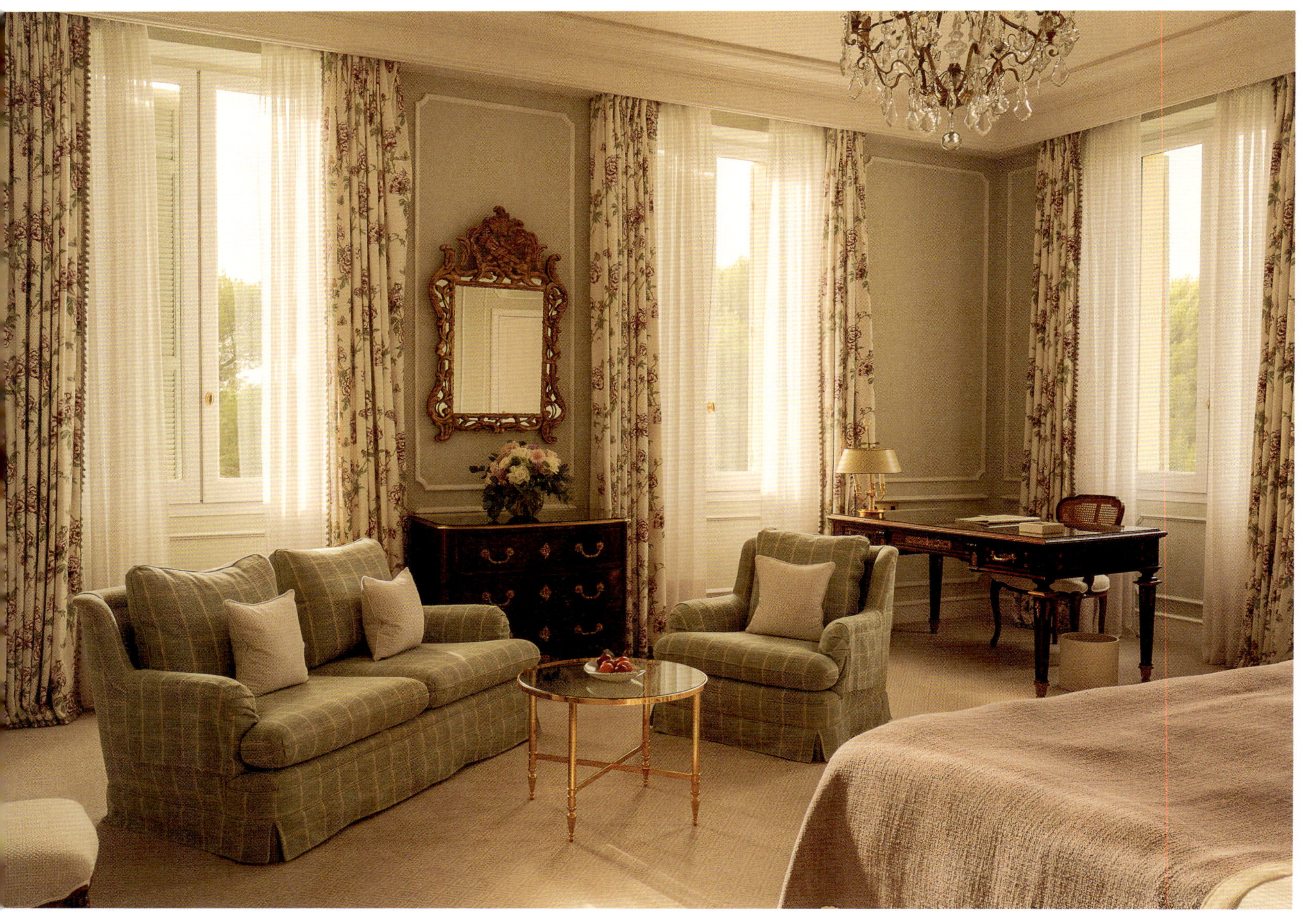

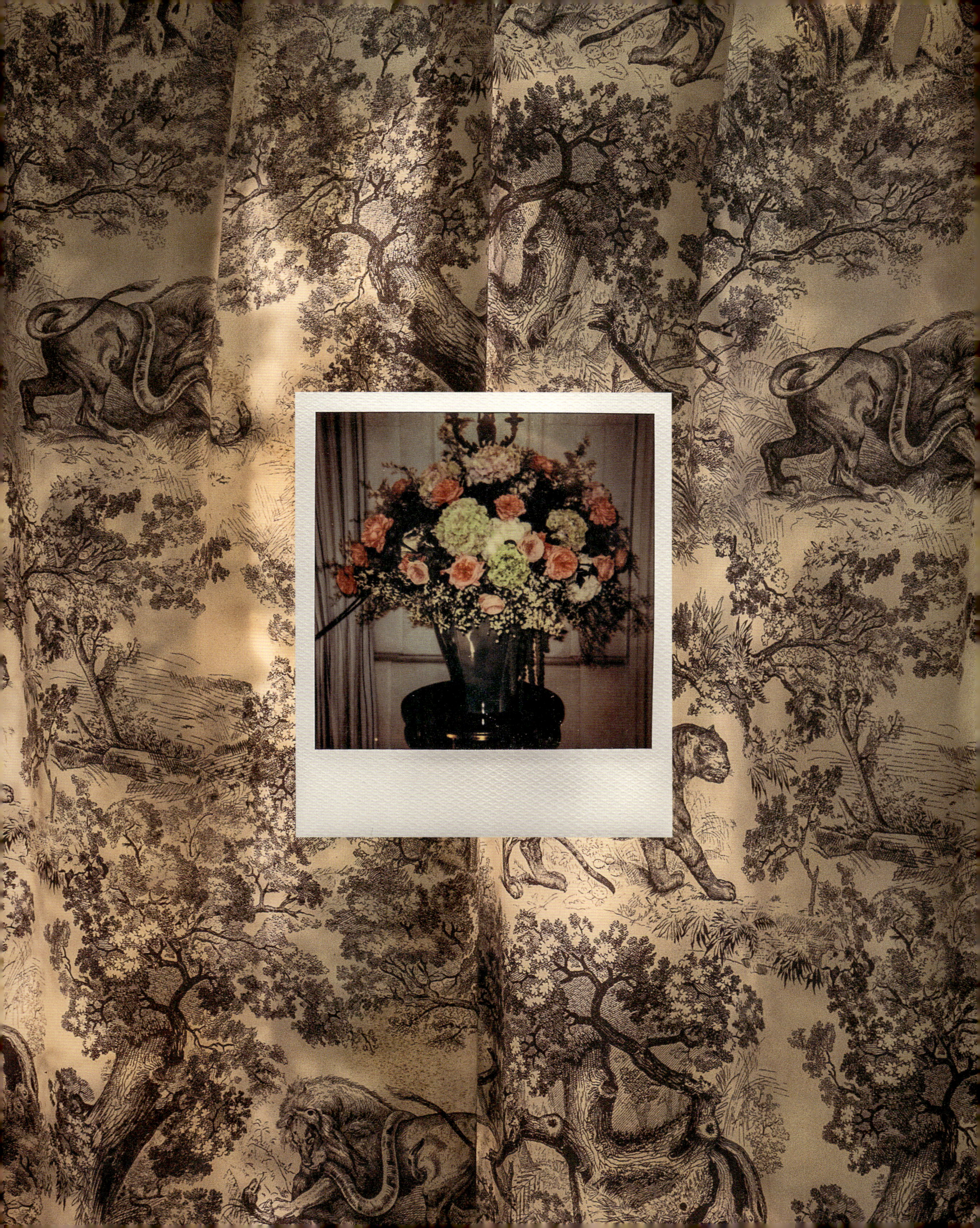

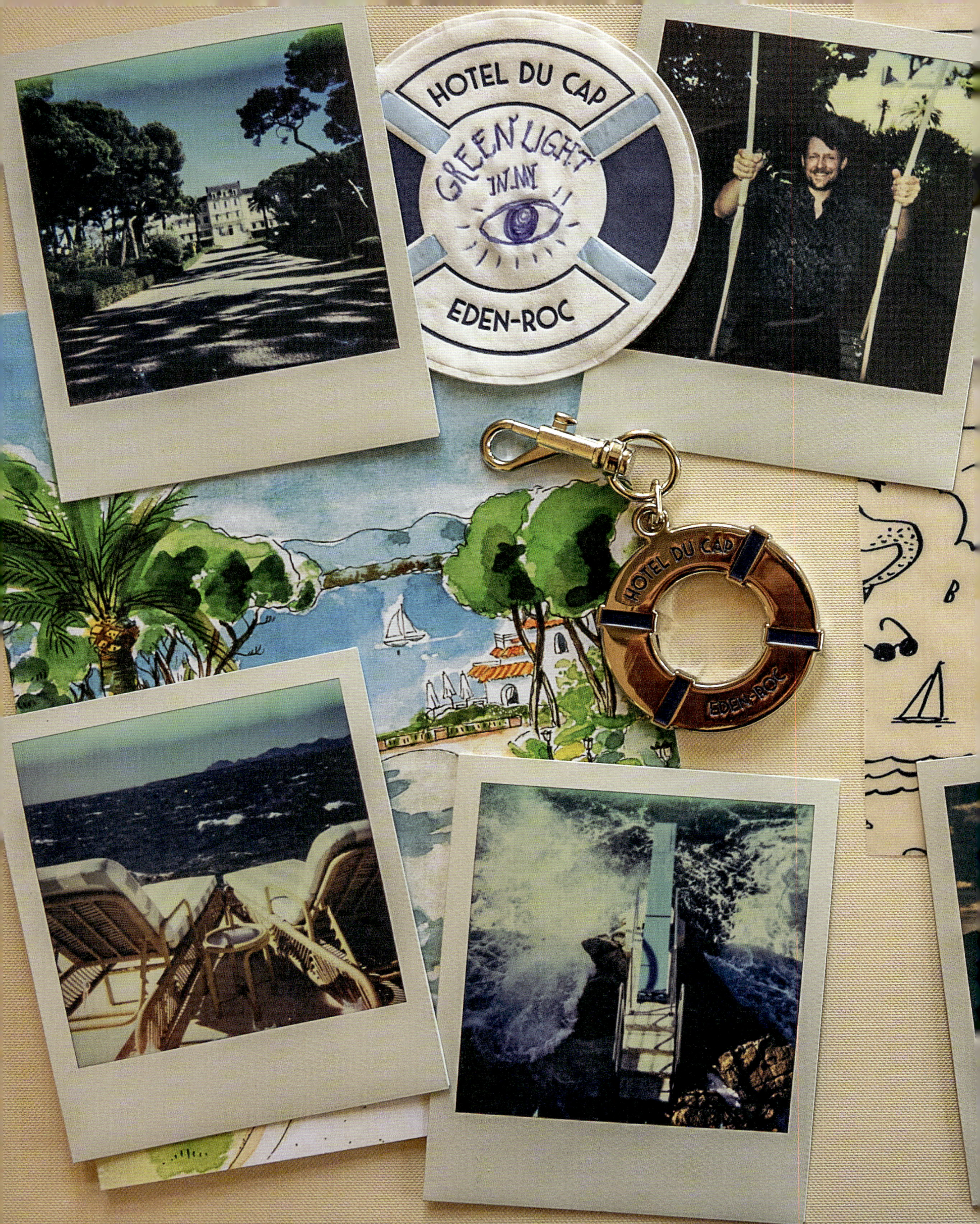
HOTEL DU CAP
GREEN LIGHT
EDEN-ROC
HOTEL DU CAP
EDEN-ROC

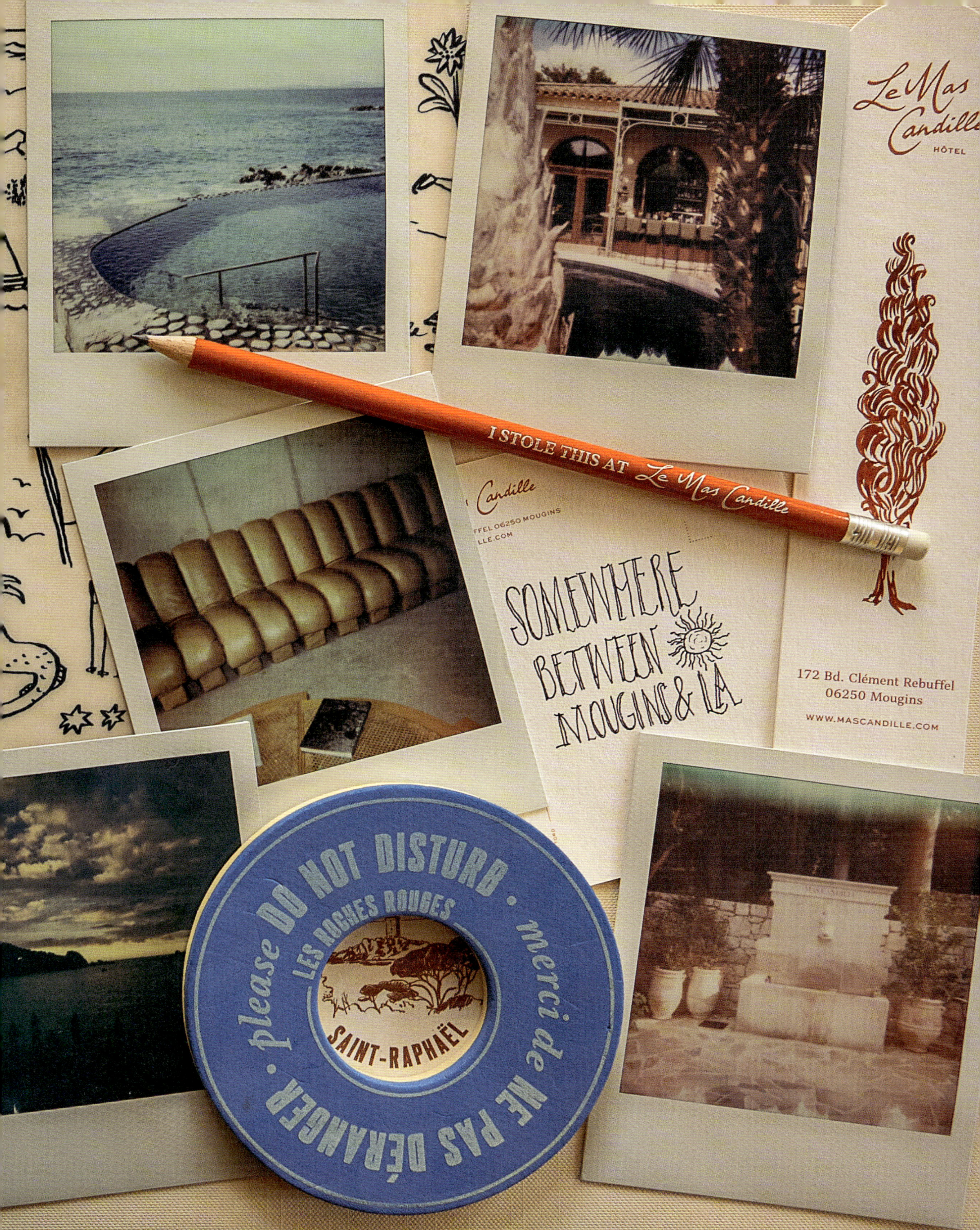

Le Mas Candille
HÔTEL
I STOLE THIS AT Le Mas Candille
SOMEWHERE BETWEEN MOUGINS & LA
172 Bd. Clément Rebuffel
06250 Mougins
WWW.MASCANDILLE.COM
please DO NOT DISTURB · merci de NE PAS DÉRANGER ·
LES ROCHES ROUGES
SAINT-RAPHAËL

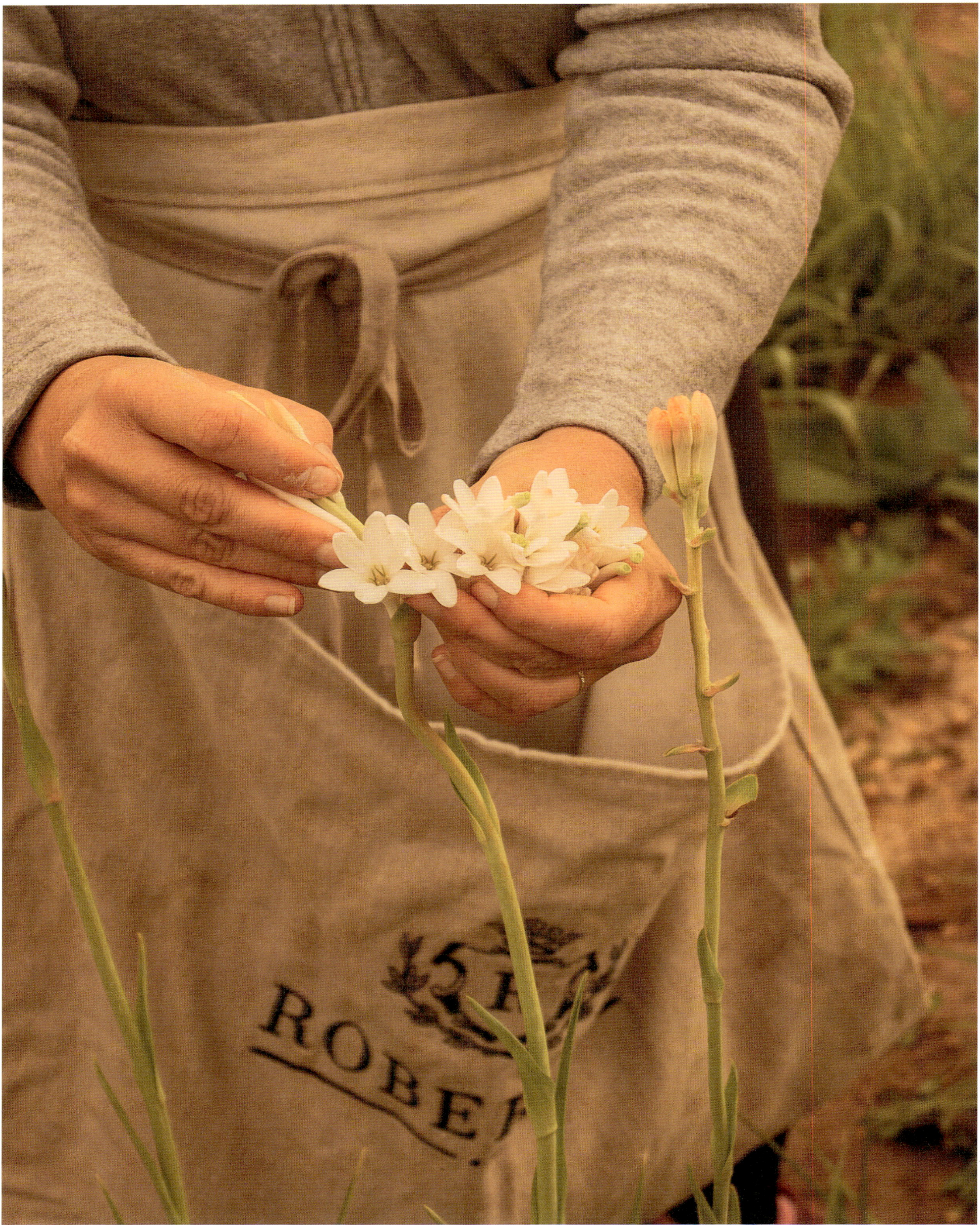

MARIEJEANNE

CÔTE D'AZUR

MOONLIGHT EXTRACT

Well before dawn, we depart for what may be the most sensual stop on our itinerary: Grasse, *cité des parfumeurs*. The route veers inland, threading through the foothills until a town reveals itself tucked against the folds of the terrain. Grasse's charm lies not so much in its visual but rather in its olfactory appeal. The town's every fiber is dedicated to scents. Here are seated the world's oldest and most influential perfumeries, their success nourished by mineral-rich soil and steep terraces that catch the sun and coax the fabled *Jasminum grandiflorum* to blossom across the fields.

We pull up beside one of those very fields. The sun has barely cleared the horizon, and dew still pearls on an emerald sea, yet the rows are already astir with pickers. They have been at it since the wee hours. Their motions are gentle but deliberate as they pluck each bud and slip it into wicker panniers. Jasmine is best gathered before sunrise, as the scent is strongest when the white blossoms catch the moonlight, luring nocturnal pollinators. Higher up the slope, we find Georges, the youngest bud of the Maubert family, owner of Robertet, one of Grasse's most storied maisons de parfum. He ushers us—and the morning's haul—to their factory, where tons of blossoms vanish into iron distillation columns. Inside, their *âme*—the purest breath of their essence—is coaxed out until only a few drops of extract remain: concentrated, pristine, and priceless. Those drops, blended into the most exquisite compositions, are coveted by the world's great fashion houses. But Georges keeps some for his own label, MarieJeanne named in honor of his grandmother. Why sit at the source and let others have all the finest quality? MarieJeanne's perfumes are pure and potent, each built on just a handful of notes—an ode to jasmine, iris, or lavender at its most piercing. We leave Grasse under the influence of its charms, convinced that no other city on earth is as utterly devoted to a single craft.

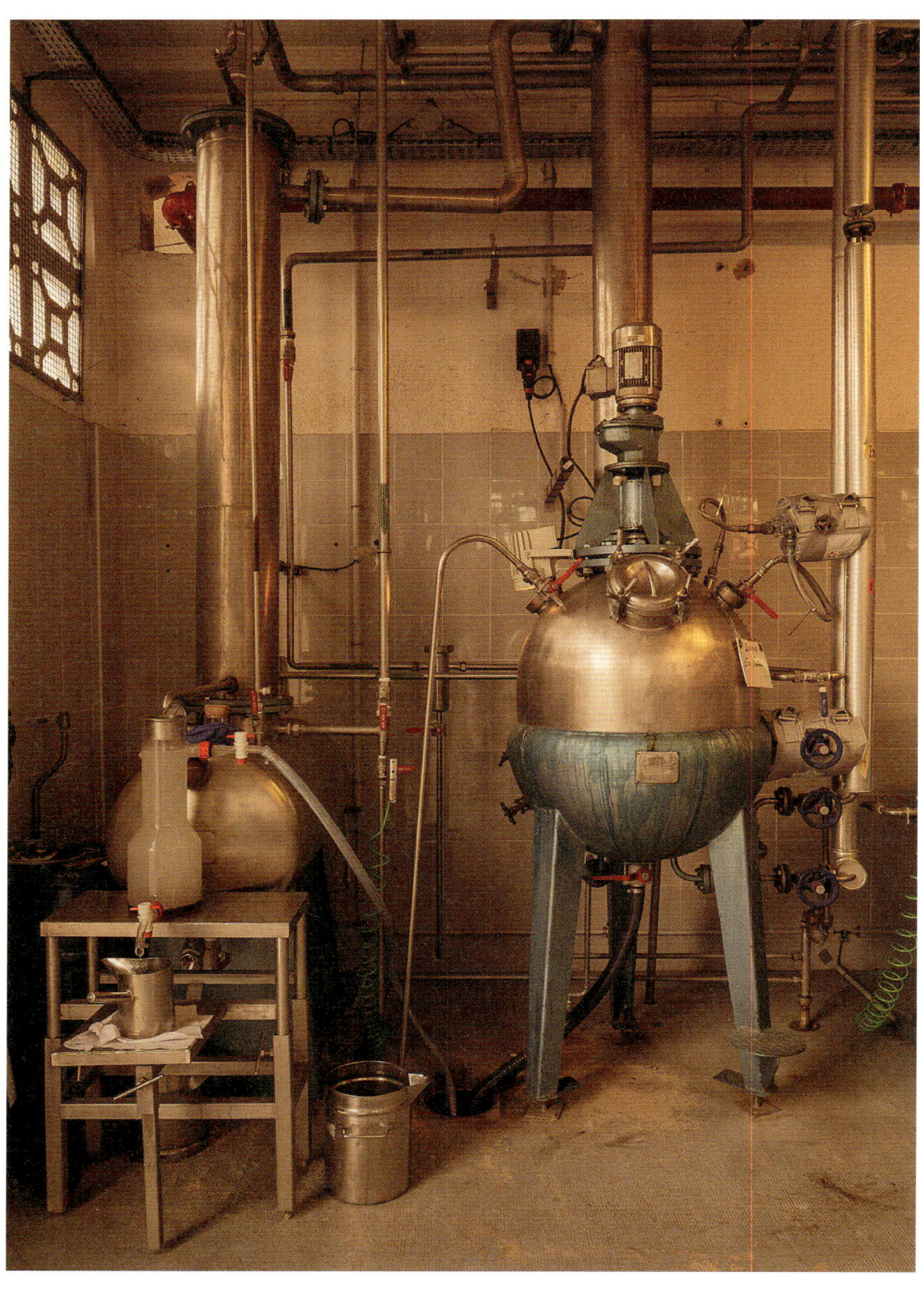

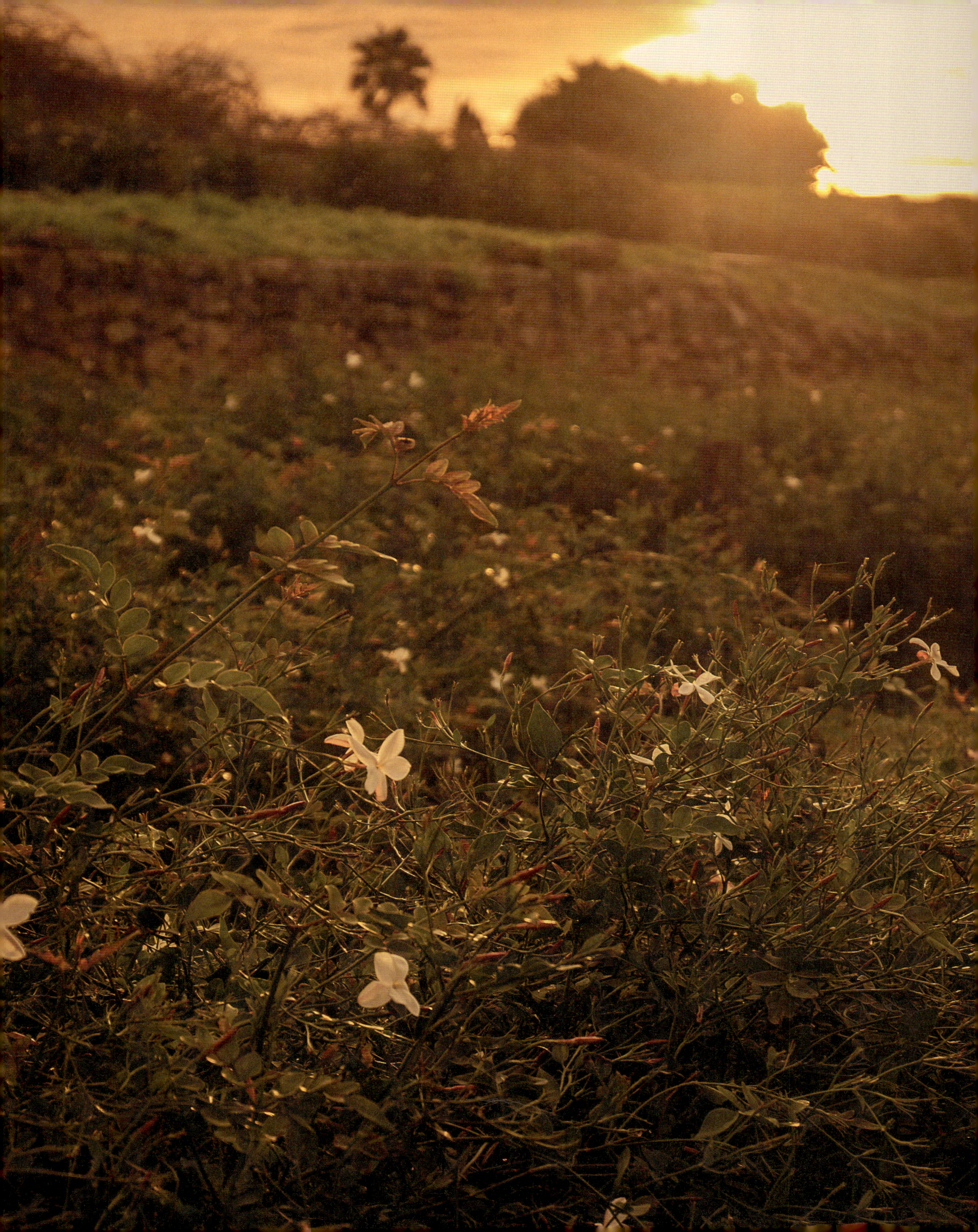

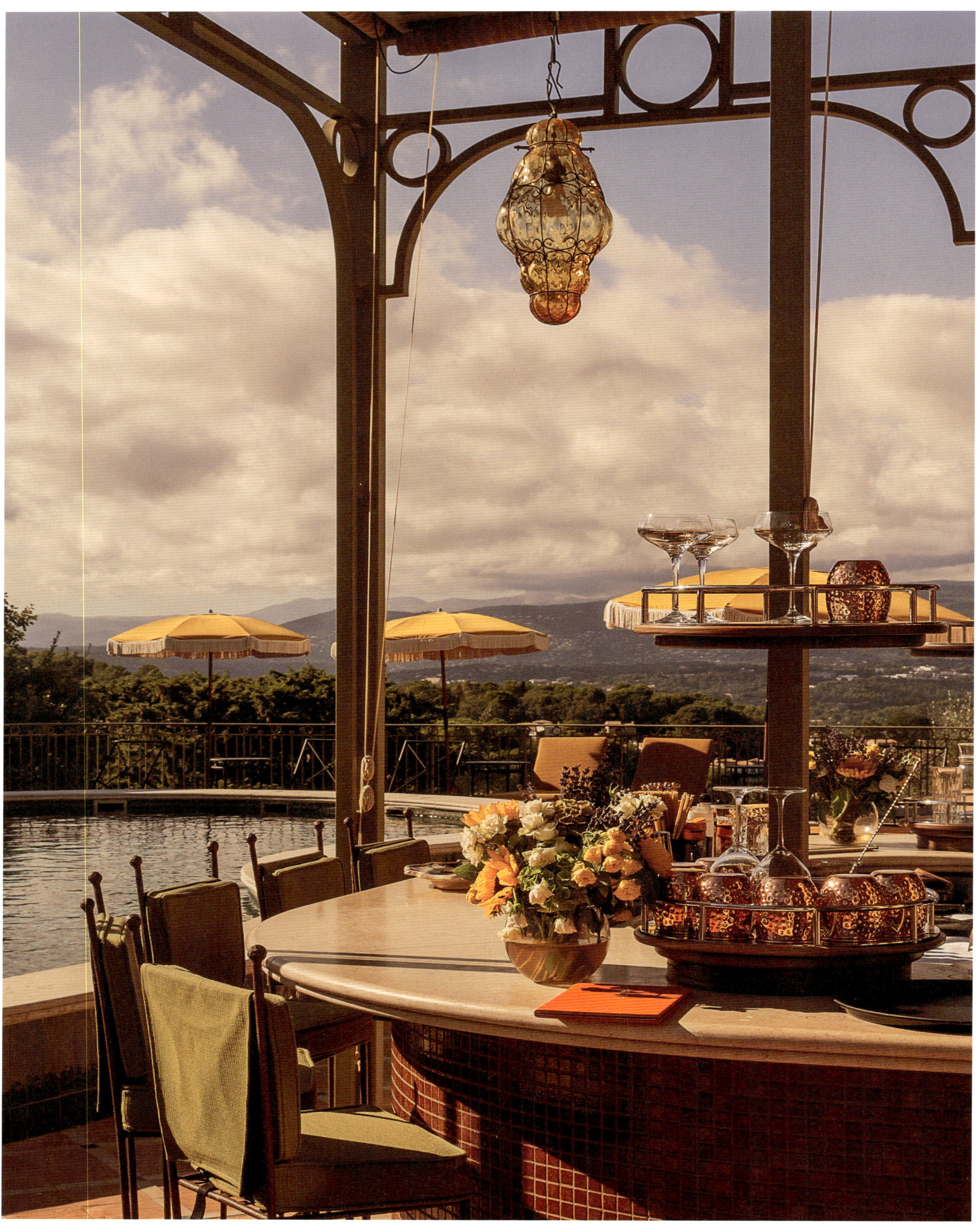

LE MAS CANDILLE

CÔTE D'AZUR

MOUGINS & LOS ANGELES

The scents of Grasse still linger, and we find ourselves reluctant to return to the coast. Too peaceful is the embrace of the tranquil hills of the hinterland. A glimpse of Mougins ushers us off the highway—but the picturesque hilltop village, famed as Picasso's final abode, is not our destination today. Instead, we arrive at Le Mas Candille, just outside the walls of the old town. Spread across ten acres of gently rolling landscape, this hideaway's cohesive, modern design helps you get over the glitz and bustle of the Riviera. Interior design rising star Hugo Torro has thoroughly reimagined the long-established hotel, cooly blending Côte d'Azur elegance with laid-back California. The reception sits within the original farmhouse at the heart of the property, welcoming us with warm ochre walls, leather-trimmed tables, polished mahogany, blind mirrors, and golden velvet—a nod to the American style of the 1960s and '70s, yet unmistakably Provençal. This bold aesthetic runs through the entire hotel—from the suites to the restaurant decked out in emerald-green and carmine-red wood paneling, to the library with its collection of French classics lining heavy black wooden shelves. There's nothing held back here and no qualms about luminous colors. Le Mas Candille thus stands in striking contrast to the coastal restraint we've experienced so far. The warm afternoon sun beckons us outside, to the bar beside one of the resort's two swimming pools. The Doors hum softly from hidden speakers as a waiter brings us spicy margaritas. Before us, beige tassels flutter gently from yellow parasols in the warm breeze. In the distant hills lies Grasse, yet we could easily be gazing at the Hollywood Sign across the hills of Los Angeles.

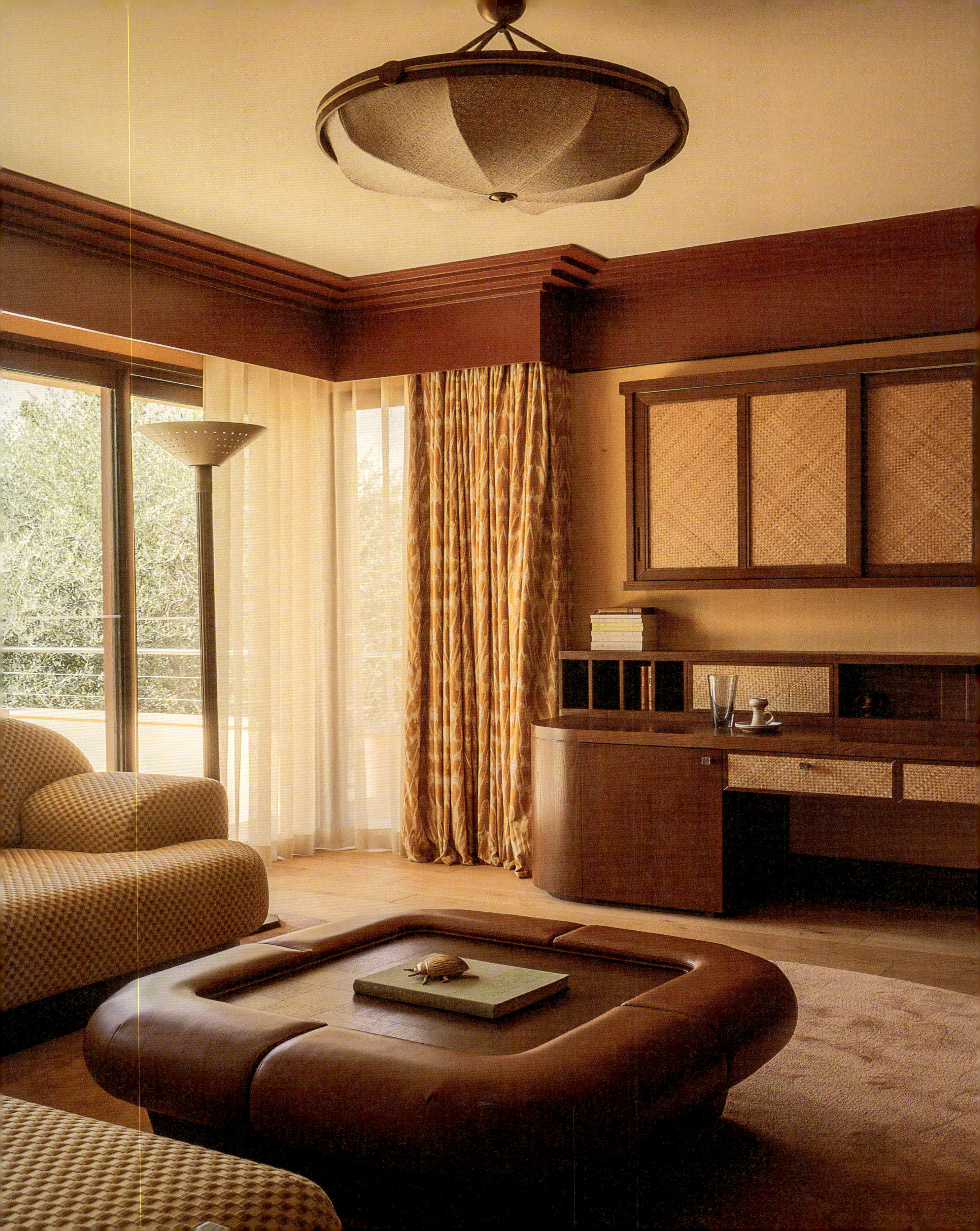

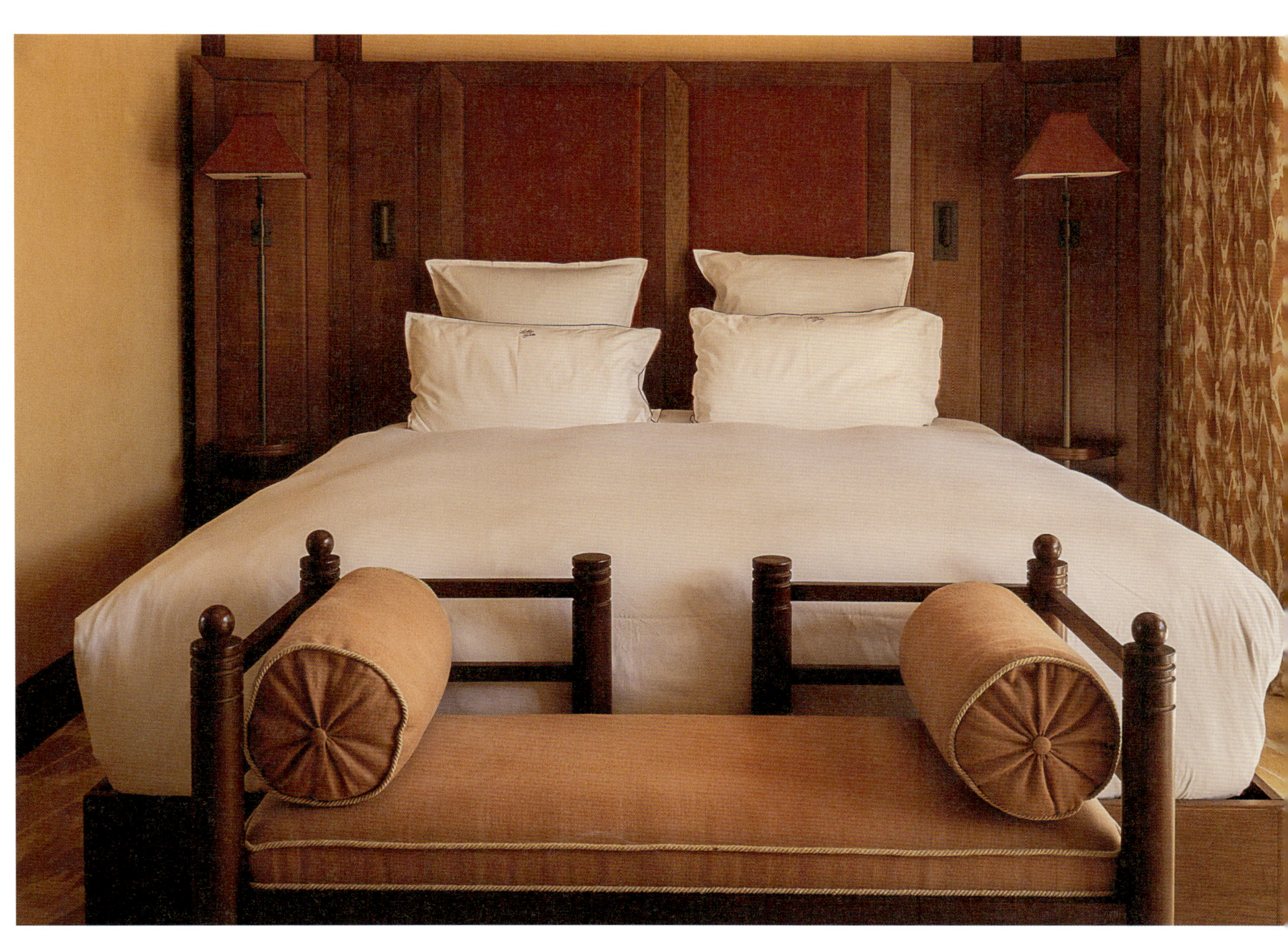

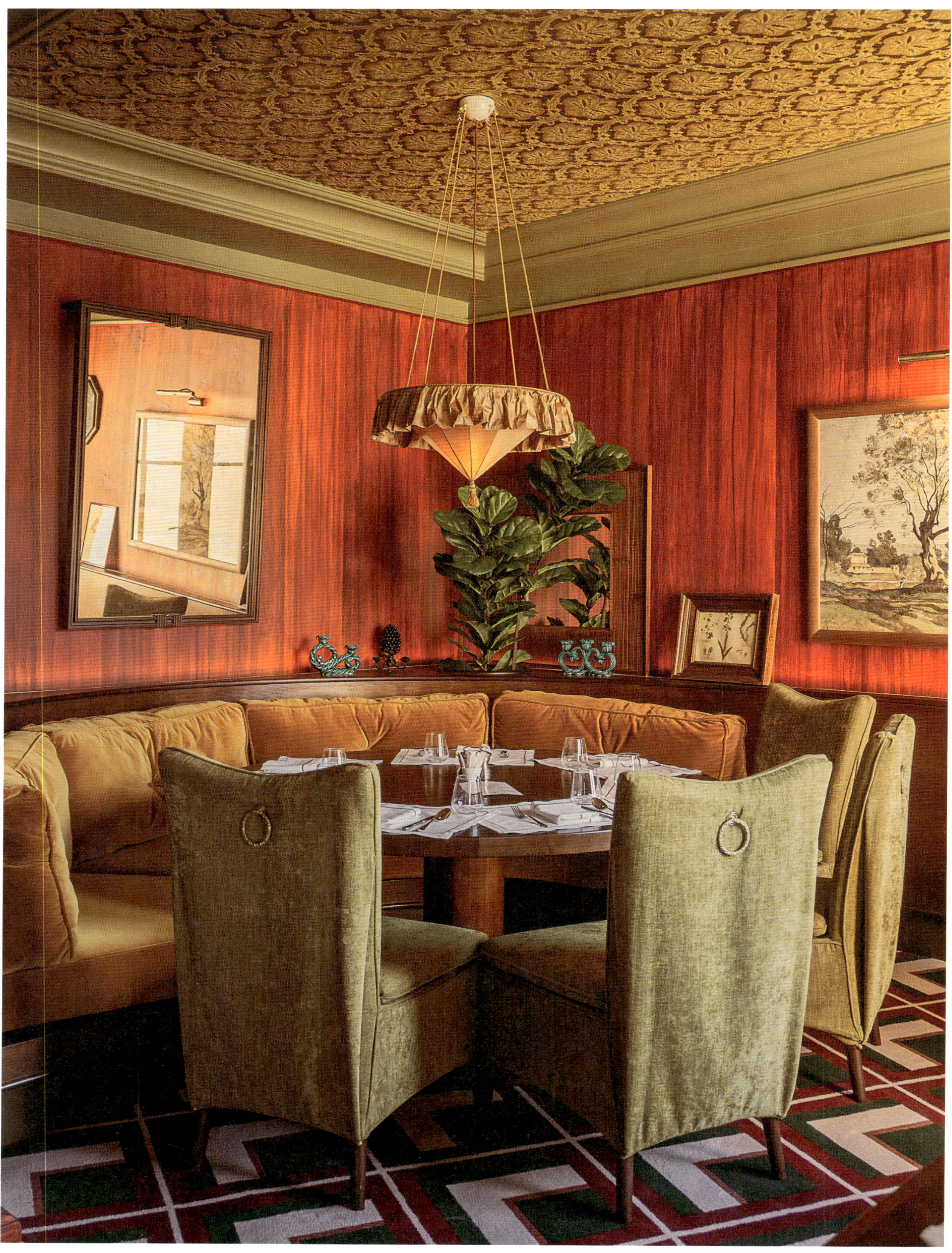

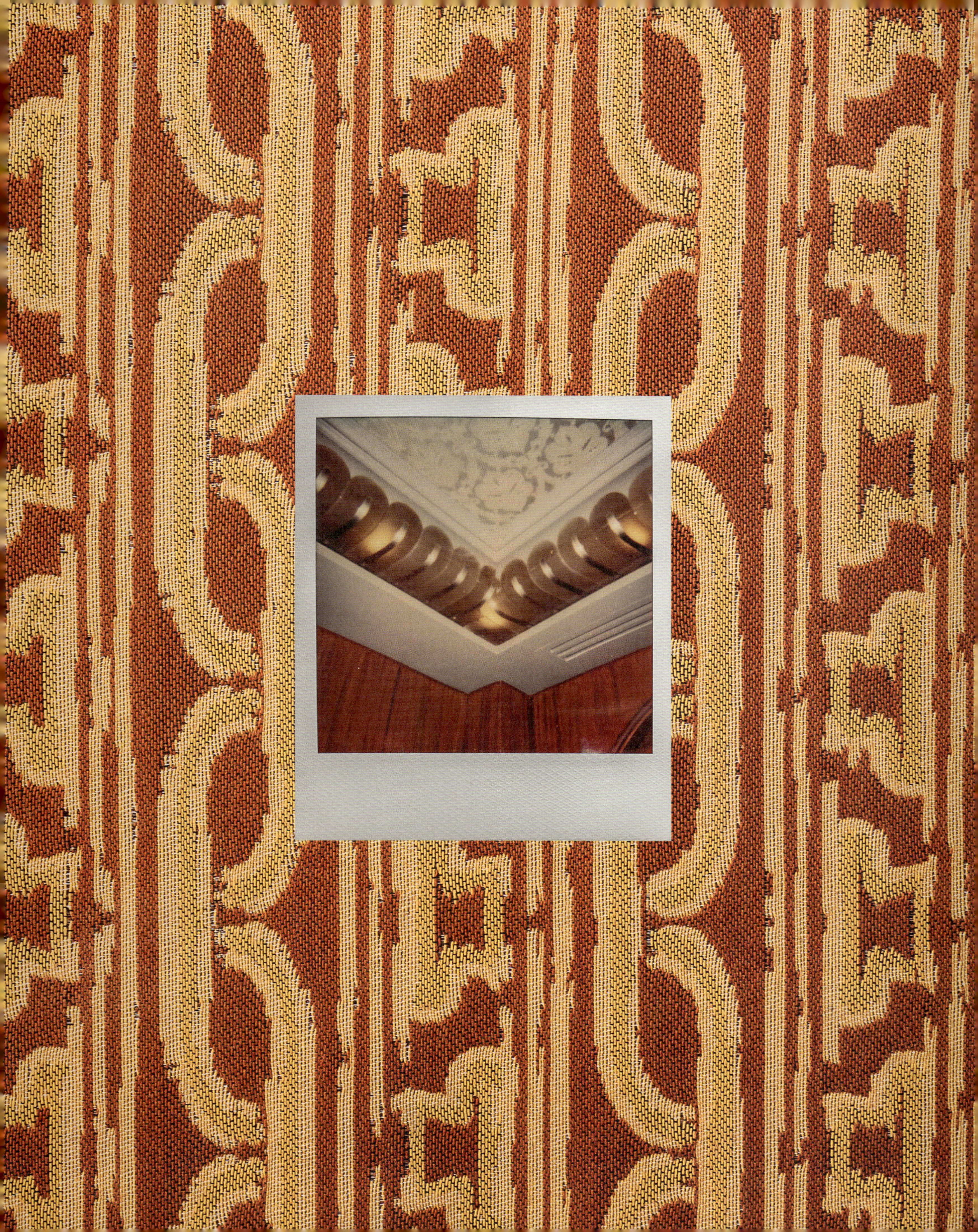

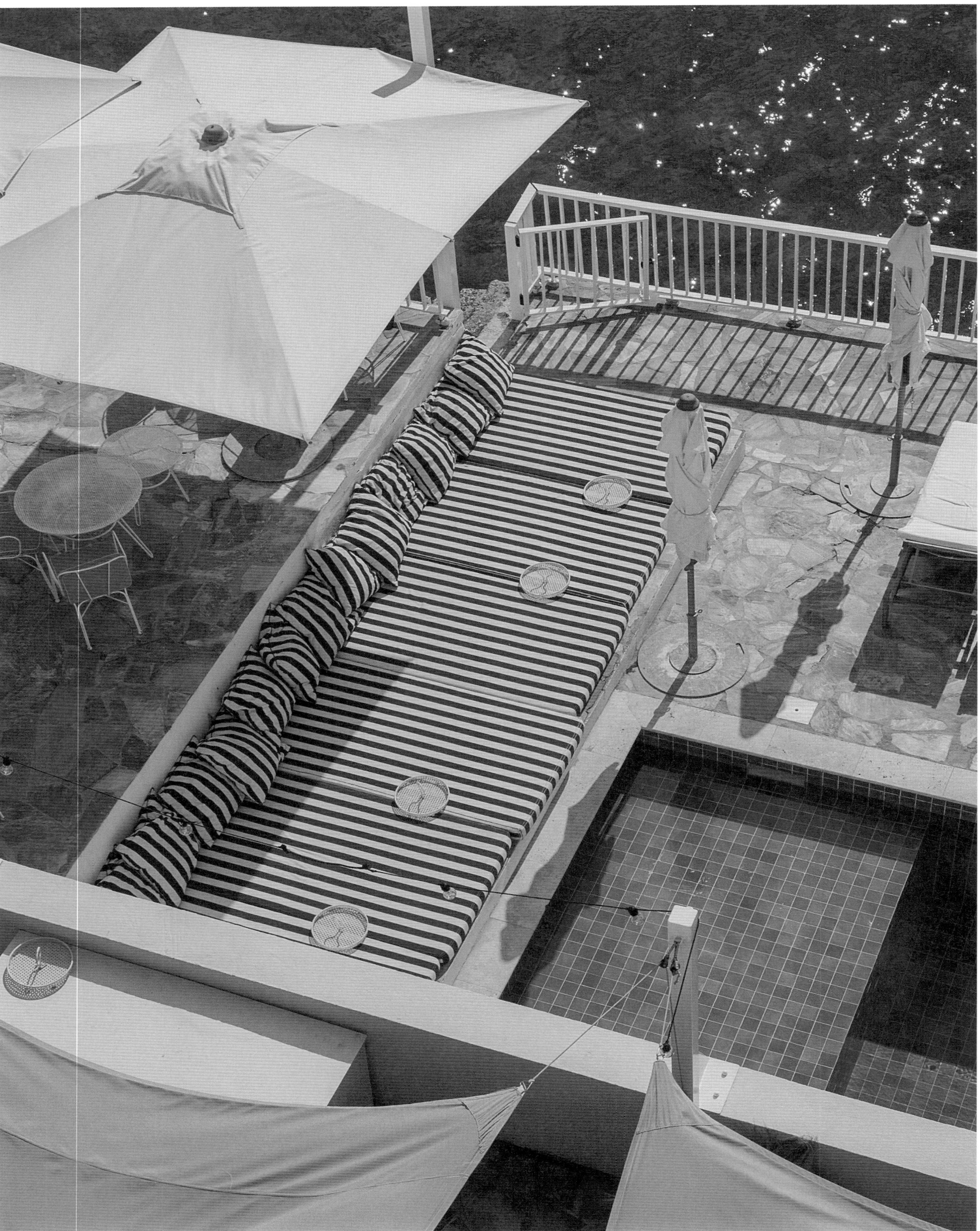

LES ROCHES ROUGES

CÔTE D'AZUR

SUN BLEACH

It's back to the coast for yet another change of scenery. From Cannes, we follow the coastal road eastward. Here the rugged Massif de l'Esterel dominates the horizon, tumbling dramatically down to the sea. Precipitous red cliffs at water's edge, ancient cork oaks lining the roadside, the dusty air shimmers beneath the midday sun—creating a Côte d'Azur reminiscent of California and Arizona at the same time. Just outside Saint-Raphaël, our journey ends at a hotel aptly named after this red-rock massif: Les Roches Rouges. The hotel, a striking white modernist structure from the 1950s, is uncompromisingly minimalist inside, with every line and angle perfectly oriented toward the restless azure sea. In the reception area, we pass the iconic curved leather couch known affectionately as the *Tatzelwurm*—named after a mythical creature that terrorizes the German-speaking Alps—a piece so coveted by interior-design enthusiasts that some would contemplate lawless activity to possess it. Upstanding citizens that we are, we instead take the elevator down three floors to the hotel terrace, where white chairs sit beneath cheerful yellow sun sails. It's far too hot to lounge in the sun, and we soon find ourselves craving a dip in the seawater pool, unquestionably the hotel's signature feature. Hewn directly into the rocky coastline, it nestles right at the water's edge; waves crash against its borders, occasionally washing small sea creatures into its waters—today's visitor is a tiny octopus. Later, we rinse the salt from our skin back in our room. The rooms and suites echo the hotel's minimalist aesthetic, dressed in clean white with balconies featuring two vivid-yellow butterfly chairs—an exclamation of color against the white walls and boundless blue sea. We awaken the next morning to a spectacular pink sunrise. Overnight, the sea has grown fierce, hurling waves onto the terrace and sending sprays against our windows. Yet Les Roches Rouges reveals itself to be equally captivating under stormy skies: a restorative refuge where stress and mundane concerns bleach away in the relentless sunshine or are carried off by salty blasts of wind.

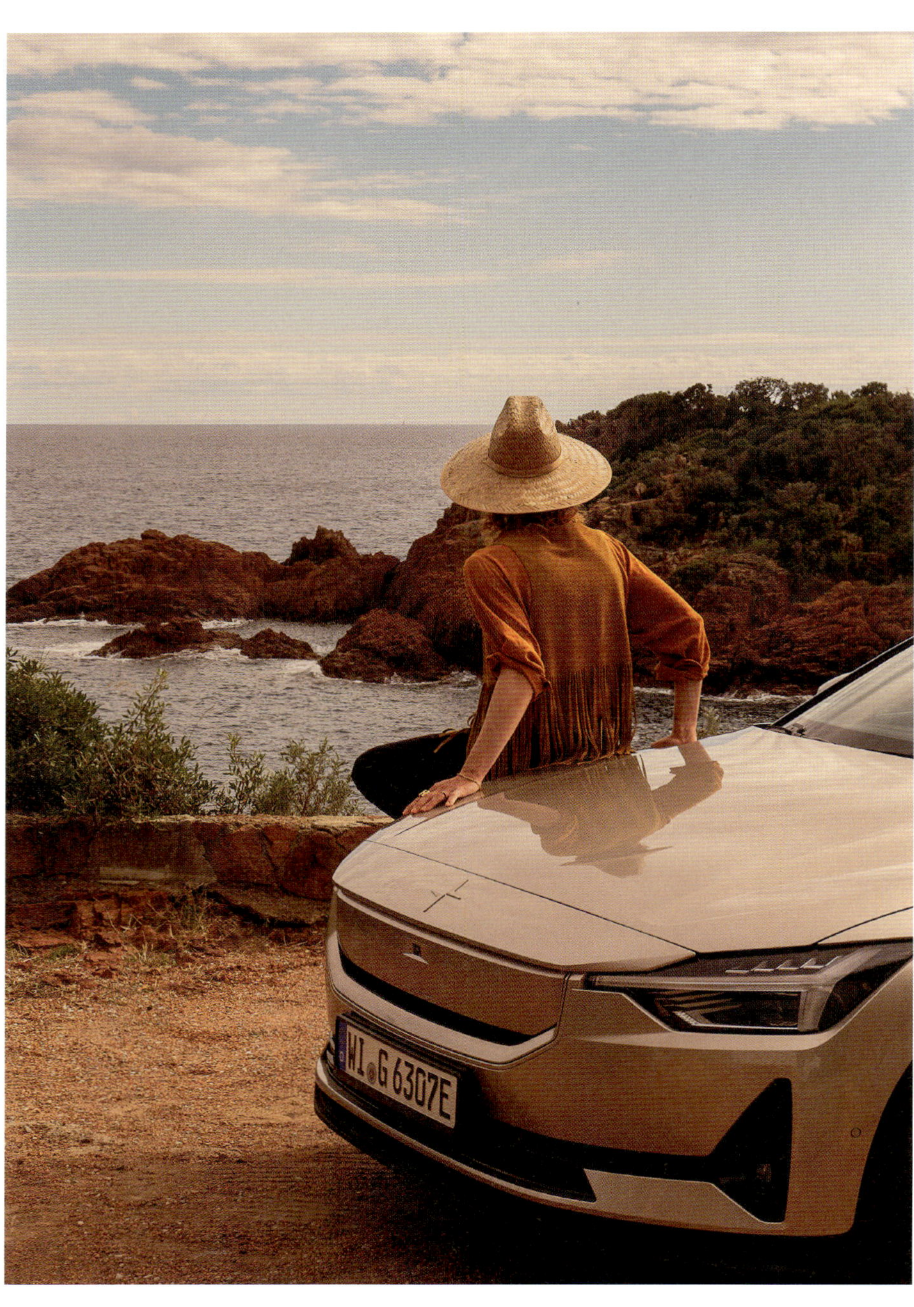

Before we arrive in Saint-Raphaël, we pull over in our Polestar at a dusty rest area. Here, the red rocks of the Esterel massif tumble so dramatically that we have to stop to appreciate the abrupt, rugged aspect of the Côte d'Azur, yet another of its many facets. Cannes is only 15 km away and yet couldn't be farther.

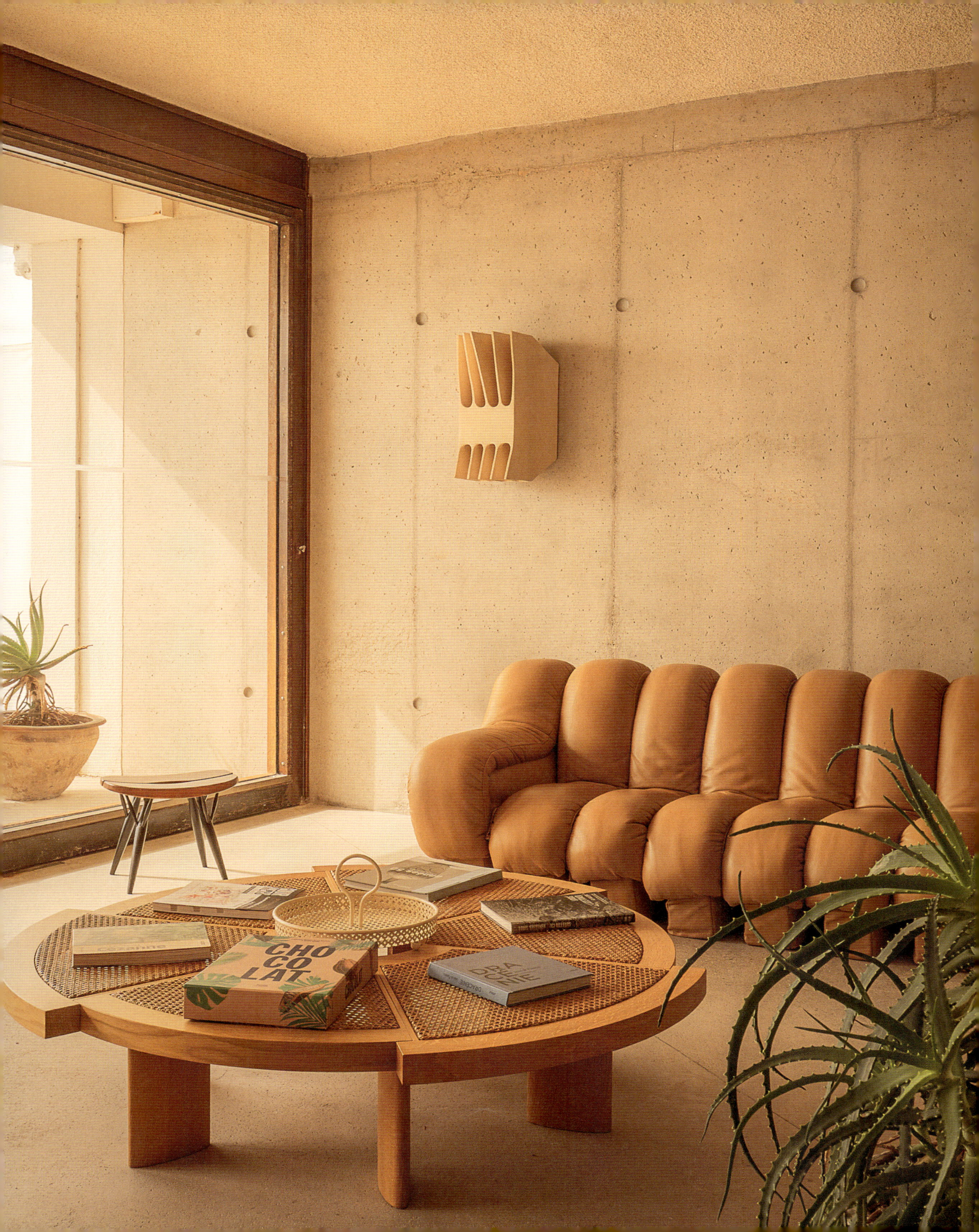

Cézanne
CHO
CO
LAT
DRA
DE
DUNIE
DRACENIE

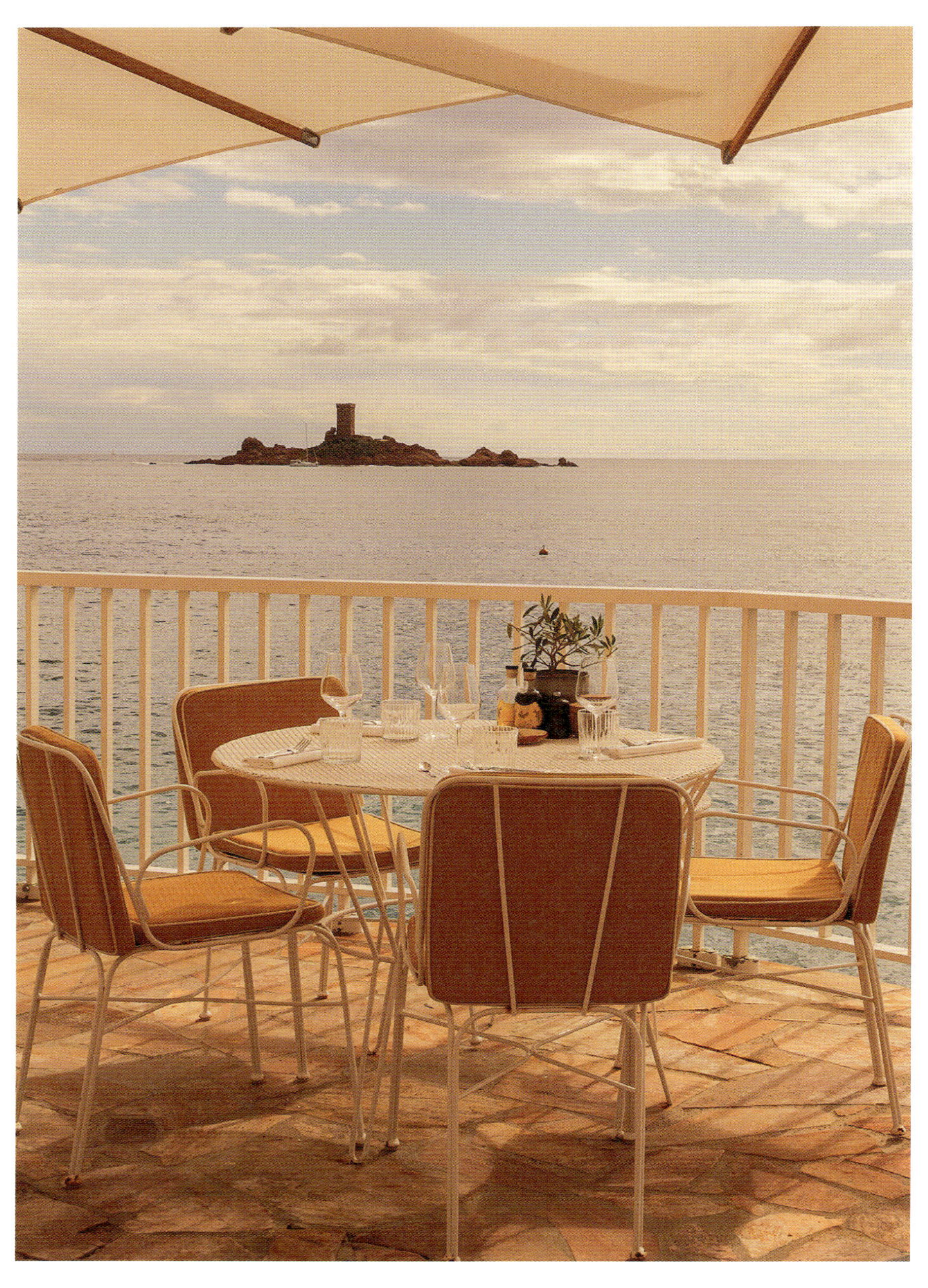

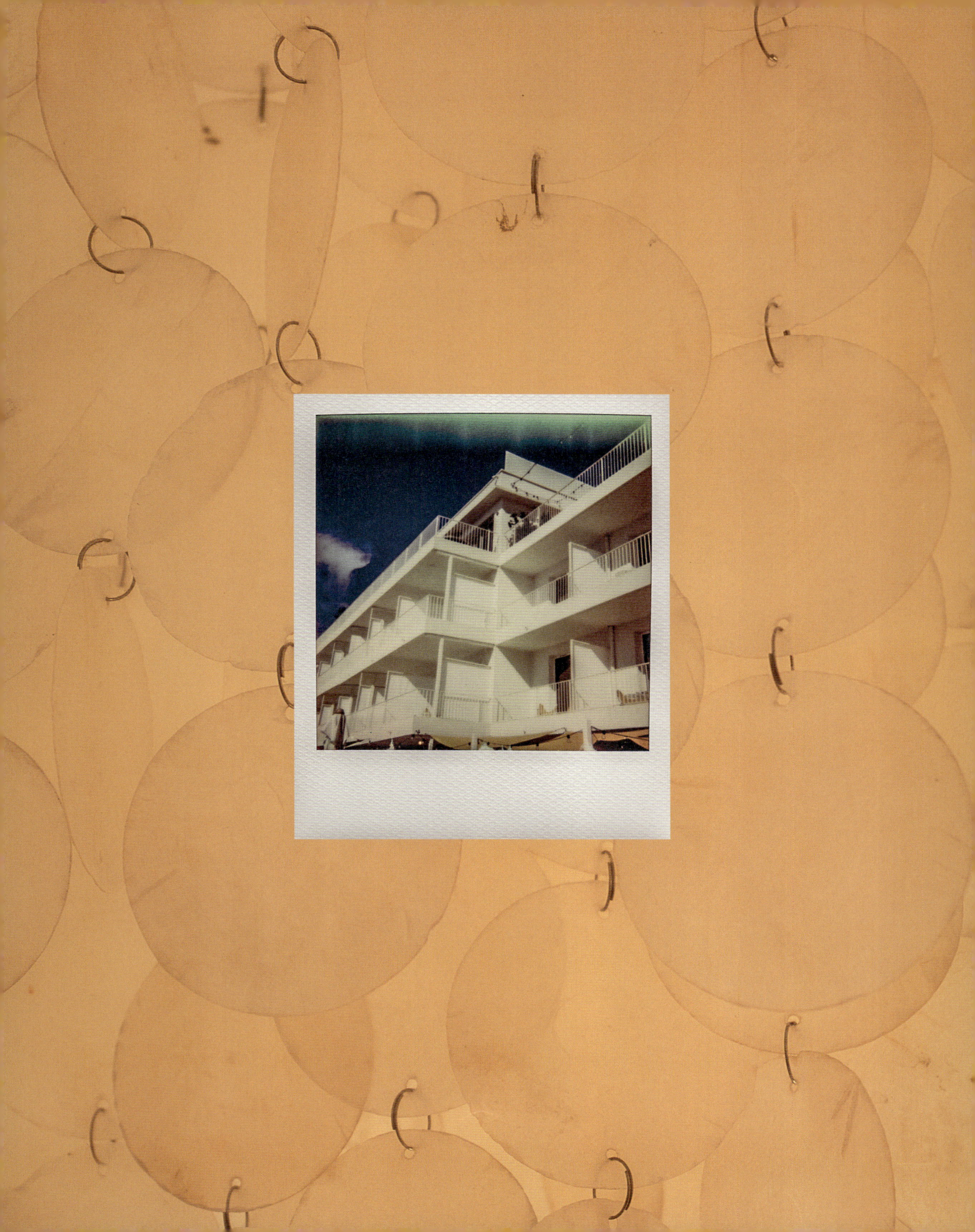

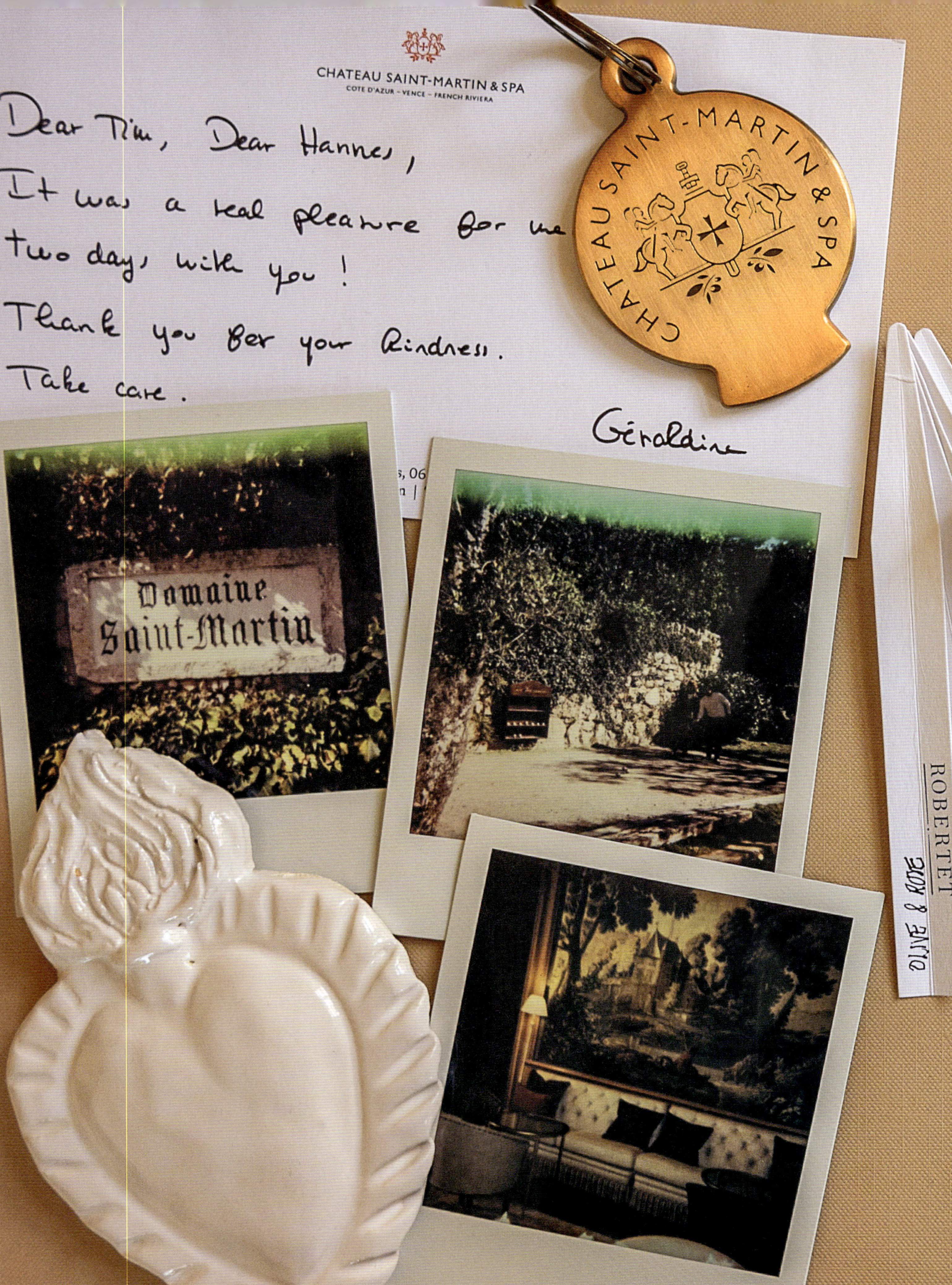

CHATEAU SAINT-MARTIN & SPA
COTE D'AZUR – VENCE – FRENCH RIVIERA

Dear Tim, Dear Hannes,
It was a real pleasure for me
two days with you!
Thank you for your kindness.
Take care.

Géraldine

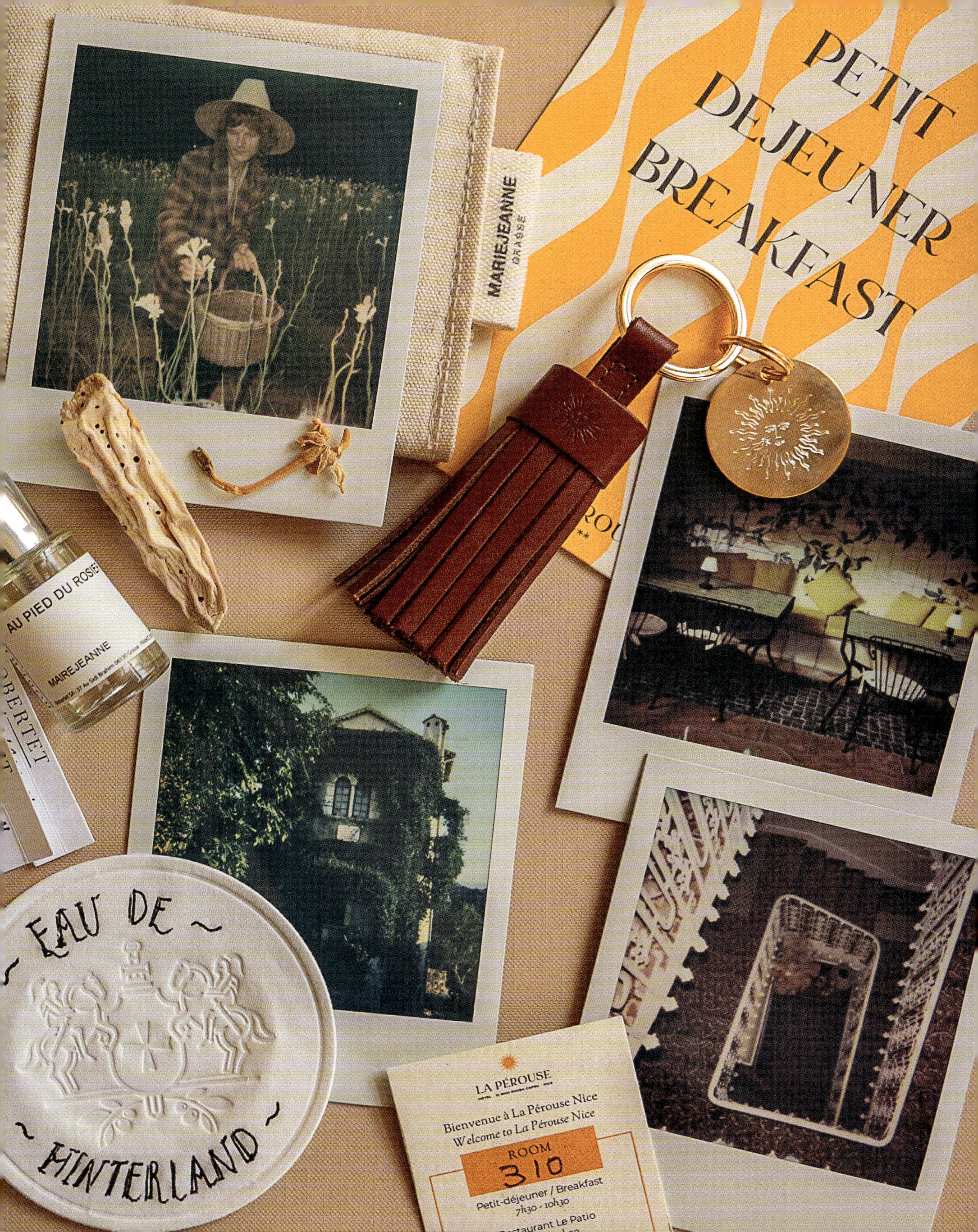
PETIT
DEJEUNER
BREAKFAST
MARIEJEANNE
GRASSE
EAU DE
HINTERLAND
LA PÉROUSE
Bienvenue à La Pérouse Nice
Welcome to La Pérouse Nice
ROOM
310
Petit-déjeuner / Breakfast
7h30 - 10h30

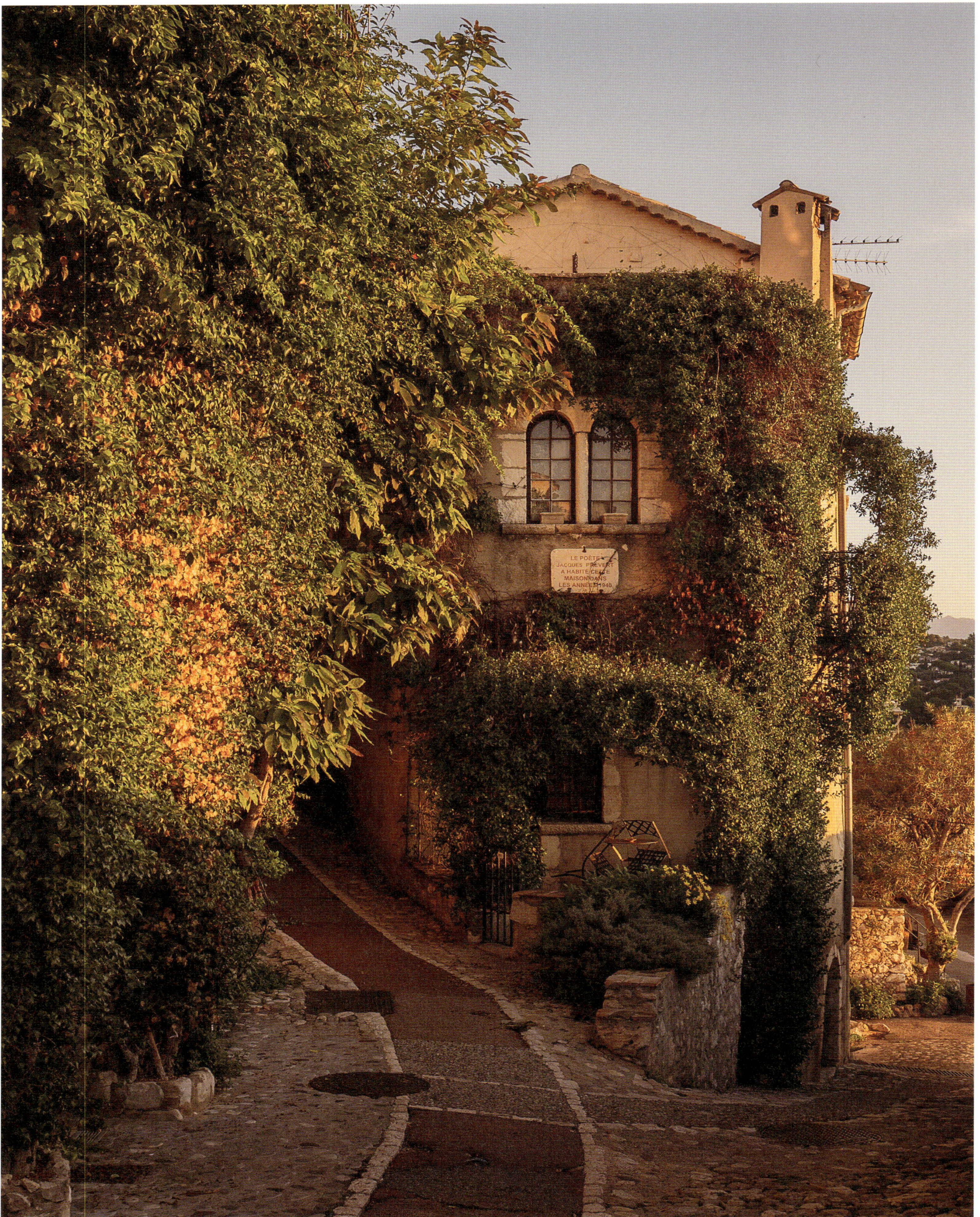
LE POÈTE
JACQUES
A HABITÉ
MAISON
LES
1940

SAINT-PAUL-DE-VENCE

CÔTE D'AZUR

A JEWEL IN THE CROWN

We set off early once more, tracing another sweeping route along the coast past Cannes and Antibes, heading toward Nice. But before we explore the coastal city in detail, the inland charms beckon us once again, drawing us to the artists' haven of Saint-Paul-de-Vence. For decades, this medieval hilltop village, encircled by imposing stone walls, has captivated France's greatest artists. Marc Chagall made it his home, producing some of his most renowned pieces here over two decades. Matisse, Calder, and Picasso were frequent visitors, famously staying at La Colombe d'Or. Just outside the village gates stands the Maeght Foundation, one of France's earliest and most significant private art foundations, full of sculptures by Braque, Miró, and Giacometti. As we step inside the village, the first rays of sun break through, the air still cool with morning dew. We enter a not-yet-fully-awake Saint-Paul-de-Vence—it's just us and a handful of cats roaming its narrow, cobblestone alleyways and twisting staircases leading to the heart of the village. Artists' studios line the main streets, and prestigious galleries from across the globe keep outposts here. Grapevines trail romantically along the façades of charmingly crooked houses—no apologies for quintessential French kitsch. We must have chosen the ideal time to catch some of that magic that lured generations of artists here. Saint-Paul-de-Vence is an idyllic jewel among the hills, where creativity thrives behind sturdy medieval stone walls. Appropriately, we end our tour with a leisurely *petit déjeuner* at La Colombe d'Or. Marc and Pablo would surely approve.

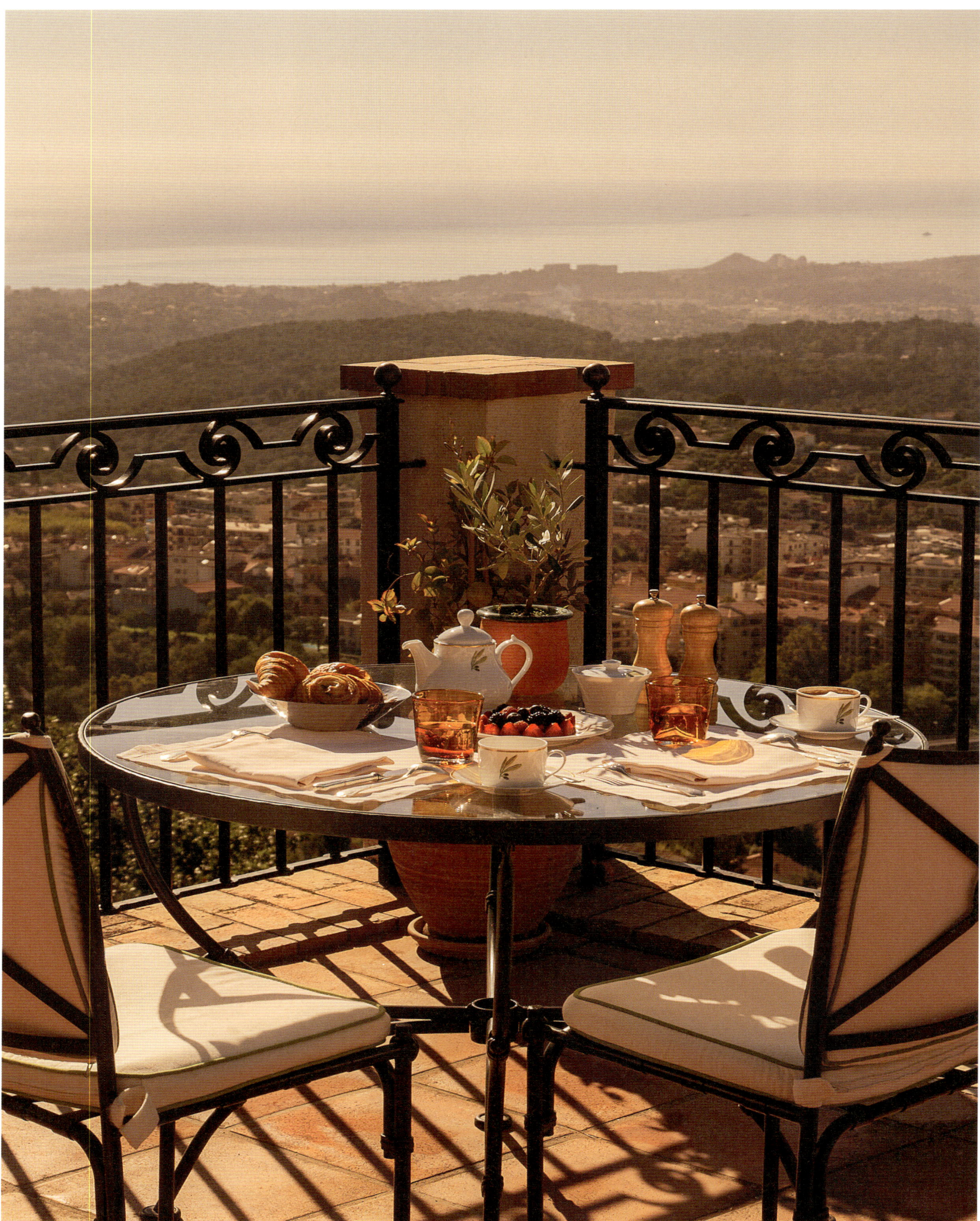

CHÂTEAU SAINT-MARTIN

CÔTE D'AZUR

THE ROMANTIC

From Saint-Paul-de-Vence, we venture deeper into the hinterland. The roads grow narrower, the hairpin turns sharper, and high above, Château Saint-Martin already looms, blending almost seamlessly into the side of a mountain. This secluded retreat is the sister property of the glamorous Hôtel du Cap-Eden-Roc—though perhaps a more introverted, nature-loving sibling of the grand hotel, and like us, hopelessly romantic. The winding ascent ends at an imposing black iron gate, beside which stand the weathered, crumbling remnants of an old gate with a red drawbridge and fragments of a 900-year-old complex that long ago was a base and sanctuary of the Knights Templar. The Templars may be long gone, but in their place, the Oetker family has opened one of its elegant Masterpiece Collection hotels. Rust-red grapevines wrap gracefully around the château, with its earth-toned tiled roof and green shutters. The pale green entrance hall opens into the coral-colored lobby, where lavish bouquets—meticulously arranged by the hotel's in-house florist—spill dramatically over an enormous root-wood table. Here we're greeted by Geraldine, the heart and soul of the establishment, who guides us onto the hotel terrace, where a leisurely second breakfast awaits, along with an unrivaled view. Miles of Provençal countryside stretch below, merging gently into the blue Mediterranean and offering a direct line of sight clear to Cap d'Antibes. Enchanted by the vista and the buttery croissants as well as by Geraldine's quiet charm, we go exploring. We drift through the Michelin-starred restaurant Le Saint-Martin, the wood-paneled bar draped in heavy tapestries, and finally ascend spiral stair-

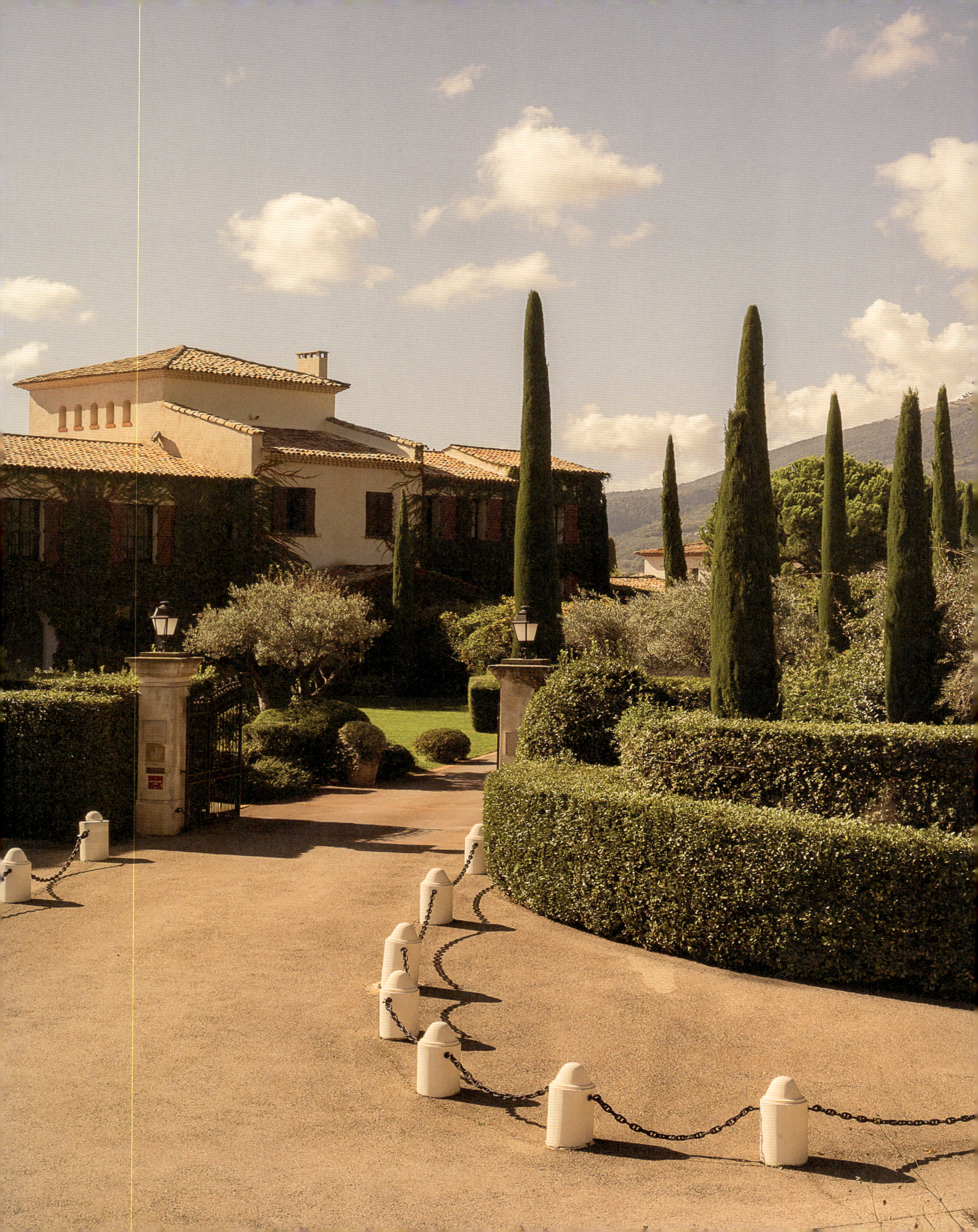

cases and winding corridors to reach our airy room. It proves to be an idyllic retreat for the two of us: The view on one side gazes across the sweeping landscape below the château, on the other side the rugged mountains and the surrounding, lovingly manicured park. Solitude reigns. At Saint-Martin, you are for yourself and surrounded by pure romance. This becomes clear when you play boules in the garden and take a dip in the whirlpool, sheltered under a vine-covered pavilion with a stunning view of the coast. Although our honeymoon was years ago, we feel like we are on a second one here.

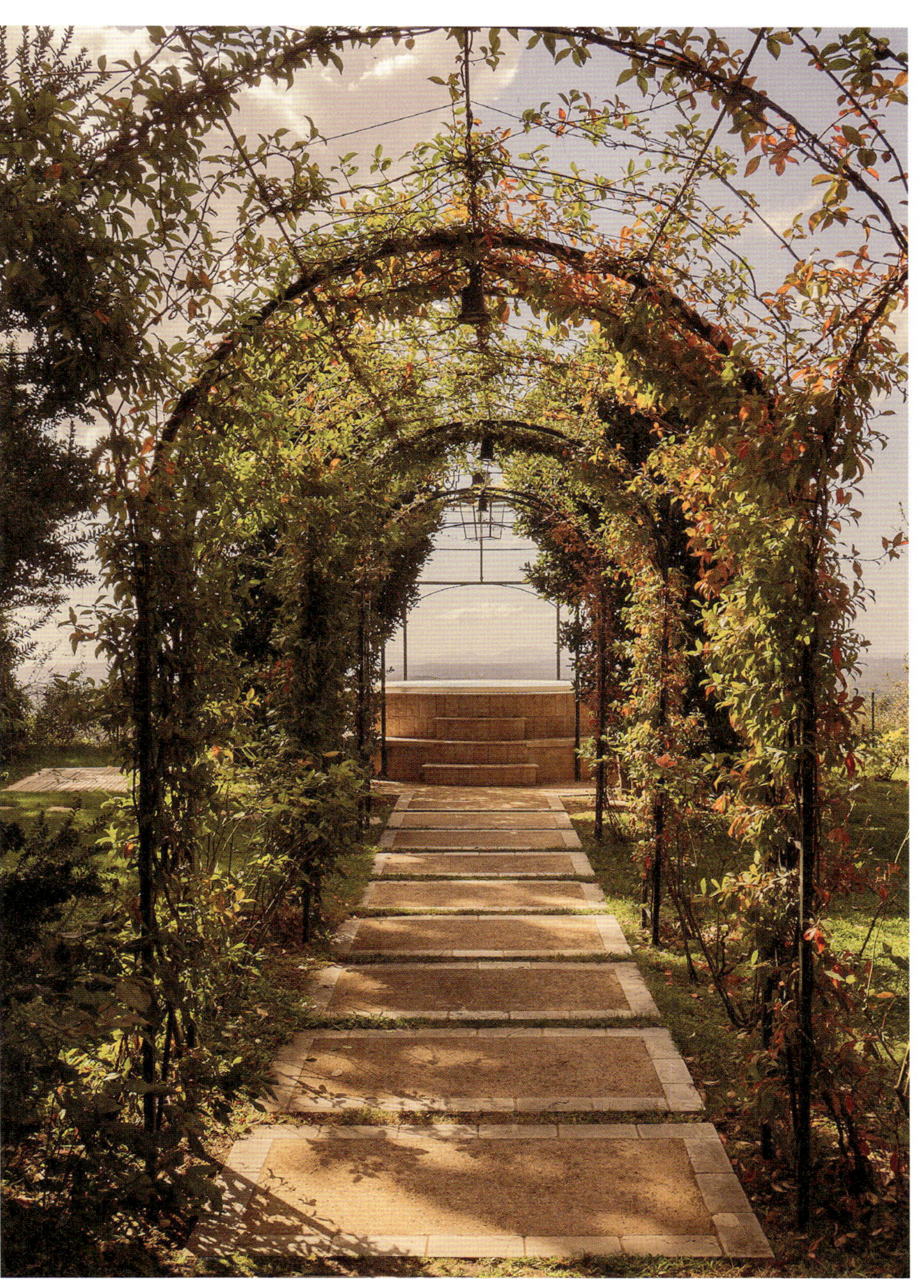

After we set eyes on the jacuzzi—beneath a vine-covered pavilion with a view of Antibes—our conclusion is firm: the Château Saint-Martin is the paramount honeymoon hotel, whether for newlyweds, veterans of long marriages, or singles romantically liaised with themselves.

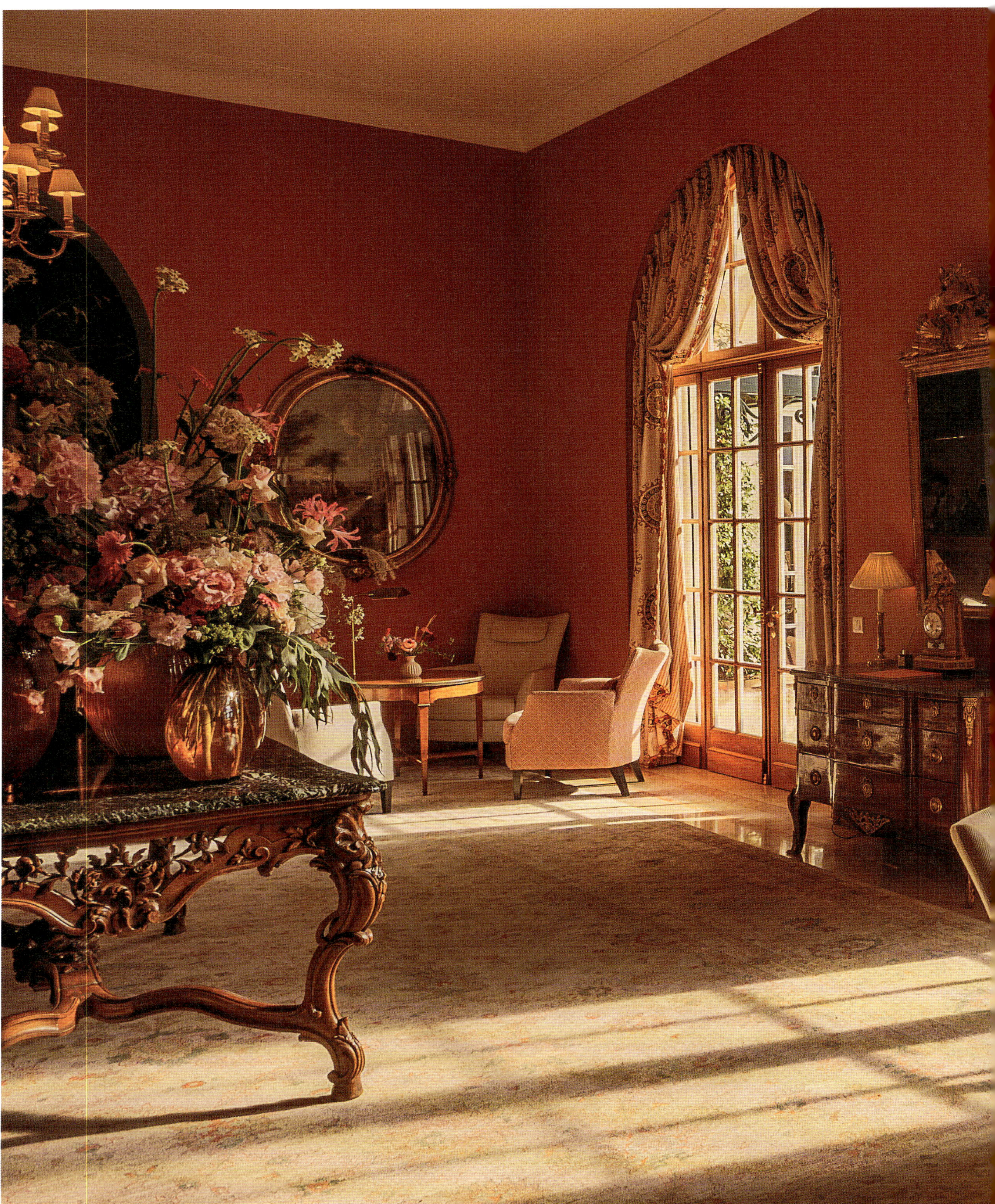

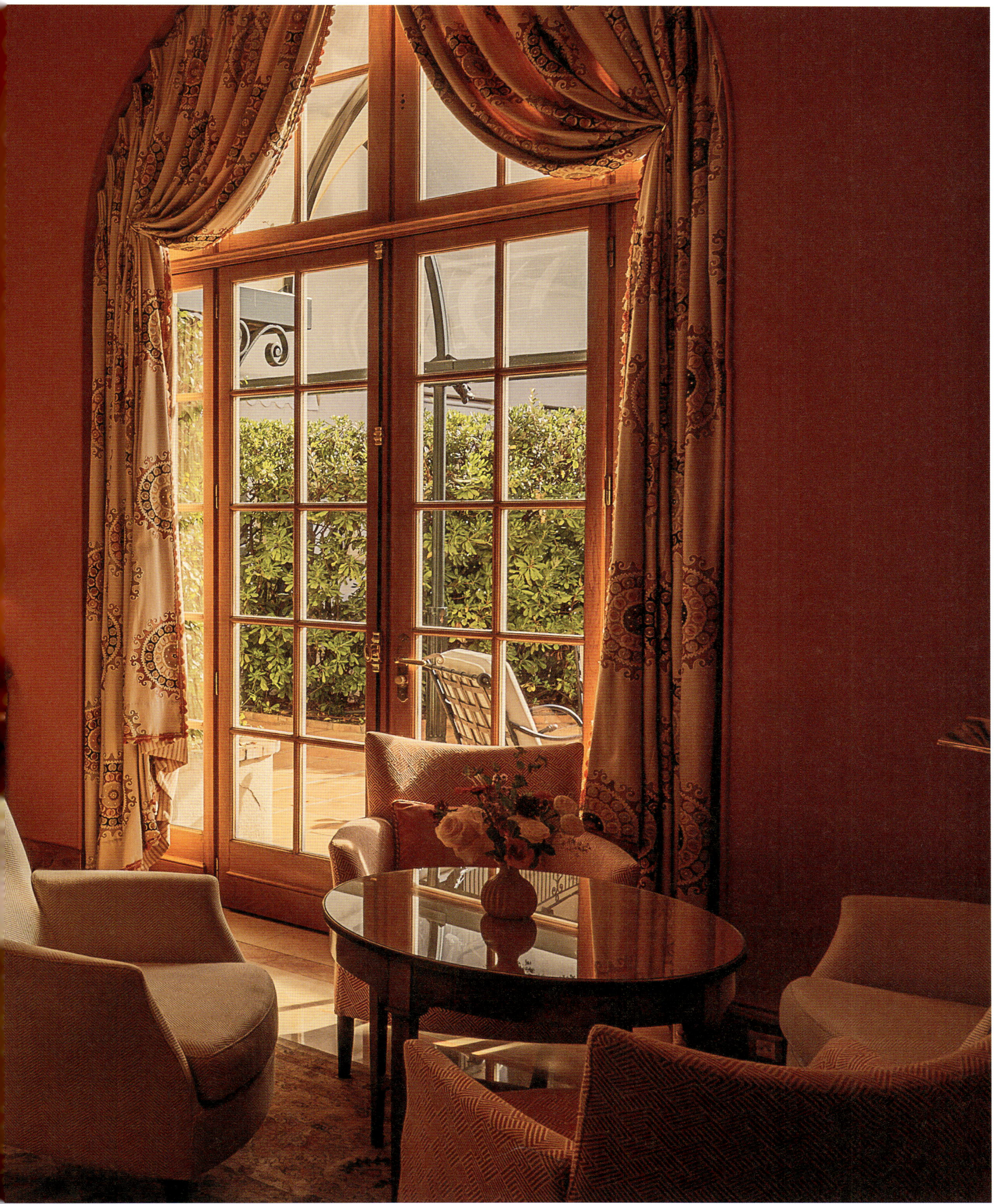

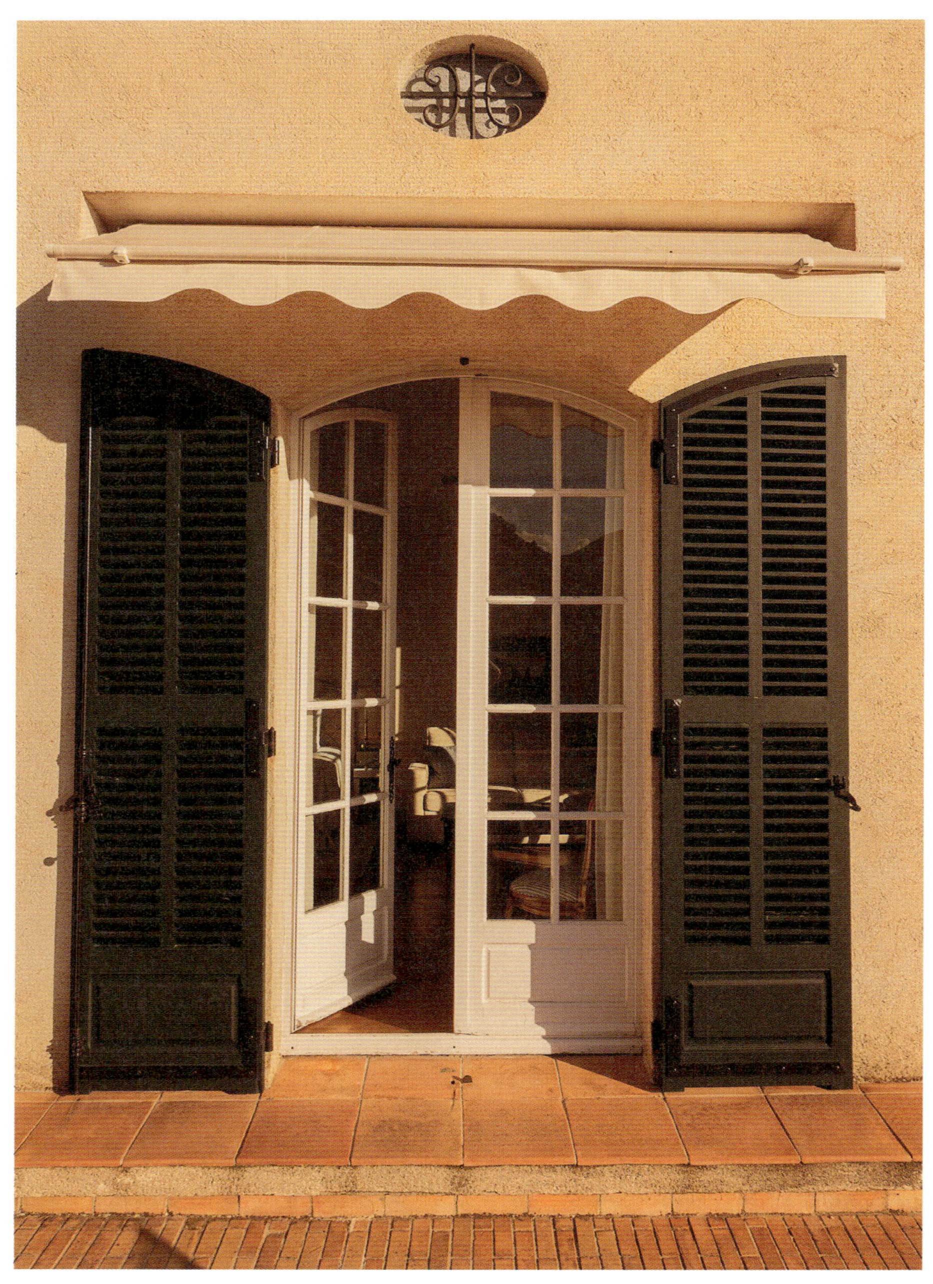

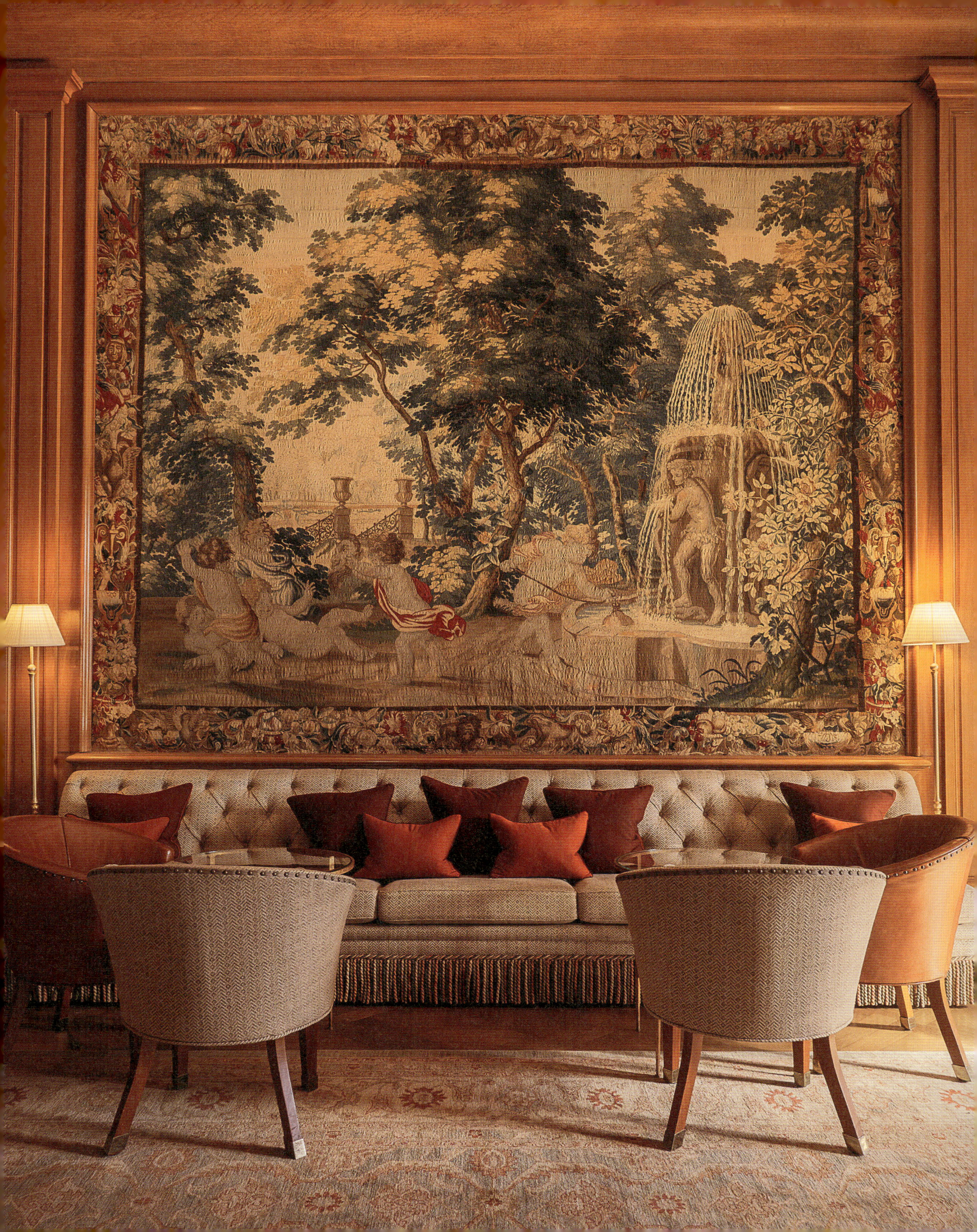

N I C E

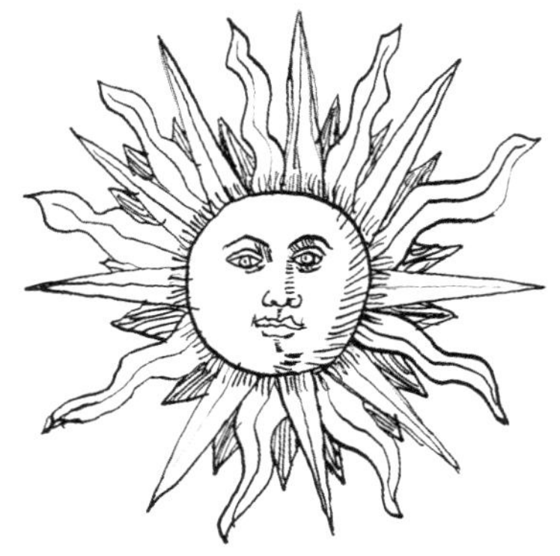

We're paying extra-special attention to two cities along the Côte d'Azur: on the eastern side, Nice, on the western side of the broad coast, Saint-Tropez. But why Nice? It could just as easily have been Cannes, even Monaco. But we think neither of those cities can hold a candle to Nice in terms of sheer variety and historical charm. Perhaps it's a lingering echo of Italy that makes Nice feel so reassuringly familiar to us, that keeps drawing us back to its long shoreline and azure waters. There's no water that color anywhere else.

The ancient maritime city of Nice was once an important—and long-disputed—trading center. It came under Italian rule for centuries and was part of the Kingdom of Sardinia before finally becoming part of France in the latter half of the nineteenth century. These Italian roots, which, to look at this grand city, may not be immediately apparent, reveal themselves layer by layer. Architecturally, they show in the colorful Mediterranean façades down along the old harbor, in the vibrant tiles at the cathedral, and in the narrow streets of the old town, which feels more like Siena than anywhere in France. But the Italian spirit is most vivid in the Mediterranean delicacies at the city's flower market (yes, flower market) and in interactions with the locals, who carry themselves with a touch of warmth just slightly above the French national average. But neither does it actually feel like Italy; the city's identity is too richly interwoven with other cultures for that. The British, flocking here for the health benefits, lent their name to the famous Promenade des Anglais. Russians came to the coast, fleeing cold winters and revolution. It's precisely this eclectic mix that makes Nice irresistible and deserving of its own chapter.

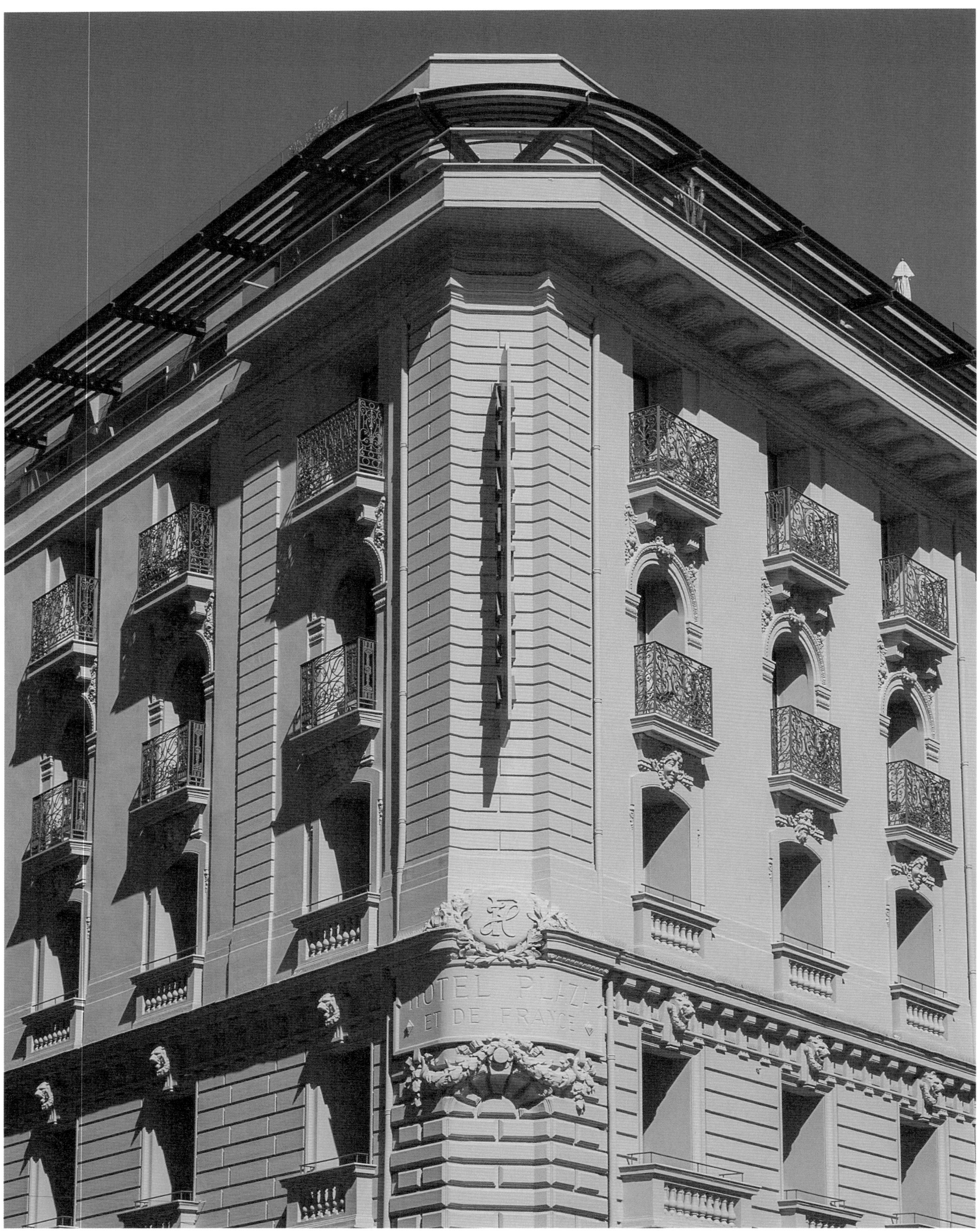
HOTEL PLAZ
ET DE FRANCE

ANANTARA PLAZA

NICE

THE METROPOLITAN

Naturally, the first thing we do in Nice is strike out down the Promenade des Anglais. This splendid boulevard runs for miles beside the dazzling blue sea, past grand hotels and stately casinos. When the Albert I Garden comes up on our left, we turn onto Avenue de Verdun and make our way toward the seemingly endless Belle Époque façade of the Anantara Plaza. This hotel is simply inescapable for anyone picturing gilded Nice in its turn-of-the-century glory.

Built in the mid-1800s, the Plaza changed owners a few times before Charles Dalmas—yes, the man behind the Carlton in Cannes and the Palais de la Méditerranée in Nice—turned it into a full-blown landmark in 1913. A friendly team ushers us into the rotunda, all metropolitan polish with updated Art Deco elements. Of all the stops on our circuit through the south of France, this place has the most international vibe. We feel like we could be in Manhattan—until the elevator lets us out onto the rooftop terrace and we snap back to the reality of Nice as palm trees, the vibrant green park, and the azure-blue of the Mediterranean stretch out below. Lunch upstairs is oysters and sushi; afterwards we settle on our little balcony with macarons and iced lattes. From here we can see the carousel in the park turning and hear its nostalgic organ music. But there's no time for idle sentimentality. The Plaza has booked us on its trademark activity: an auto-rickshaw tour. We're a little skeptical at first, but then we meet our profoundly cool driver. With the Ramones blaring from tiny speakers, our ride through the old port and tight streets is extremely hilarious and surprisingly informative. We even put in a pit stop at the antiques market, where we load up on vinyl and a few weathered books. A pretty perfect intro to Nice, really.

New York on the inside, Nice on the outside: The Anantara may be the most metropolitan of all the hotels we've seen on our tour. It *is* a plaza. But when you open the windows and step onto the small balcony to admire the azure expanse that lies beyond the palm trees, when you hear the music from the carousel in the park, you know it's Nice.

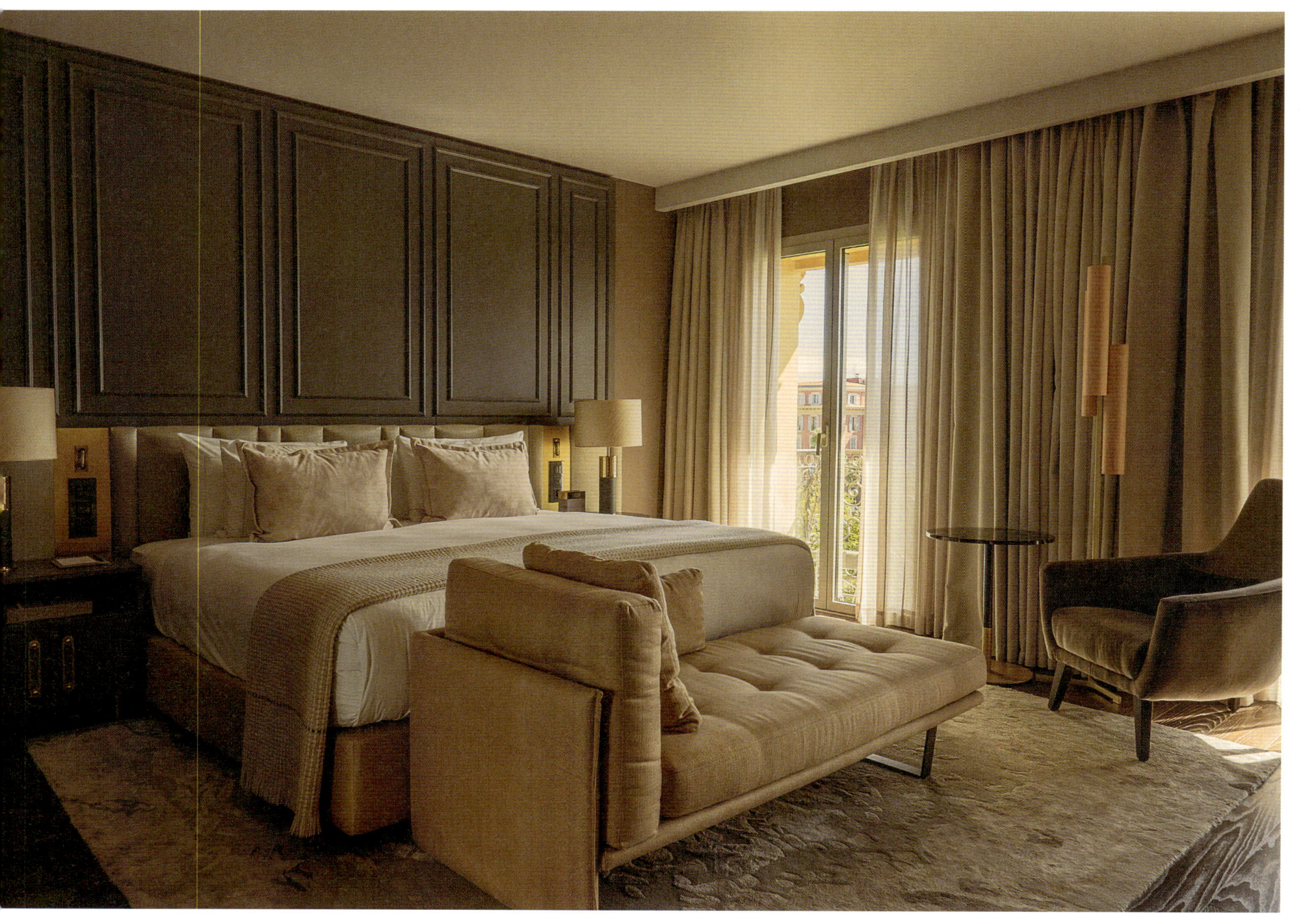

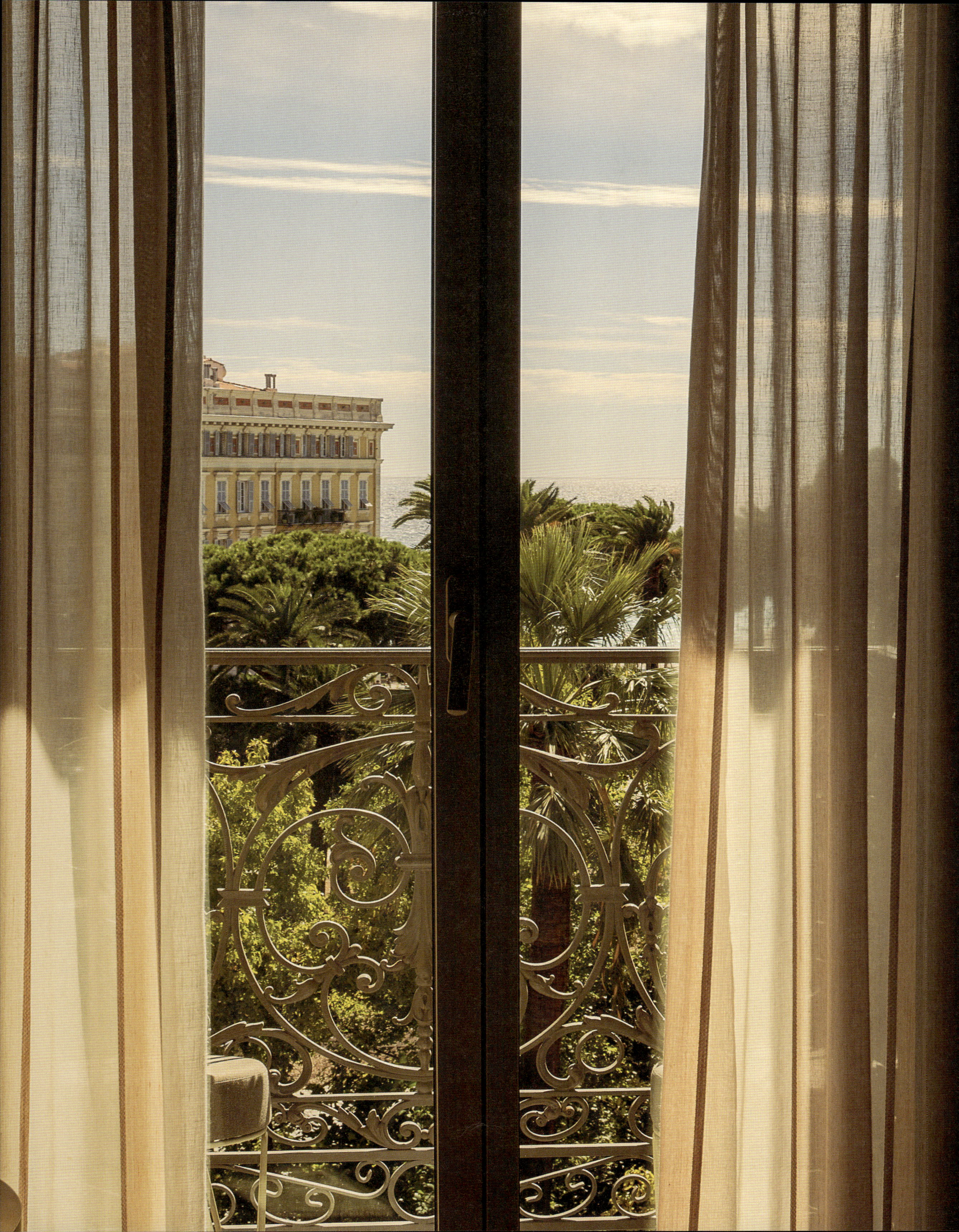

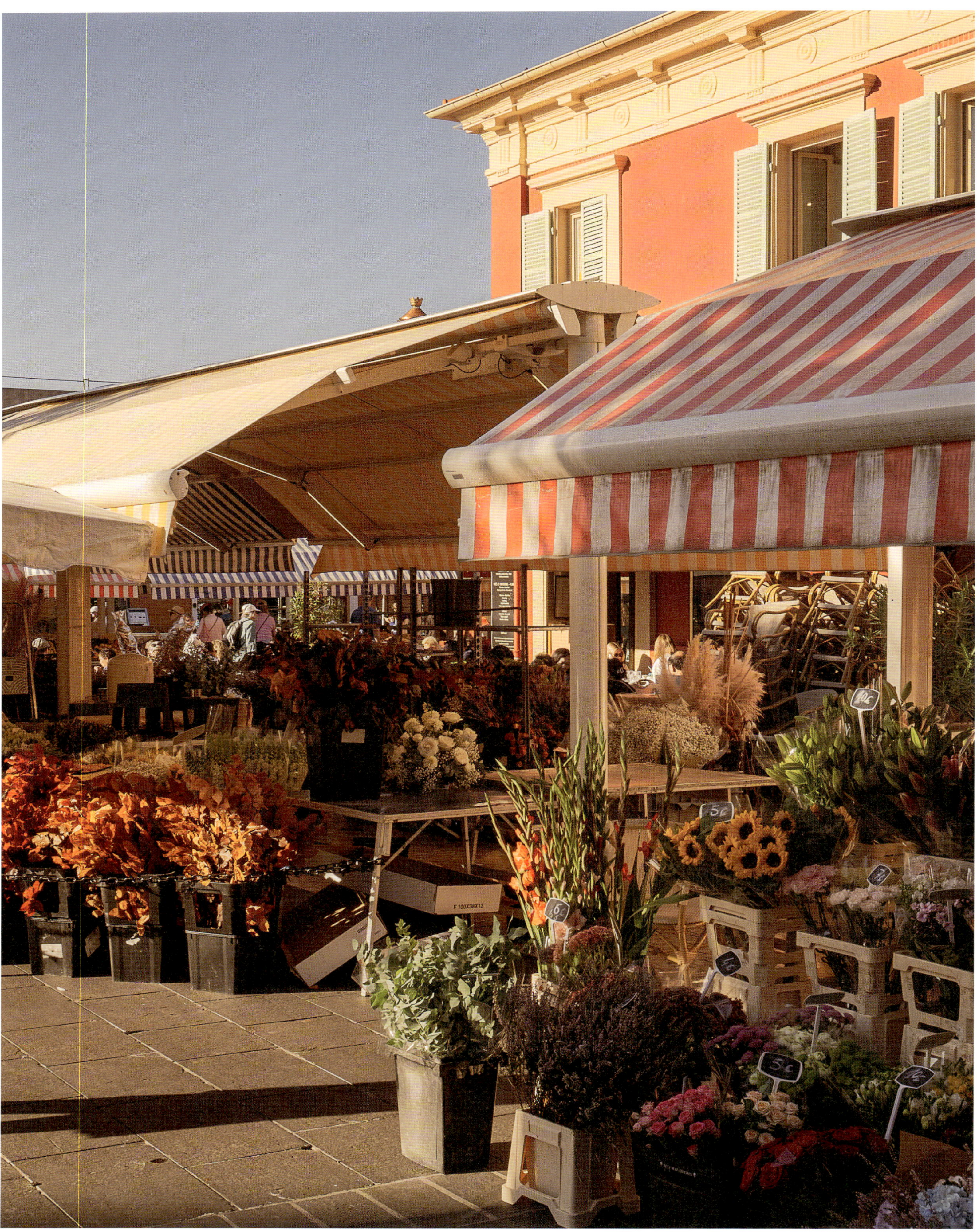

MARCHÉ AUX FLEURS

NICE

CULINARY SOUL

We linger over a second *café* on the terrace at the Anantara, taking in the sea, the park, and the tiled rooftops of Nice's *vieille ville*. Next on the agenda is the Marché aux Fleurs, the daily flower and food market in the heart of this port town. It's a short stroll from the hotel past the grand opera house and straight into the bustle of the historic center. On the Cours Saleya, vendors are already hoisting their colorful awnings. The air carries the scent of freshly cut bouquets and the aroma of still-warm Niçoise pastries waiting to reveal some of the city's edible soul. The stalls go on for almost a kilometer beneath striped canvas and the balconies of neighboring cafés. The first visitors are already threading their way around one another, equal parts tourists and locals getting their shopping done. We see two policemen on bicycle patrol dismount to grab a slice of *pissaladière*, a Niçoise onion tart thickly topped with black olives. Everywhere you look, the merchants' tables are piled high with everything Nice and the surrounding countryside have to offer: bunches of tuberose, big dahlias, delicate roses; just-picked zucchini flowers; tomatoes ranging from lemon yellow to nearly black; and the first mushrooms of the season from the mountains. By the time we make it past the market and the bakers' stalls, we're utterly seduced: first, a slab of *socca*—a local staple made from chickpea flour, hot from the oven—then a few crisp fried raviolis with black tapenade, and finally *macaron de Nice*, which are less refined than their more typically French cousins, but warmer, and with a distinctly Italian soul. A perfect reflection of Nice itself.

Every Tuesday through Sunday, insights into Nice's culinary traditions accumulate at the Marché aux Fleurs: Mediterranean, as much Italian as French, mouthwatering food to satisfy every heart's desire; fresh-cut flowers, vegetables, and fruit; socca and pissaladière as far as the eye can see.

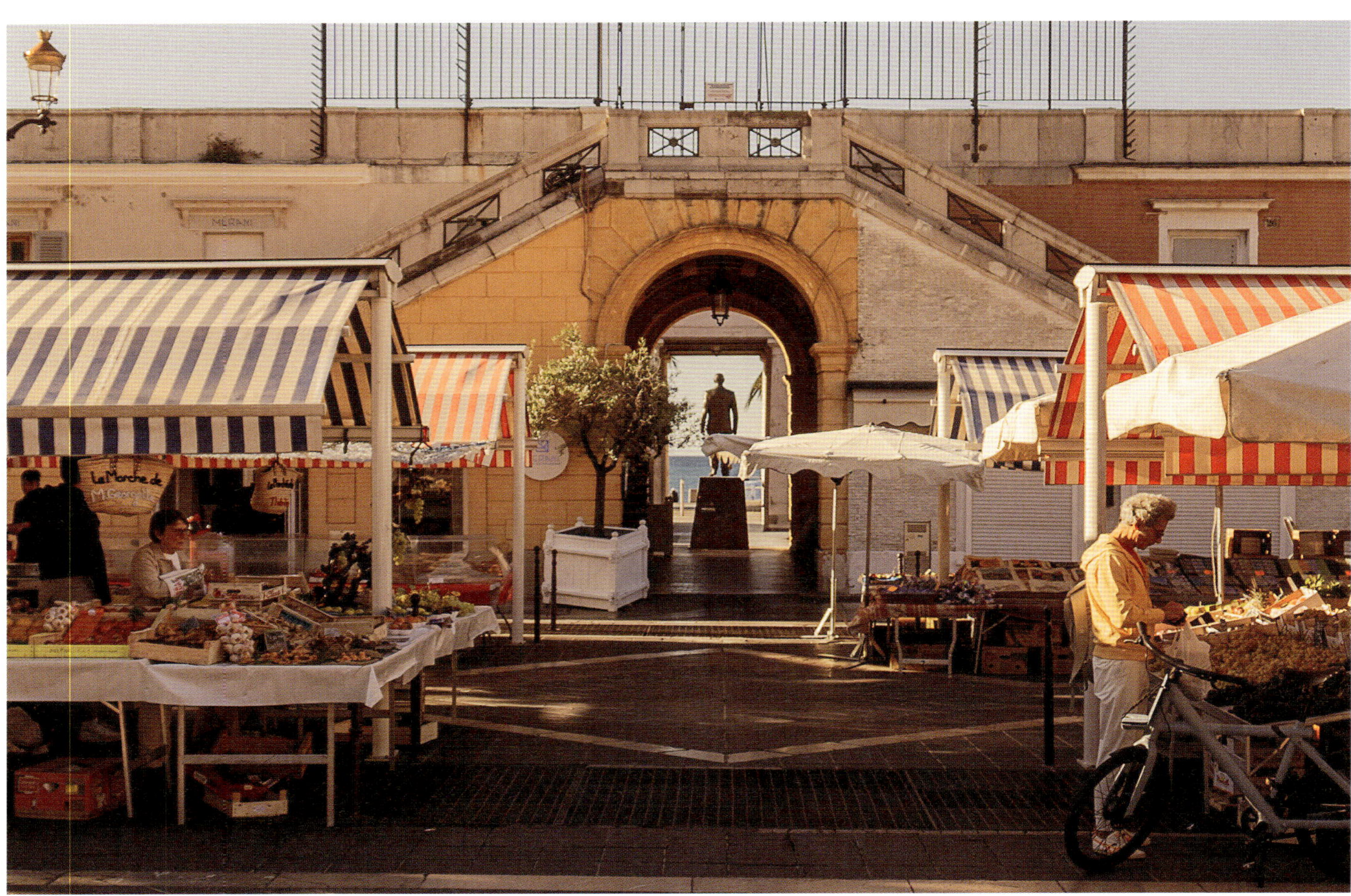

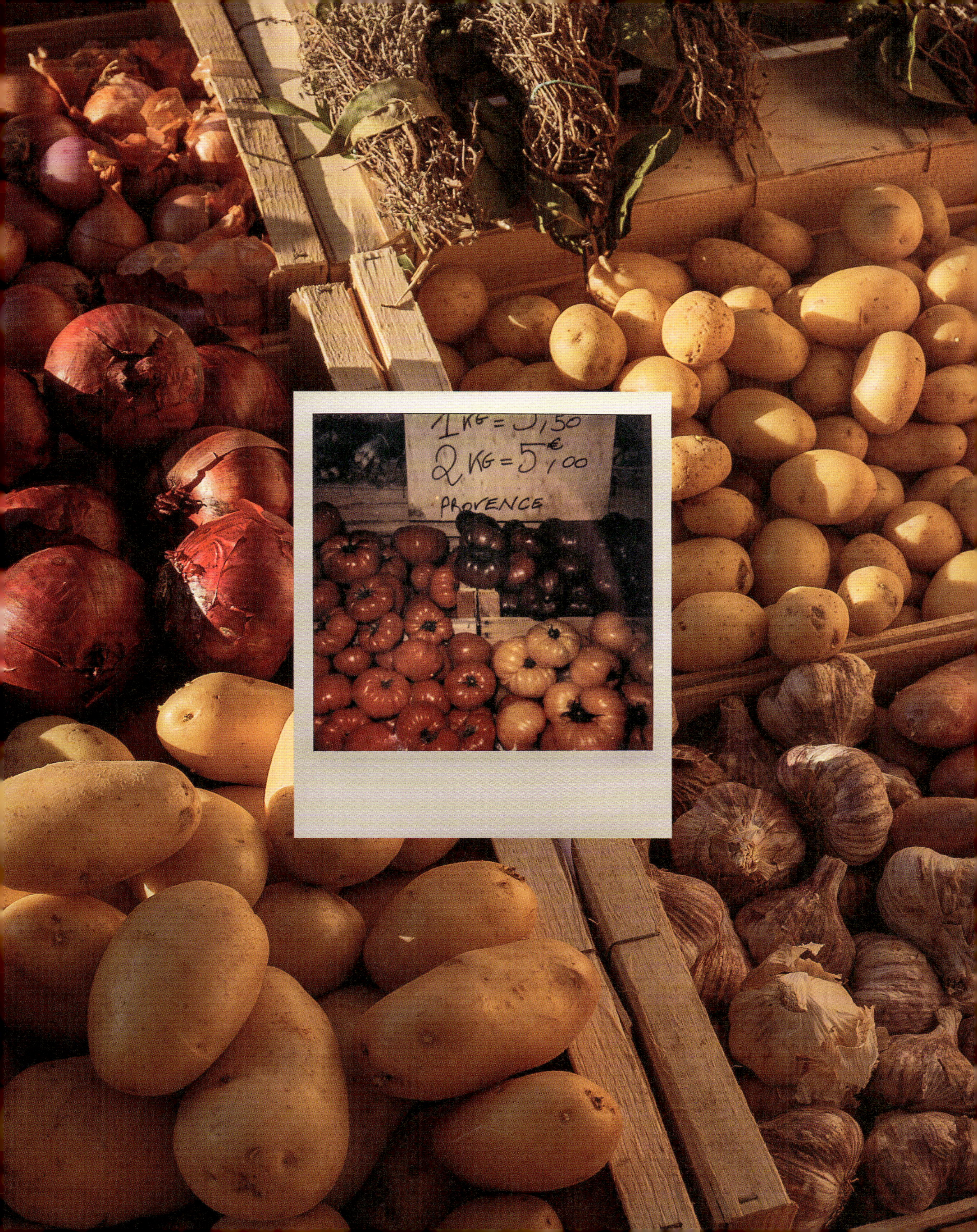
2 KG = 5€,00
PROVENCE

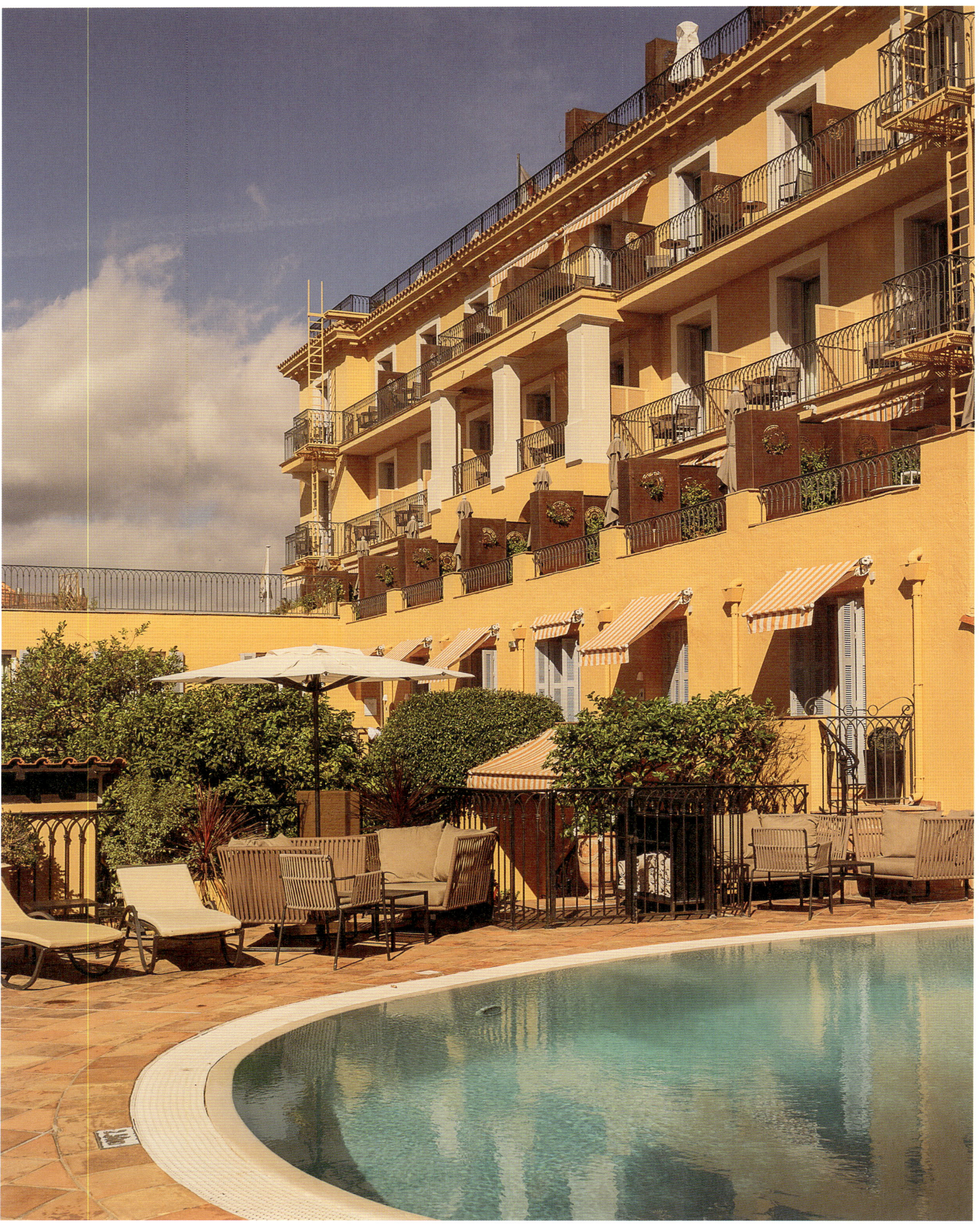

LA PÉROUSE

NICE

BATTLE FOR THE VIEW

The hotels of Nice are locked in a centuries-old rivalry, which is a struggle for the best view of the azure Baie des Anges. The matter is settled as far as we're concerned. The prize can be claimed by the next stop on our tour of Nice. We drive out to the end of the Promenade des Anglais, where, at the tip of the Quai Rauba Capeu—so named for the hats the brisk wind whisks from tourists' heads—we locate an unassuming entrance.

La Pérouse has been a fixture in Nice for decades, long before anyone was saying things like "boutique hotel" In 2023, it finally received the makeover everyone had been waiting for. This is where design duo Friedmann and Versace made their first foray into hotels, to give La Pérouse a bold new identity: chic, contemporary, and in the moment. The interior is full of organic curves, stripes, lathed burl wood, coral and shell motifs, rustic hand-painted ceramics and tiles, eclectic colorful rugs—it's part Picasso, part Cocteau, part Dufy, and a true ode to the south of France. We take the first of three lifts to the sixth floor, then wind our way through twisting corridors until we reach the inner courtyard, where a pool and restaurant await. The bar gleams with a mosaic of shells and coral, glittering in the yellow light cast by the lemon trees. It's only now we realize the hotel quite literally scales the cliff and how its 53 balconies crane upwards toward the sun. After a quick drink by the pool at the base of a cliff, we're keen to see the view from our suite. A short detour and two more lifts later, we arrive. Over the years, the hotel has embedded itself into the rock face—but every step through the maze is worth it.

Tourists ascend hundreds of steps to take in the Nice panoramic view from the old fortress next door. We, on the other hand, reach the same elevation by stepping onto our rooftop terrace. Slightly different vantage point, but with 180 degrees of uninterrupted blue and blazing sun, our gaze alternates between the promenade and the sea.

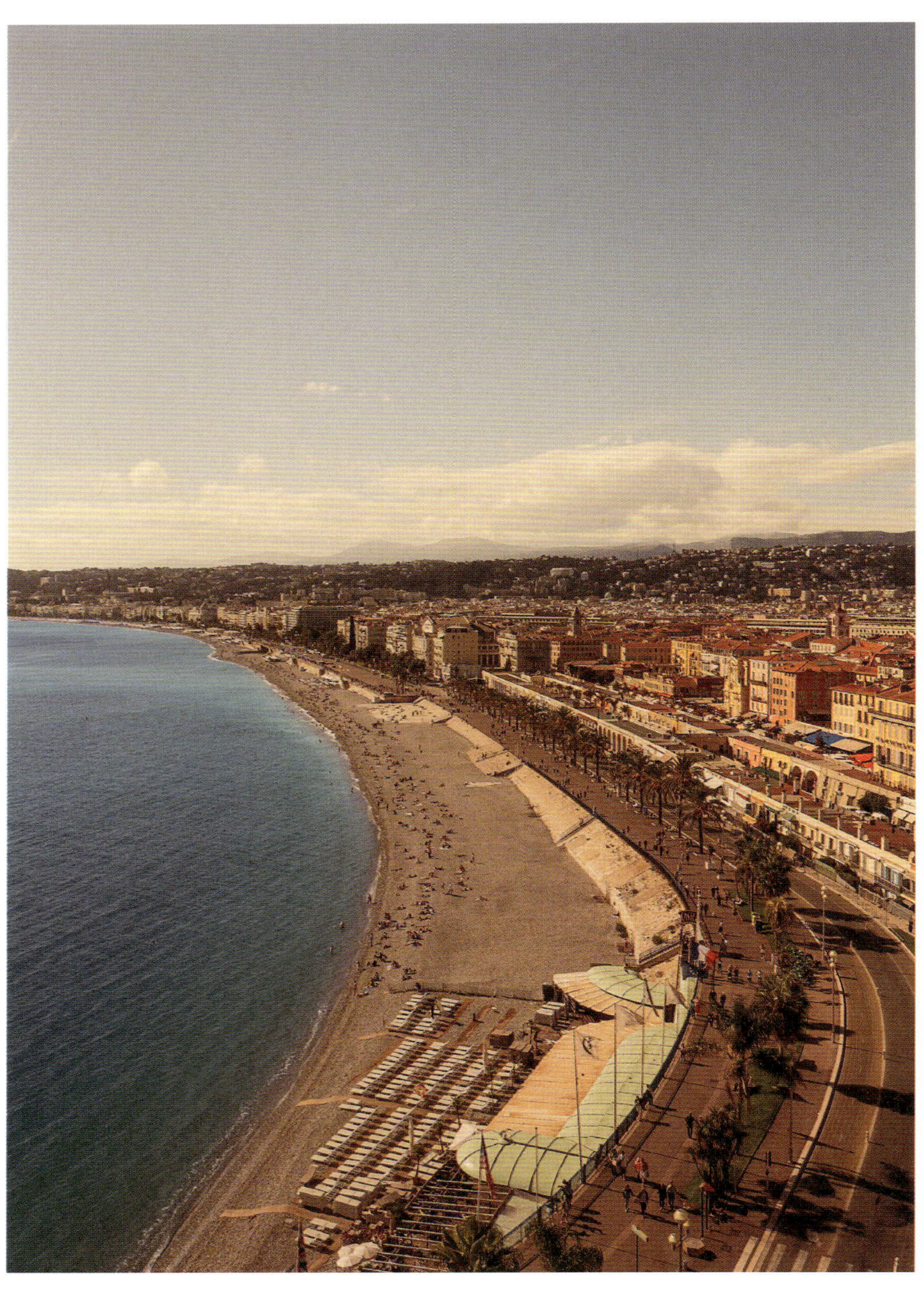

La Pérouse's location, on Quai Rauba Capeu, already provides the best views of Nice. But Friedmann & Versace have hooked it up with an interior that's trendy even as it reflects the essentials of Provence. They've done it up completely into a boutique hotel with a prime view.

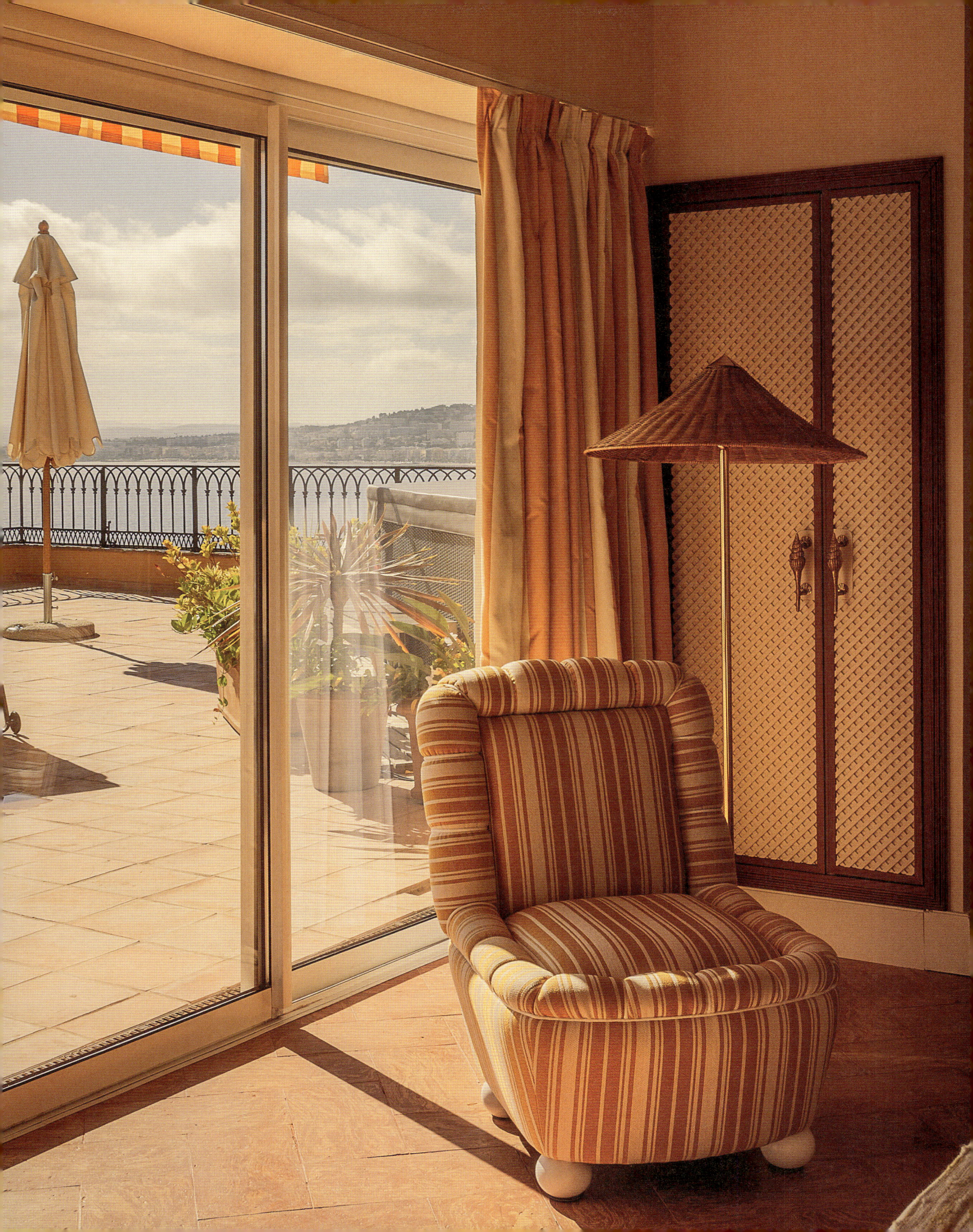

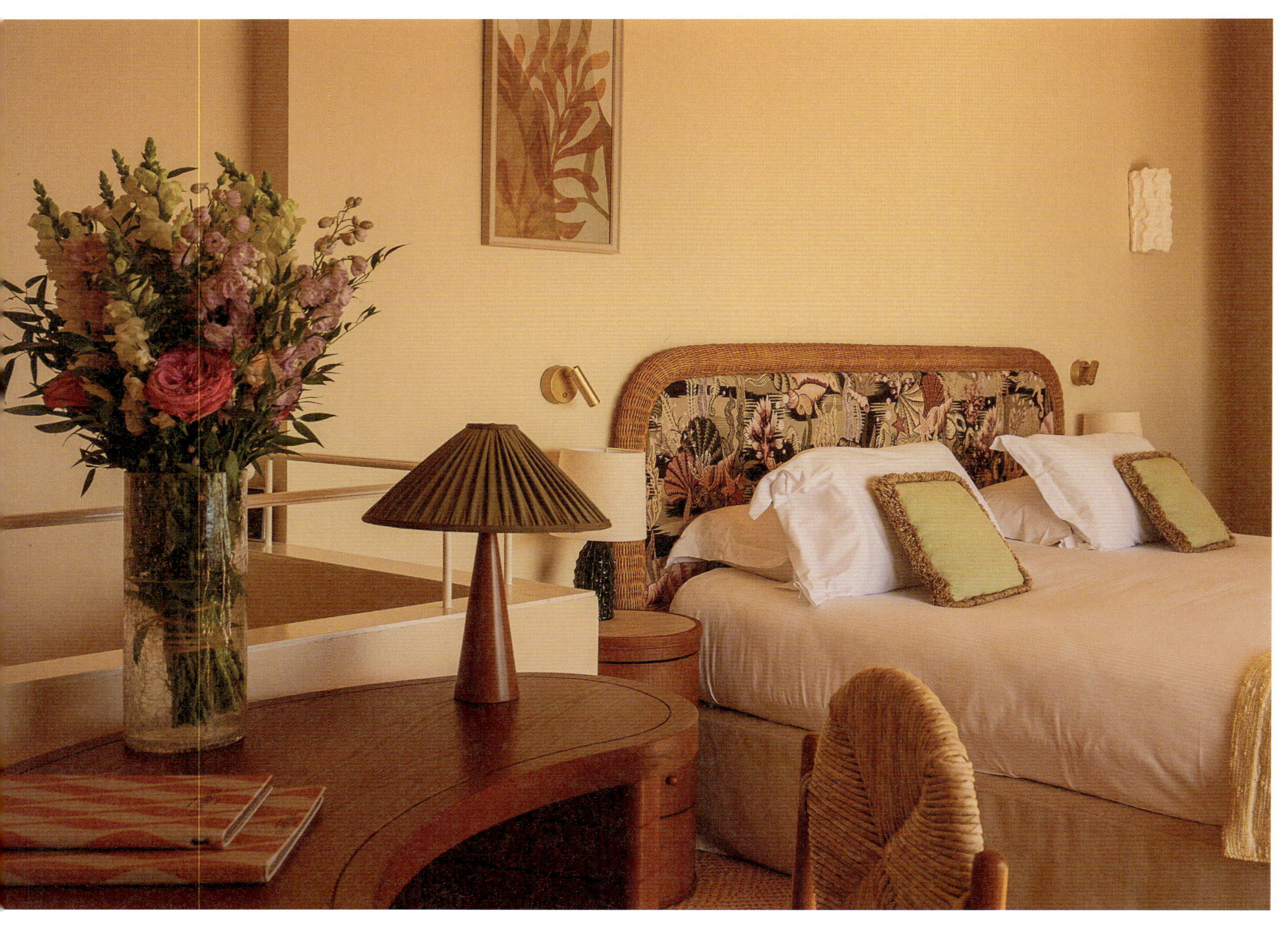

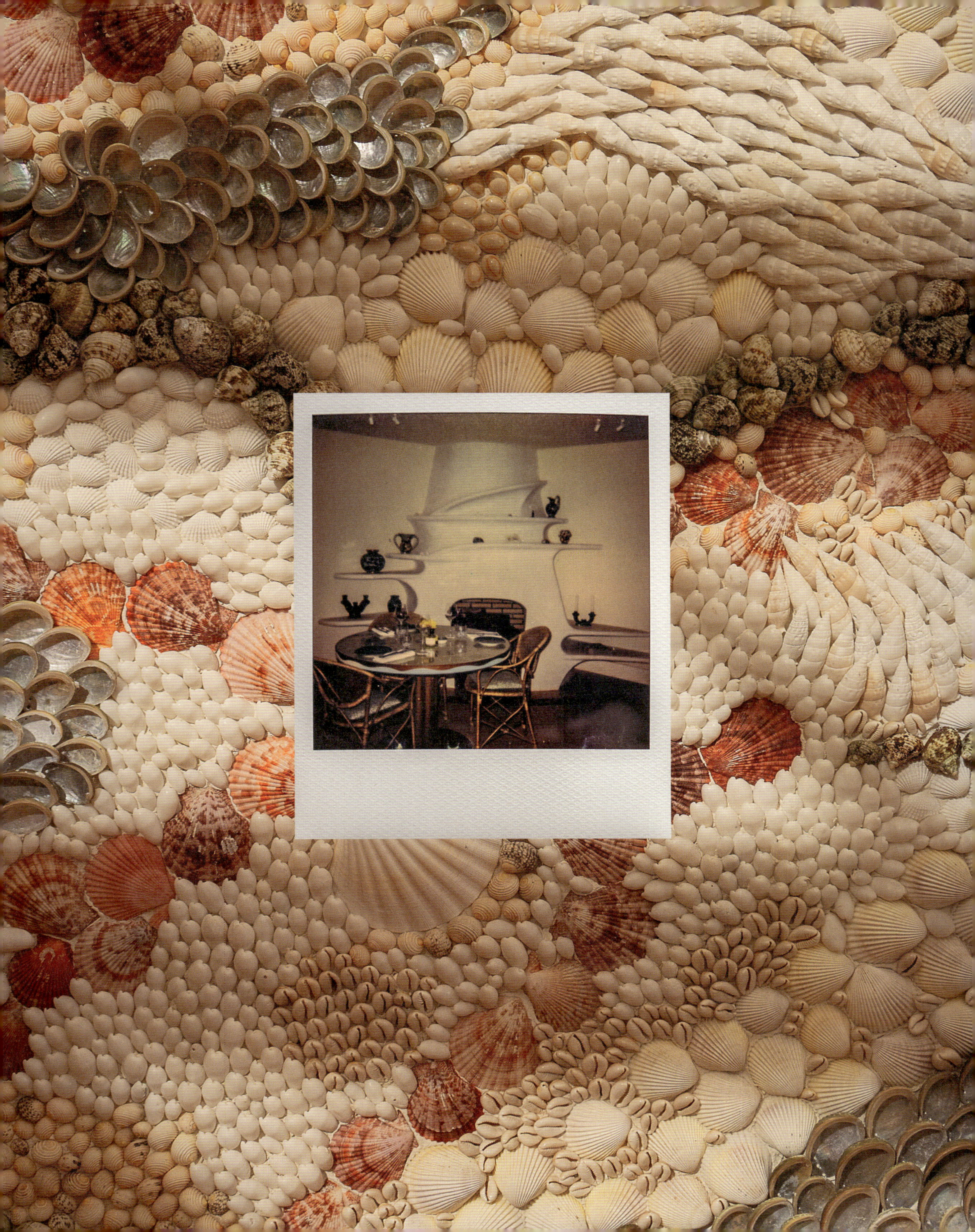

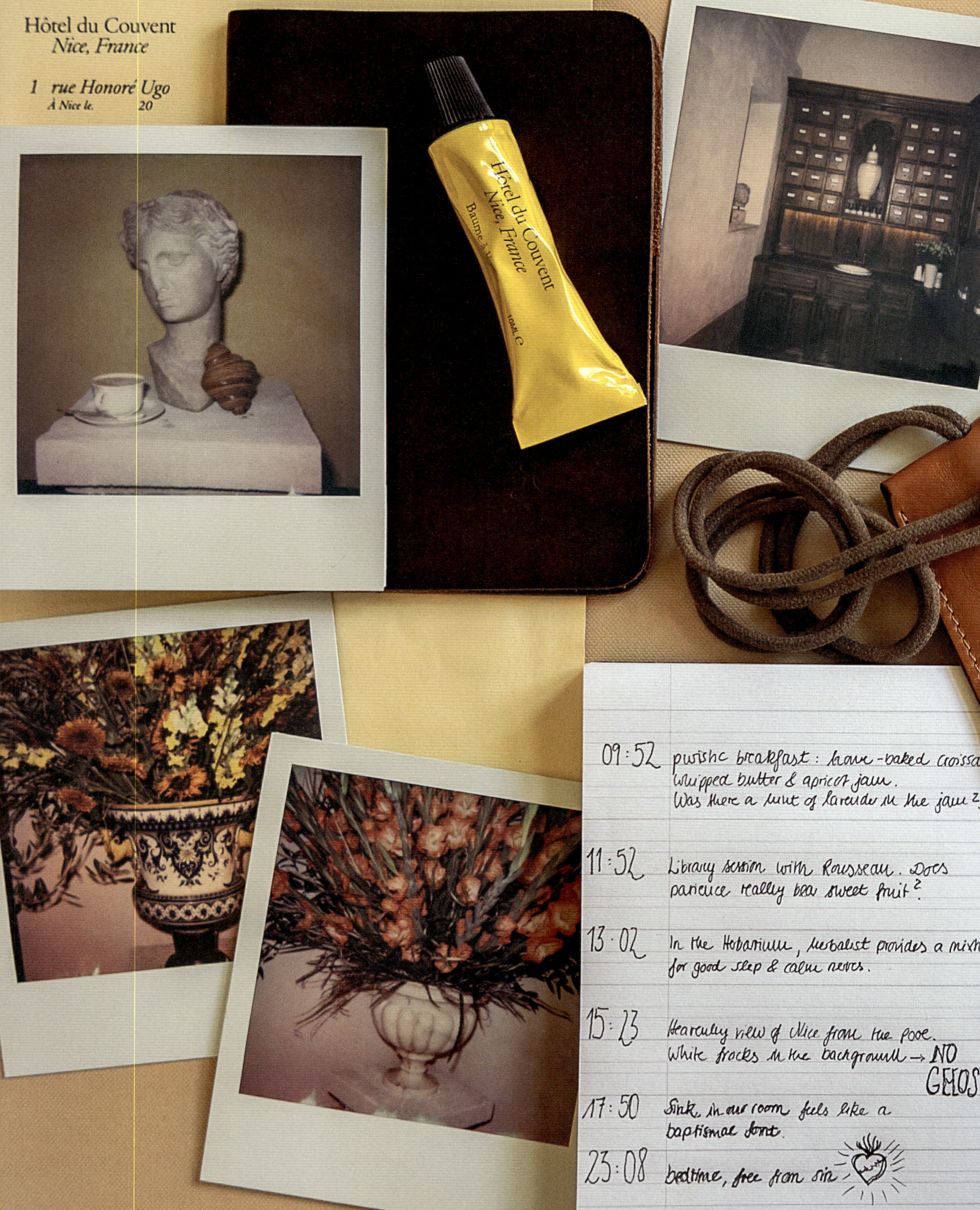

Hôtel du Couvent
Nice, France
1 rue Honoré Ugo
À Nice le. 20
Hôtel du Couvent
Nice, France
Baume à l
10ML e
09:52 parishc breakfast: home-baked croissa
whipped butter & apricot jam.
Was there a hint of lavender in the jam?
11:52 Library session with Rousseau. Does patience really bear sweet fruit?
13:02 In the Herbarium, herbalist provides a mixt
for good sleep & calm nerves.
15:23 Heavenly view of Nice from the pool.
White frocks in the background → NO GELOS
17:50 Sink in our room feels like a baptismal font.
23:08 bedtime, free from sin

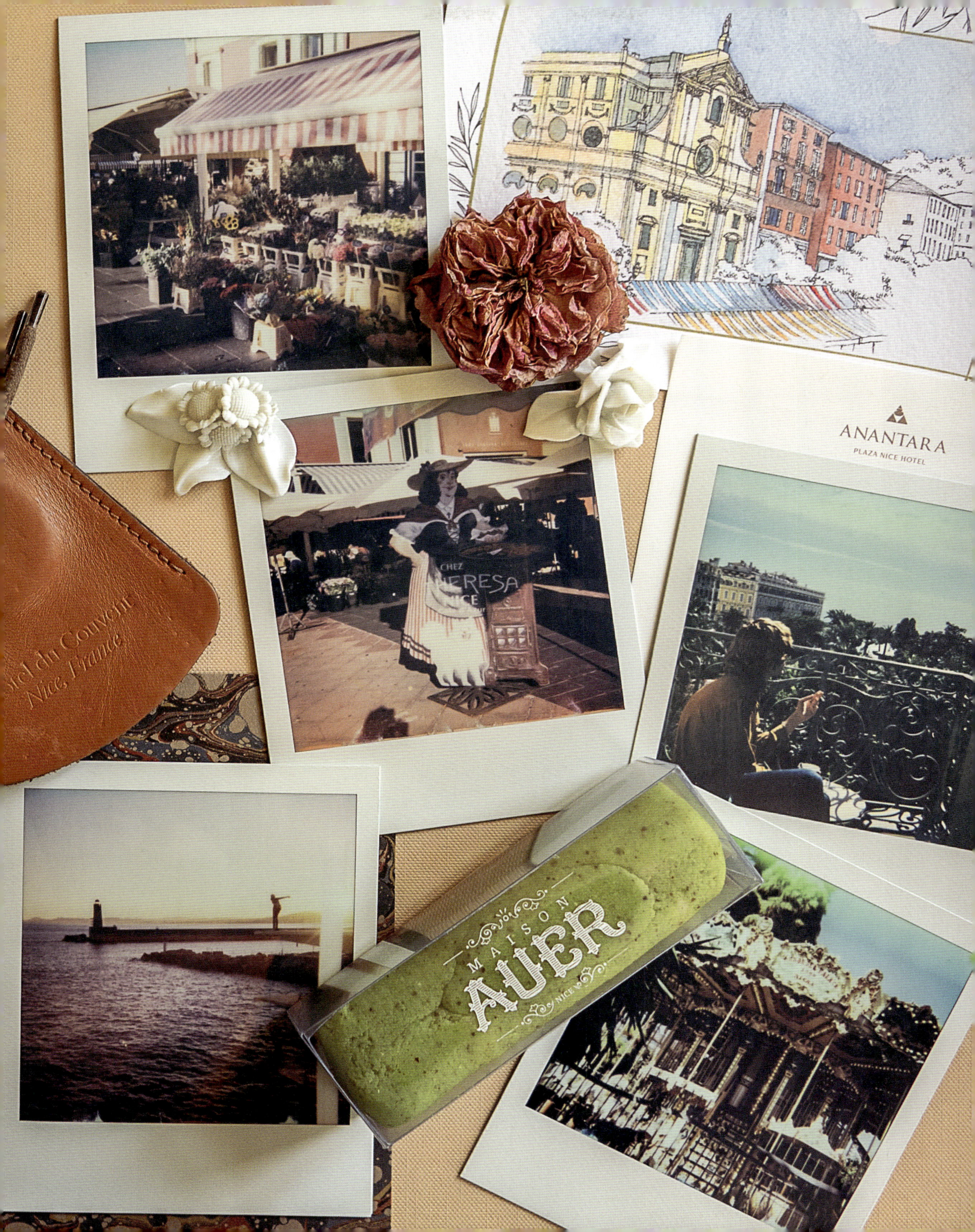
ANANTARA
PLAZA NICE HOTEL
MAISON
AUER
NICE
Nice, France

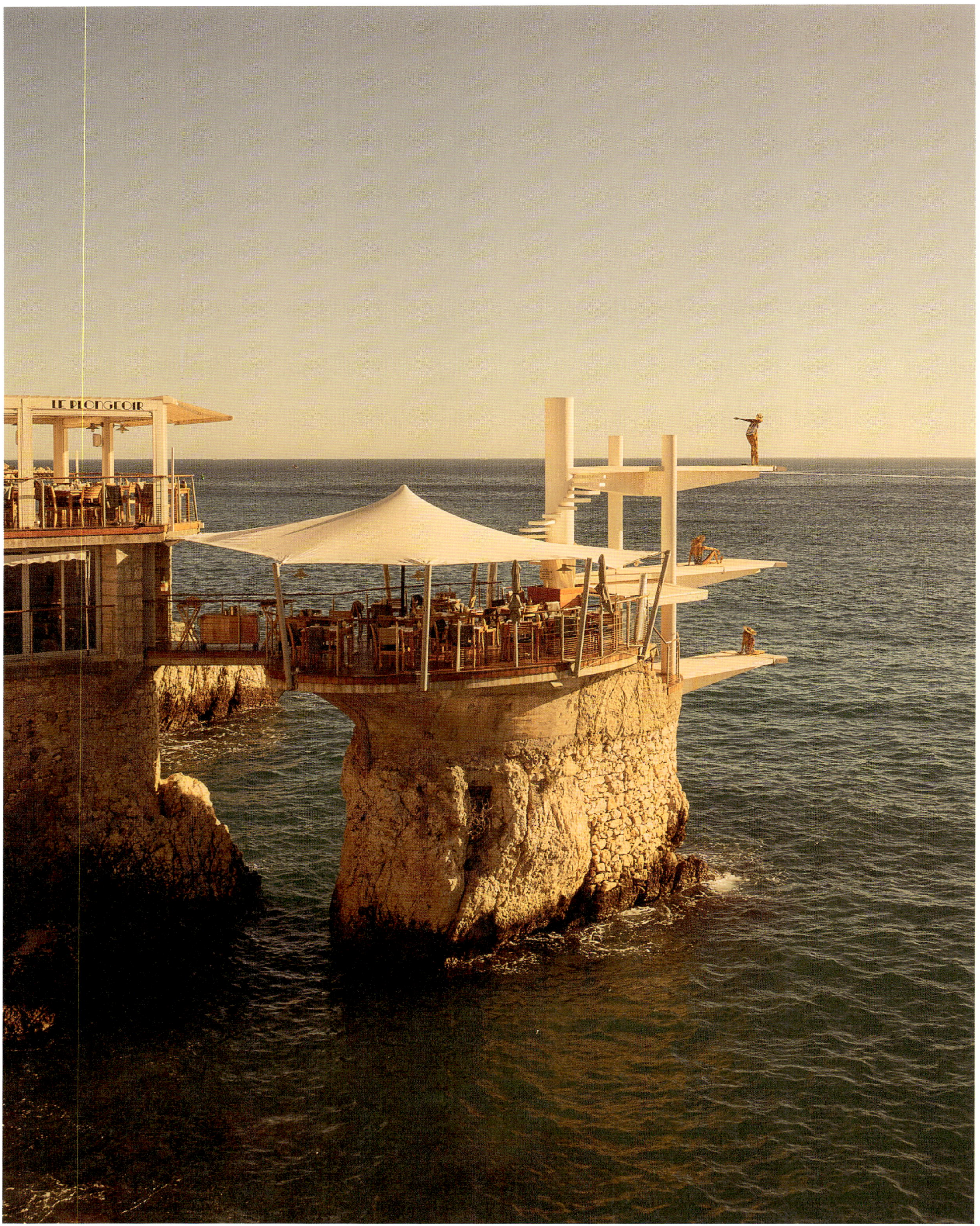
LE PLONGEOIR

LE PLONGEOIR

NICE

FIRST CLASS

Around five o'clock in the afternoon, we begin to contemplate going for a walk and getting an early dinner. We walk along Quai Rauba Capeu toward the Port of Nice. Amid the commotion of the harbor, brightly painted fishing boats steal the spotlight from ridiculous-looking mega-yachts and hulking cruise ships. A quirky local ordinance says every little skiff has to sport its own color scheme. The sun is still blazing, attracting locals to every sliver of beach—no matter how tiny or how rough the cobbles—to be slapped around in the choppy water, aided only by a swim cap. Near one of these beaches, we see two huge rocks spanned by a skinny footbridge. The near one supports a pavilion that's been cut into the rock; the far one supports a small terrace shaded by a sun sail in front of a three-tiered diving platform. We seem to see the silhouettes of people getting ready to dive. Since the early 1900s, the twin rocks have served as a stage for whimsical architecture: During the Belle Époque, a stylized miniature sailing ship lay secured to the top, where people could come for afternoon tea. In the 1940s, it was replaced by the Art Deco diving tower. Fast-forwarding to the 2010s, the shy but charming Marc Dussoulier rescued the crumbling tower, grafted a restaurant onto the rocks, and turned this spot into Nice's ultimate photo opportunity: Le Plongeoir. Marc ushers us up a snug staircase to the top deck. Tonight's lineup is just-caught *pulpo*, fried zucchini flowers, and burrata, local delicacies every morsel of which is sourced from purveyors that Marc knows personally. The restaurant fills quickly, wall to wall; reservations must be made weeks in advance. Beneath our plates, waves crash against the rocks while the diehards keep doing laps in their swim caps. As the sun goes down and paints the sky orange, it sharpens the illusion of divers out on the platform, which is created by small metal figurines.

After dinner winds down, we weave our way around the line of supplicants and down to the recently launched bar at the base of the cliff. We each order a First Class—bourbon, cachaça and pineapple juice—as if there were a more fitting way to describe our perfect dinner on the deck at Le Plongeoir.

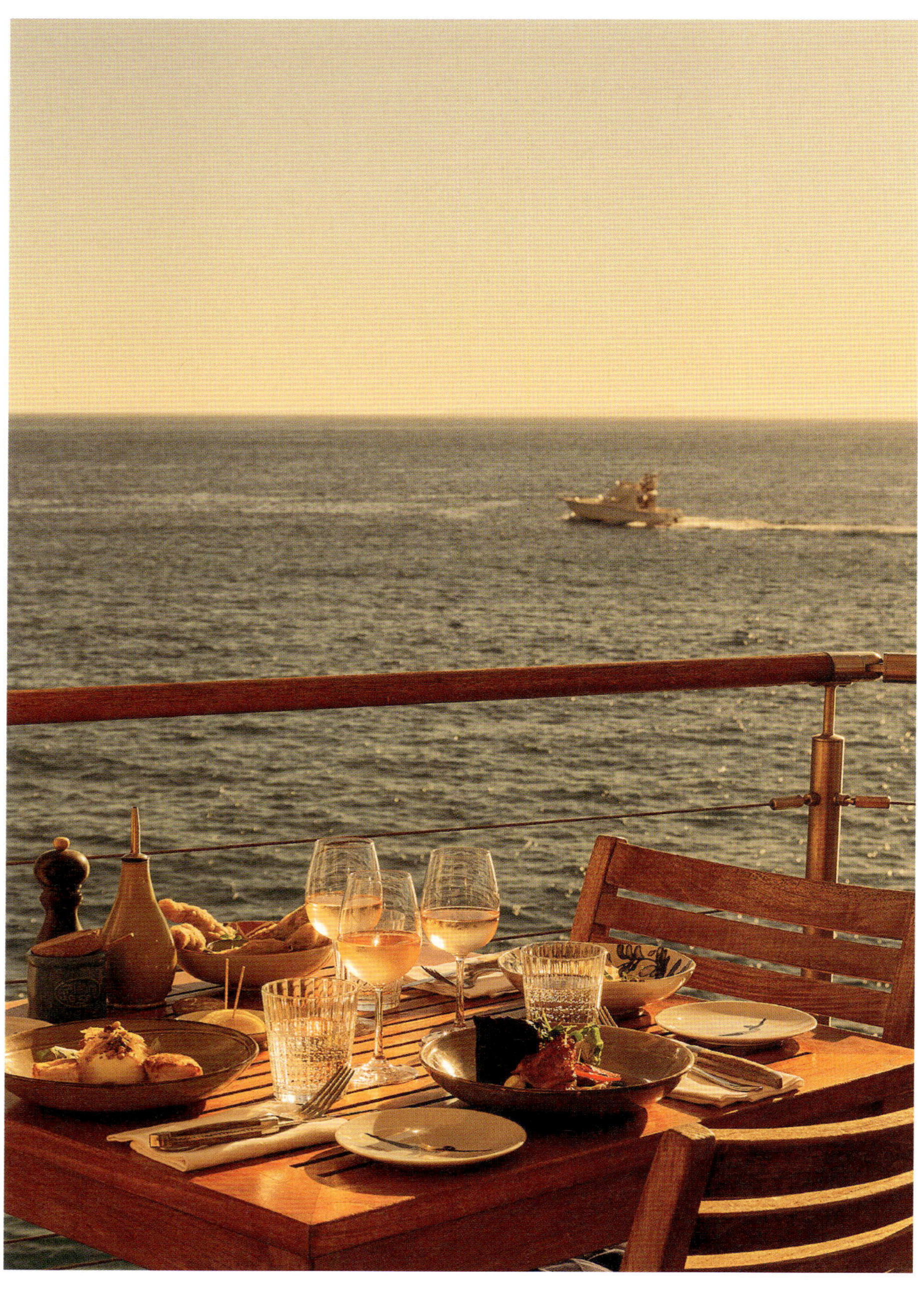

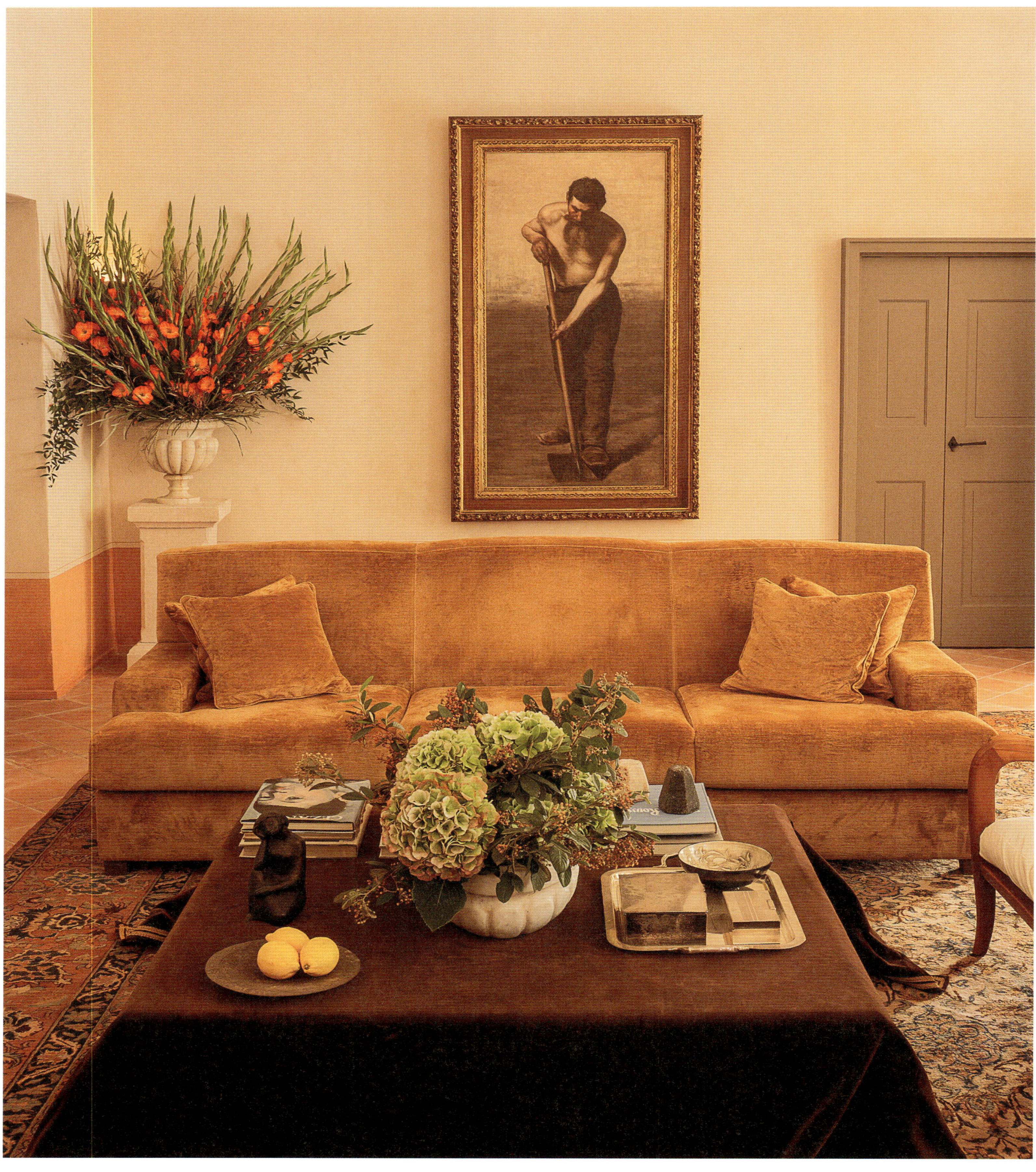

HÔTEL DU COUVENT

NICE

CONVENT CLUB

Nestled in Nice's old town, in a former convent just beneath the ramparts, sits what is arguably the most uncompromising hotel on our circuit. Opened in 2024 after a long closure, Hôtel du Couvent was radically transformed by Festen Architecture, the celebrated interior design duo who keep appearing on our itinerary. On this project, they've executed their vision with a level of radical clarity seldom seen. We enter through a massive arched gateway, our conduct silently appraised by two doormen who are watching what is probably France's most exclusive abbey. Beyond them lies a courtyard dappled in the shade of fruit trees, sand-washed walls with olive-green shutters, and sun-struck colonnades. The hush feels intentional, a salve for the soul. Everything here is reduced to a devout minimum, clean and pure. To our right is a heavy door that leads to the house's own herbarium, where personalized blends of herbs are mixed from stores in old apothecary cabinets. The convent draws us inexorably deeper: old wooden elements, heavy brown velvet; old editions of Rousseau and coffee-table books of Cézanne are presented on silver trays with freshly picked lemons. Probably the most stylish flower arrangements we've seen on our tour tower out of large amphoras: huge, pale hydrangeas, cardinal-red gladiolus, wildflowers cut from the garden, and shimmering lunaria. In their monkish brown robes, vermilion aprons, and soft slippers, even the staff of this part sanctuary, part hotel look sworn to aesthetic vows. The gravel path crunches beneath our feet as we ascend to the terraced gardens, each level thick with flower beds and looping zucchini vines. At the crest, among olive trees, lies a pool where a leafy, half-hidden

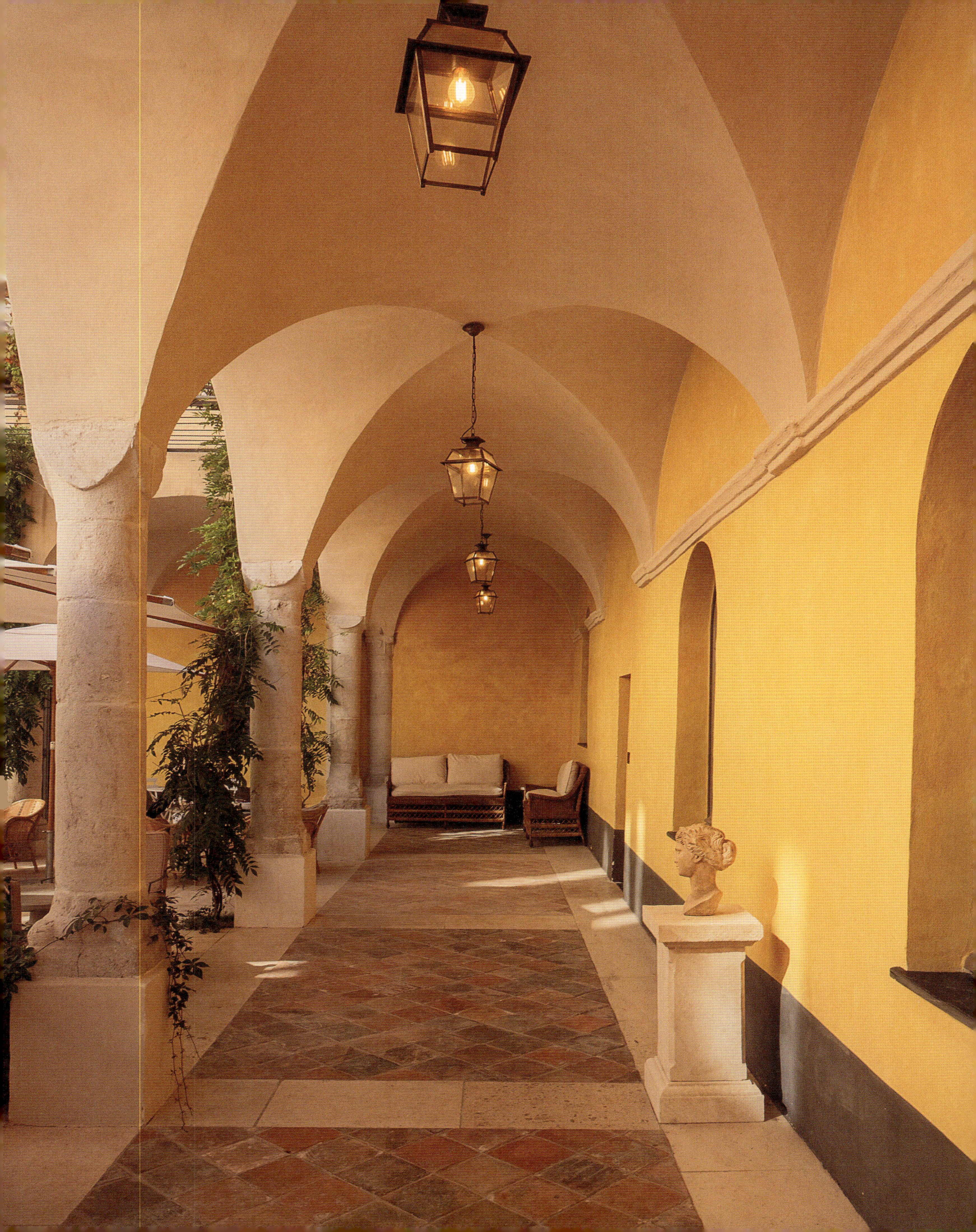

view of Nice and the hotel below us reveals itself. Two white-clad figures step through a wooden door onto the garden's lowest terrace. They're not ghosts, but monks who still reside in the remaining wing of the neighboring convent. The hotel's concept holds together beautifully, offering considered, almost ethereal, luxury in a place of general ostentatiousness. Our little retreat ends the following morning. It could feel like we've checked out of a house of quiet reflection, except that the doormen could be bouncers at the most exclusive club in Berlin. For some, that's all the same anyway.

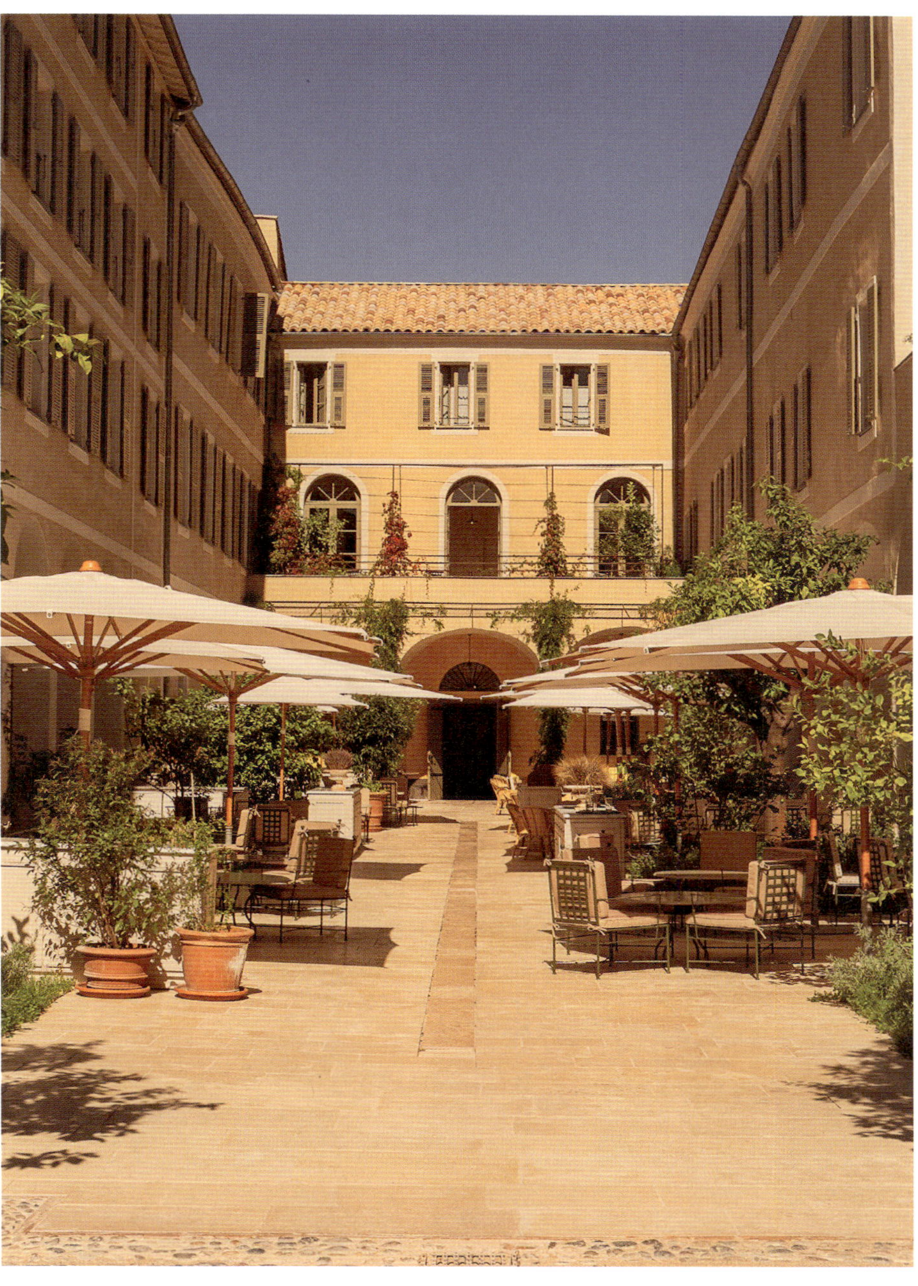

The convent theme plays out radically at Hôtel du Couvent. They have their own herbarium, entered through a door off the cloister of the main building, and next to that is a bakery: blends of aromatic herbs, yeasted breads, and monks that you sometimes come across in the garden.

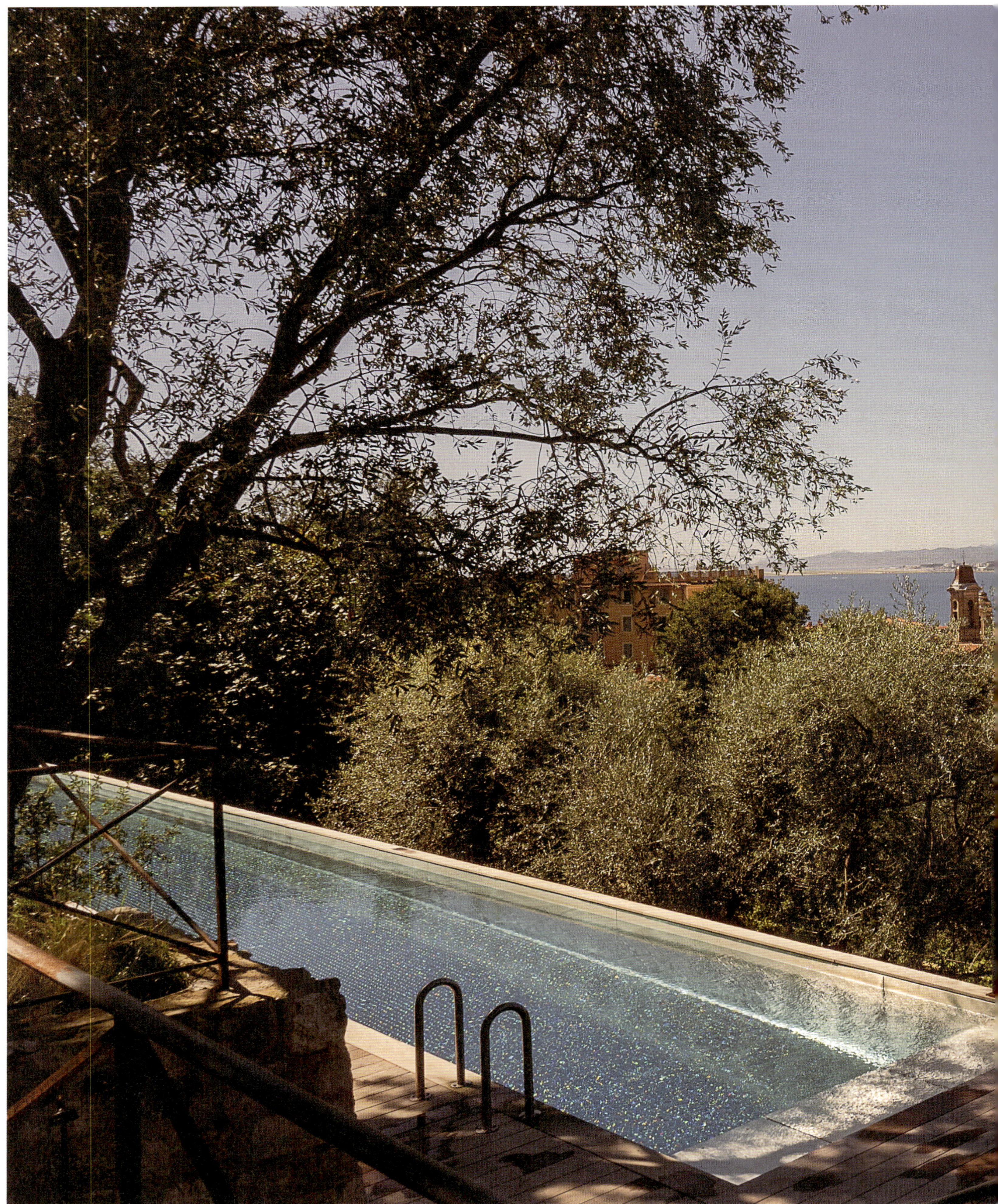

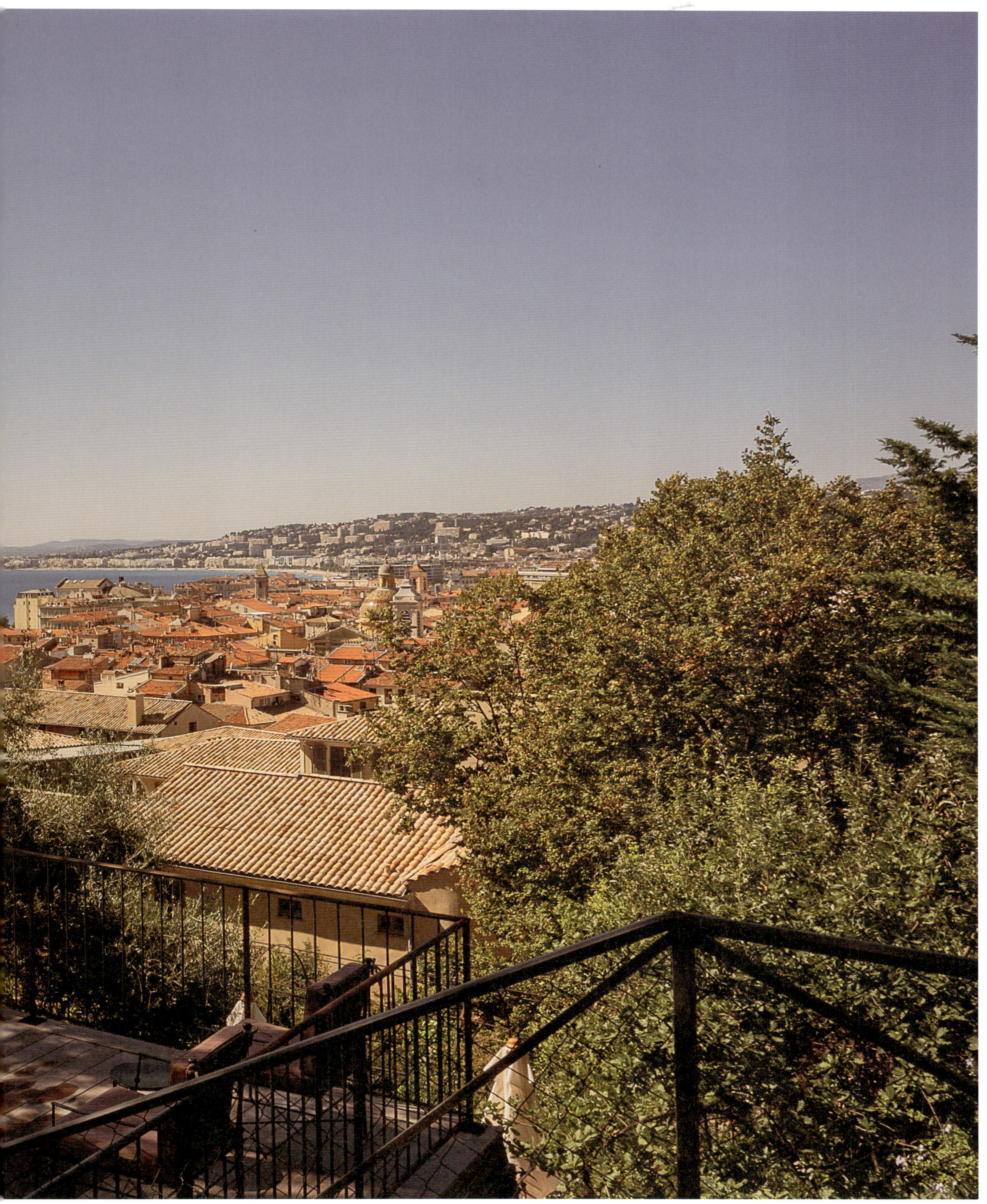

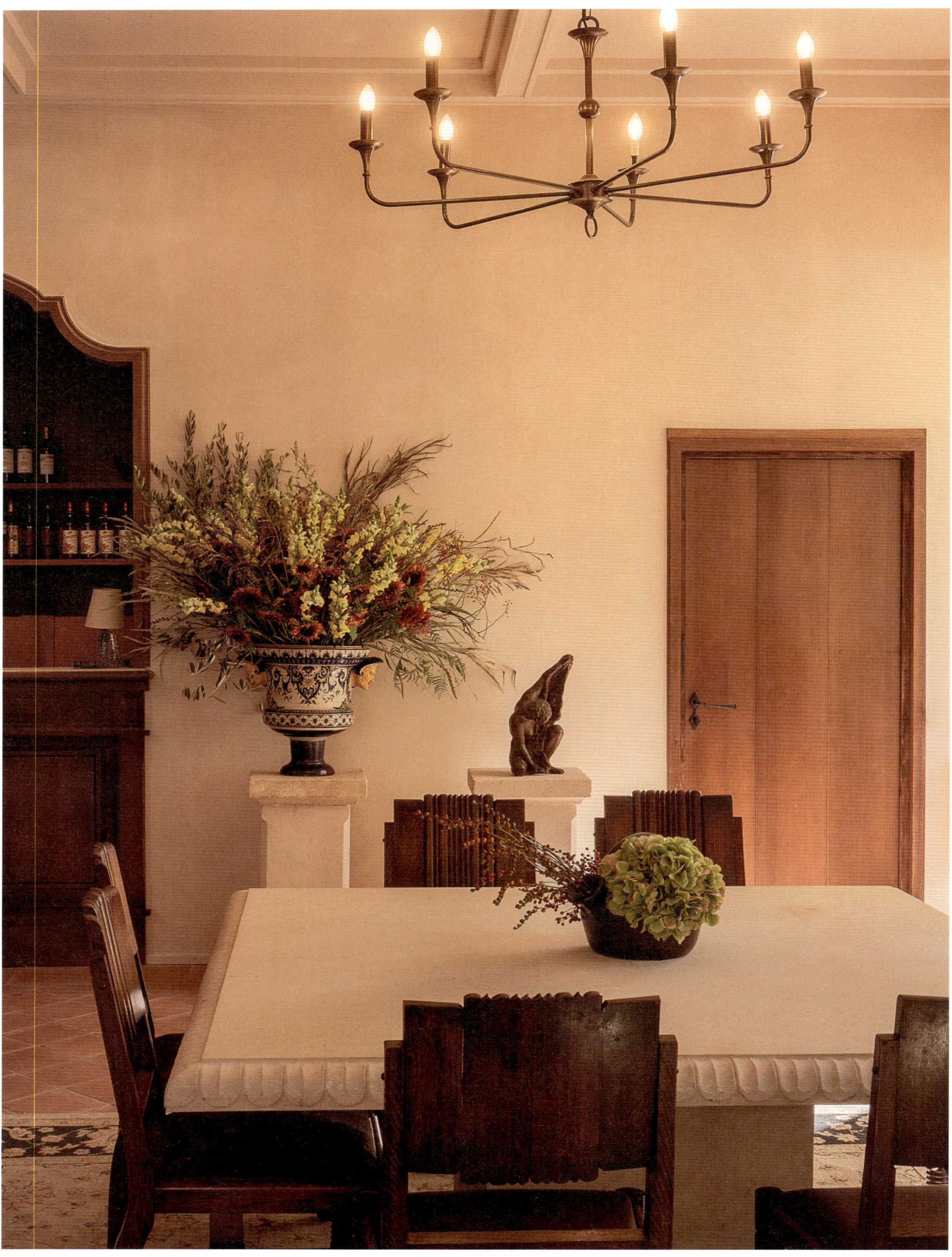

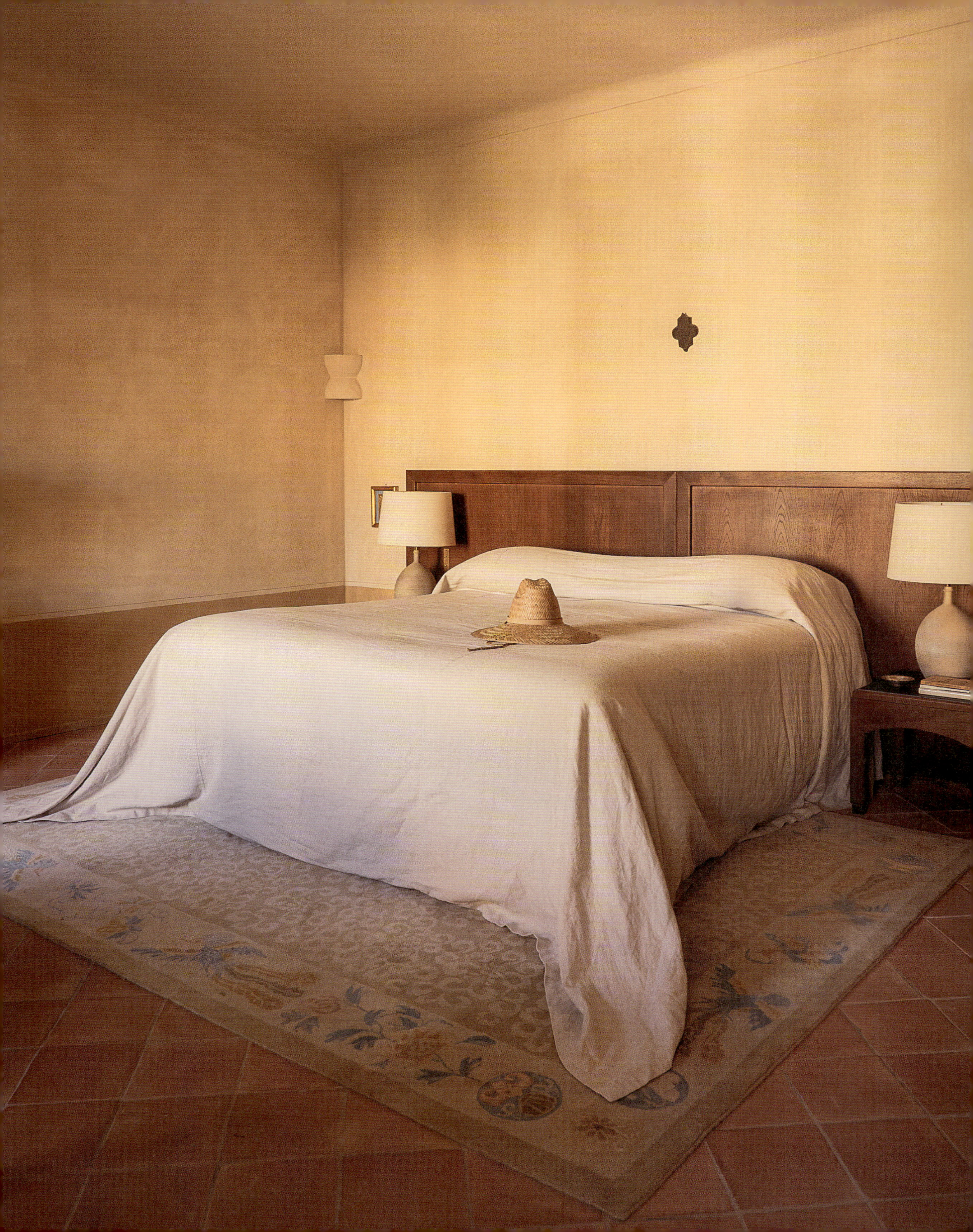

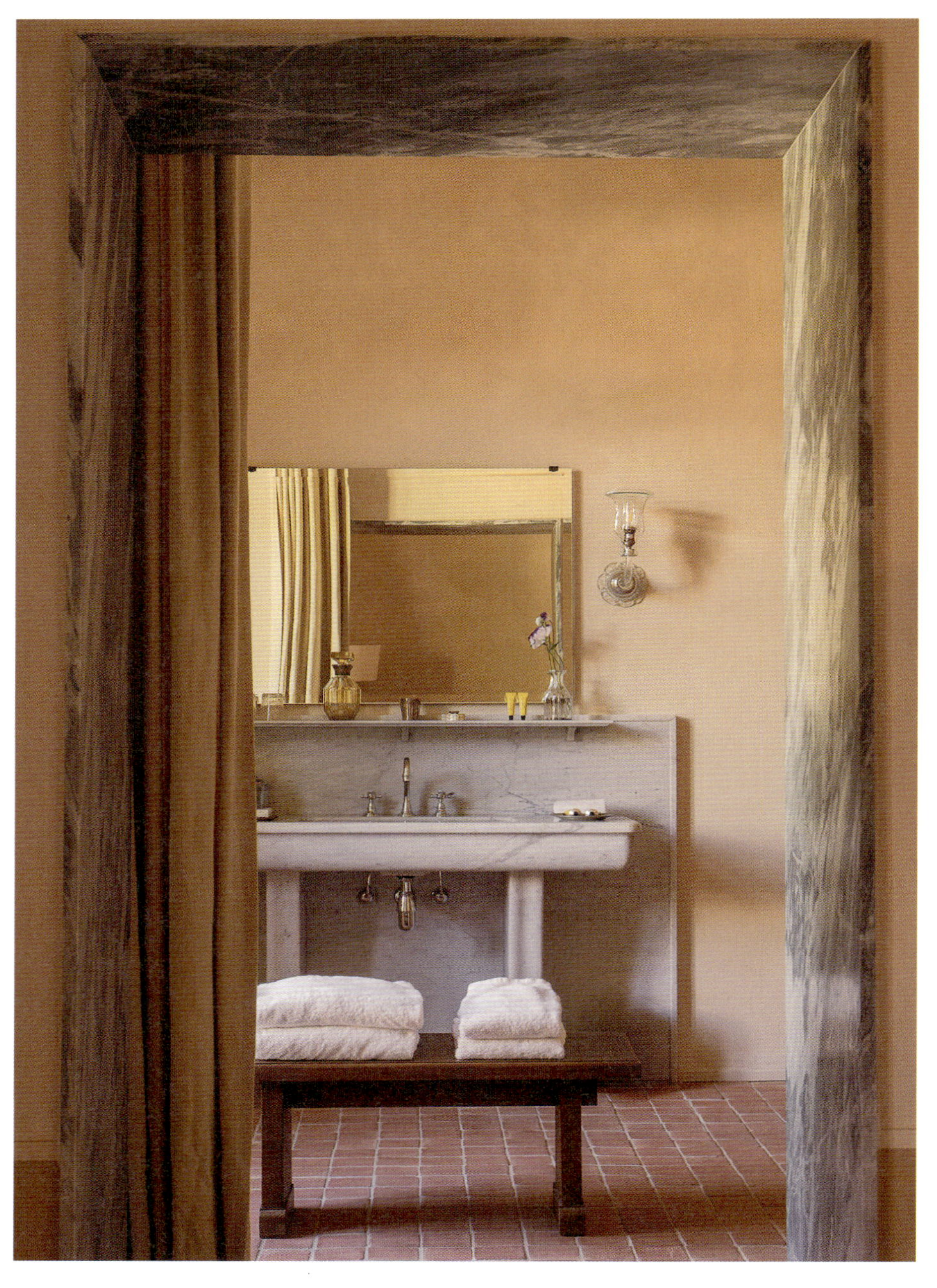

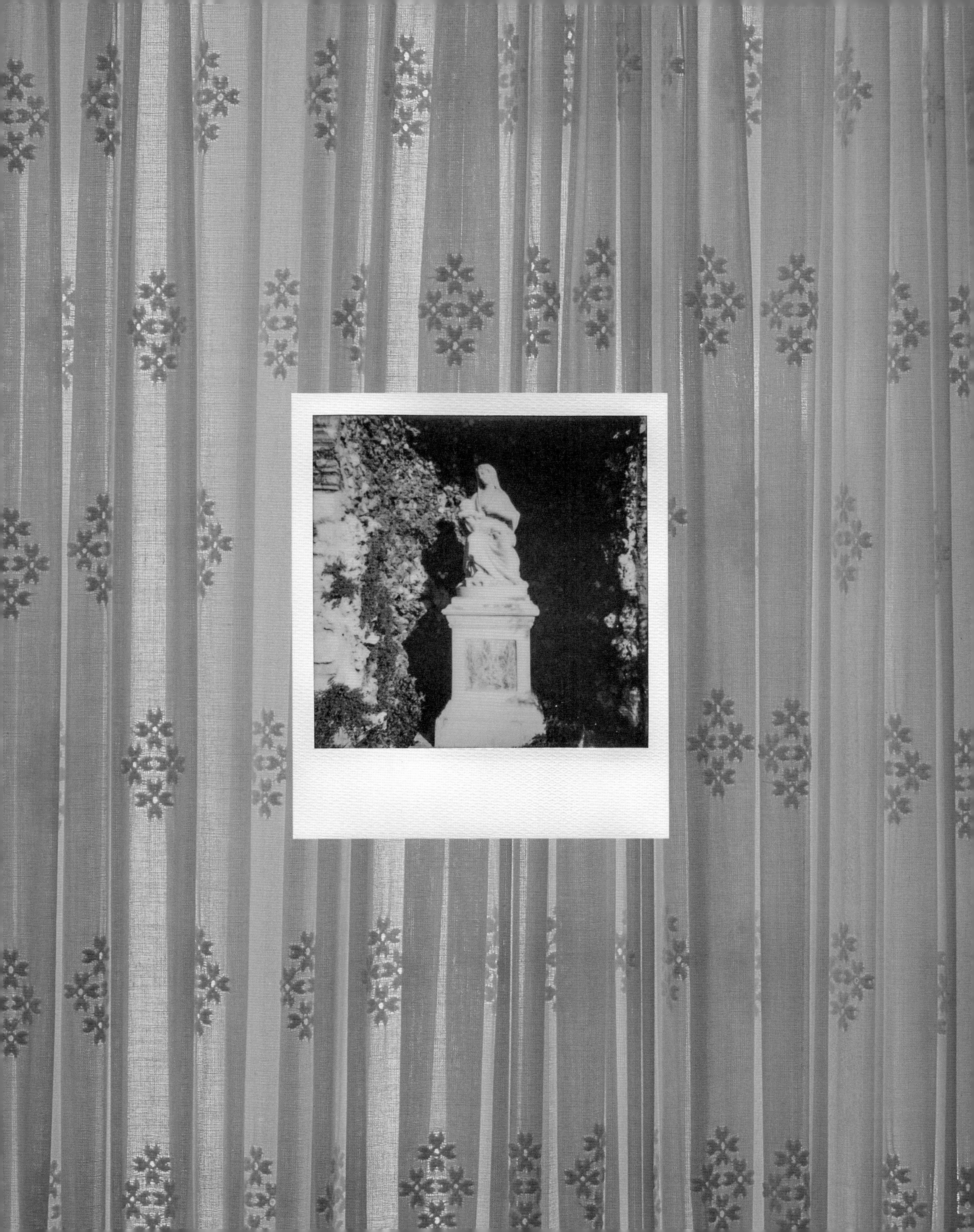

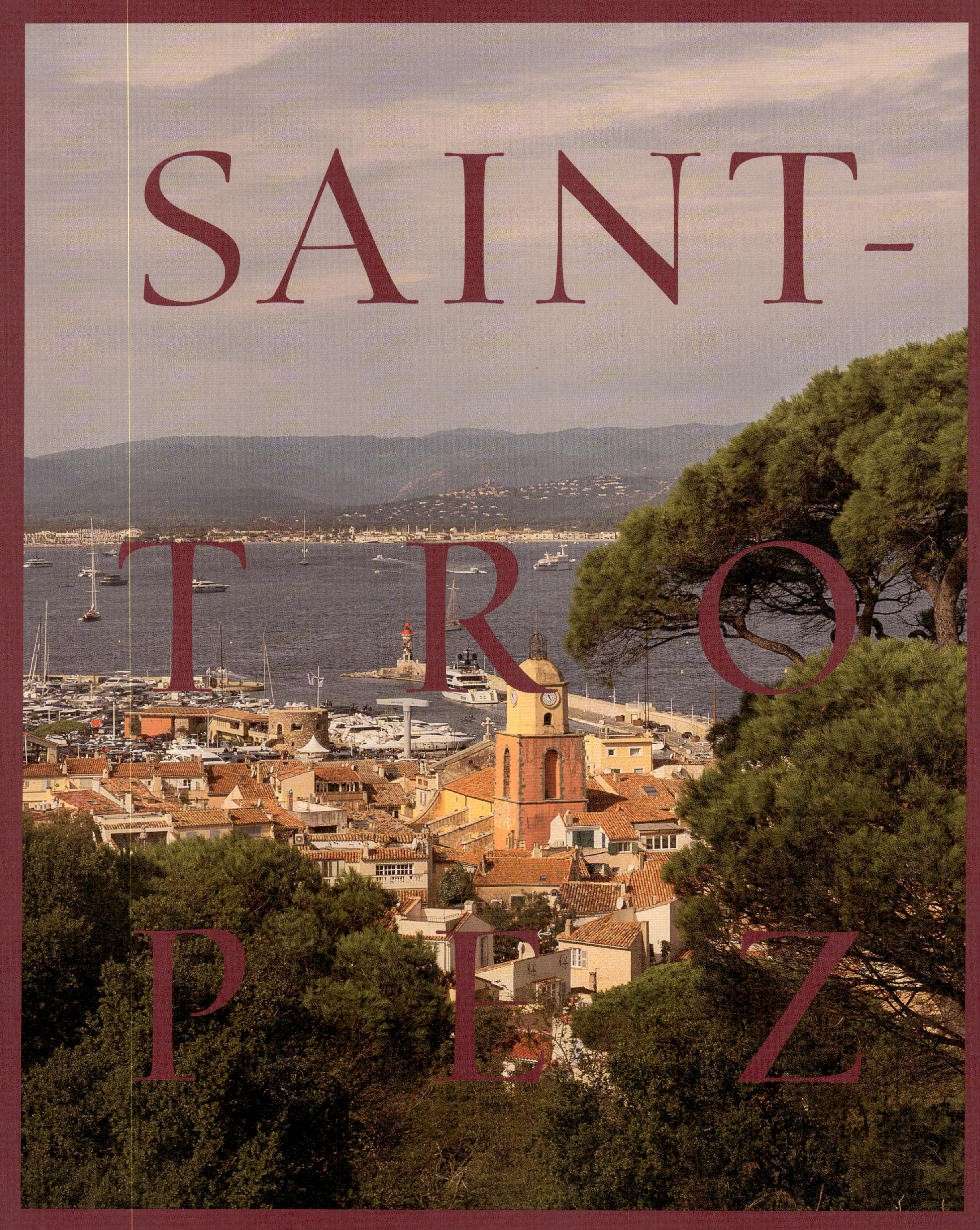

SAINT-TROPEZ

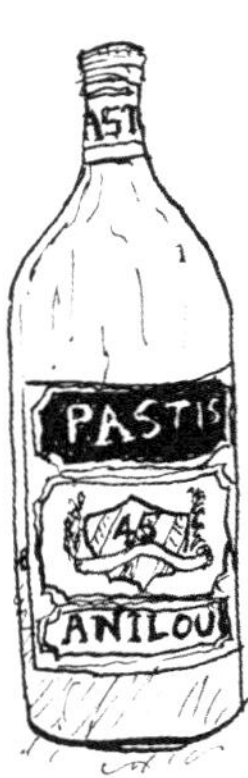

We leave Nice at one end of the Côte d'Azur and once again drive the entire coast end to end. We pass all the places we've been—all the pearls in the chain—in the form of road signs: Antibes, Mougins, Grasse, Saint-Raphaël. At Fréjus, the gnarled pines become the predominant landscape feature, there are larger ships at sea, and helicopters buzz across the sky: all signs that we are nearing the town of Saint-Tropez, the legendary summer residence and harbor for the jet set.

Once, the old fishing village remained calmly obscure, lay motionless on its little gulf, monitored by a bastion fort and the church's cute yellow bell tower. Slowly it attracted the attention of artists like Signac and Matisse and writers like Kurt Tucholsky, who were drawn to the beauty of the hills and inspired by the white beaches. Then Brigitte Bardot came along, and everything changed. With her famous film *And God Created Woman* and her presence there, Saint-Tropez came to epitomize the lifestyle on the French Riviera: exuberant, unrestrainedly hedonistic, and perfect for the jet set. Only hypocrites would claim they were visiting purely for Saint Tropez's historical roots, and no one would believe them anyway. There is an allure to walking along the tiny harbor and seeing these disproportionately huge megayachts lying there, canvassing the boutiques in the cobblestone alleyways, succumbing to fascination with luxury or just to observe it. If that gets to be too much, you can also watch the boule players on the Place des Lices, or you can join our tribe and sit with a piece of *tarte tropézienne* in the quiet atmosphere beneath the fairy lights at the Plage de la Ponche. Saint-Tropez and environs, with white beaches lined with pine trees and reeds, has something for everyone. It's a cornucopia in miniature, the carefree essence of summer on a silver tray.

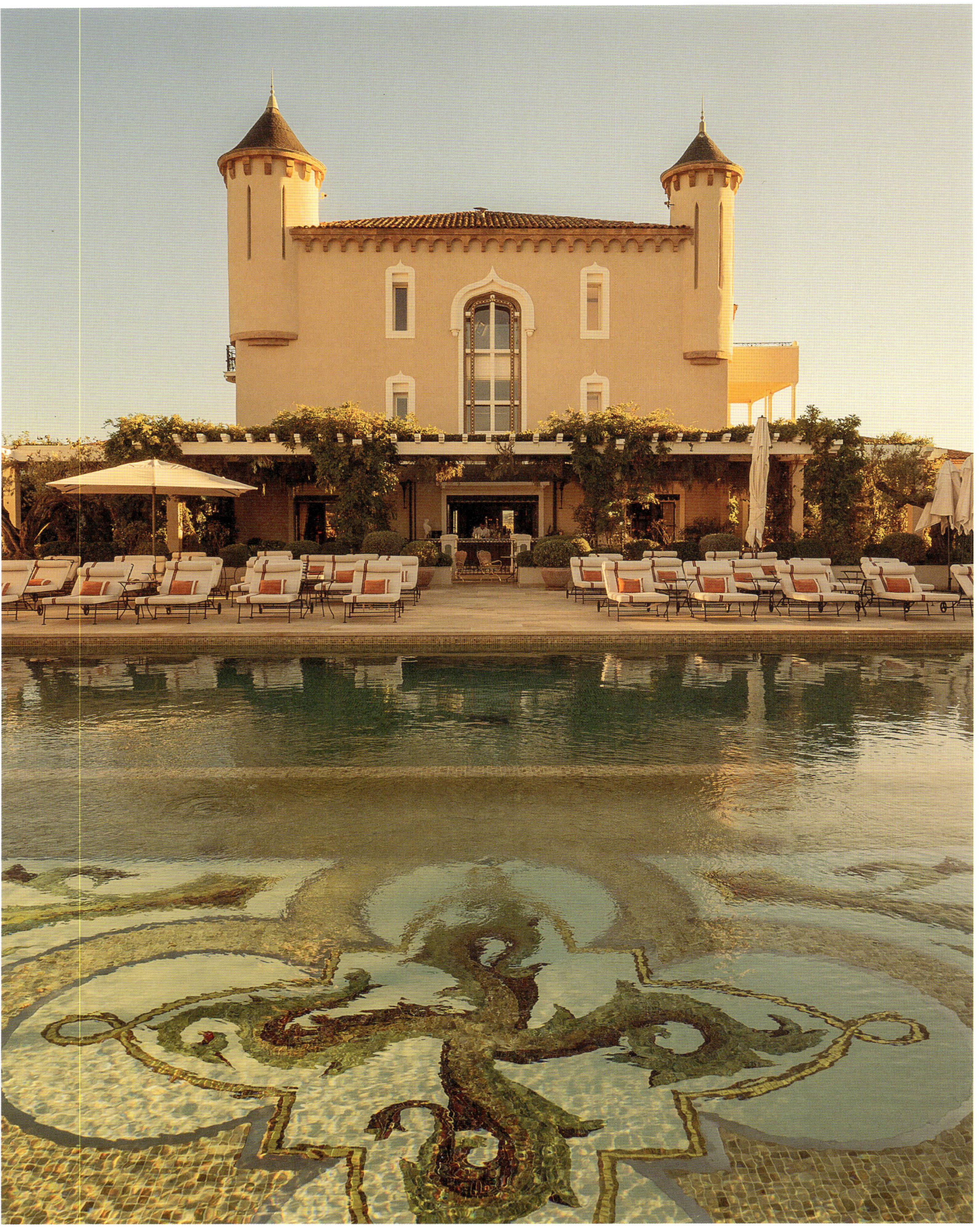

CHÂTEAU DE LA MESSARDIÈRE

SAINT-TROPEZ

CORNUCOPIA

Somewhere amid Saint-Tropez's tangle of rolling hills, secluded villas and beaches, we turn onto a long driveway leading to a majestic château with a 360-degree view of the surrounding countryside. Yet the Château de La Messardière is far more than a dreamy residence in the backcountry: It is a genuine hotel paradise where no guest's wish—not one—goes unmet. In 2019, it was inducted into the Airelles Collection, a relatively recently formed hotel group that is redefining luxury in carefully chosen locations. We step into the marble lobby and are immediately enveloped in a cloud of ambergris and incense, which is the Airelles signature scent and already etched in our memory. Interlocking glass conservatories unfold across the terraces of the château, a fresh vista of sprawling gardens, pine trees, bays and the sea opening from each successive balustrade. Among the tables of the three restaurants, guests float around—both the creative luminaries of our day and day visitors from Saint-Tropez—waiting for the conservatory doors to open and unveil the buffet. We join them and snag a table on the western side of the space. The yards-long table at La Table de La Messardière is heaping with oysters, lobsters, delicate salads, and fine cheeses in a superlative abundance and quality that also epitomizes the hotel in general. It's got everything, even pleasures you never knew you wanted: dreamy herb gardens, tennis courts, its own movie theater, a finely curated boutique and so many pools it's hard to keep track. Familiarizing yourself with all the details would take weeks. It is all pervaded by a subtle elegance. Airelles is not merely a hotel but a pure luxury brand, the kind where you just have to have it: Everything is enticing, everything is desirable. If the château can't offer something, it partners with today's most coveted names: macarons from Ladurée, oils and wines from Carla Bruni's Château d'Estoublon, pastries by Cedric Grolet. These await us in the evening, selected and arrayed on a table in our suite. There are silk nightclothes embroidered with our initials. We end the day with our wishes all come true.

They serve a lunchtime buffet on the veranda at La Table de La Messardière that could almost be a stand-in for the entire hotel. Laid out on a banquet table is a cornucopia of cravings: mountains of oysters, lobster, fresh salads, and oven-fresh pizza. For dessert, there are Cedric Grolet's famous fruits.

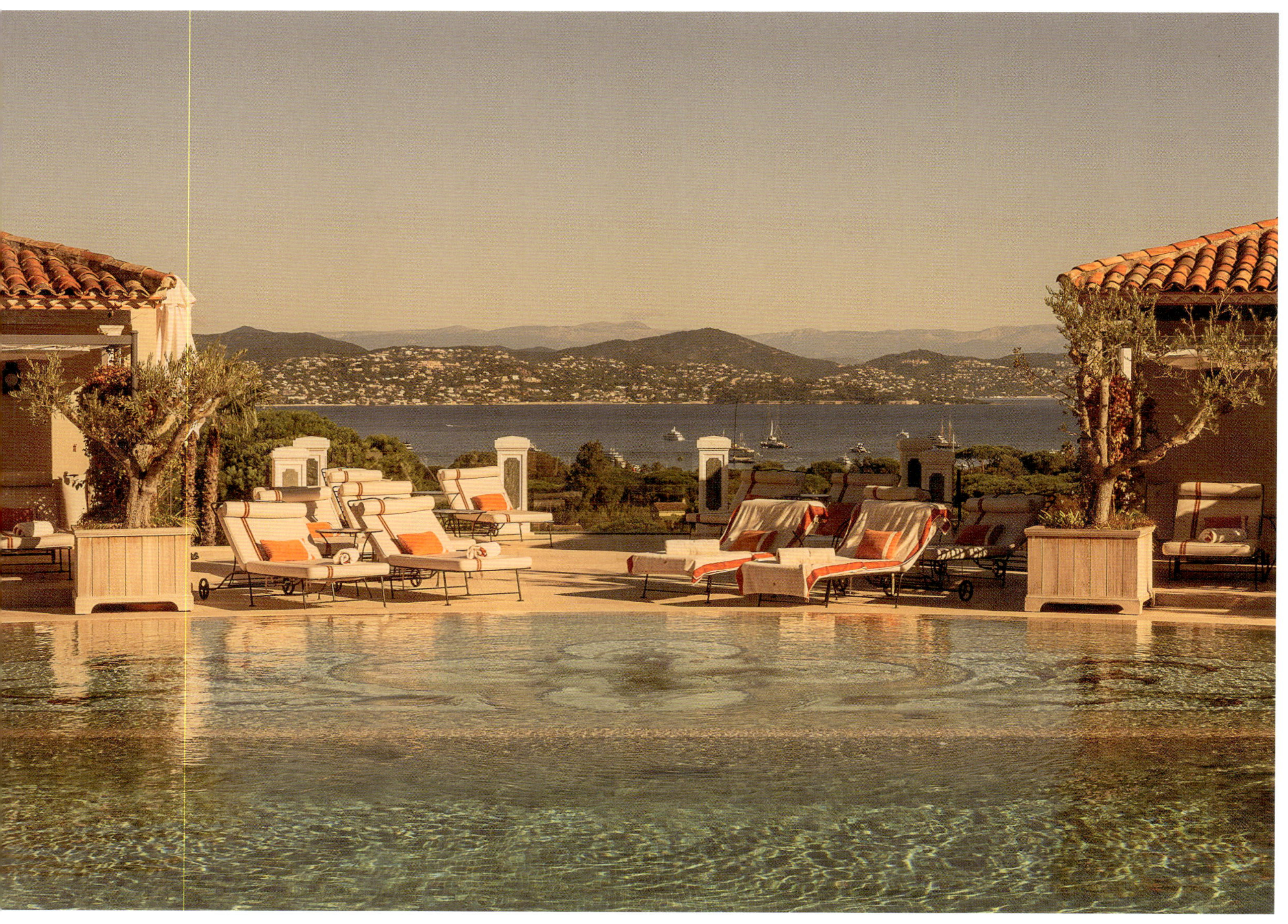

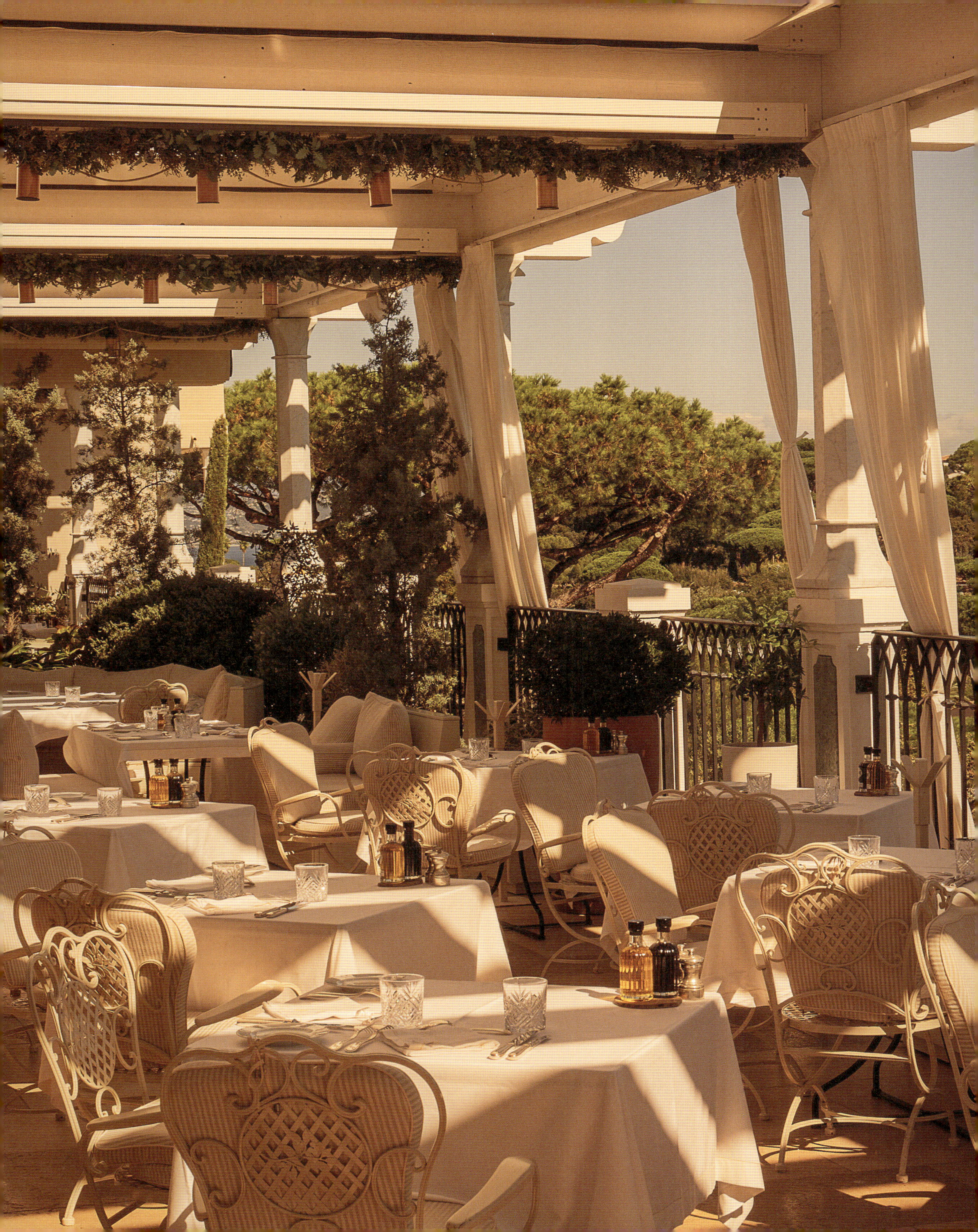

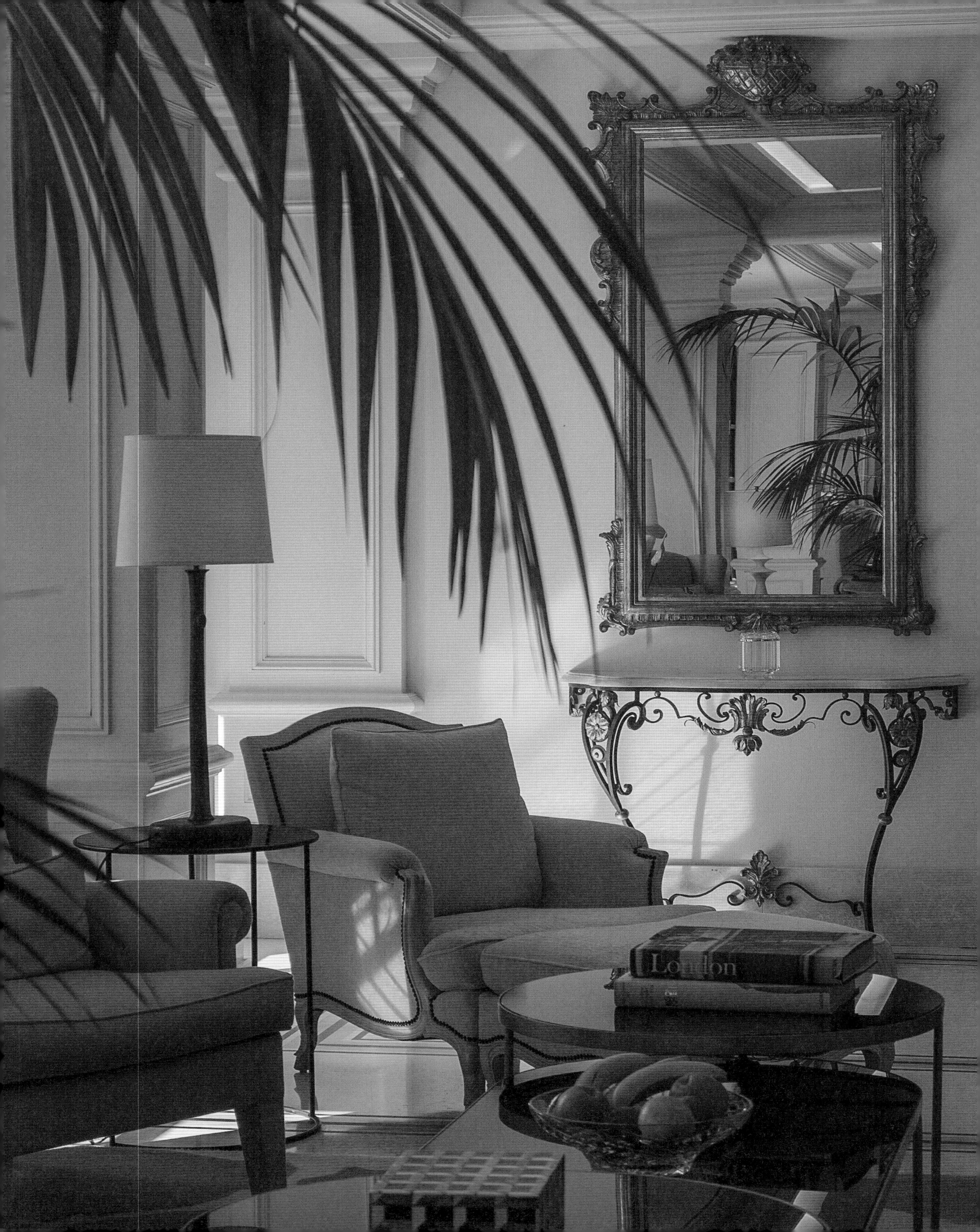
London

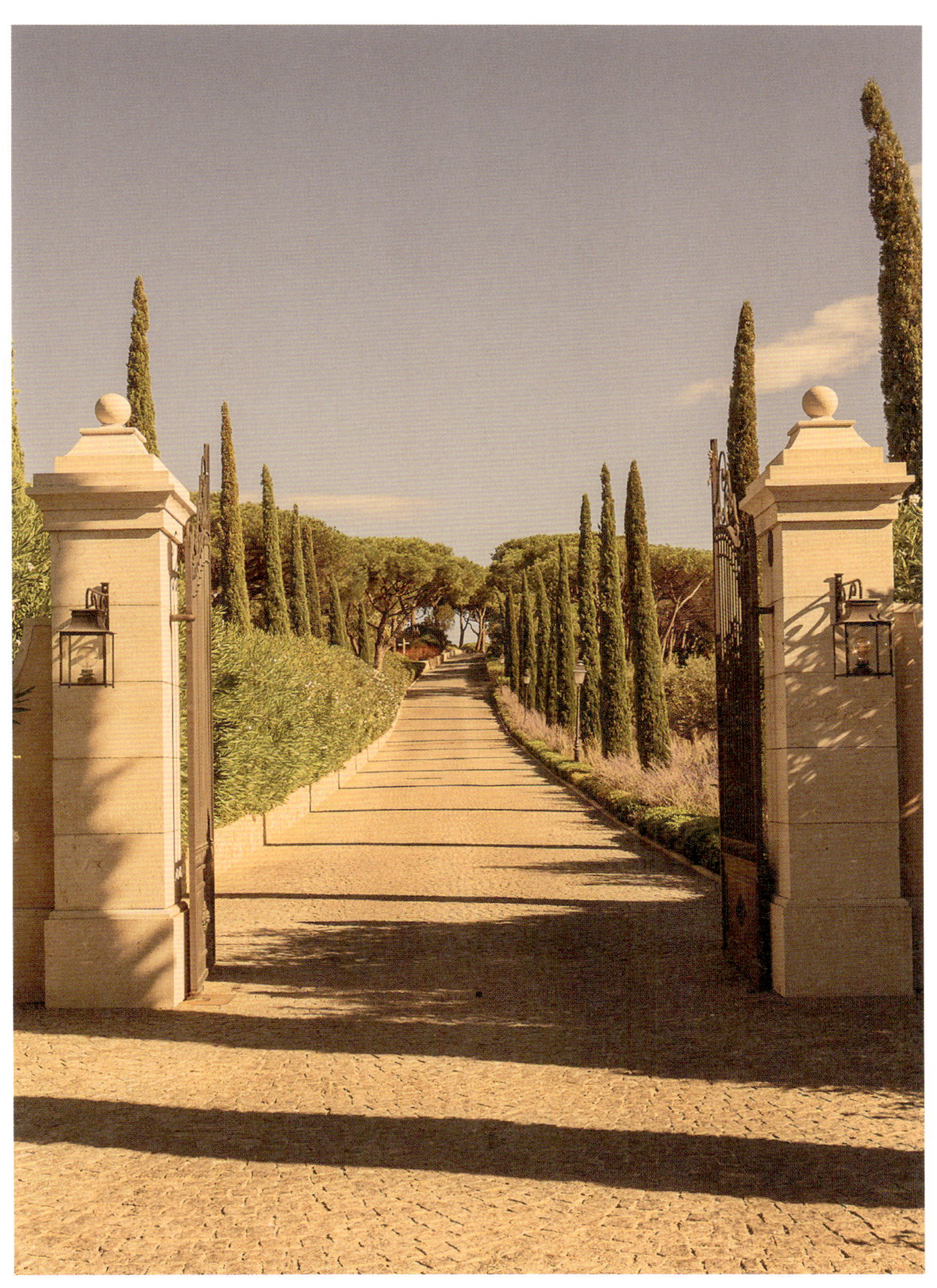

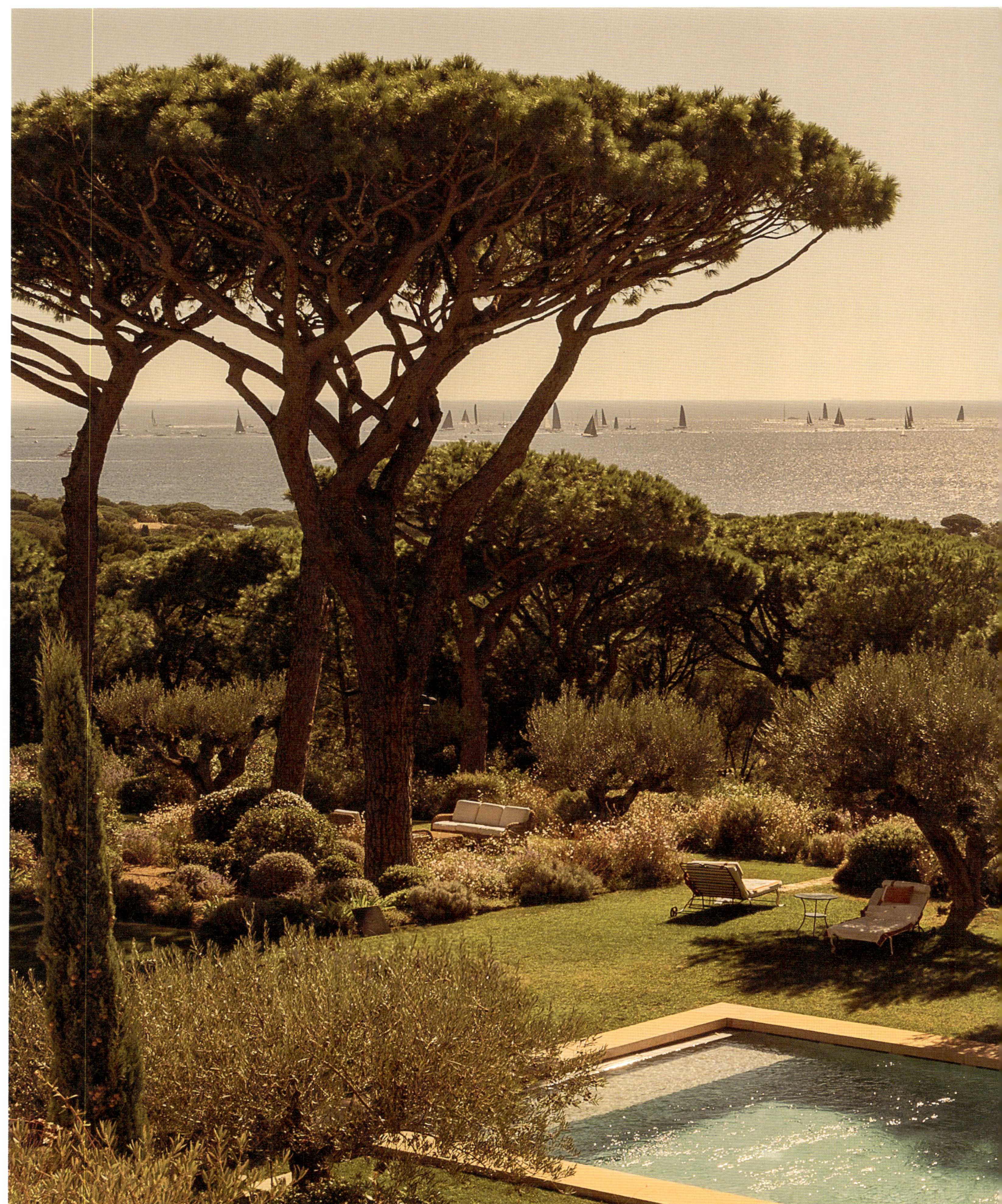

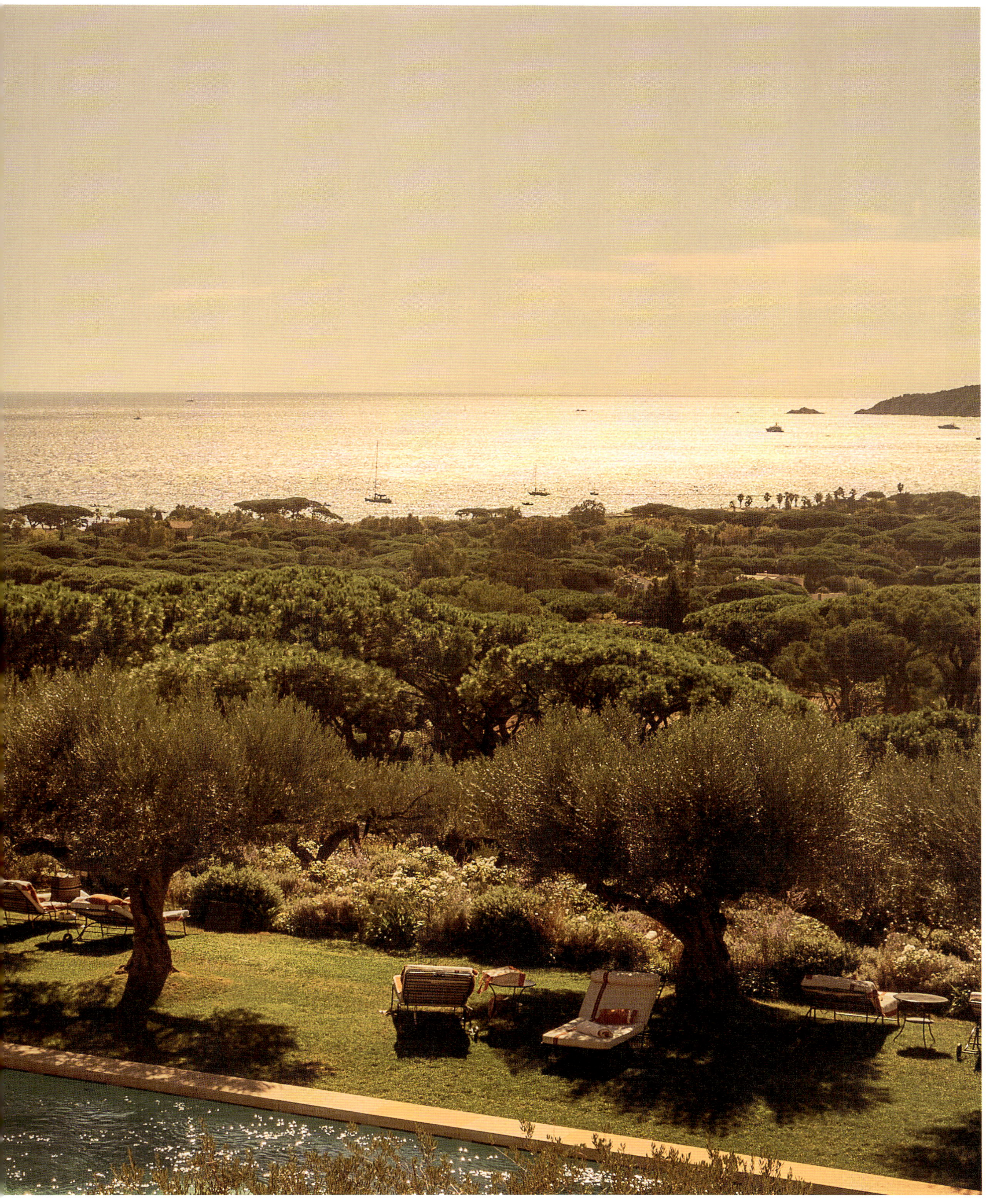

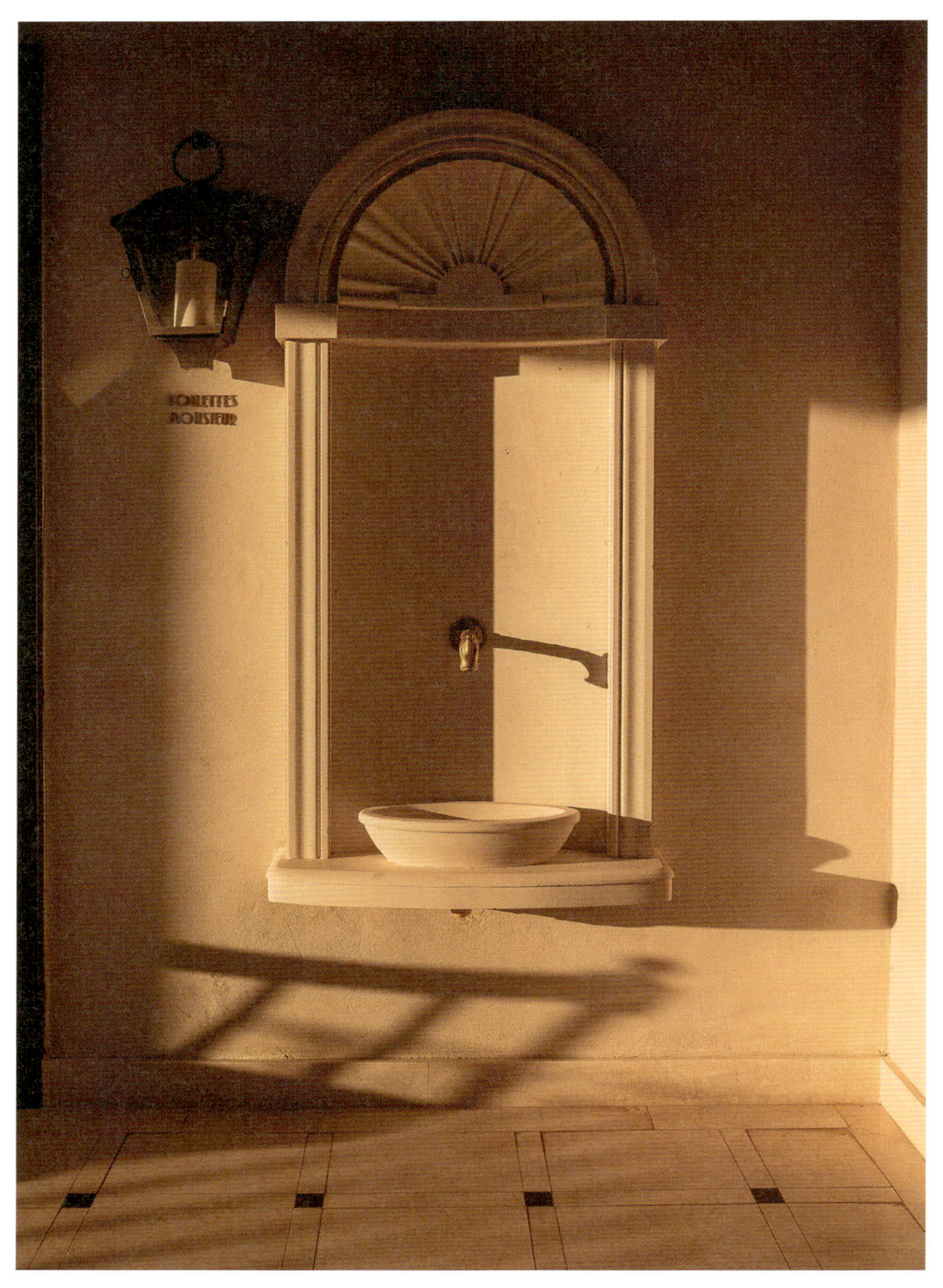
TOILETTES
MONSIEUR

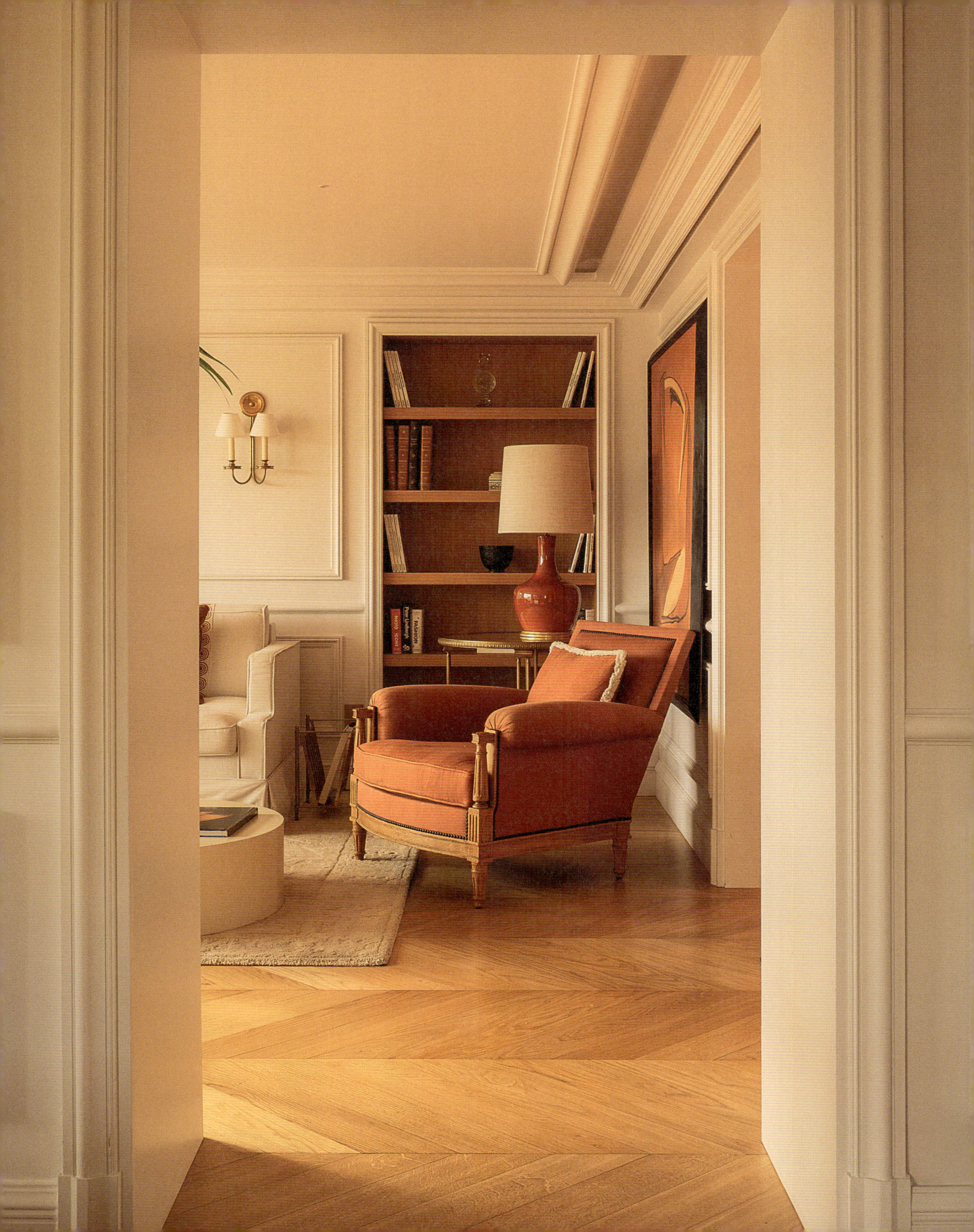
PHOTO ICONS
Peter Lindbergh
FASHION

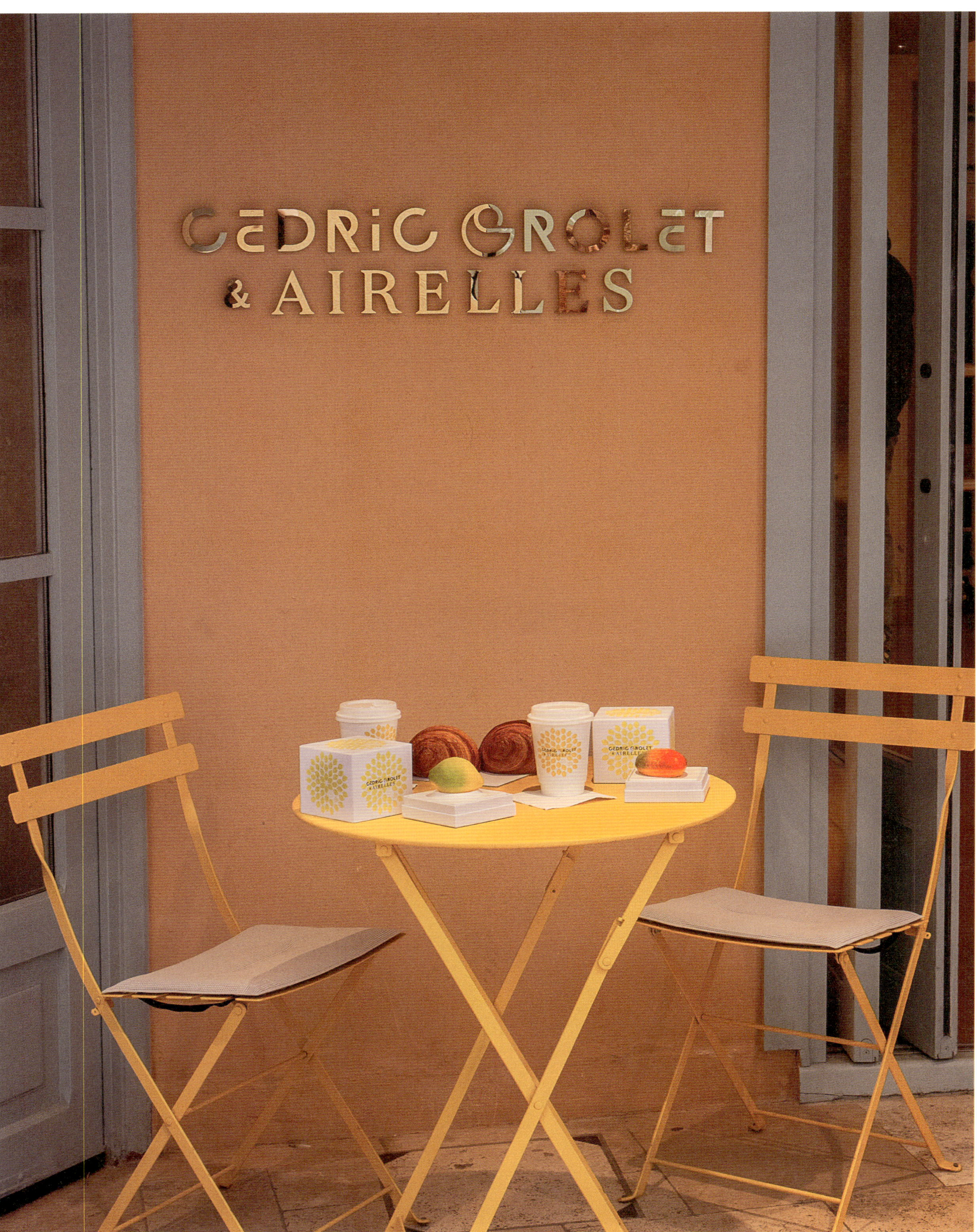
CEDRIC GROLET
& AIRELLES

CEDRIC GROLET

SAINT-TROPEZ

TROMPE-L'OEIL

We awake from a deep sleep to a room with thick crimson fabrics and creamy wood paneling illuminated by an orange sun. We only have time for a quick coffee on the balcony; the hotel shuttle is already waiting. For breakfast we are going on a trip. Yesterday, we already fell under the spell of Cedric Grolet's sweet creations at the hotel. Today, we want a tour of his works and a glimpse into the mind and soul of the megastar Parisian pâtisserie. Cedric opened his first boutique near the Paris Opera a few years ago, showcasing his exquisite pâtisserie skills on social media: modern, unadulterated, and bursting with flavor. Now, people are known to wait in two-hour lines outside his shops. Airelles wanted a piece of the action, so not only did it put his masterpieces on the menu at the hotel, but it also collaborated with him to open a Cedric Grolet shop directly in Saint-Tropez—which is where the château's black Rolls-Royce is now taking us.

The fishing village is still asleep, though a few peacocks have drifted down from the citadel to peck at crumbs in the market square—or perhaps to reclaim the city. We turn into the narrow Rue des Feniers and pull up at the door of the boulangerie to see silver plaques, yellow garden chairs and sunflowers on the blue windowsills of a weather-beaten fisherman's cottage. From the workshop on the left emerges a series of trays of twisted puff pastry—perfectly risen, lightly wobbling—being ferried to the oven on our right. The display case starts to fill up with oodles of flaky croissants, next to them *pains au chocolat* and *pains suisses*. The counter is onyx, and Cedric Grolet's showstoppers are arrayed on it like relics in a glass shrine: flawless replicas of fruit, vegetables, nuts, and whatever else gives these things their flavor. A flawless green apple rests beside a lemon; a crumply passion-fruit lies beside an obsidian-black pod of vanilla. Grolet creates optical illusions, edible trompe-l'œil; his shops feel more like luxury boutiques than bakeries. We fail miserably in our bid to sample the entire collection; all we can handle is one Paris-Brest, one hazelnut, and one vanilla-flower each before we're both flirting with a sugar coma. By now, the queue of Grolet devotees is snaking all the way to the church. Fortunately, we can rejoin the pursuit of France's hottest pâtisserie at the château later, after we've recovered from this round.

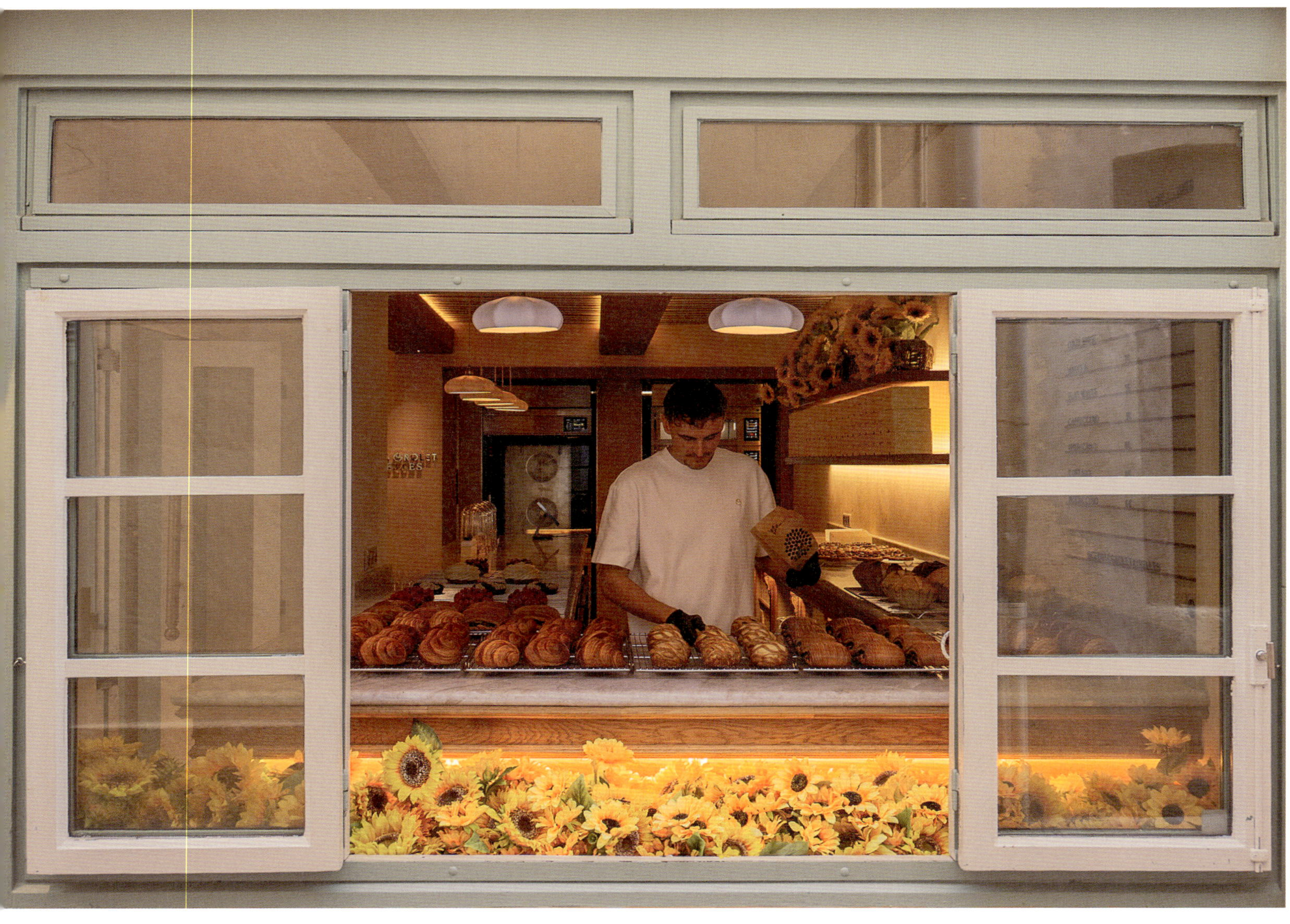

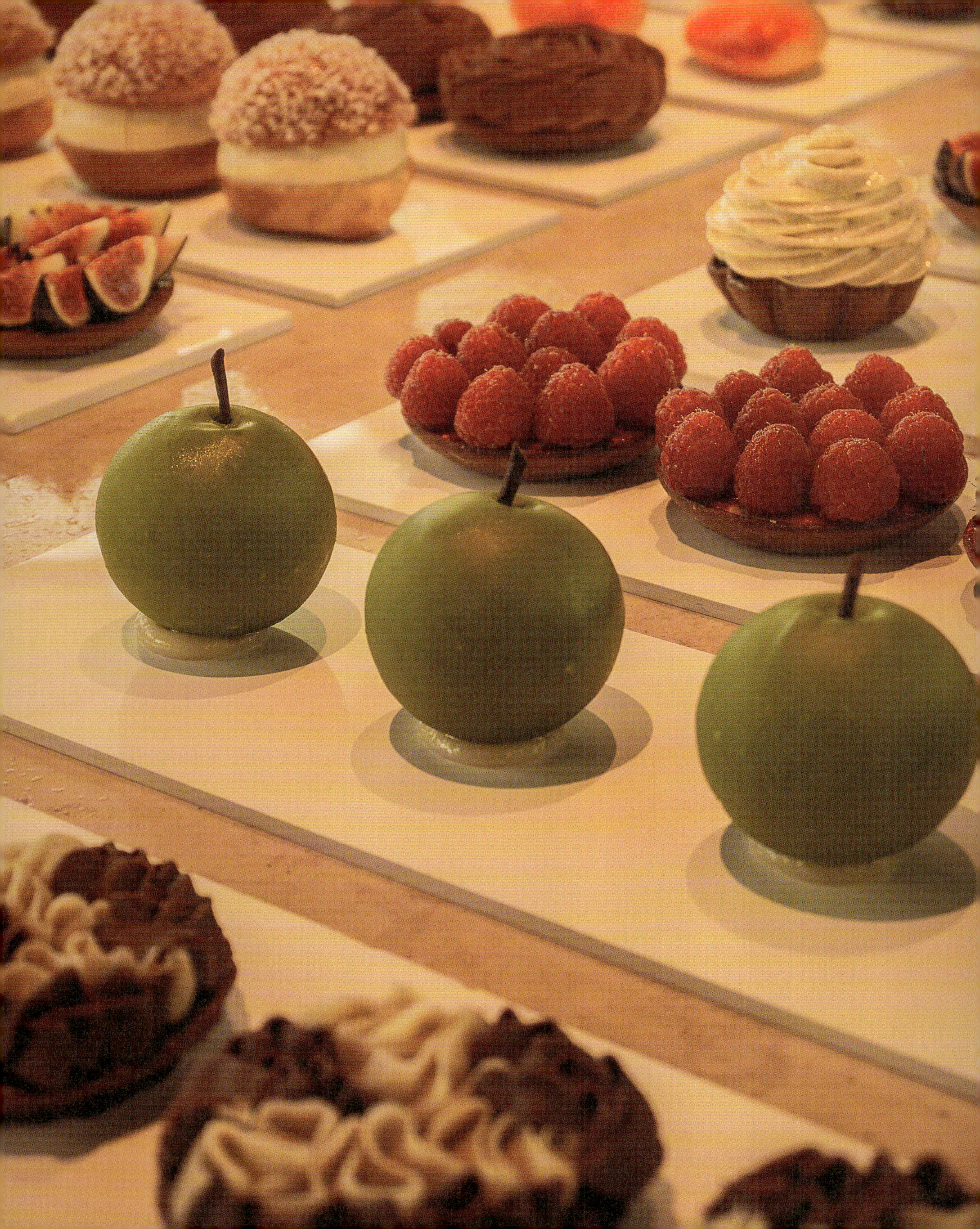

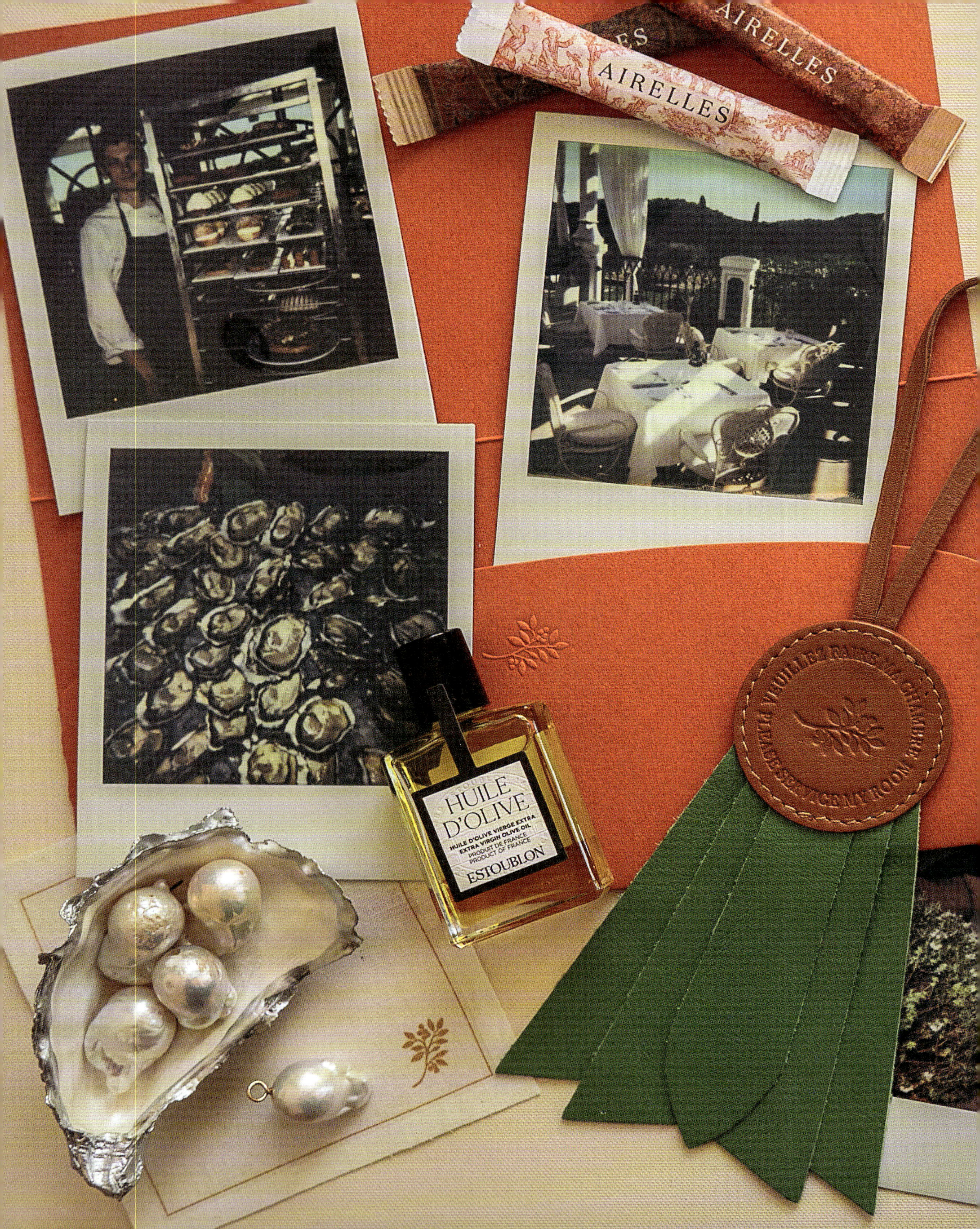
AIRELLES
AIRELLES
HUILE D'OLIVE
HUILE D'OLIVE VIERGE EXTRA
EXTRA VIRGIN OLIVE OIL
PRODUIT DE FRANCE
PRODUCT OF FRANCE
ESTOUBLON
VEUILLEZ FAIRE MA CHAMBRE
PLEASE SERVICE MY ROOM

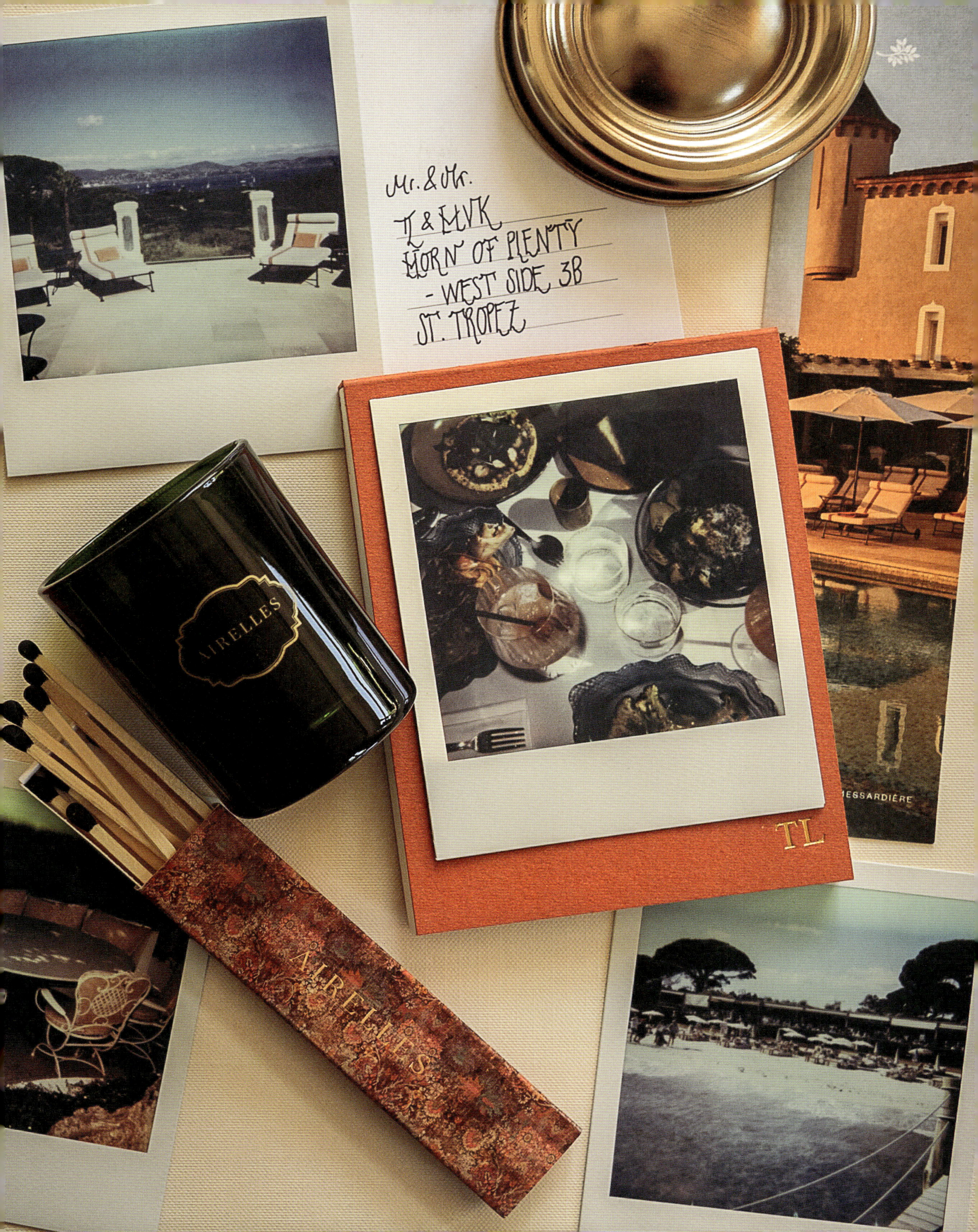
Mr. & Mr.
TL & MVK
HORN OF PLENTY
- WEST SIDE 3B
ST. TROPEZ
AIRELLES
TL
AIRELLES

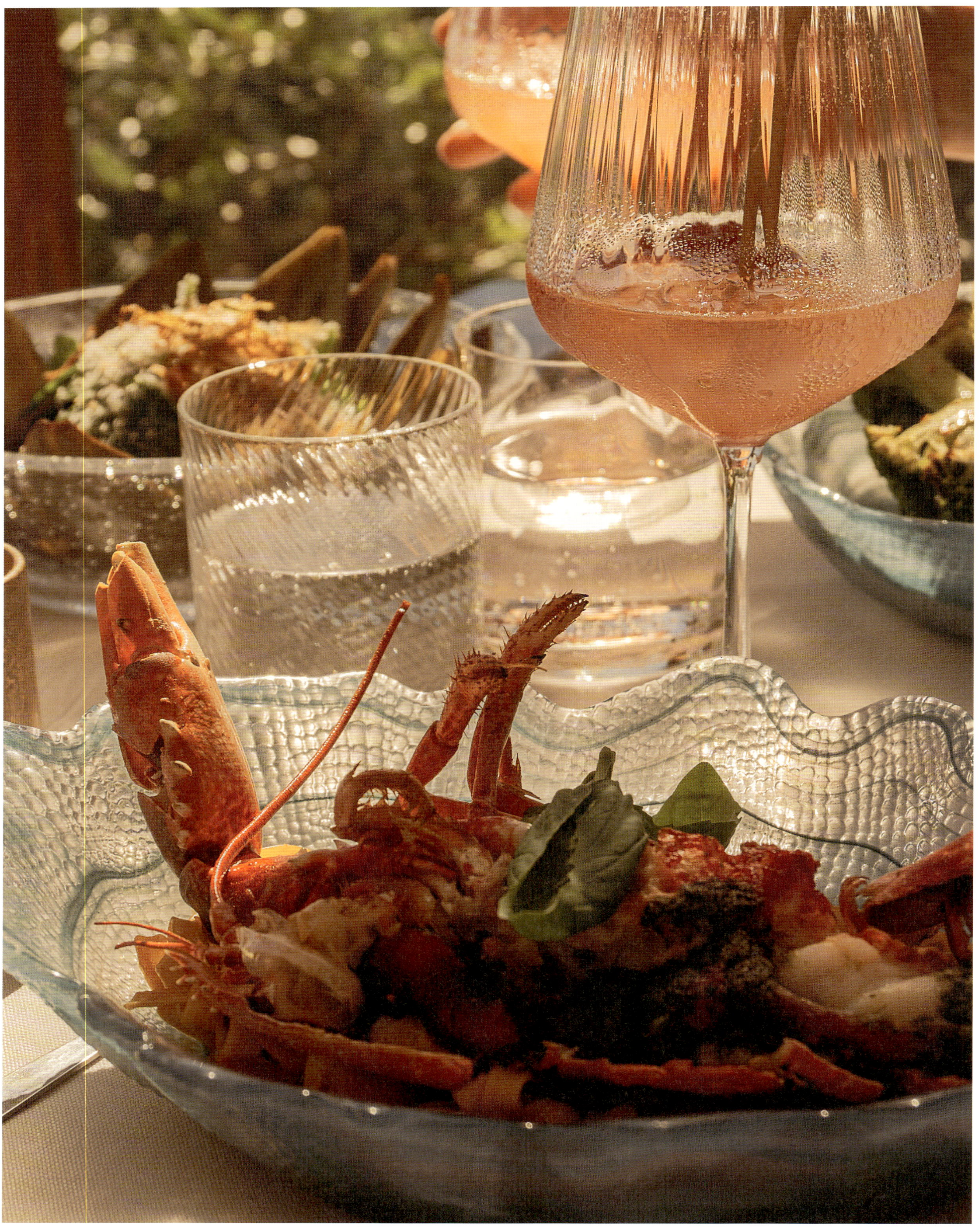

JARDIN TROPEZINA BEACH CLUB

SAINT-TROPEZ

H O T S P O T

Back at the château, we settle beside the garden pool as a warm sea-breeze stirs our still-damp hair. Substituting for our sugar rush from breakfast is now a desire to be at the beach we can see in the distance, and coming on more slowly is also a craving for a hearty lunch. Naturally, Château de La Messardière has just the thing at its own beach club at Plage de Tahiti. The same shuttle we rode in the morning takes us down. A few minutes later we're at water's edge at the Jardin Tropezina Beach Club. The restaurant doesn't seem posh or elitist but rather open and inviting. The atmosphere is set by sun-bleached wood construction, vine-covered palisades, and the strong accents of eclectic colors at the heavenly beach. Friendly staff members show us to the last available seats with an unobstructed view of the sea and the small wooden pier. Summer may be fading, but a tropical wind and temperatures in the mid-80s—that's about 30 degrees Celsius—have brought an almost unruly horde out to the terrace at the beach club to talk business or for a hedonistic lunch. I mean, why hold back? Anyway, the Jardin Tropezina attracts people from all over the region. We order chilled rosé, steamed artichokes, lobster tagliatelle, and tender broccoli hearts. Berries, iced figs with mascarpone cream, and coffee round out our perfect lunch. Replete, the crowd (if not its members) is now splitting open and melting onto the beach or taking water taxis back to Saint-Tropez. Our shuttle will wait as we snag the last of the colorful beach loungers. We're stuffed, slightly giddy, and once again, utterly content.

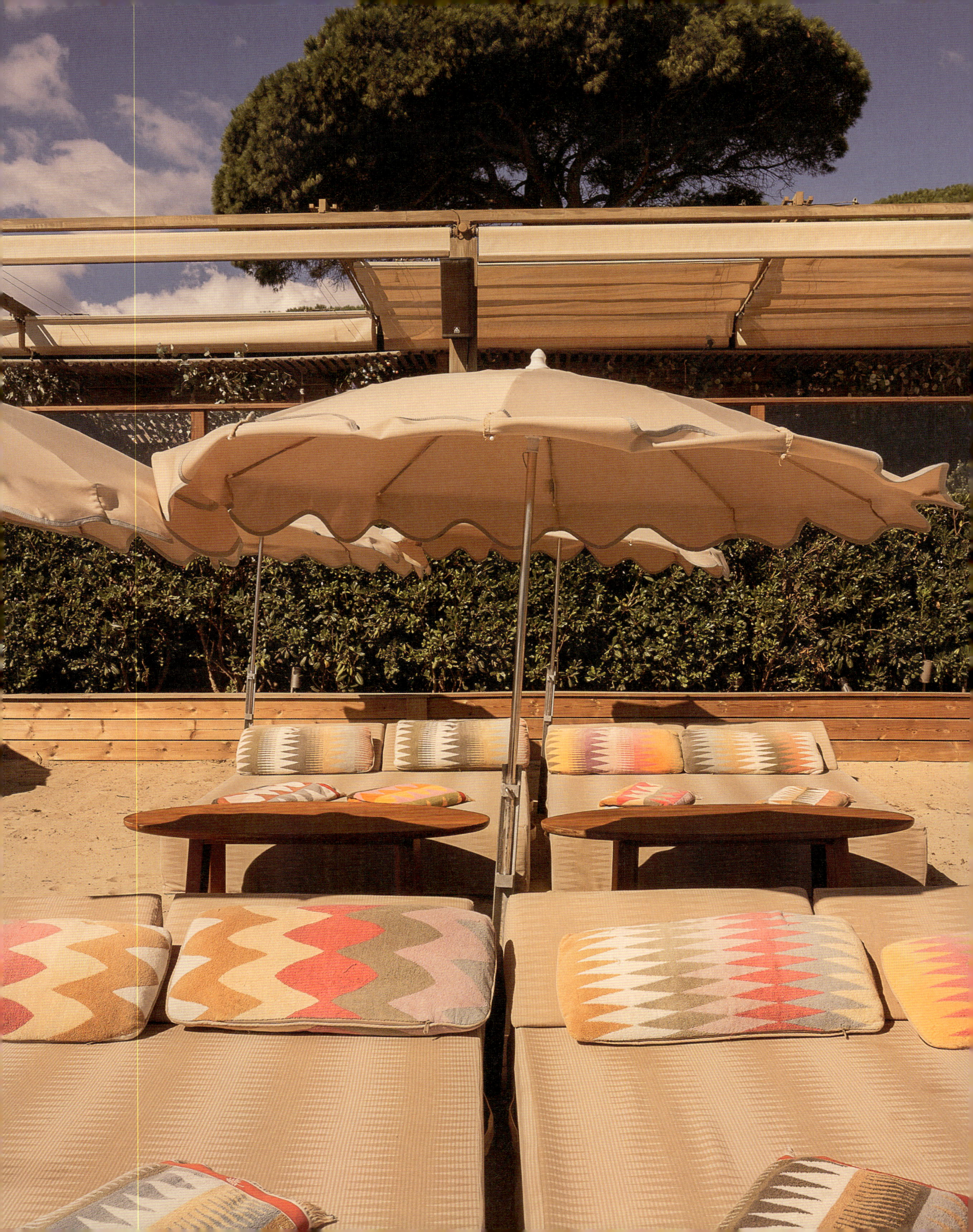

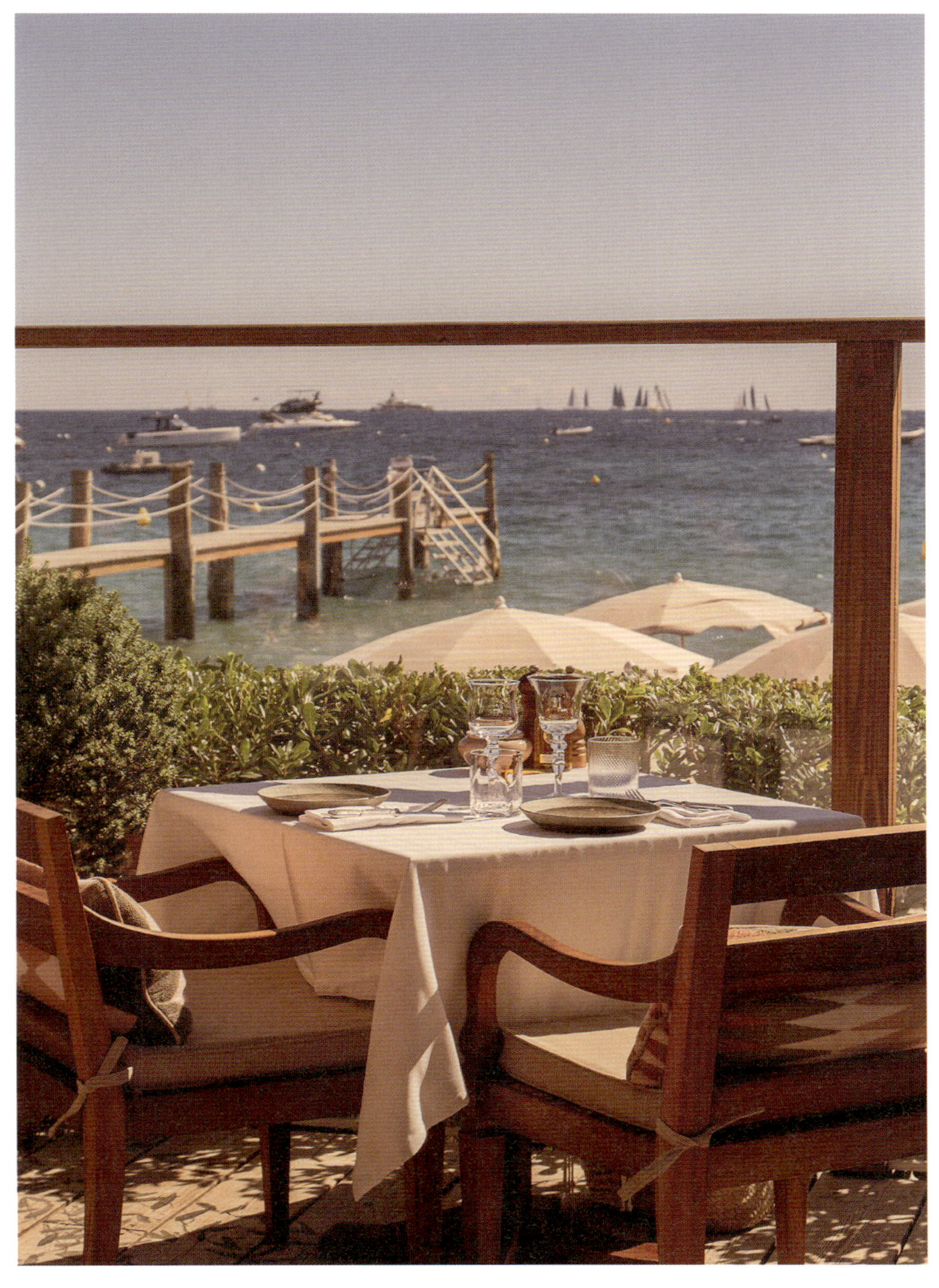

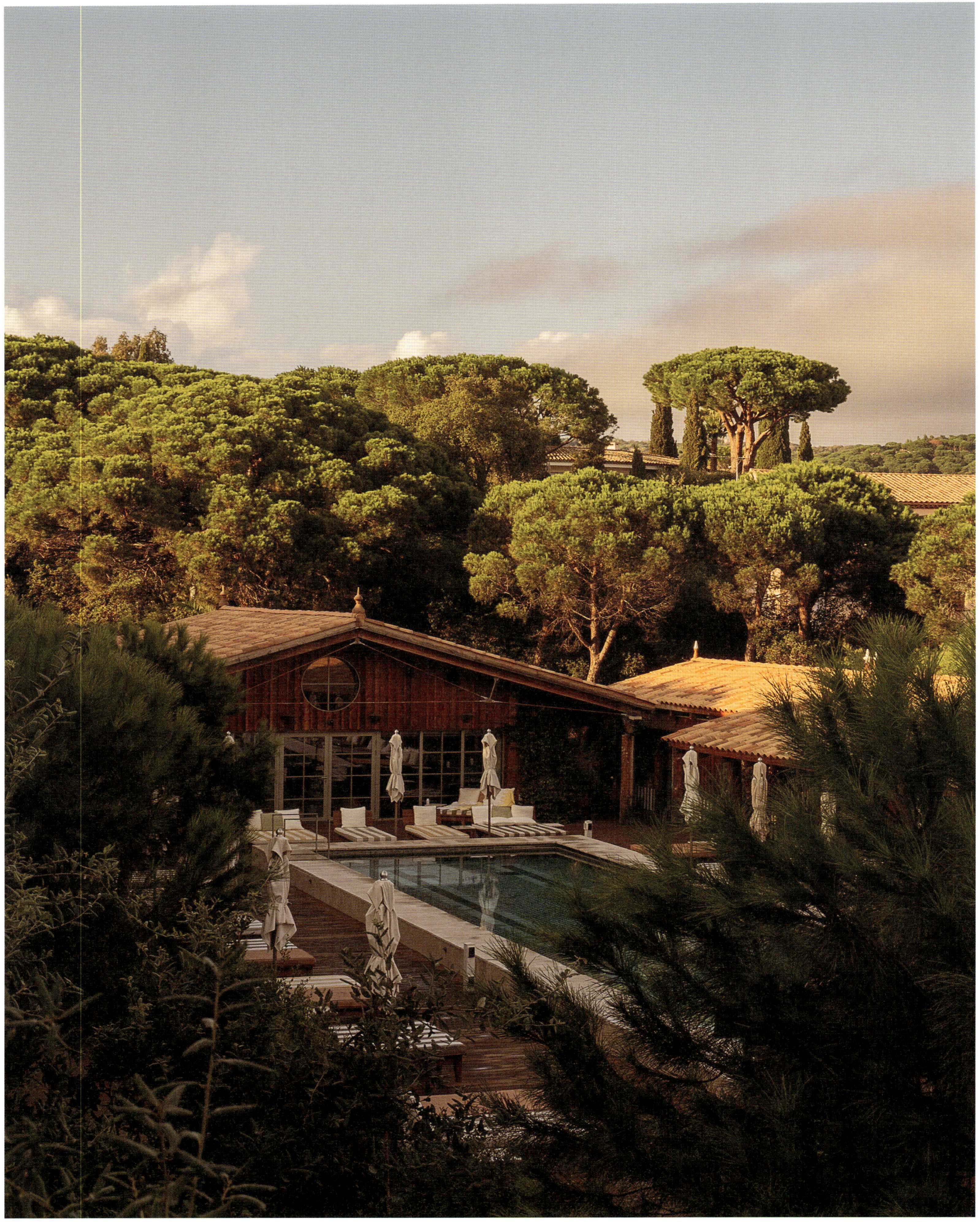

LILY OF THE VALLEY

SAINT-TROPEZ

PART OF THE PROGRAM

We need respite from the endless banquets at our last base near Saint-Tropez. It's time for a change of scenery—and to restore balance to mind and body and get ourselves chronologically situated. The countryside grows wilder and the pines thicker as we approach Lily of the Valley, yet another hotel with a very specific concept that is still firmly in the spirit of the Côte d'Azur. The hotel has devoted itself entirely to renewing and reviving its guests' spirits. It offers a holistic and perfectly conceived retreat program that is as effective as it is aesthetically pleasing. Lily of the Valley reveals the surprisingly warm touch of designer Philippe Starck, renowned for his ubiquitous Ghost Chair, who here reveals his fondness for natural materials. Our retreat begins with a tour of the grounds, an intricate network of cave-like bungalow complexes. Rooms and apartments, as well as the Shape Club, which has an Alpine feel, are connected by wooden staircases. Below lies the spa area, where the windows look onto the sports pool—it's part submarine, part submarine cathedral. If this is the heart of Lily of the Valley, then its mind and spirit live in the restaurant in the airy pavilion at the upper end of the estate. It is flooded with sunlight and furnished with a harmonious mixture of different wood furnishings and ceramics. But above all, there is an endless relaxation pool that seems to hover above the horizon of the bay. At the end of the tour, we are handed our schedule for the next few days. We are signed up for the whole program. It begins with a detailed analysis of our bodies and setting individual goals; on the agenda are fat reduction, muscle building, and increased mobility. After an intensive massage by a physiother-

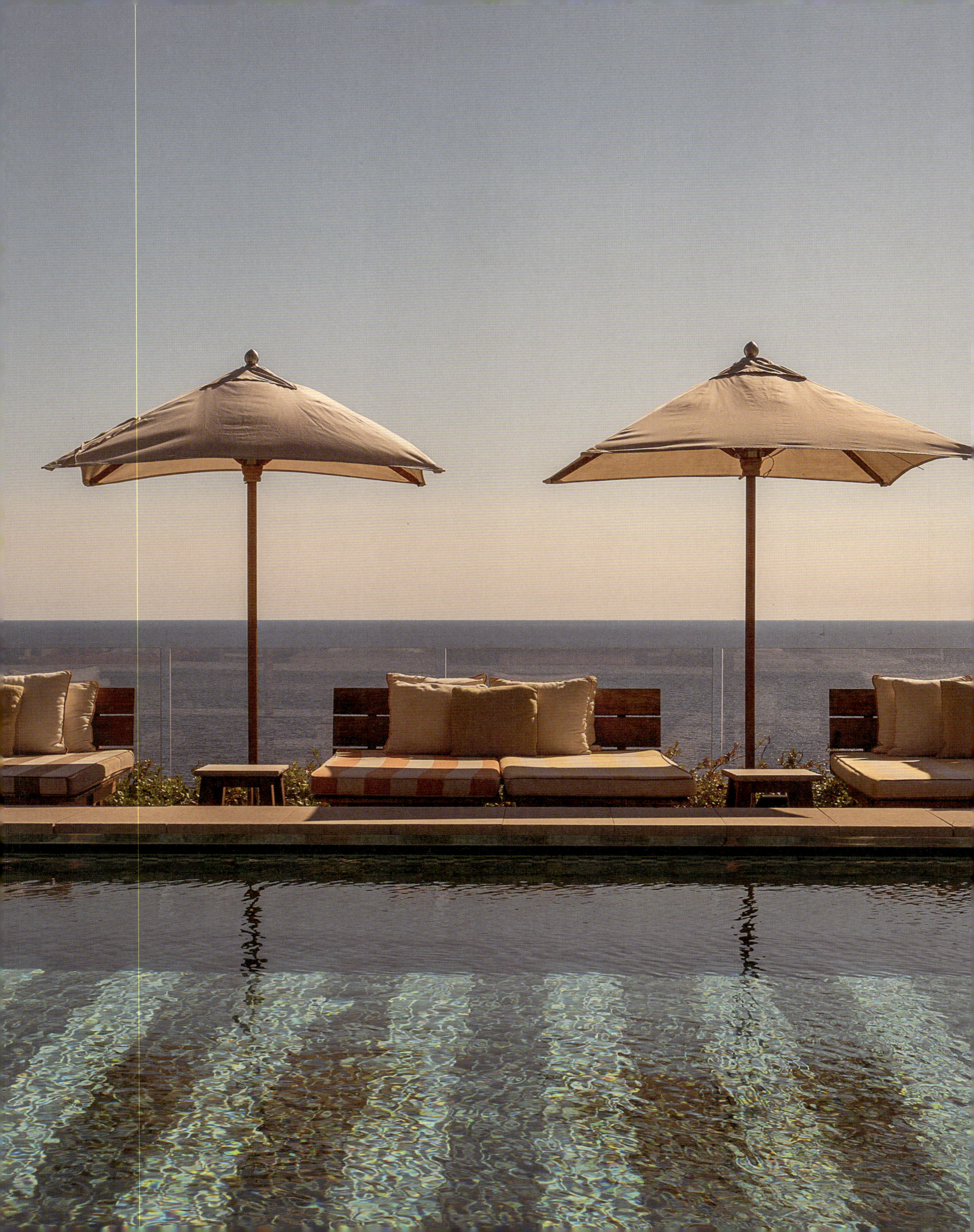

apist, we work out with a personal trainer named Yoann. In the morning, there will be a group hike, followed by yoga in the hills overlooking the bay. Lunch will be served at the beach club—with a minimum of carbs and sugar, of course—after all, we are part of the program. Blanched vegetables, lobster, fish and truffled eggs *en masse*. Fiber, protein, a curative regimen for body and spirit: they probably never look or taste as good as they do at Lily of the Valley. Two days later, we still haven't seen a single *pain au chocolat*, and at no other time on our trip have we felt better. What would happen if we spent a month here?

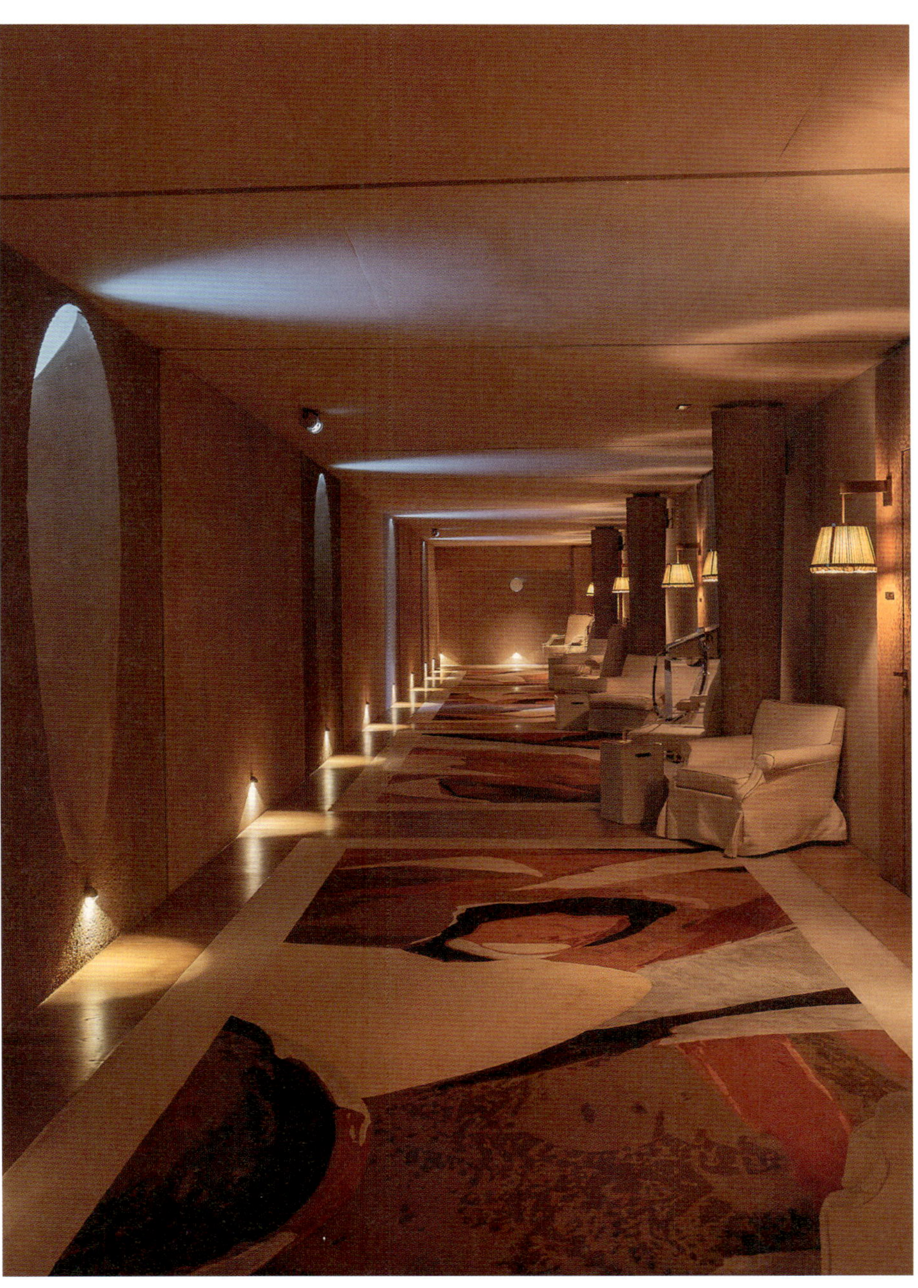

The spa at Lily of the Valley is situated directly below the pool and is fitted with large portholes that afford views of guests going through intense aquatic workouts at the surface while you try to find the right frame of mind for the intense sports massage you booked at the Shape Club. It's an underwater cathedral where self-care is the religion of choice.

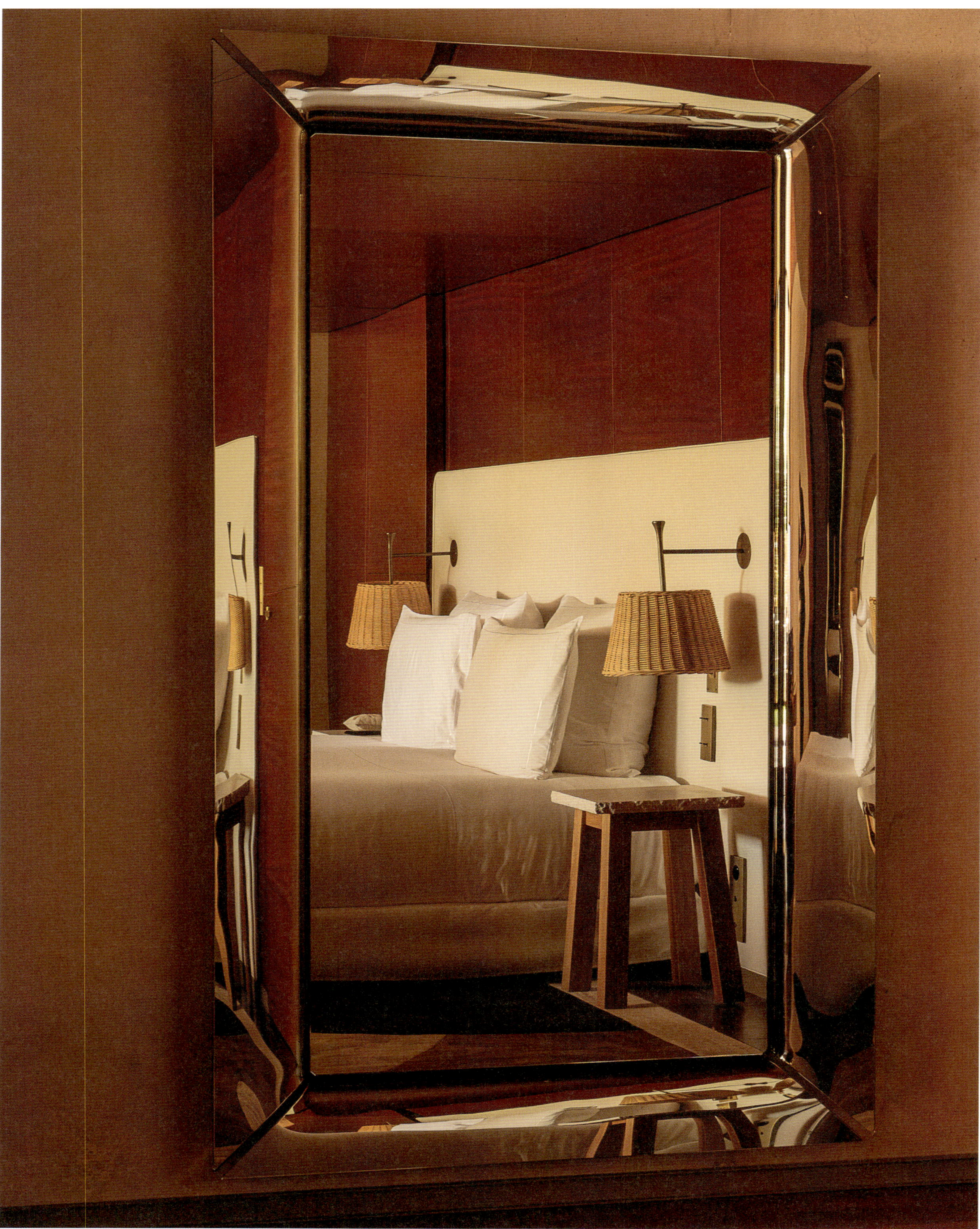

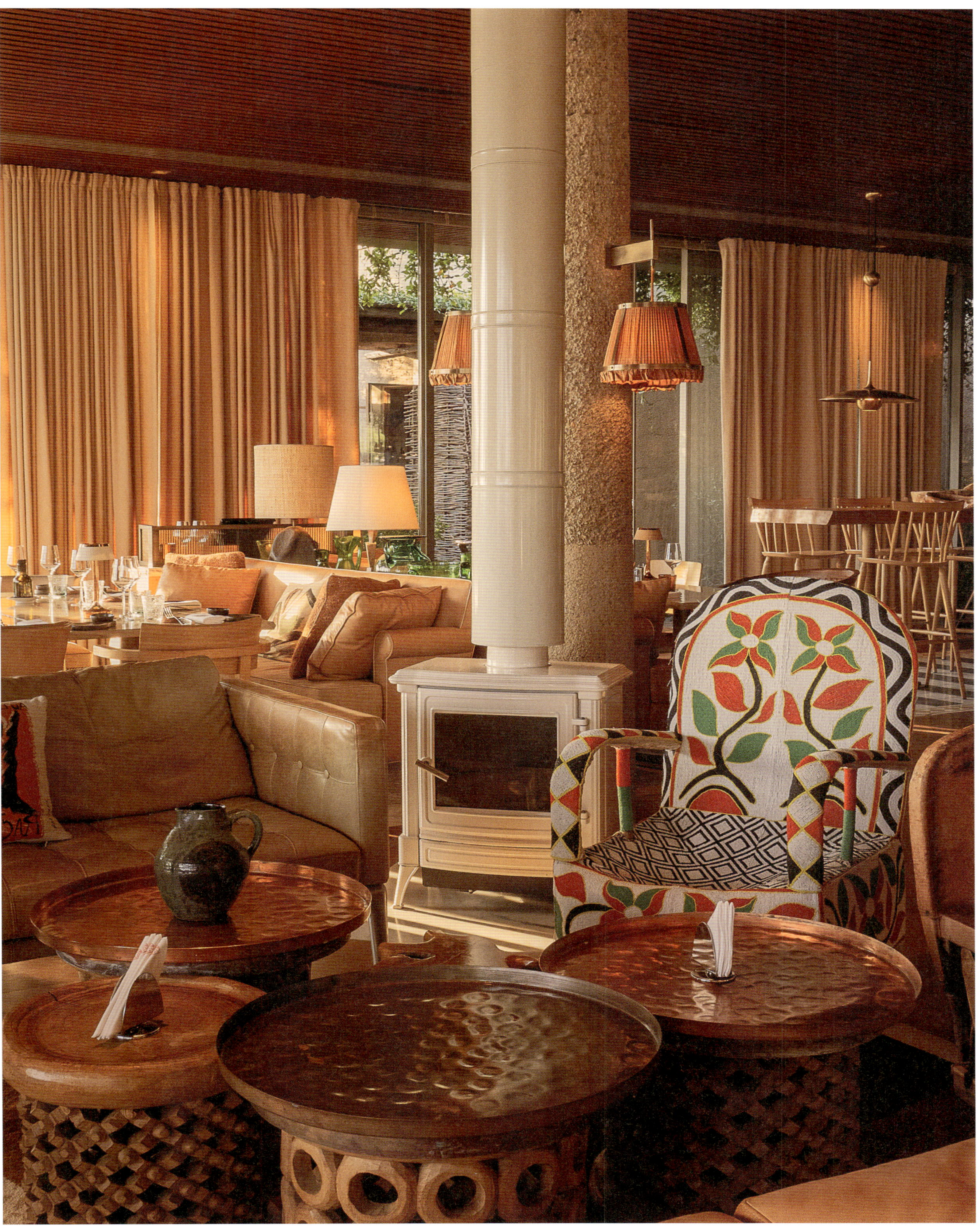

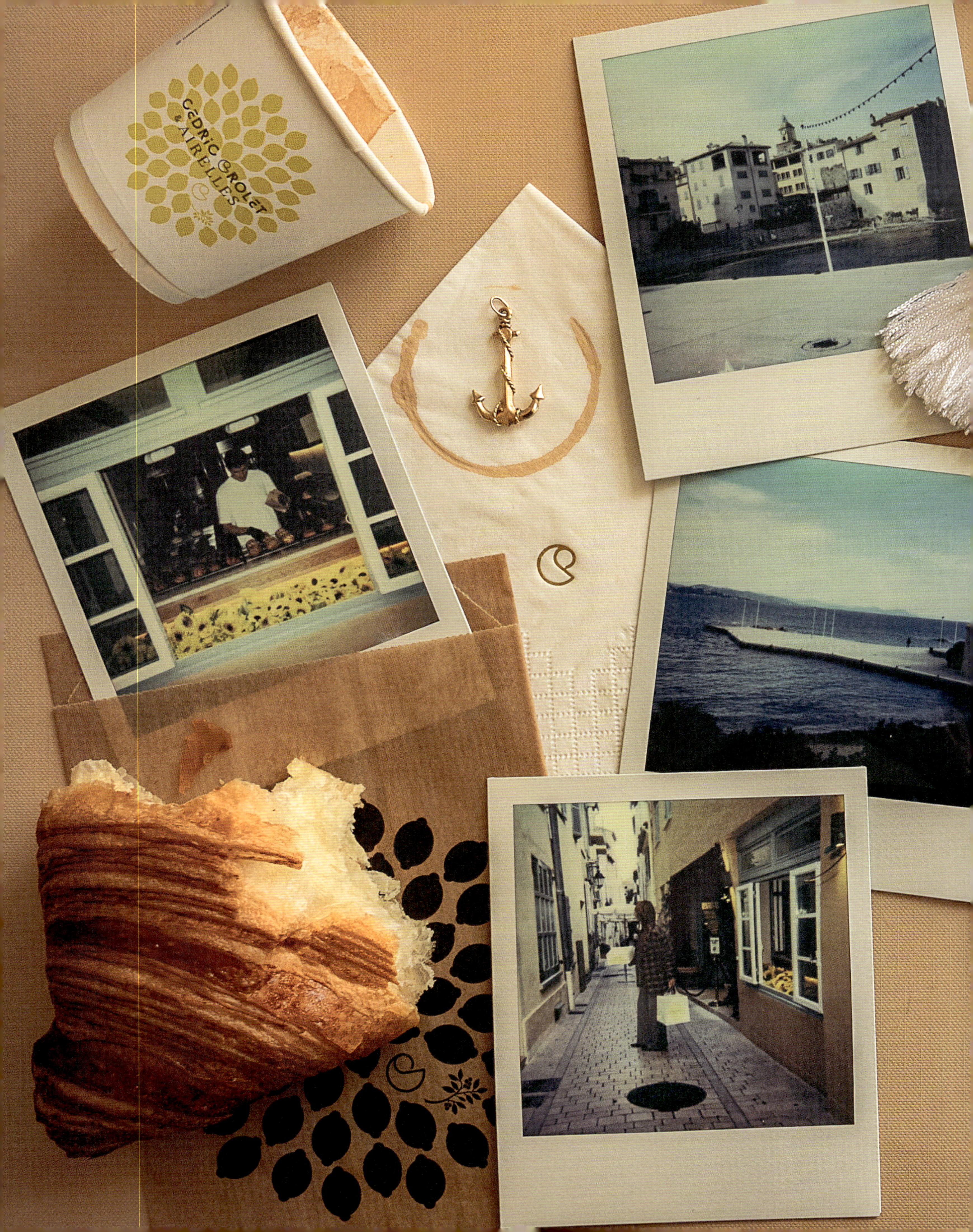
CEDRIC GROLET
& AIRELLES

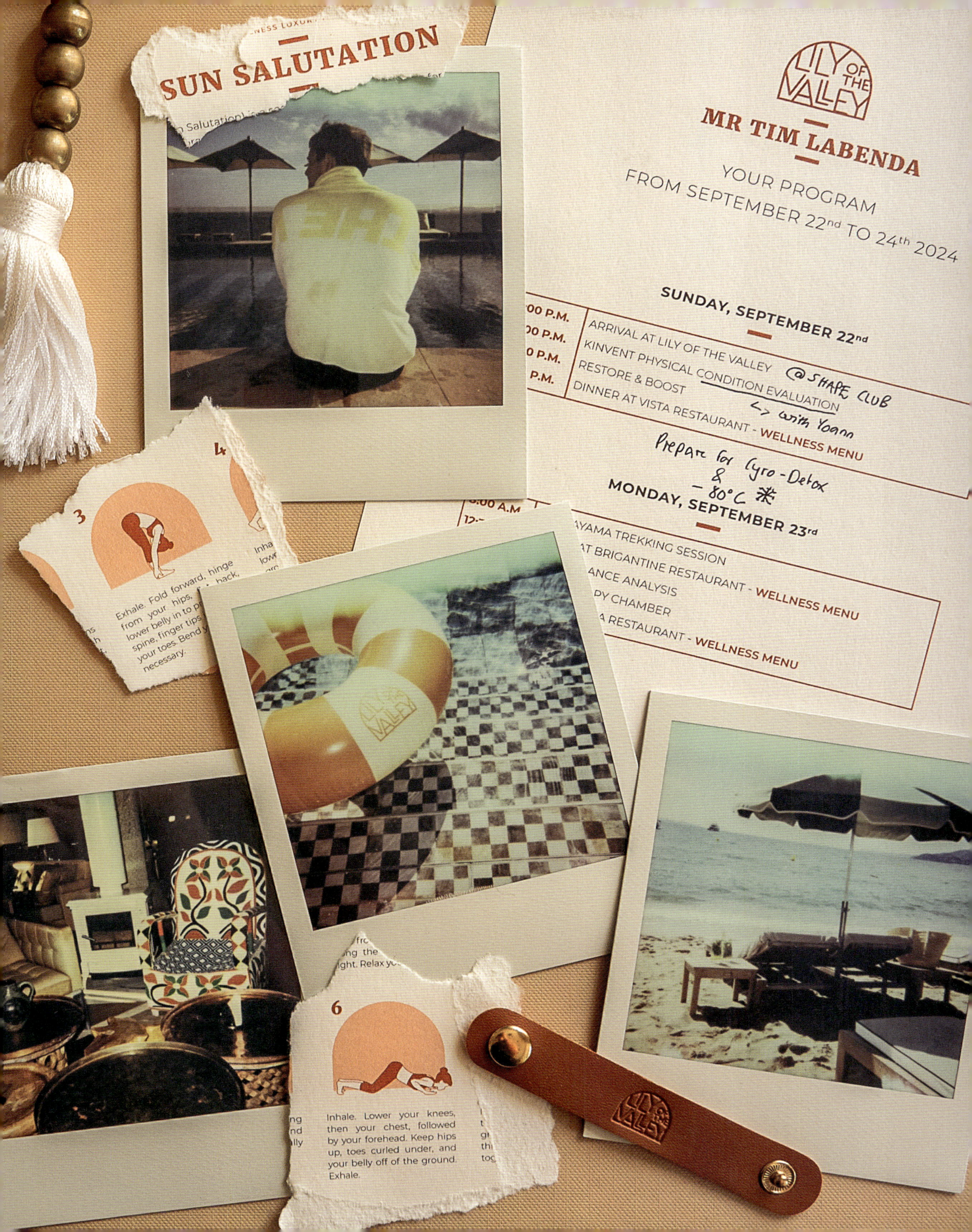
SUN SALUTATION
LILY OF THE VALLEY
MR TIM LABENDA
YOUR PROGRAM
FROM SEPTEMBER 22nd TO 24th 2024
SUNDAY, SEPTEMBER 22nd
ARRIVAL AT LILY OF THE VALLEY
KINVENT PHYSICAL CONDITION EVALUATION
RESTORE & BOOST
DINNER AT VISTA RESTAURANT - WELLNESS MENU
@ SHAPE CLUB
with Yoann
Prepare for Cyro-Detox & -80°C
MONDAY, SEPTEMBER 23rd
WELLNESS MENU
WELLNESS MENU
3
6
Inhale. Lower your knees, then your chest, followed by your forehead. Keep hips up, toes curled under, and your belly off of the ground. Exhale.

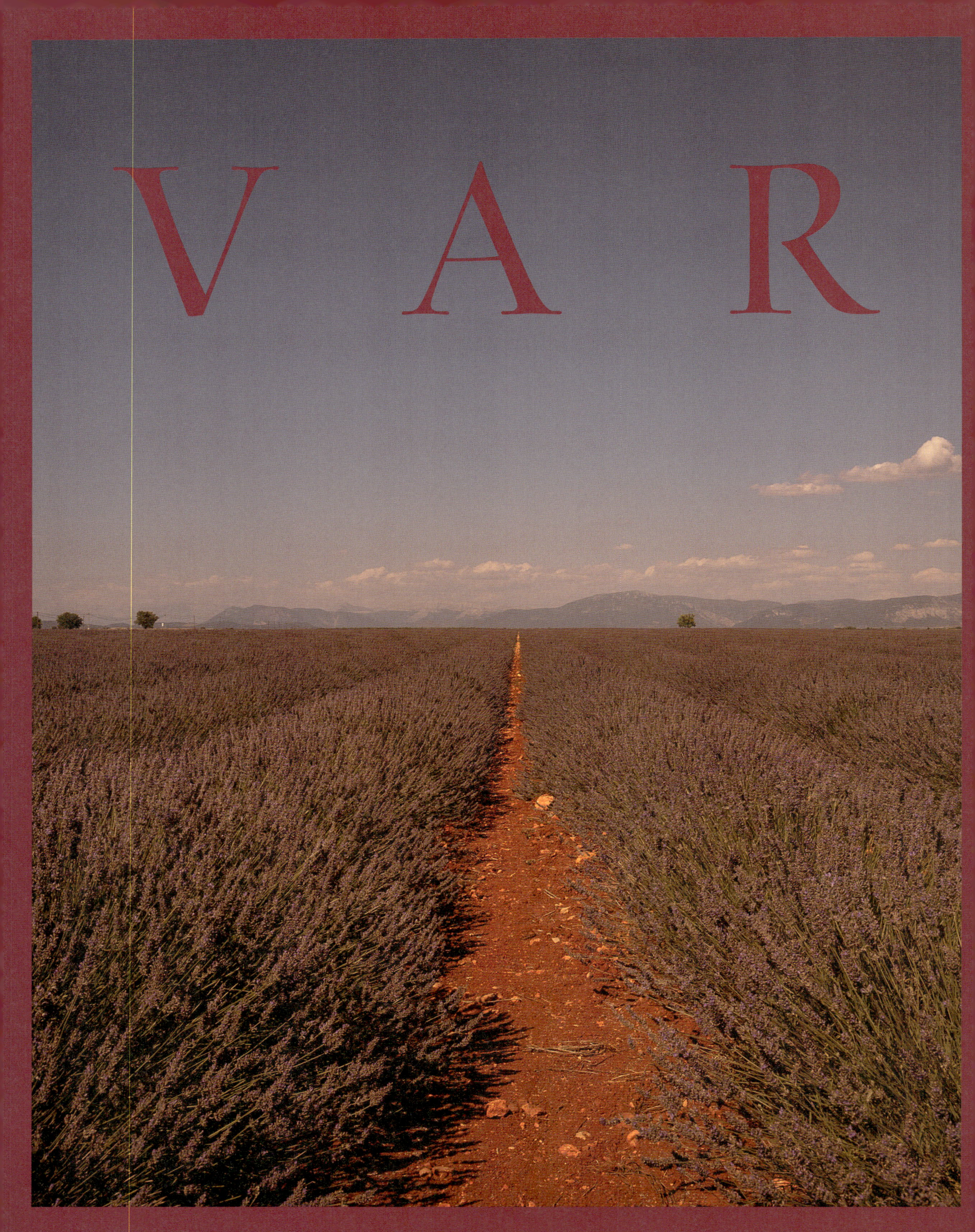
VAR

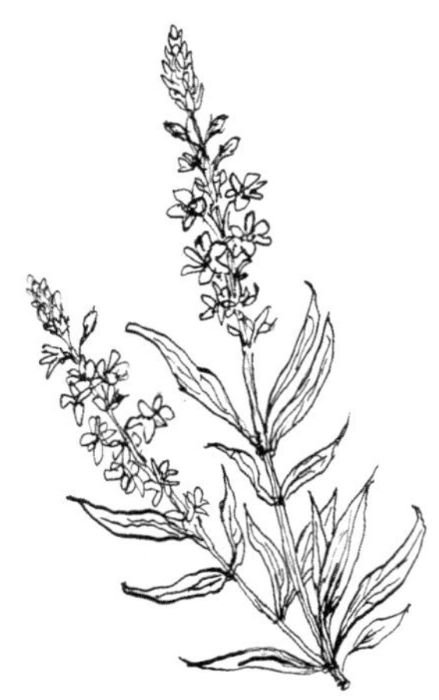

We leave the coastal environs of Saint-Tropez and set out to discover the wider *département* of Var—the agricultural heart of Provence and a gallery of its rugged beauty. Much of what defines the south of France originates here: rosé, which is summer distilled into wine; lavender, which you cannot deny immediately occurs to you at the mention of Provence; and the fruity, peppery olive oil that is the foundation of dishes from ratatouille to bouillabaisse. That Var is a supplier to so much of the region is the result of the extraordinary range of landscapes it encompasses and their unspoiled, often severe character, where all the fruits and plants can thrive.

Rocky plateaus catch the sun and coax olives from ancient trees, while dense stands of boxwood, oak and pine shelter herds of goats and encourage the growth of truffles. Red gravel and chalky soil are the perfect substrate for purple rows of lavender and vigorous grape vines. Over it all hangs an unfiltered sense of summer and holidays—unencumbered, unhurried, self-contained—as the days simply dissolve beneath the burning sun.

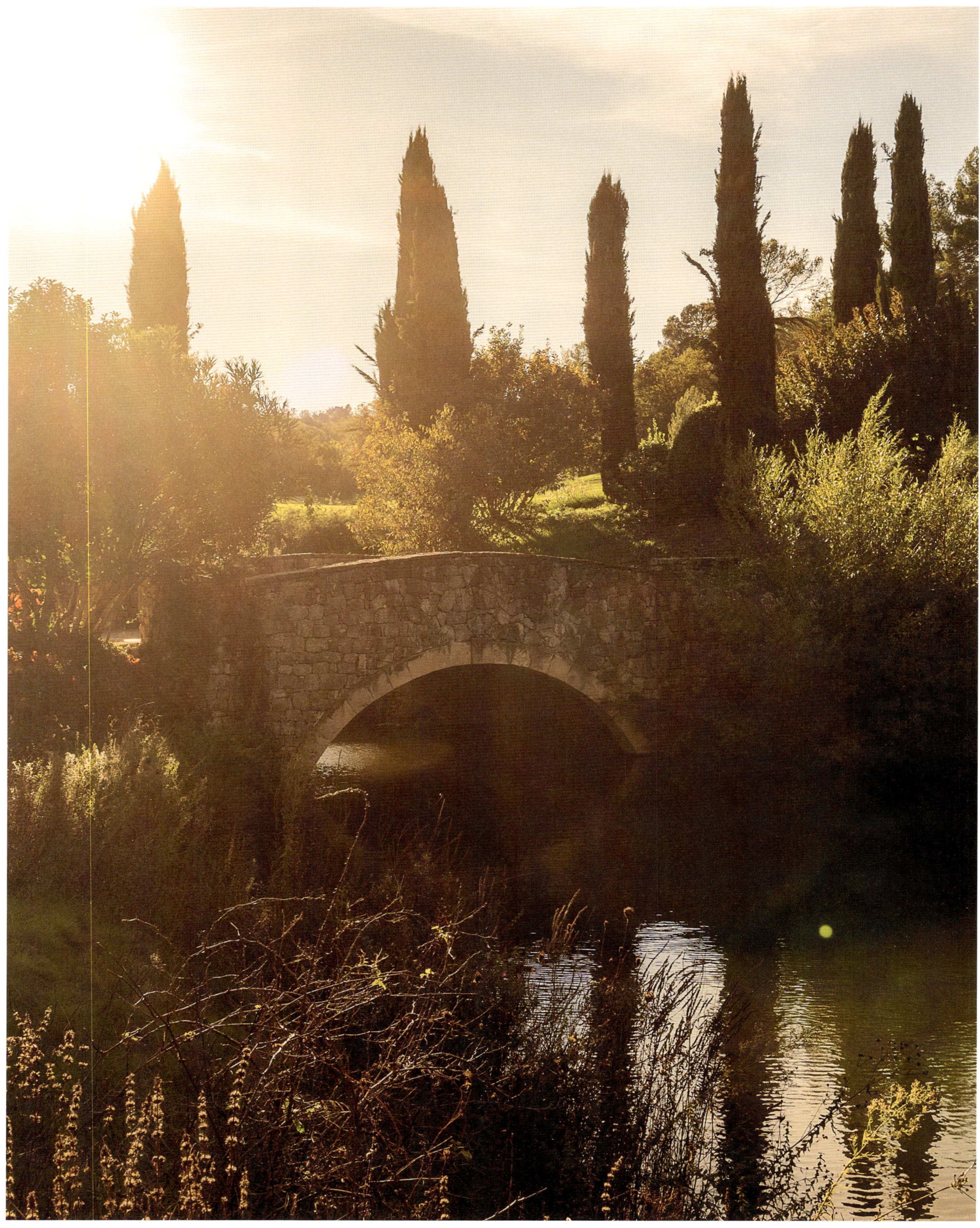

TERRE BLANCHE

VAR

B E S T B A L L

At the eastern edge of Var, where the northern reaches of the Préalpes d'Azur meet the southern slopes of the Esterel, lies Terre Blanche. We pass through a landscape of red and grey rock cloaked in dense pine forest. We arrive at the resort near Fayence. If our Grand Tour is going to include a resort, it might as well truly deliver. At nearly 750 acres, Terre Blanch is larger than Monaco. It's ginormous. Set amid the raw beauty of the countryside, spas, restaurants, villas, and suites unfold like a town in itself. But the undisputed rulers of the resort are its golf courses. There are two full courses and a dedicated training facility, which are reputedly among the best in the world. Everything here revolves around golf, to the point that we are driven to our villa in a golf cart. Now, we are not golfers by any stretch of the imagination. But we can't resist the allure of playing a round on the velvet greens and fairways, framed by scenic waterfalls and majestic stands of oaks. Our training concludes with a handicap that we are too ashamed to mention to the other professionals here. We flee the scene and set off to explore this green oasis at our own pace—may we be forgiven—just us in a golf cart, cruising past quiet ponds and startling a few herons at 10 km/h. Two hours later, hungry from playing the game of golf the way only Tim and Hannes know how, we tee off again, this time aiming straight for Le Gaudina, the restaurant at the upper extremity of the estate and our nineteenth hole. The sweet-natured staff forgives us our abominable golf skills and summons a delightful meal for us. It's our personal best ball of the day in this blissful resort bubble of Terre Blanche.

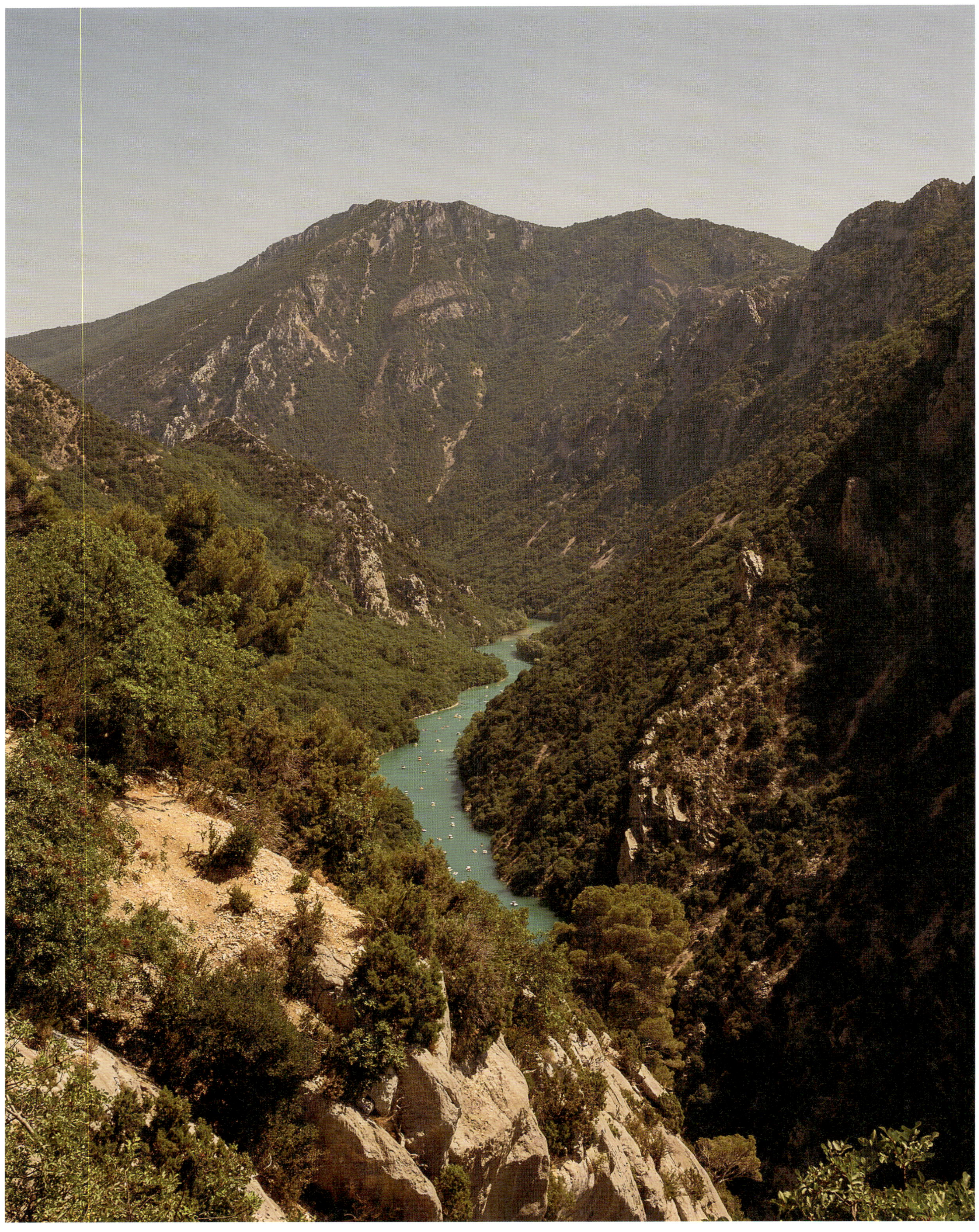

GORGES DU VERDON

VAR

CLIFF DIVERS

From Terre Blanche, it would be less than an hour's drive straight across Var, heading due west, to our next overnight stop. But to the north lies Verdon Regional Nature Park, which marks the border with Alpes-de-Haute-Provence and is the reason for our otherwise irrational pathfinding. To see the wild beauty of the Verdon Gorge is worth any length of detour. Our car winds sharply up the switchbacks as the trees yield to smaller and sparser vegetation: white bedrock blanketed here and there by moss; burly boxwoods; sometimes a free-roaming herd of goats or sheep. As soon as we reach the first plateau, the landscape falls away again before us, and the view from the road opens onto the milky-blue waters of the reservoir Lac de Sainte-Croix. Old camper vans and RVs park haphazardly along its stony shoreline, conjuring a misty vision of the south of France in the late 1960s.

We stop at the Pont du Galetas, which is the best viewpoint of the Verdon Gorge. This is Europe's deepest canyon, 700 vertical meters from floor to rugged rim in some spots, at times approaching a sheer drop, before the river pours into Lac de Sainte-Croix. The sun burns our faces as we stand gazing upon ice-blue waters, the reservoir at our backs, the rest of the frame filled by blank rock walls.

It's an almost unreal panorama, broken only by the colorful commotion of pedal boats fighting their way upstream. Sunburnt teenagers scramble over the rocks, fiercely competitive about who can pull off the highest dive, the most somersaults, the wildest mid-air spin. It's pure midsummer chaos—carefree, yelling, and very tempting. For a moment, we consider going in ourselves. But we decide against it, get back in our car, and look ahead to plunging into the sea of purple flowers waiting at our next stop.

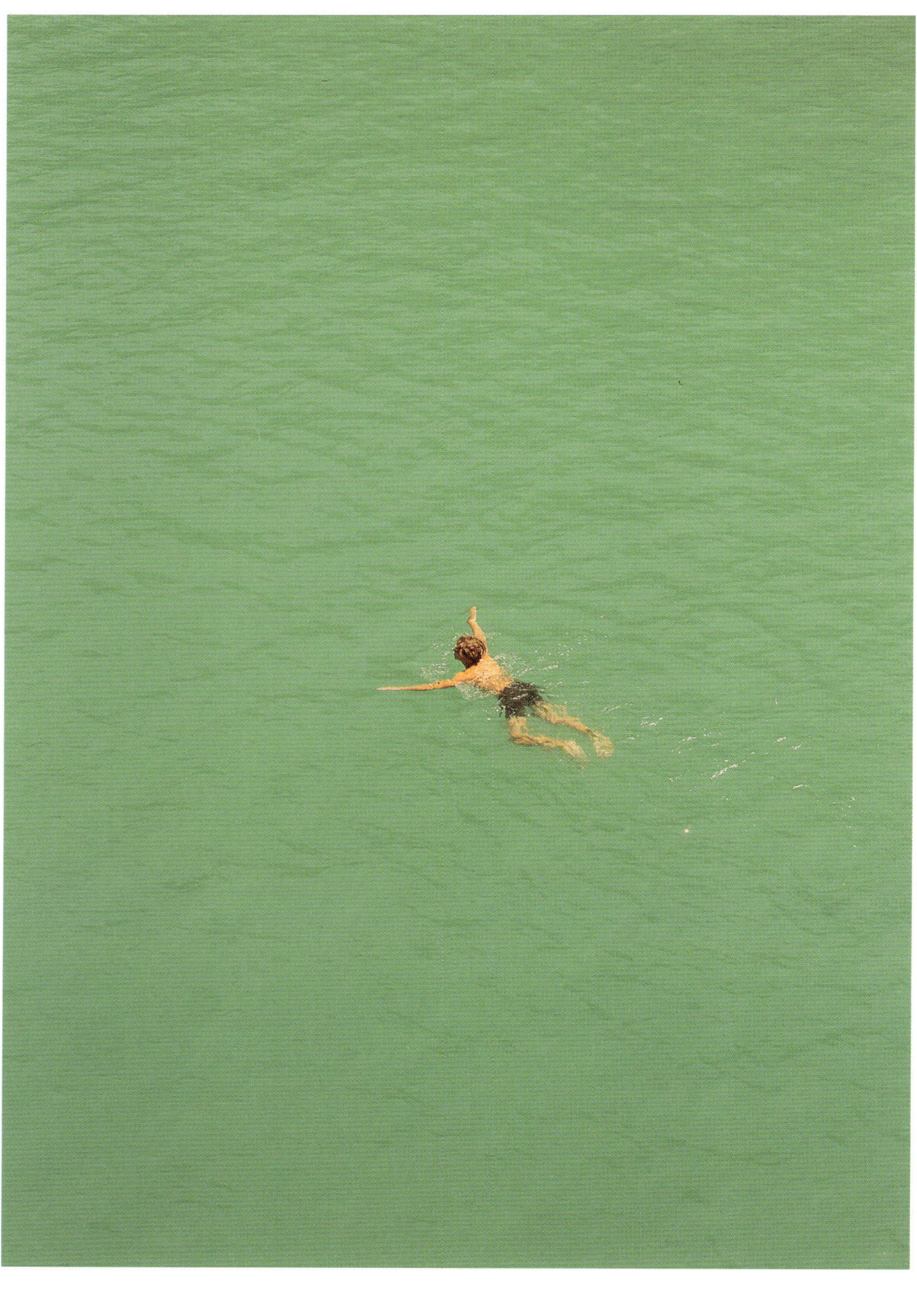

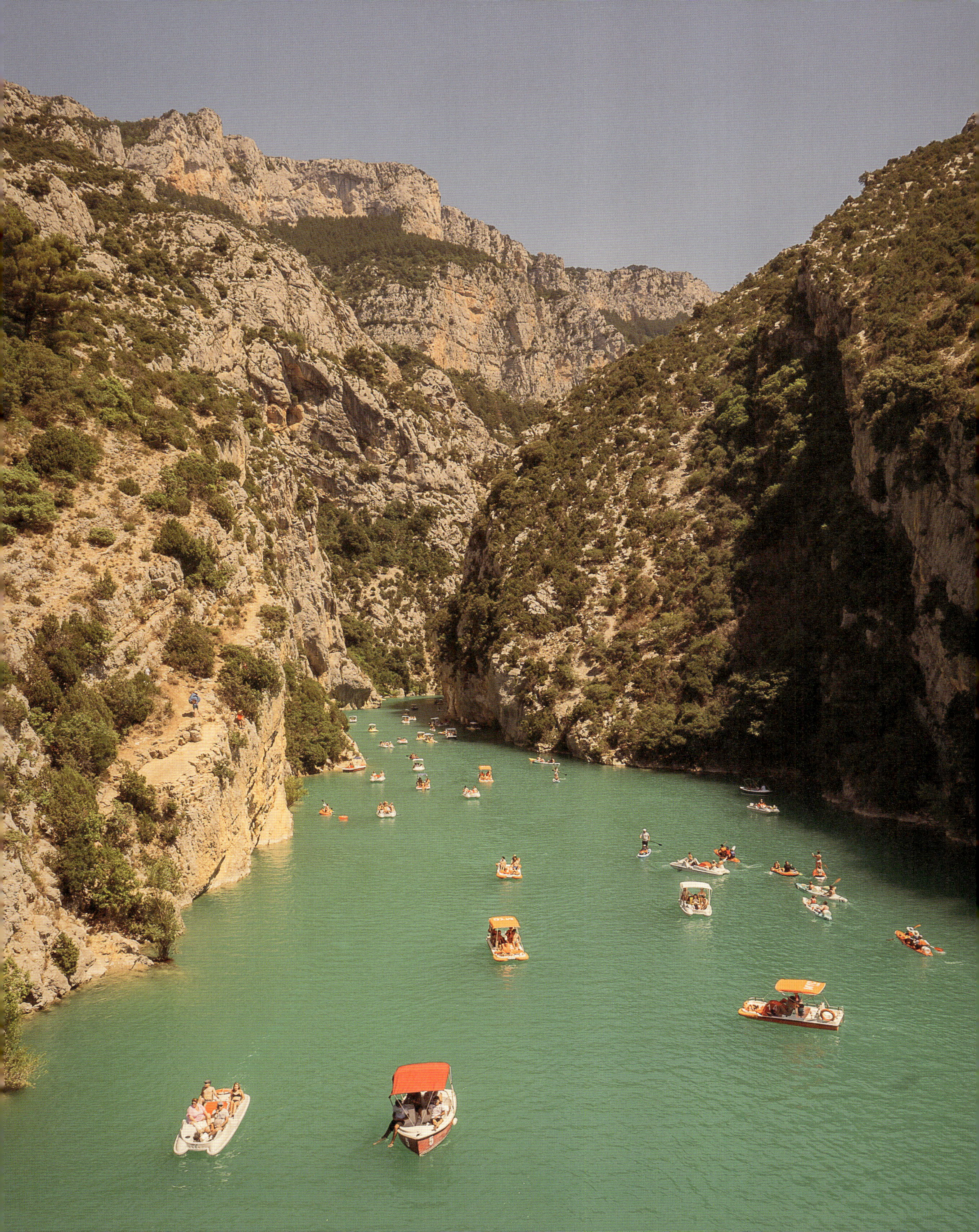

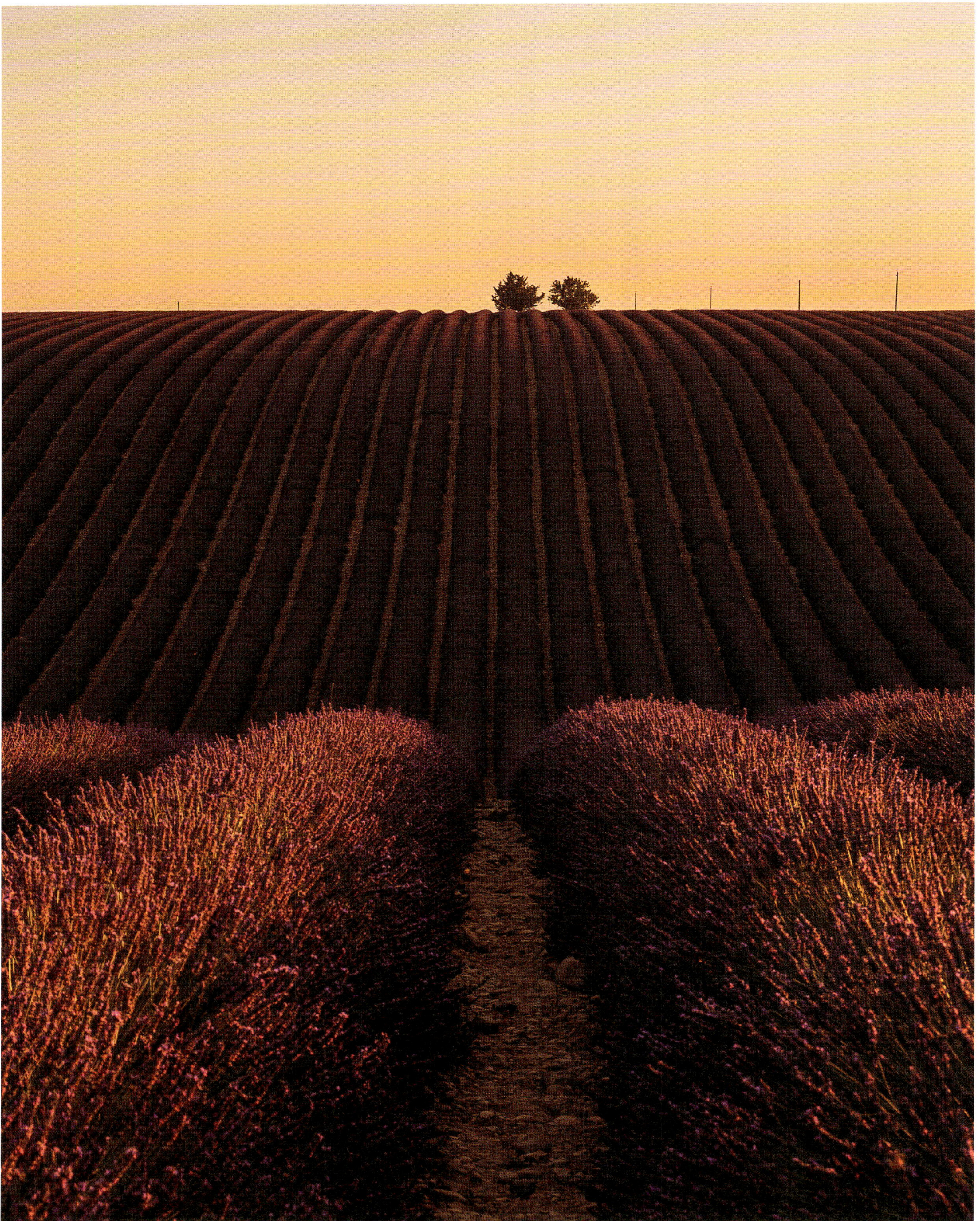

PLATEAU DE VALENSOLE

VAR

PURPLE VELVET

If Provence were a color, it would be purple. It's the second week of July, and the Valensole plateau is swarming—with tourists, with bees, and with tractors gearing up to harvest one of Provence's most treasured crops: lavender. We're not far from the lake. The road rises briefly, the mountains and rocks fall away, and the landscape is now an undulating plateau. We round a bend and see our first splash of purple. Lavender grows here on red gravel, in precise rows, amid the hum of insects and the sharp, heady scent of its blossoms. Around the town of Valensole, those purple patches expand into broad carpets that stretch to the horizon like acres of heavy, deep-violet corduroy. A strange stillness hangs over the scene, an almost unearthly calm, a silence that nothing—nothing, that is, except the shouts of the farmers desperately attempting to chase tourists out of the fields so that no influencers wind up in the crates with the harvest—could pierce. We can take a hint, so we move on to Valensole, where preparations for the big lavender festival are in full swing. Bright pennants flutter above the old town, and the shops are overflowing with every imaginable lavender-scented product: soap, honey, perfume, oil, even wax tablets to discourage moths. We buy a handwoven lavender thing in the shape of a flask and have a lavender ice cream on the square. Is it touristy? You bet. Is it cliché? No doubt. But it *is* unique. We eventually ride off into the not-just-proverbial sunset and find the perfect field: a magical swell of lavender stretching to the horizon, glowing in the golden evening sun. Alone we aren't, but who cares.

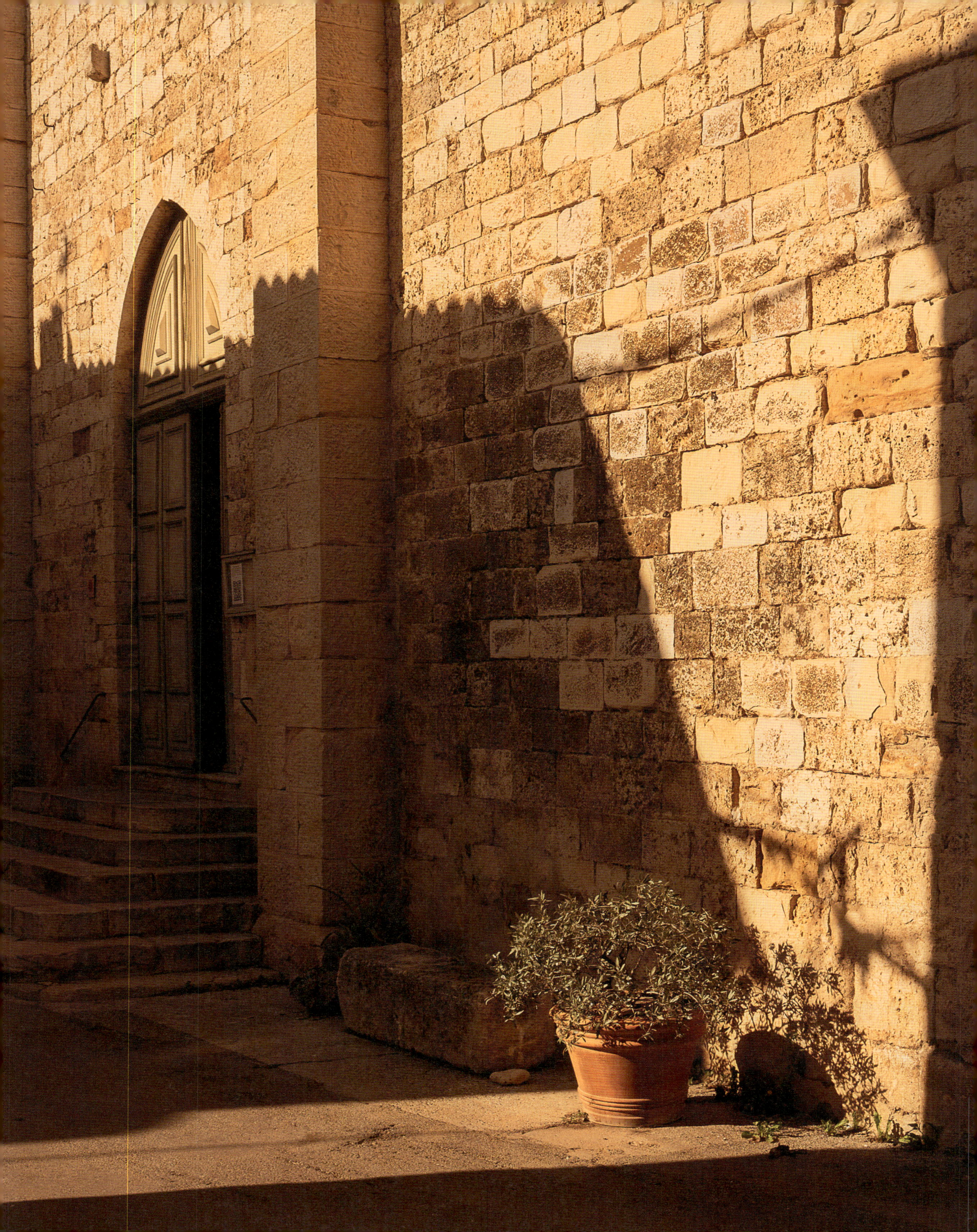

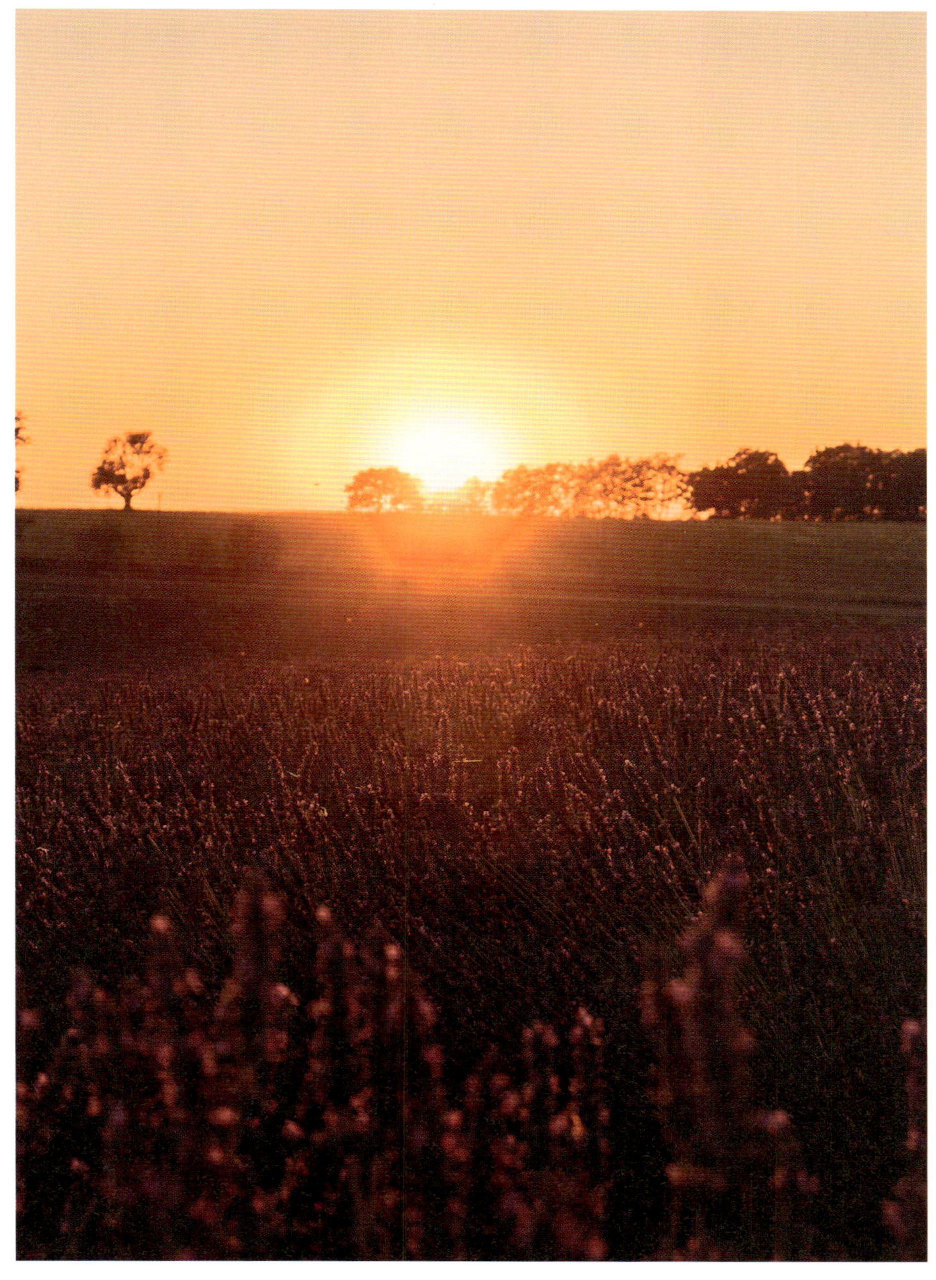

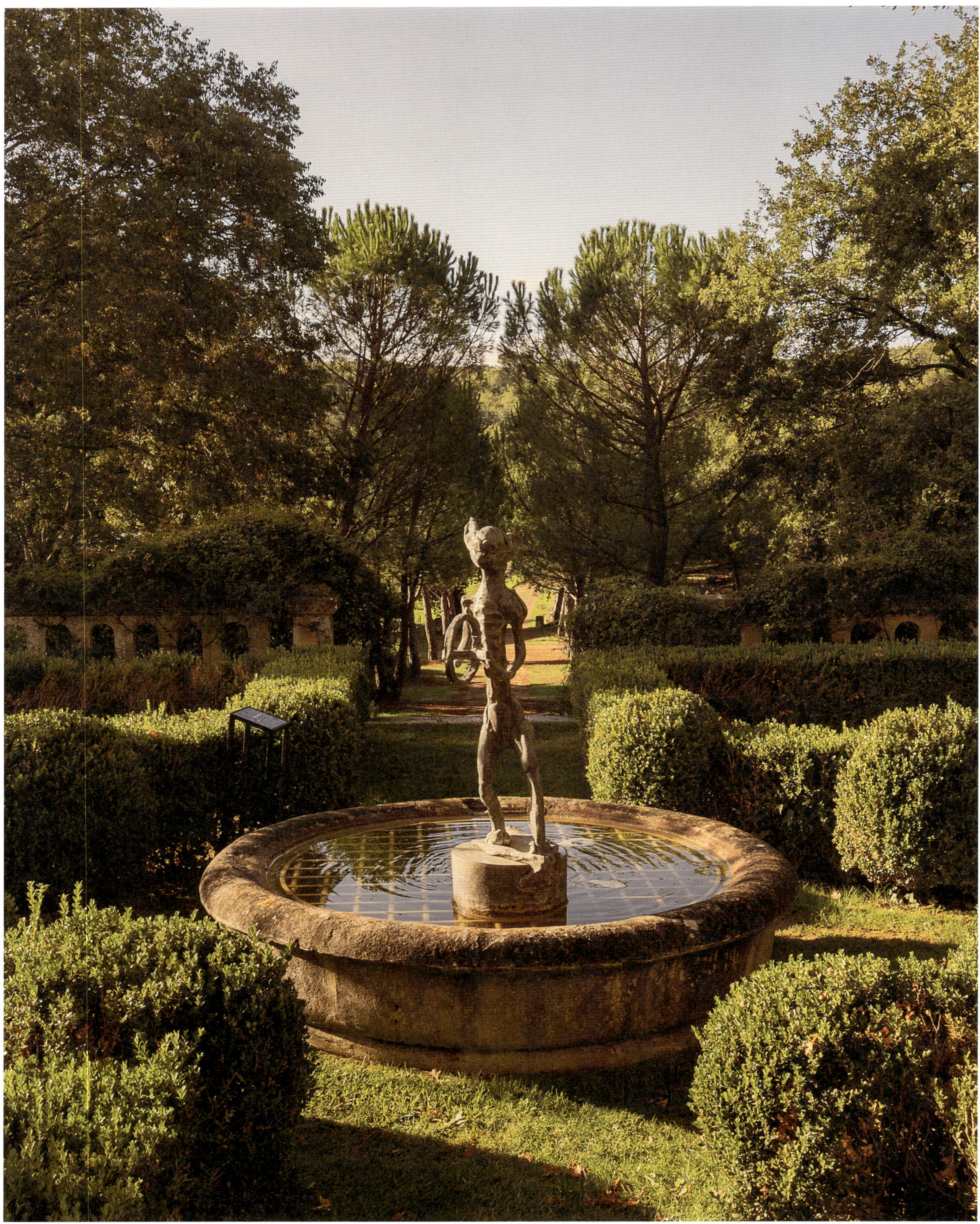

PEYRASSOL

VAR

WURM & GRENACHE

Besides lavender, the south of France is synonymous with art and rosé wine, and we'd already had more than our share of both on this trip. But nowhere blends the two quite like the Commanderie de Peyrassol. It's a ninety-minute drive from Valensole, down off the plateau and into the gnarled oak forests around Flassans-sur-Issole. Large white flags bearing red crosses guide us off the main road and into the woods on a rough gravel path that eventually leads to the winery. This fertile land has been cultivated for thousands of years. Once in the hands of the Romans, then the Knights Templar, and later the Order of Malta, the 2,100-acre estate was eventually purchased by wine lover and art collector Philippe Austruy, who turned it into a personal retreat—the ultimate combination of his two great passions.

At the heart of the estate, we reach an old château surrounded by vast vineyards, stone walls, and a dense, rugged phalanx of truffle oaks. It's the perfect soil for Cabernet Sauvignon, Sémillon, Grenache, and uninhibited creativity to thrive. Art installations are scattered across the estate, housed in three separate galleries. More than just a winery, Peyrassol is home to the largest open-air gallery in Europe, featuring works by rising talents and big names alike, from Erwin Wurm to Anish Kapoor. The modernity merges at just the right angle with the estate's deep historical roots as a winery. Our visit begins with a guided tour of stone cellars where rosés, whites, and reds mature in stainless steel, oak, and clay vessels. We might have enjoyed one too many sips of Clos Peyrassol at the wine-tasting afterwards—the estate's signature rosé. At the courtyard bistro, we fill up on grilled vegetables, a tapenade from local olives, and soft cheese from that herd of goats over there, before we climb aboard a horse-drawn carriage for a tour of the grounds. Horse Vulcano and whip Philippe drive us down endless rows of vineyards and past art that someone has placed at every turn. By the end of the day, we collapse into bed at an old hunting lodge in the forest called La Rouvière, where overnight guests can recover from the whirlwind of art and rosé.

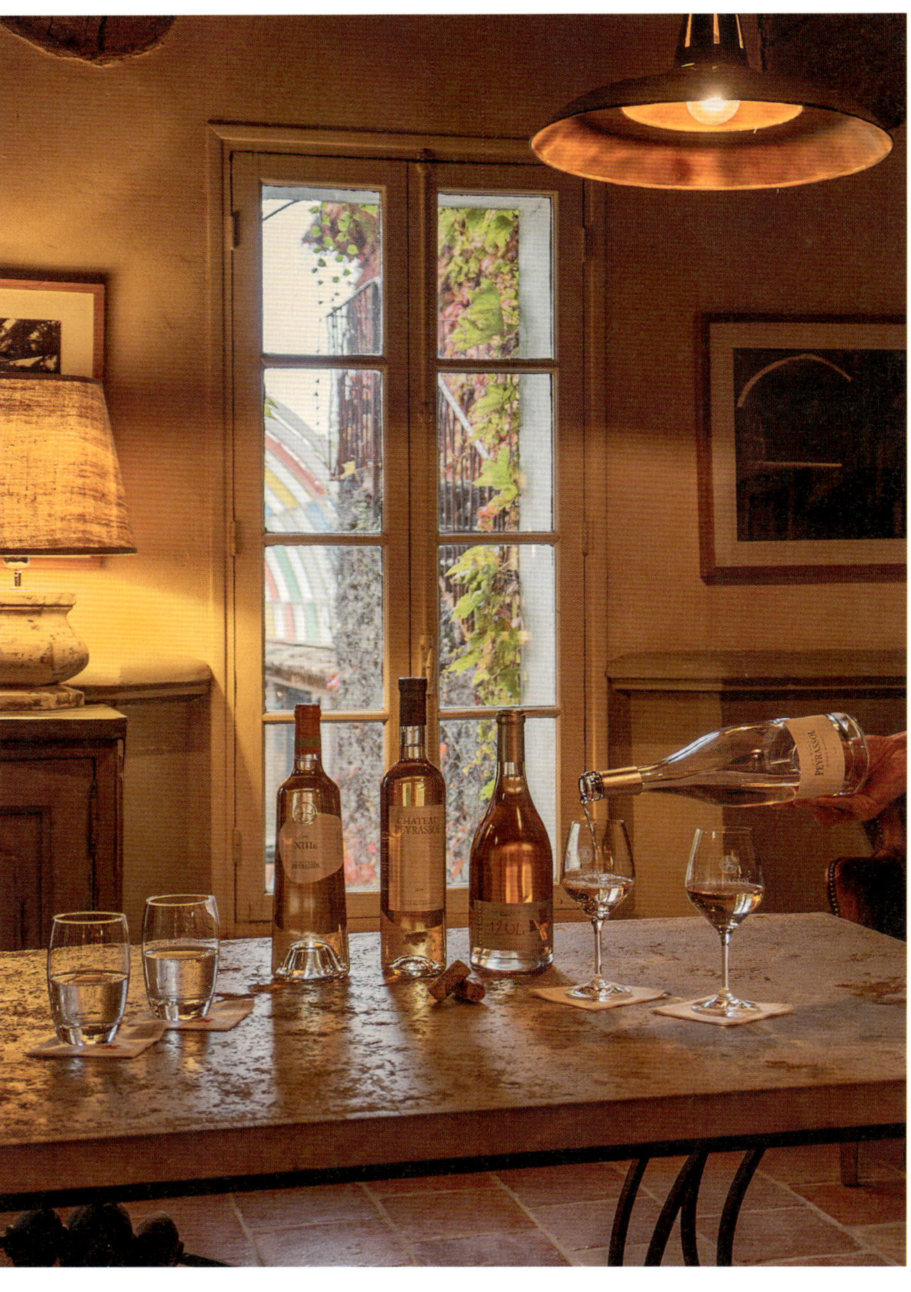

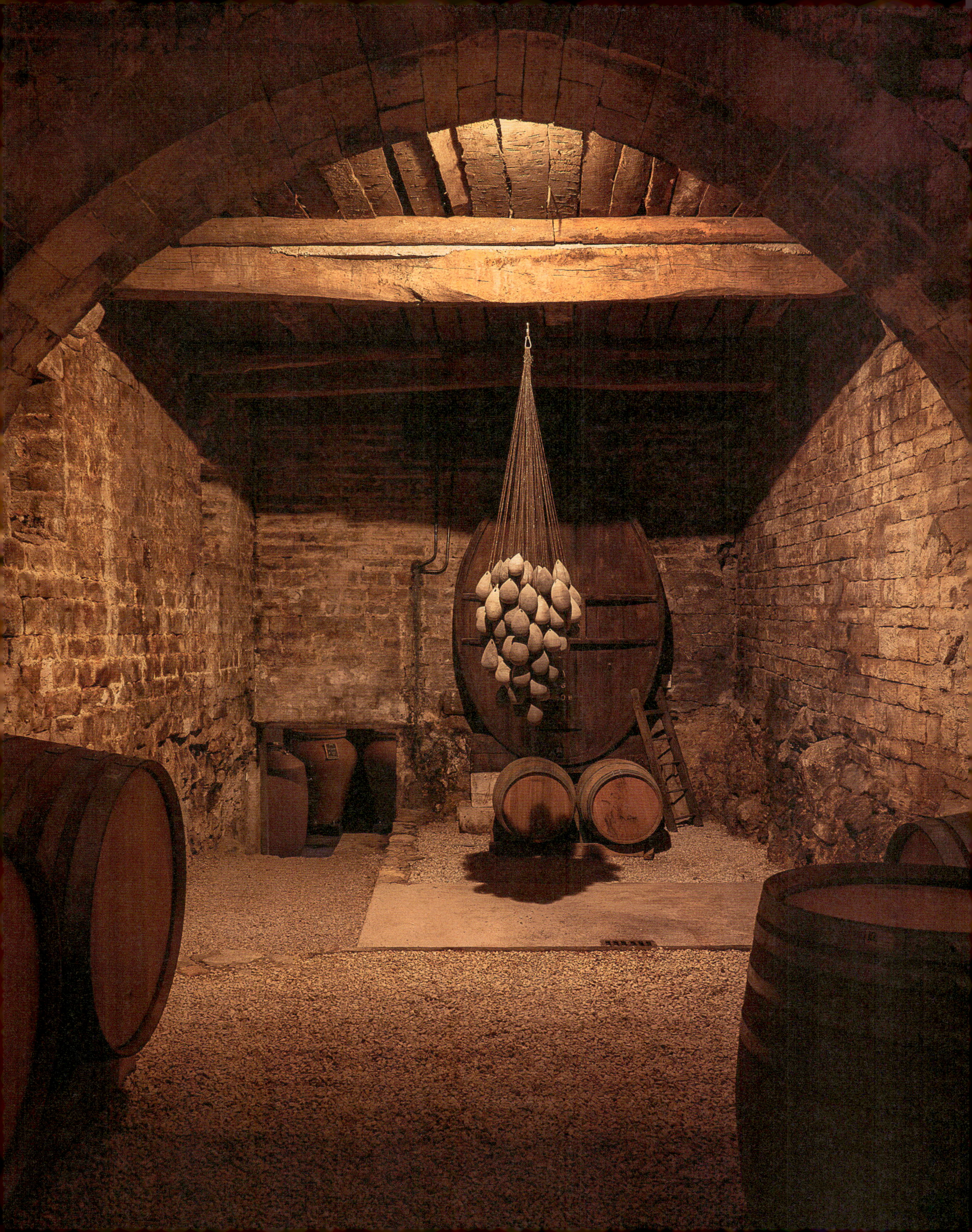

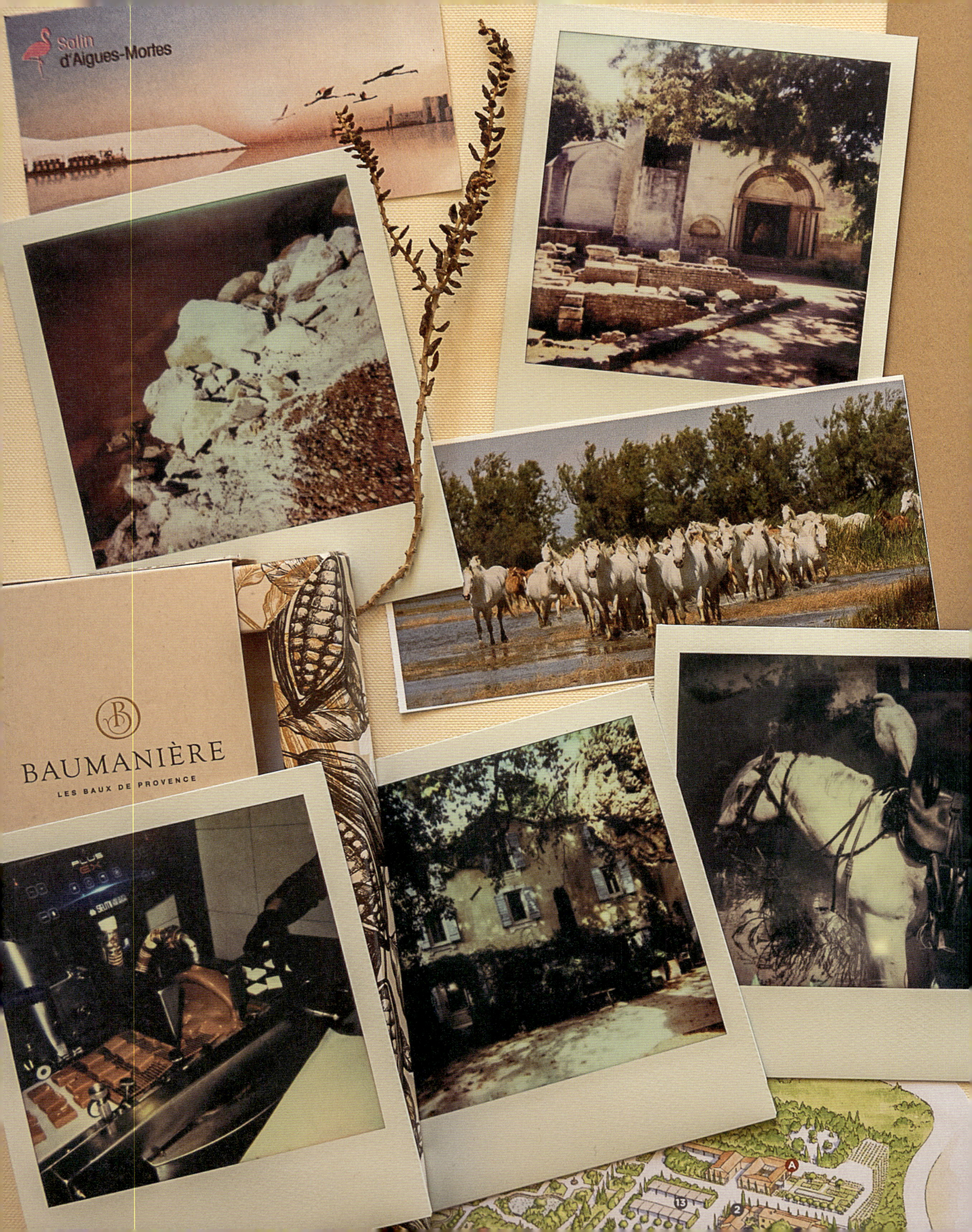
Salin d'Aigues-Mortes
BAUMANIÈRE
LES BAUX DE PROVENCE

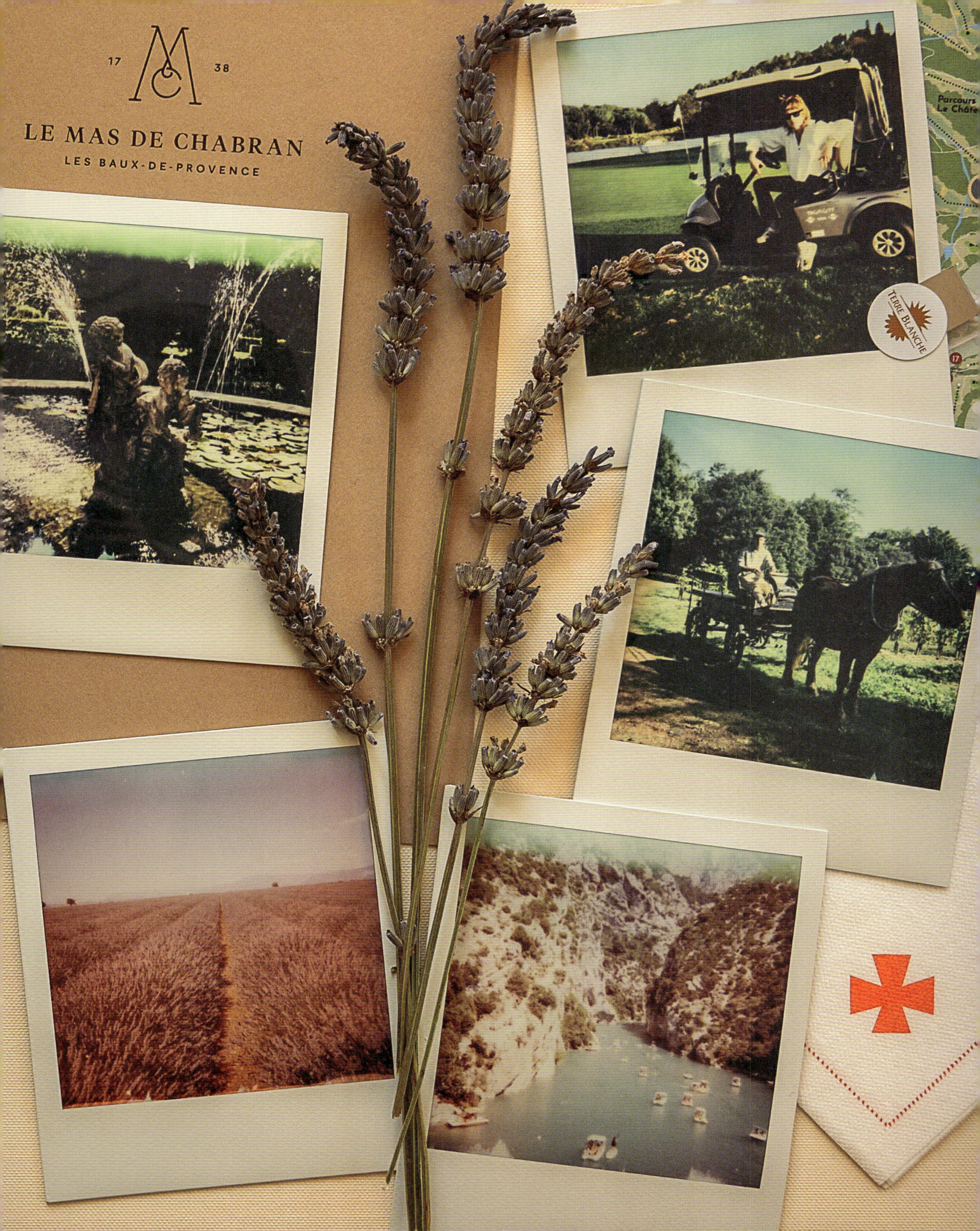
17
38
LE MAS DE CHABRAN
LES BAUX-DE-PROVENCE
TERRE BLANCHE

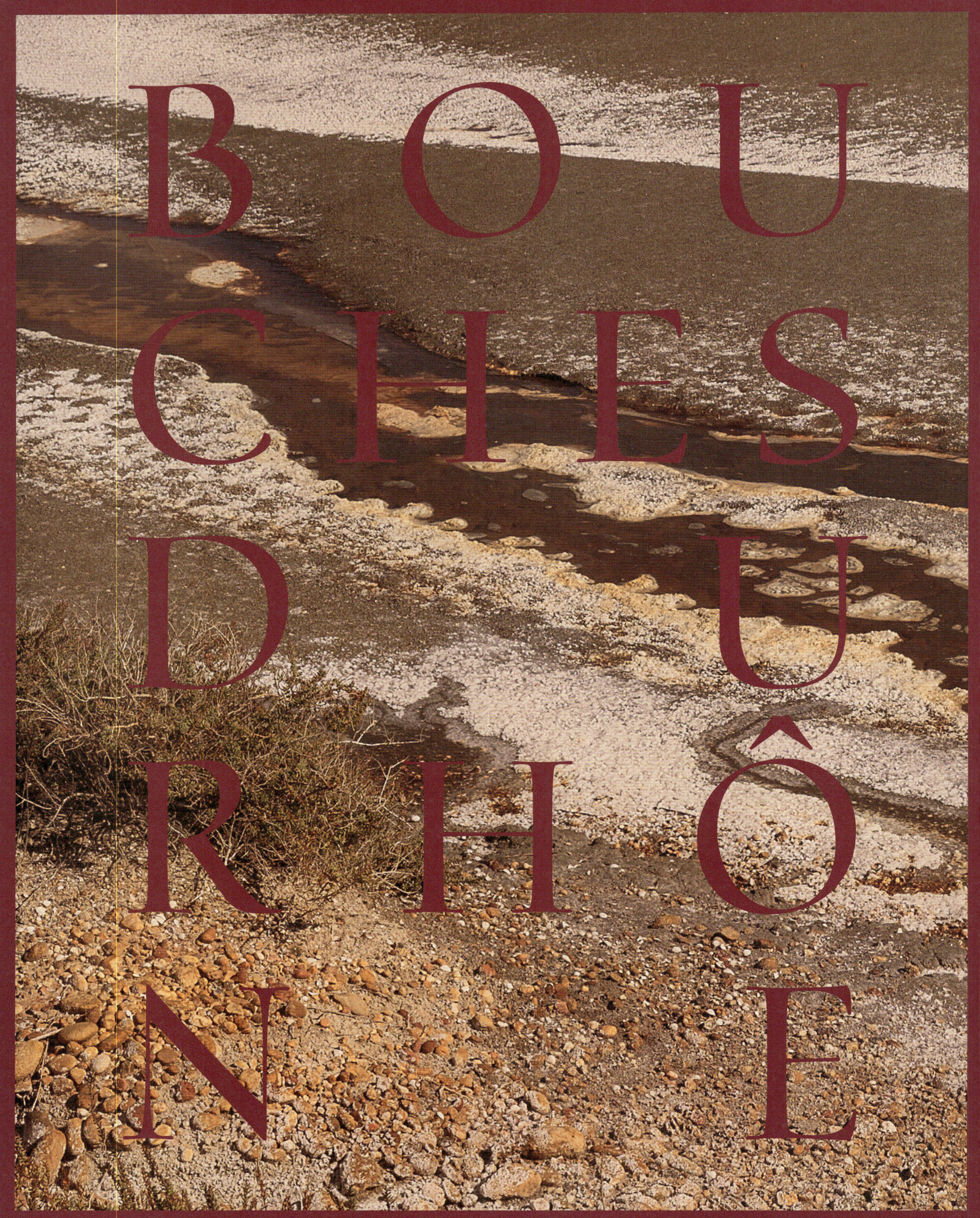
BOU
CHES
D U
RHÔ
N E

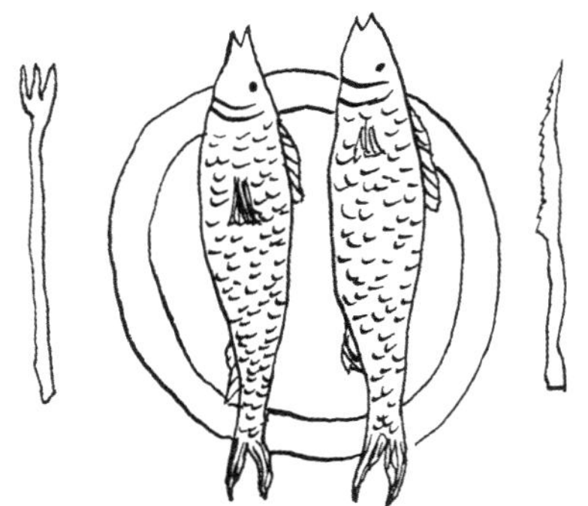

From le Var, we advance to the westernmost point of our journey, on a jaunt to experience yet another facet of Provence, possibly one of its most remarkable. This is where the Rhône—France's largest river by discharge volume—forms a natural boundary with the neighboring département of Gard as it fans out into a vast and intricate delta towards the south. We're in the region known as the Bouches-du-Rhône, meaning the mouths of the Rhône. The spectacle could hardly be more different than what Provence has shown us so far. The vast wetlands of the Camargue in the west form a salty, marshy paradise for flamingos, wild white horses, and matadors who are devoted to their beloved bulls. To the east, near Marseille, the classic Provence aesthetic still comes through, stony and rugged, but slightly sweeter. The rich diversity has inspired visitors since antiquity. Ancient Greeks and Romans founded major settlements here—Arles, Aix-en-Provence—and spun myths about the rocky Alpilles, the founding of Marseille, or the river gods who loved to bathe in the Rhône. We manage not to fall into the river, and we will visit Marseille—France's second-largest city and a bourgeoning pilgrimage site for design lovers—on another tour. For now, we're content to watch pink flamingos scraping salt from the surface of reddish waters, wander around Roman necropolises, and fill our bellies at France's most legendary culinary institution.

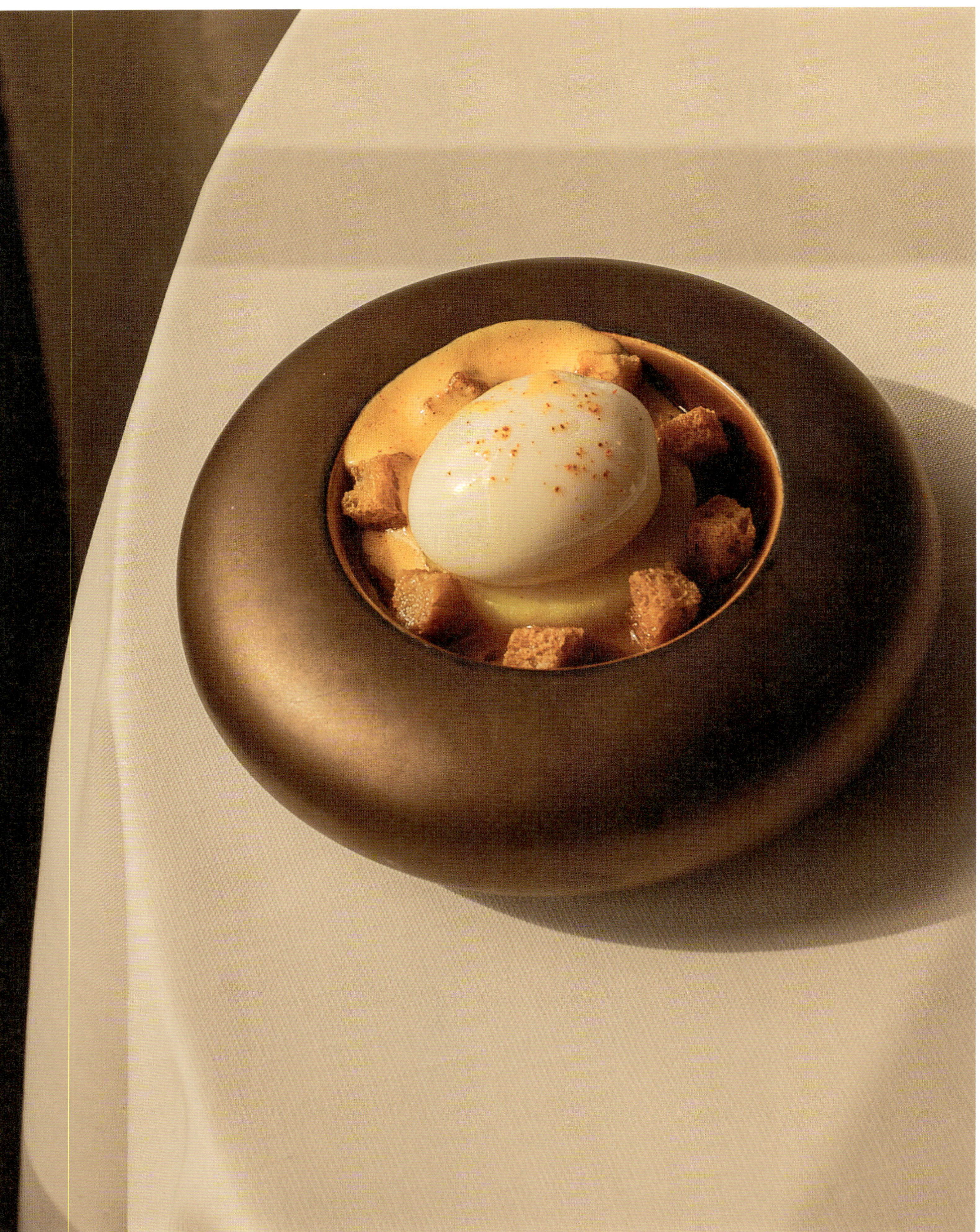

BAUMANIÈRE

BOUCHES-DU-RHÔNE

CONNAISSEUR

We round the southern foothills of the Alpilles. The landscape is rugged and outcroppings of white rock form spines on long ridges. Greek mythology holds that Zeus hurled down stones from the sky to save Heracles, laying what would ultimately be the foundation for one of the most beautiful villages in France: Les Baux-de-Provence. In the green valley just below the village, we arrive at our destination: Baumanière—or more precisely, its restaurant, L'Oustau de Baumanière, one of the world's rare few to have scaled the heights of three Michelin stars. Since 1945, this temple of gastronomy has welcomed connoisseurs, artists, high society, and the occasional monarch, all drawn by a delicate craftsmanship of indulgence. But Baumanière is not (only) about cuisine. Bit by bit, owner Jean-André Charial has expanded the legendary restaurant to include a hotel, a spa, a *chocolaterie*, a ceramics studio, and even its own fruit and vegetable farm. He's created a microcosm of flavor. We walk around the spacious estate, strolling in lush, almost enchanted gardens shaded by centuries-old plane trees and past farmhouses now reimagined as elegant suites. At last, we reach our room, which used to be Jean-André's studio in the old Charial family home. Its minimalist interior and avant-garde flair essentialize the high intellectual standards of Baumanière.

The evening sun casts a golden glow on the rocks. It's what we've been waiting for: time to make our way to L'Oustau. We enter the hallowed halls and see portraits of Queen Elizabeth II on the walls alongside hand-painted menus by Jean Cocteau. They were both regulars here, and this evening they silently witness us taking a feast. It's going to be seven courses, each one a story unto itself, complete, precise, in perfect harmony with the ceramic tableware from the restaurant's own workshop. Over the next four hours, the layered universe of Baumanière reveals itself, crossing our plates in a complete symphony of pleasure.

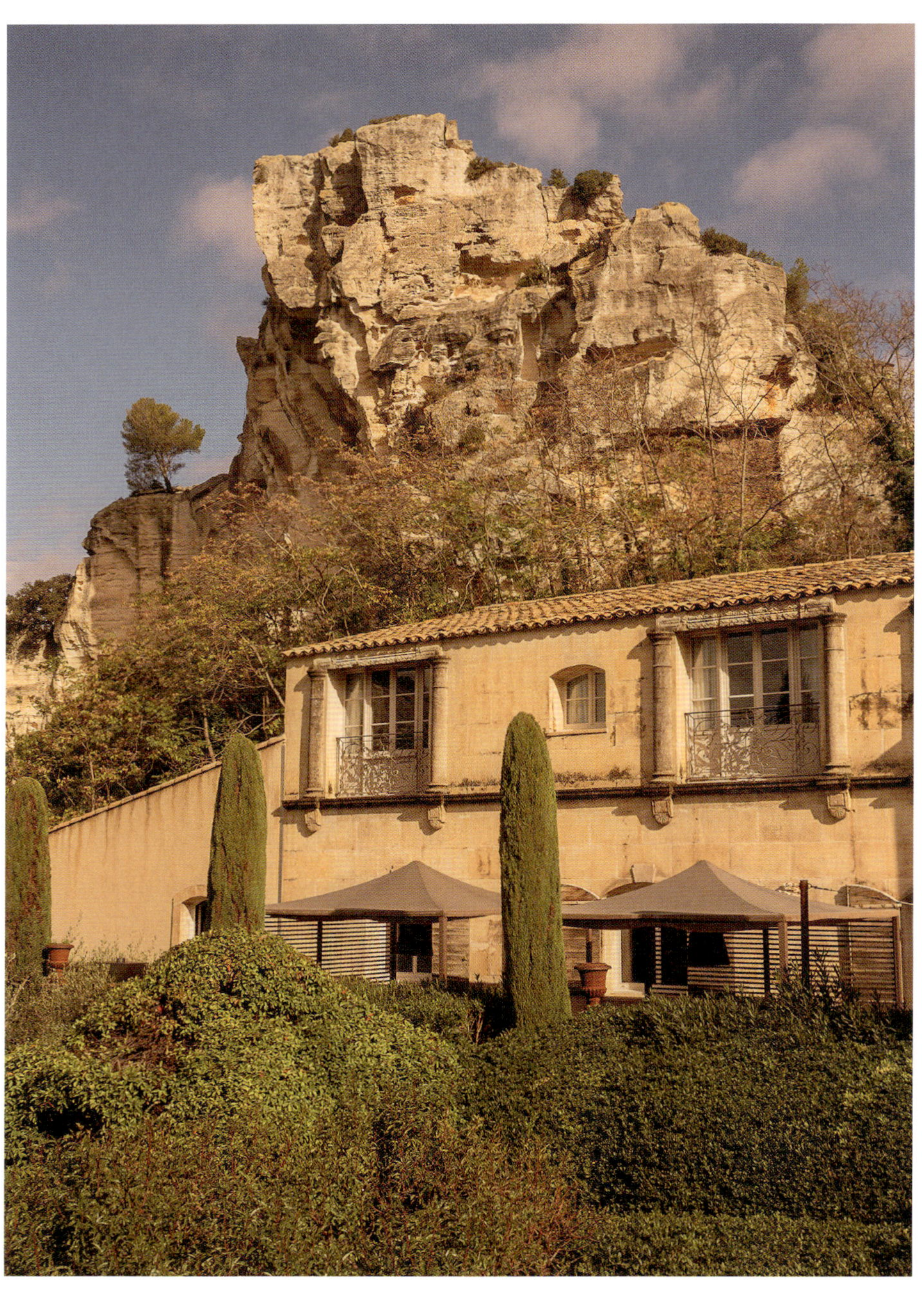

The Baumanière centers around its three-star restaurant, L'Oustau. Situated at the base of the cliffs below the village of Les Baux-de-Provence, this institution is in the perfect spot for a stopover en route from Paris to the Côte d'Azur. It will expose you to the highest echelons of craftsmanship in the art of indulgence.

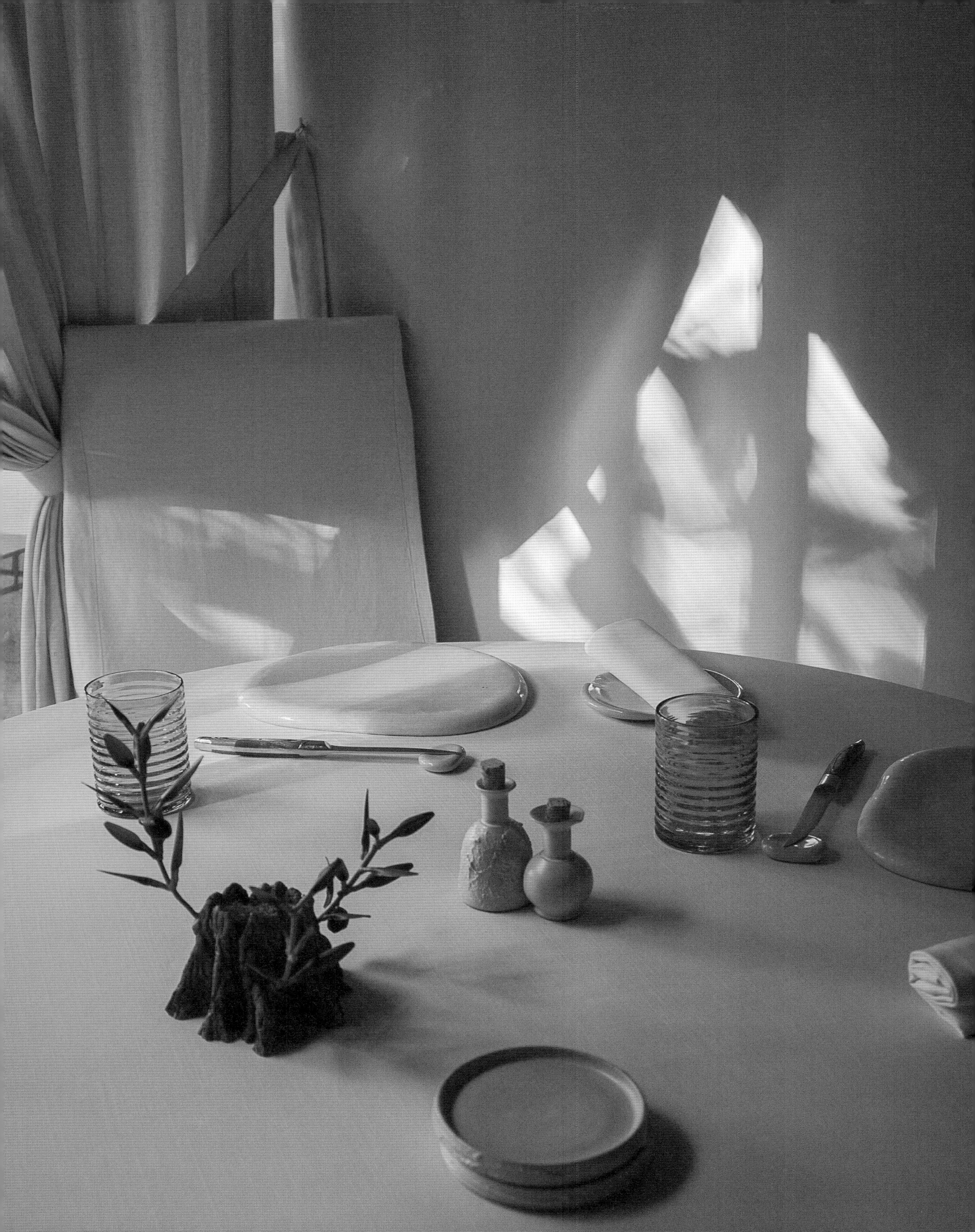

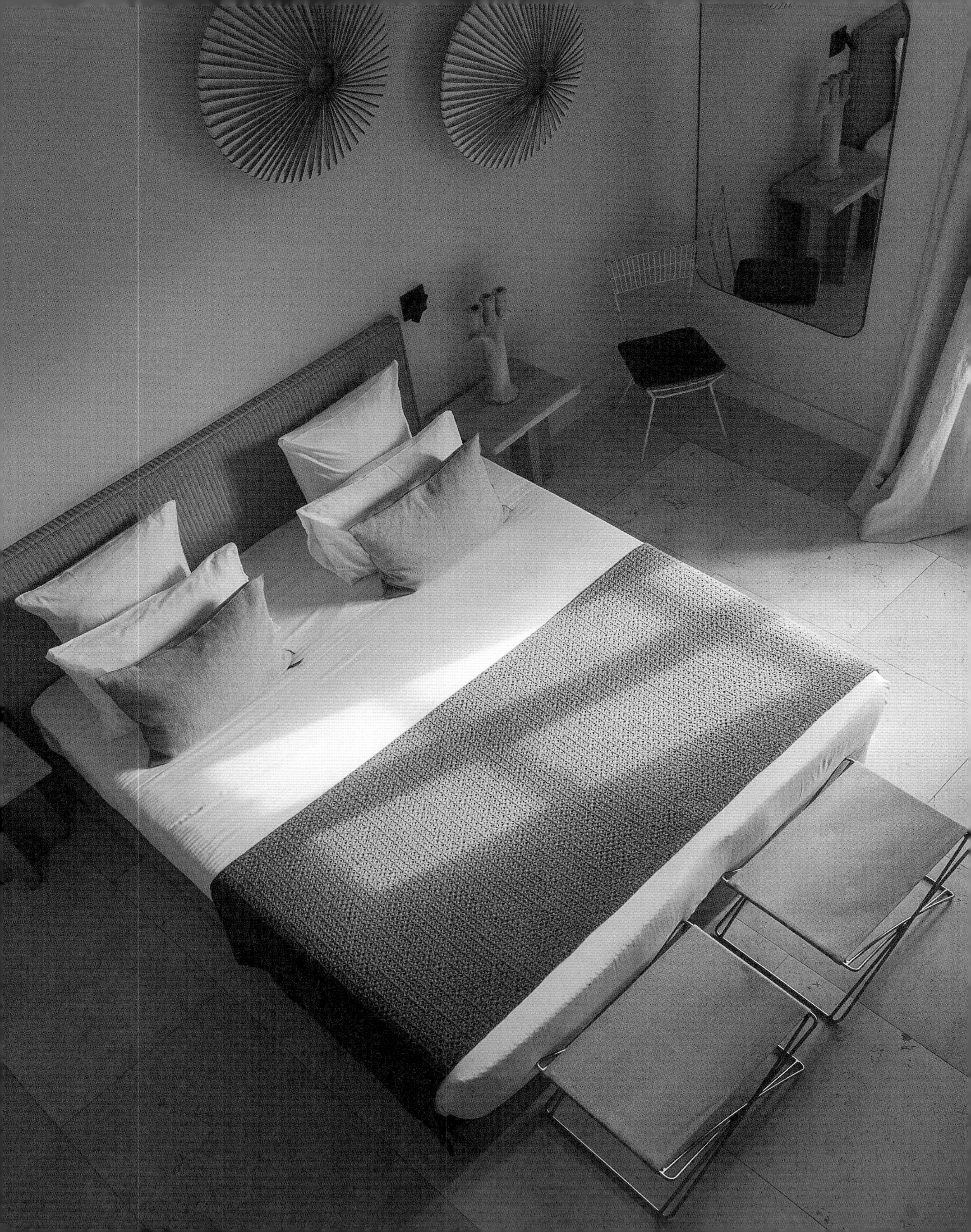

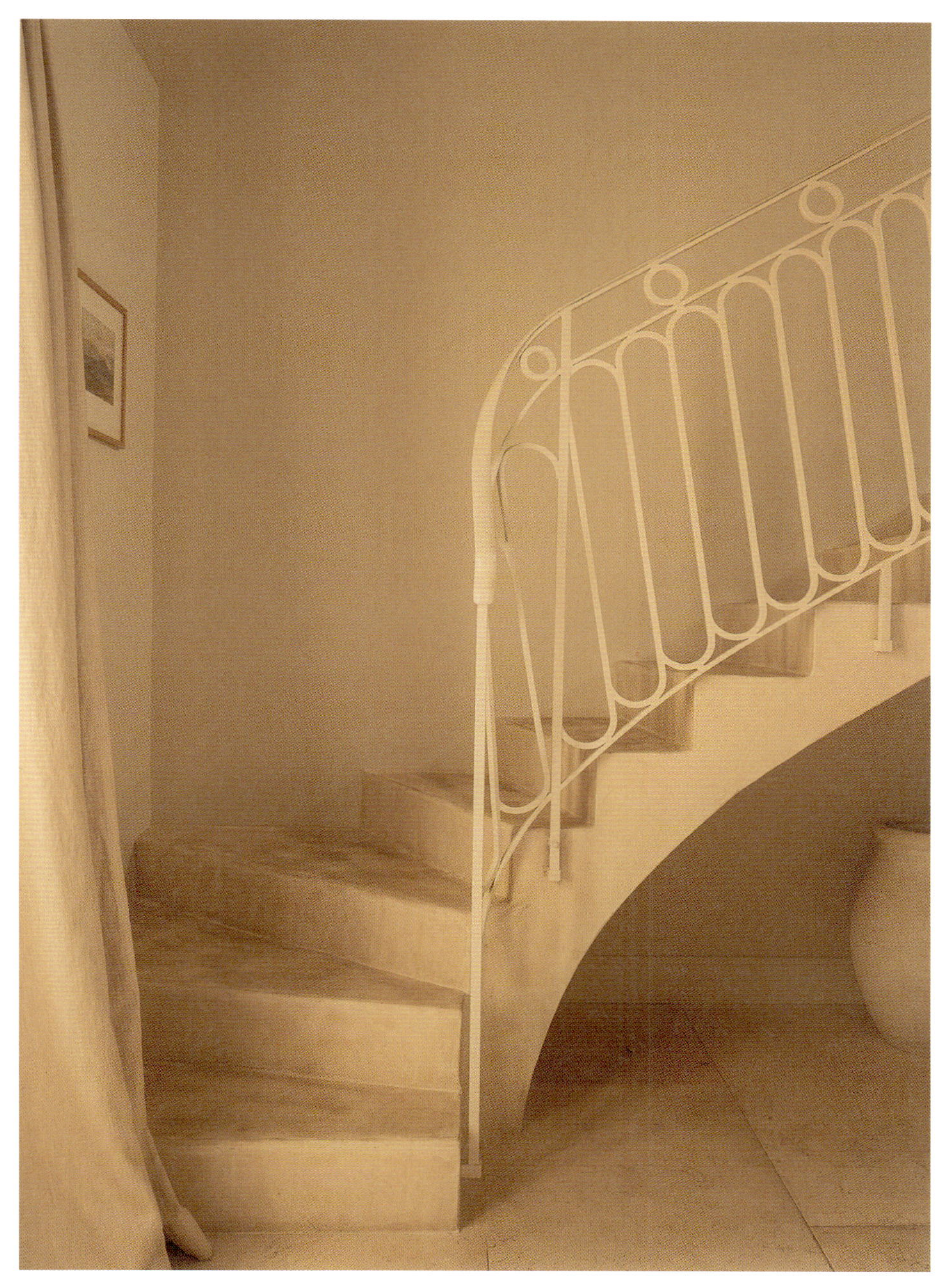

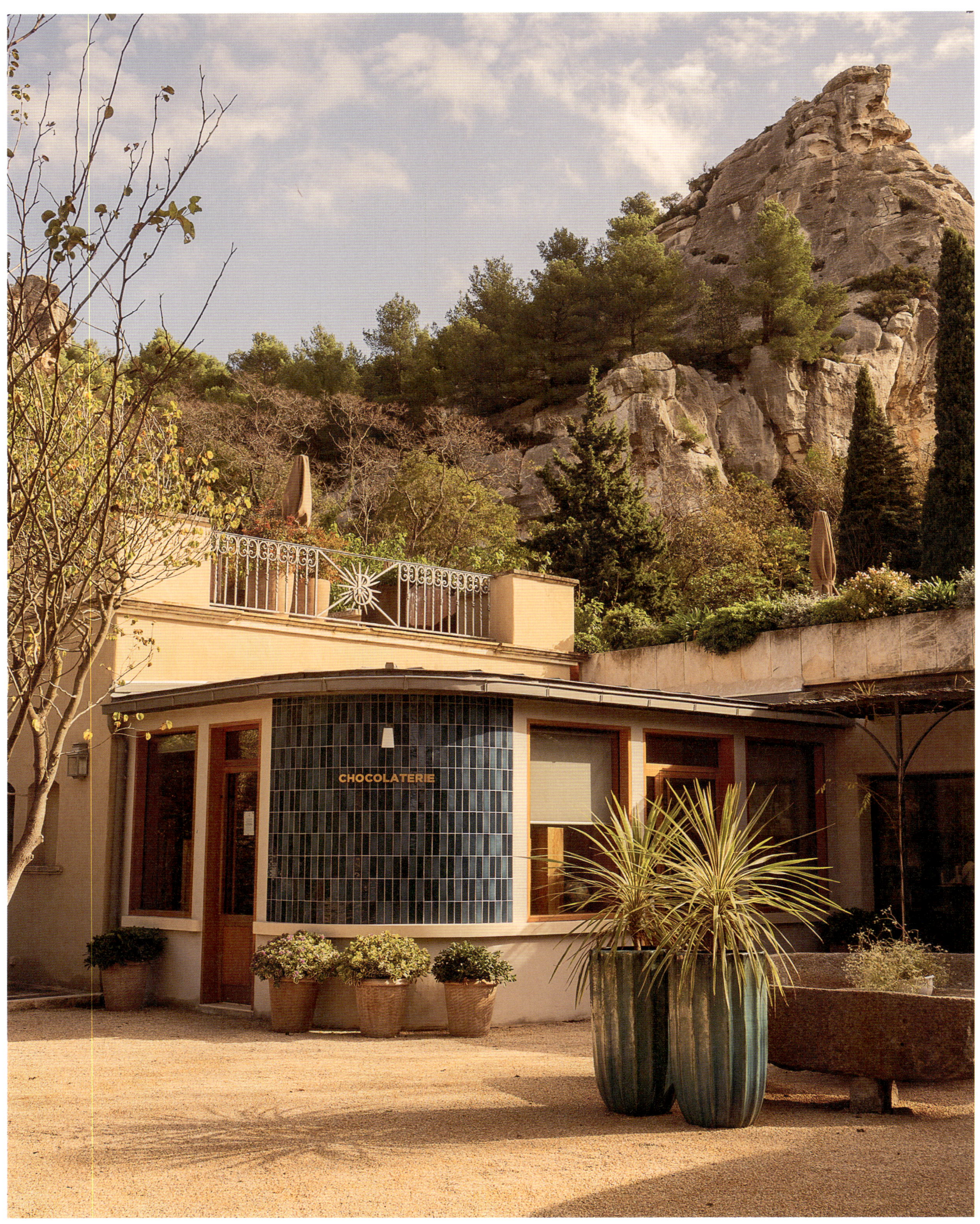
CHOCOLATERIE

LA CHOCOLATERIE BAUMANIÈRE

BOUCHES-DU-RHÔNE

CHOCOLATE BALANCE

Even the world's finest dinner would fall flat without a dessert. If it were up to us, every course would be composed of sweet delicacies. Come what may. Let us become ill. Let some big-shot chef disapprove. But anyway, at Baumanière there's a reasonable sense of balance. *Chef pâtissier* Brandon Dehan's creations are every bit as dazzling as the dishes that *chef de cuisine* Glenn Viel creates. The devotion to dessert at Baumanière ramped up to the point that they opened their own *chocolaterie*, which in just a few short years has won them just about every major award in the world of chocolate. And that's exactly where we're headed—for lunch. The *cheffe chocolatière*, Justine, receives us on a natural platform adjacent to the pottery studio and overlooking the vegetable gardens. Her manner is as enchanting as her flawless chocolate creations. Inside a blue-tiled, 1960s-era bungalow, she and her staff consummate the art of chocolate in the classic form of pralines, chocolate cicadas, and chocolate-glazed candied oranges and nuts. Every creation is pared back, no-fuss, celebrating pure flavors of popcorn, caramel, smoked hazelnut, or the essential aromas of Alpilles mountain herbs. The Salon du Chocolat et de la Pâtisserie opens in Paris in two weeks, and production is in full swing. An army of marshmallows marches along an iron conveyor belt, straight into a curtain of molten chocolate that coats them in silky brown. Justine's assistants tease pralines from their molds, laminate pastry, or whip ganache into airy peaks—it's the pinnacle of chocolate craft, absolute precision. We're in paradise. This is the coronation ceremony of our festive run at Baumanière.

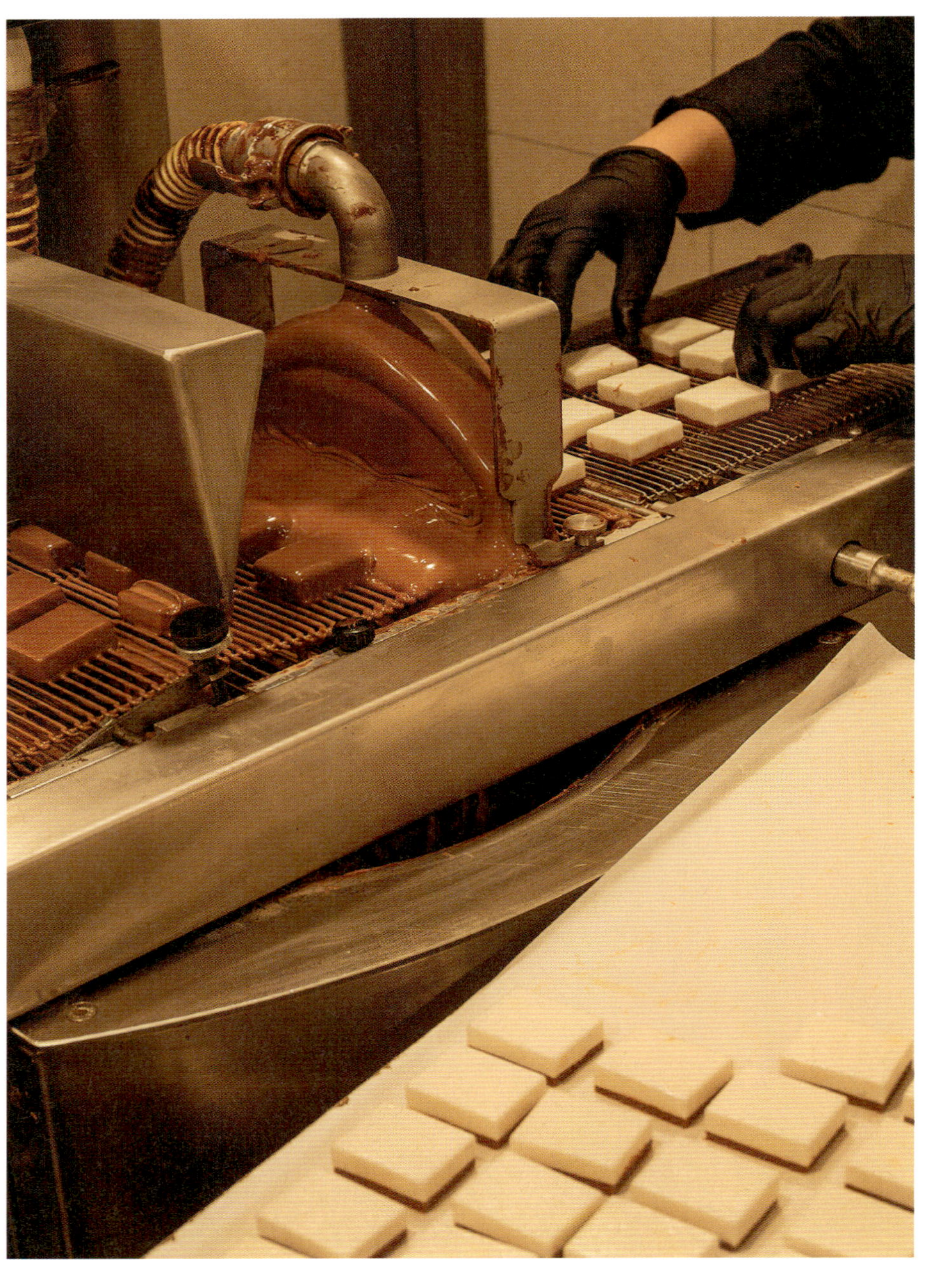

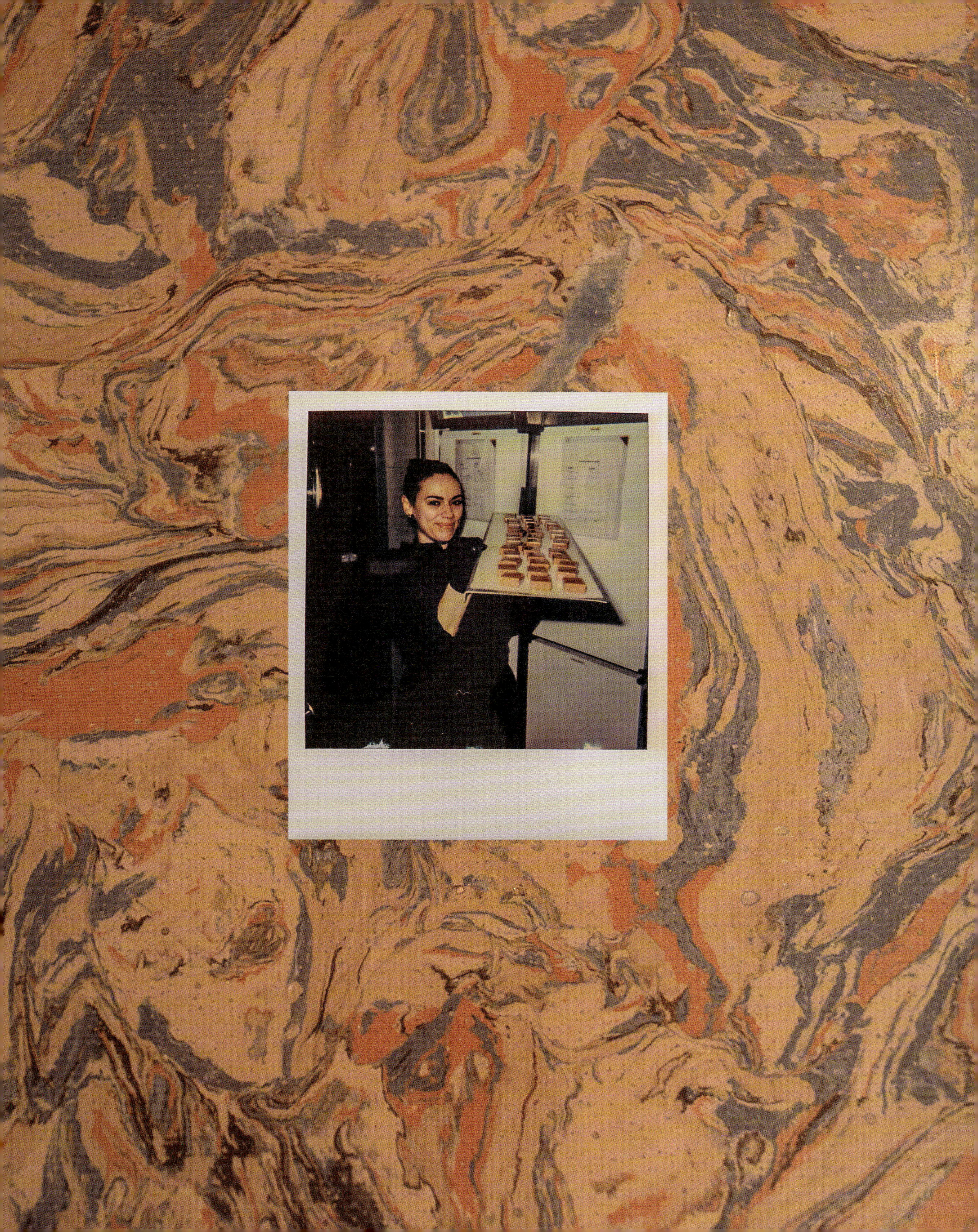

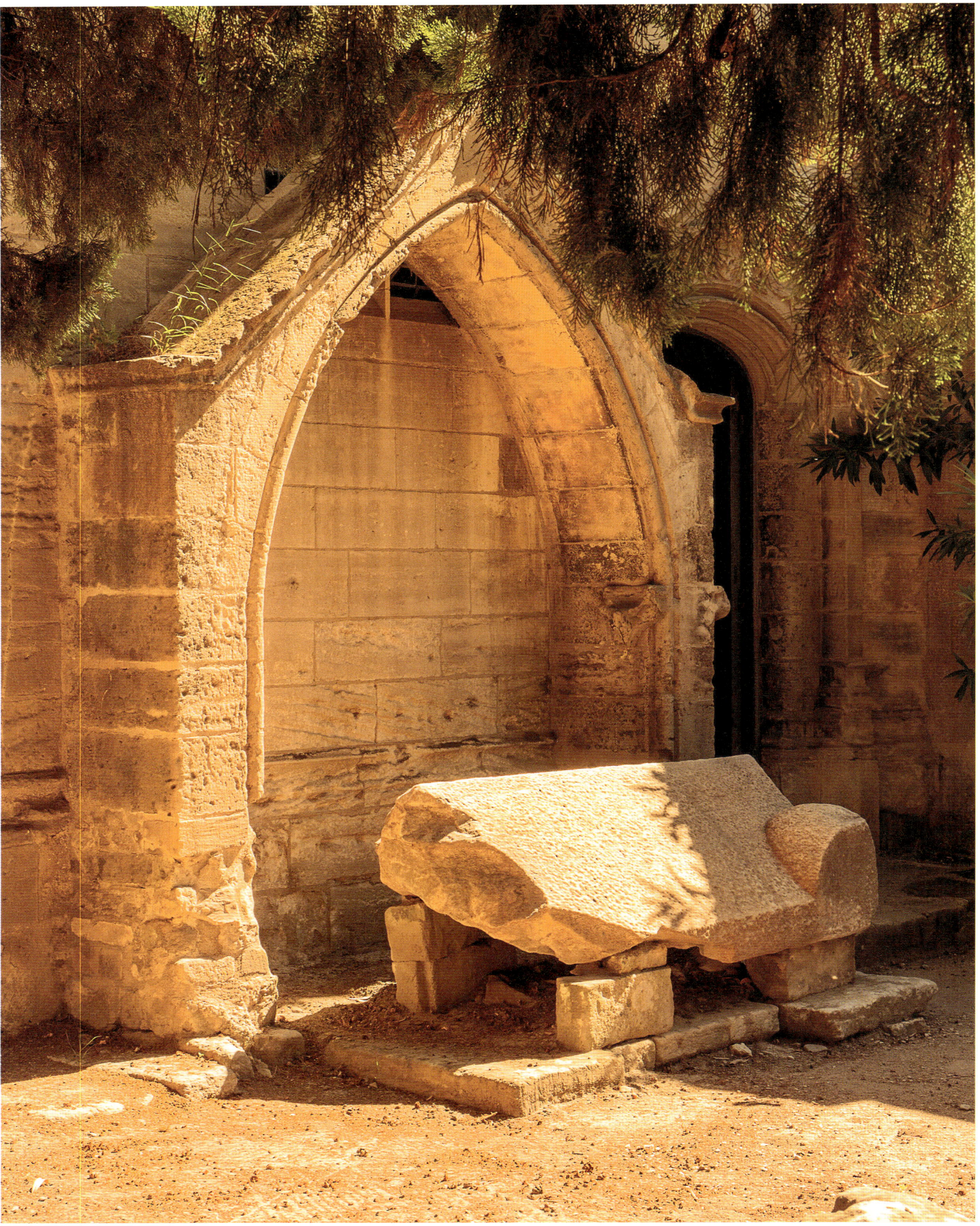

ALYSCAMPS

BOUCHES-DU-RHÔNE

ELYSIAN FIELDS

Our journey toward the Camargue takes us to Arles. We're in the mood for a stroll, to see and be seen like on the Champs-Élysées. But instead of the streets around the imposing colosseum or the amphitheater of this former Roman provincial capital, we've selected a destination that, at first glance, feels rather less Parisian. And yet it has more in common with the Champs-Élysées, the "Avenue of the Elysian Fields", than one might think. We're bound for the Roman necropolis of the Alyscamps, the name of which shares an origin with its Parisian counterpart. It's all about the Roman afterlife. Roman nobles were being laid to rest here long before the fourth century, until a Roman chancellor was martyred and this spot not far from the center of Arles became a pilgrimage site as well as the ultimate—literally the final—status symbol, with Roman high society vying for a spot they could occupy when they were dead. The undertakers may have left thousands of years ago, but the place is still magnetic. In Victorian times, aristocrats would parade along the Alyscamps on Sundays, showing off their stylish clothes. Van Gogh and Gauguin made several paintings of the scene. Gucci actually staged a runway show here a few years ago. Today, it's our turn. We walk down the long promenade at midday in the shade of old plane trees. Their branches cast dappled shade down neatly laid rows of stone sarcophagi. The chain of crumbling monuments is unbroken. They are traces of a bygone world, and yet there's no sense of morbidity at all. It feels more like a traipse through the past, with an element of reflection and, in its own quiet way, a charming encounter with our own fleeting existence.

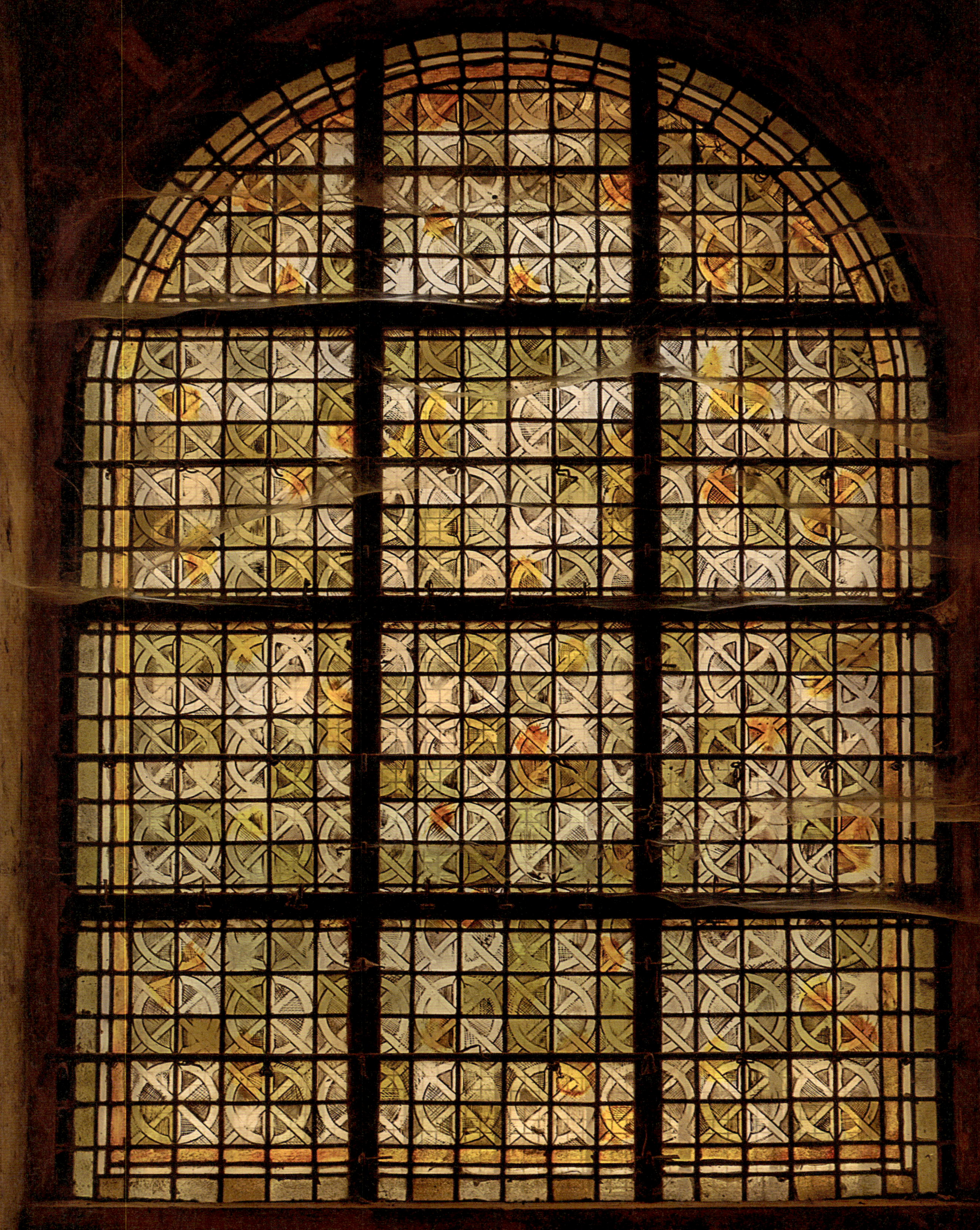

Time seems to stop as we step into the large chapel at the end of the promenade. It's just us two souls, surrounded by Gothic fragments and Roman sarcophagi, bathed in the dim glow that filters in through old leaded windows. Which reminds me: The Alyscamps has its fair share of ghost stories. More than once, there have been sightings of a lady in white. Perhaps, she just wanted to show off her new dress and didn't feel like going all the way to Paris.

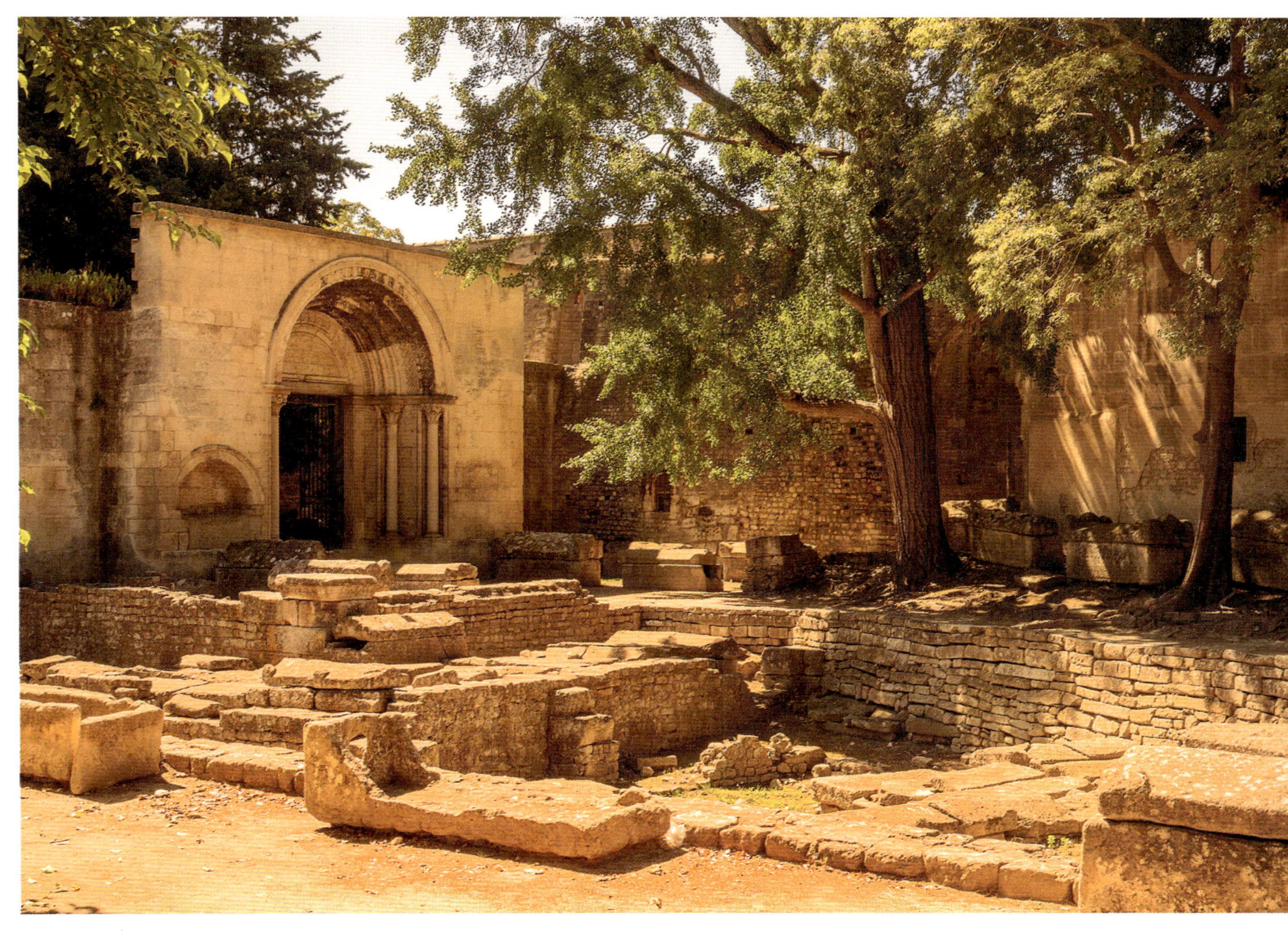

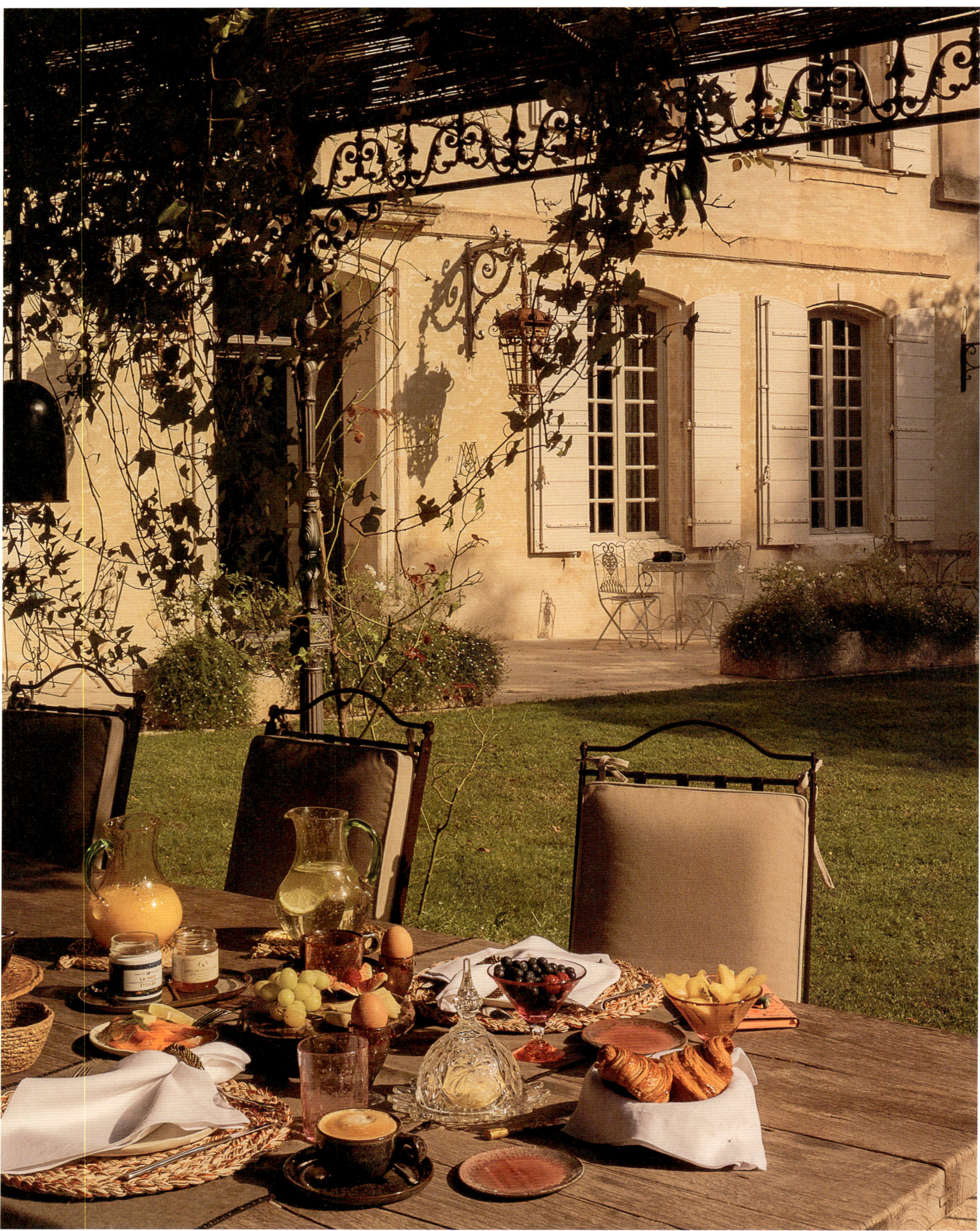

MAS DE CHABRAN

BOUCHES-DU-RHÔNE

WORLD TRAVELERS

Our stop in Arles was quick. What we need now is a base from which we can explore the Camargue. We find exactly what we're looking for just outside the small village of Maussane-les-Alpilles. Mas de Chabran isn't exactly a hotel but rather a new kind of luxury retreat, far from not only prying eyes and crowds but also from the usual clichés. And yet it's also firmly planted in the regional character. It was conceived by Liliana and Alain Meylan, a celebrated interior design duo who fell in love with Provence, bought three historic estates, and created a place where there was no pressure to compromise on their design vision. The result is pure curated luxury for their guests—a vacation sensation. For two days, we get to call Mas de Chabran—the flagship building in the collection—our own, quite literally, for the former olive mill, which can accommodate sixteen guests and has sprawling gardens, a pool, a chapel, and a tennis court, is only available as a complete package deal. Who hasn't dreamed of occupying a Provençal country estate? The majestic Mas comes into view at the end of a long avenue lined with chestnut trees. In the foyer, we are greeted by the innkeeper. A sea of irises spreads out on our right, a spacious French country kitchen on our left, and straight ahead, a stone staircase leading to the upper floor. It takes us nearly an hour to explore all eight bedrooms and the various dining halls, salons, living spaces, and the private spa beneath the roof. It's not ostentatious; it's elegant, cosmopolitan, and obsessed with materials, art, and culture. The interiors feel like a cross between a New York gallery and the eclectic collection of some aesthete world traveler. The innkeeper hands us the keys and will

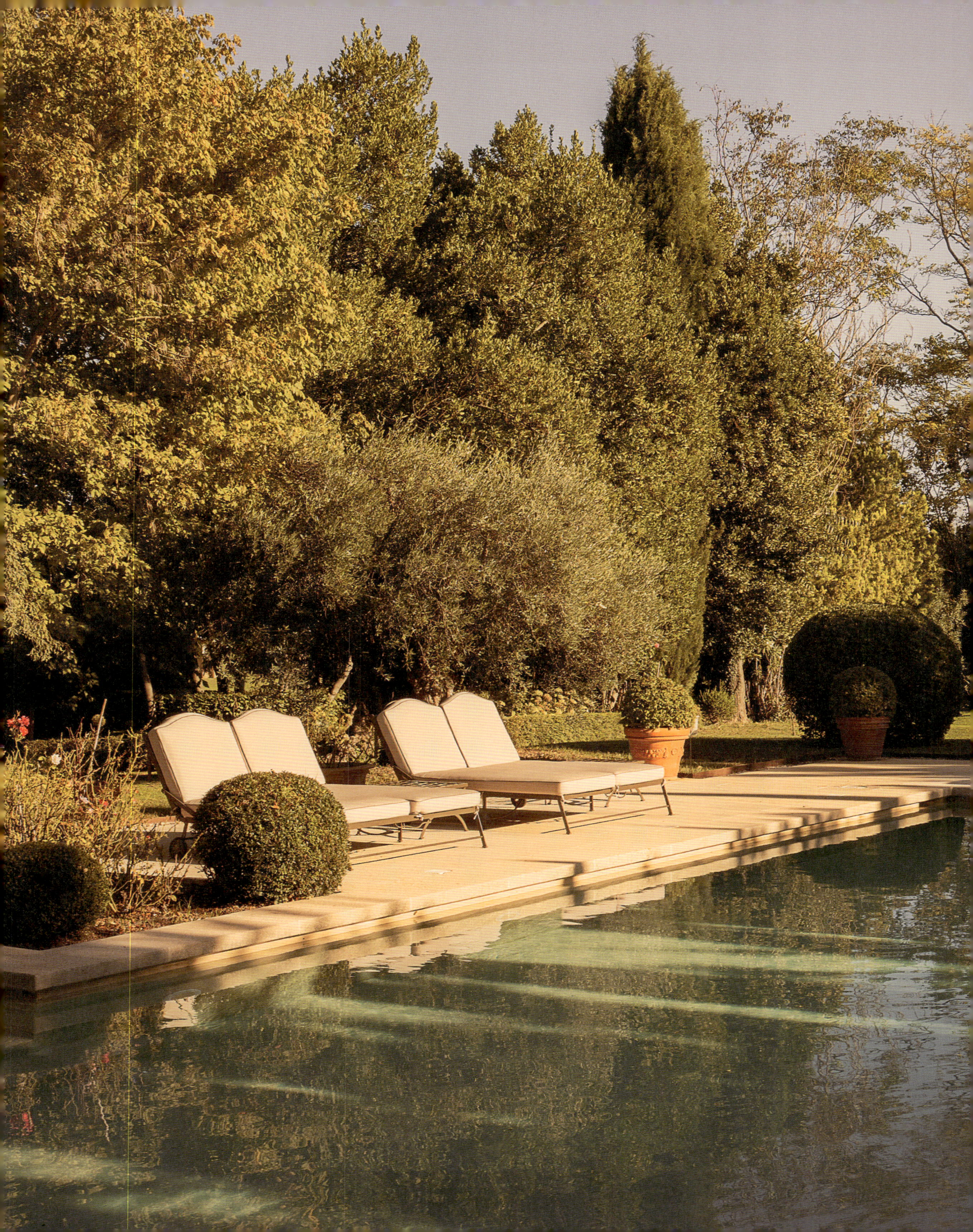

return at breakfast. For now, the villa is entirely ours. Eating cheese and drinking wine from the village, we spend the rest of the evening on our terrace. (You heard me.) The fountain murmurs, and two owls call to each other from the tall chestnuts. It's not without melancholy. Even as a couple, we're putting our estate to its best use. But it's impossible not to imagine the good it would do to have this house full of family and friends.

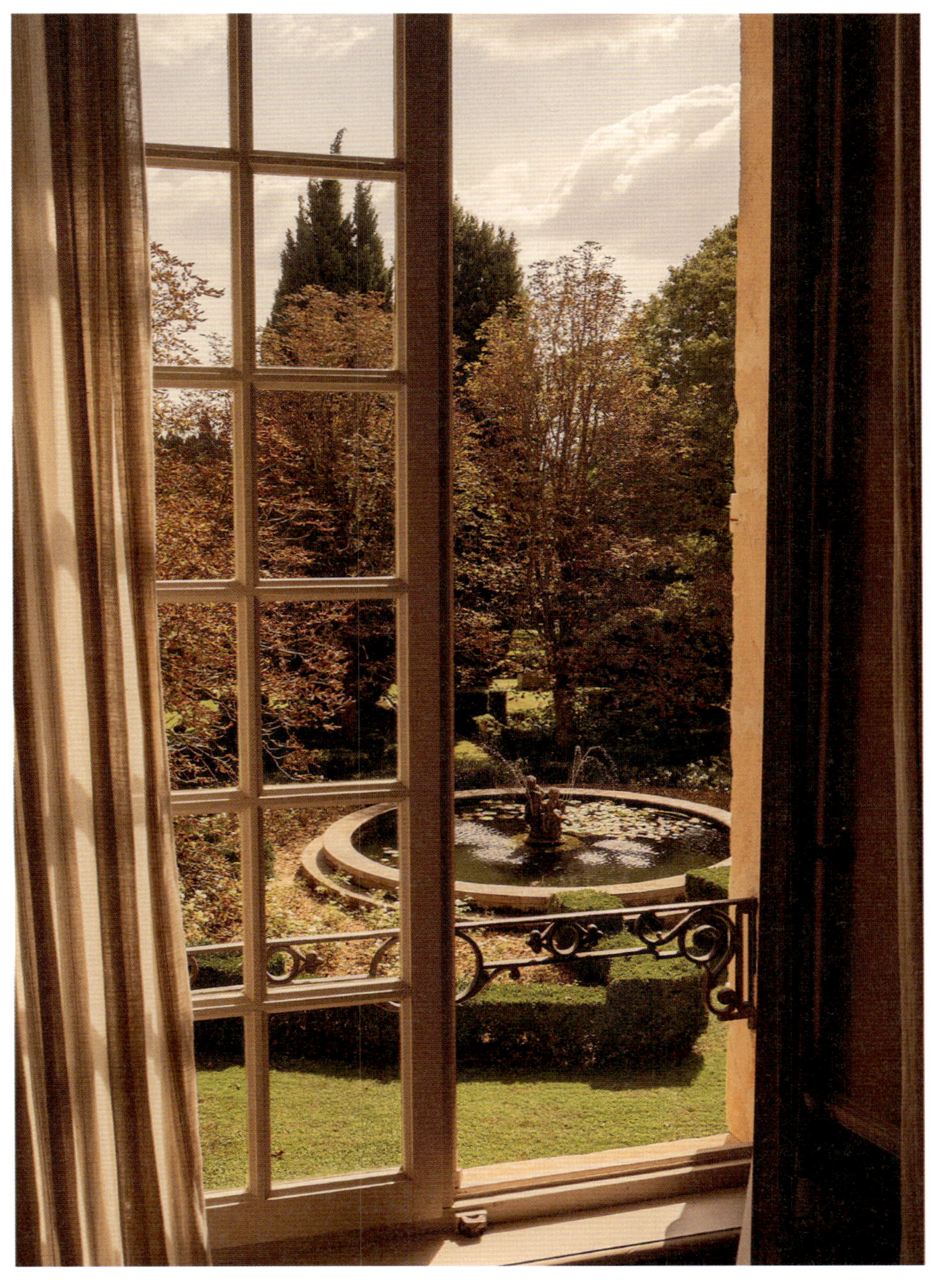

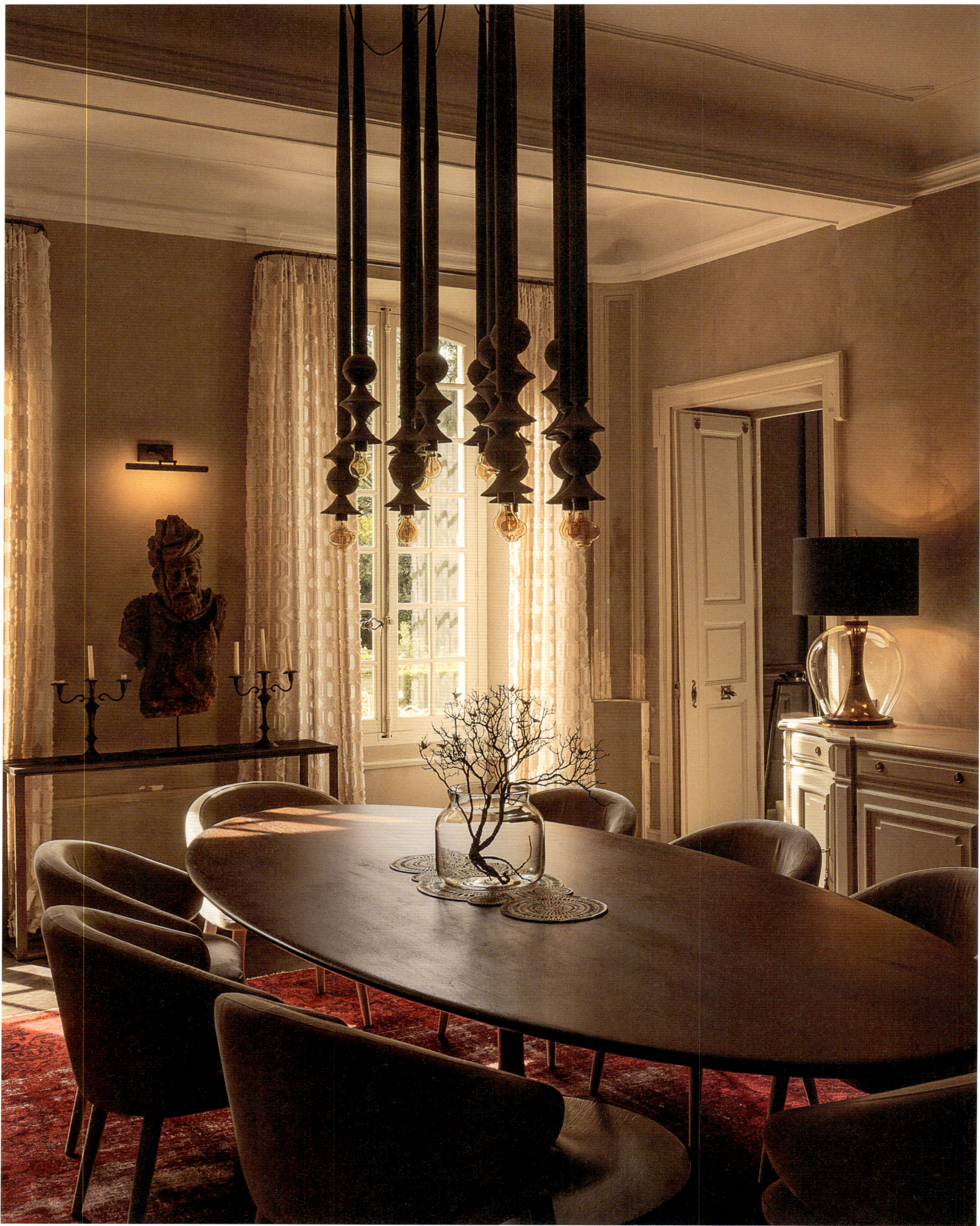

This living room is at the center of an enormous country estate with room for sixteen guests. Arched ceilings, remnants of the old oil mill, and an exquisitely curated interior as if the owners were acquisitive world travelers: the calling card of the interior designers Liliana and Alain Meylan, creators of the Mas de Chabran.

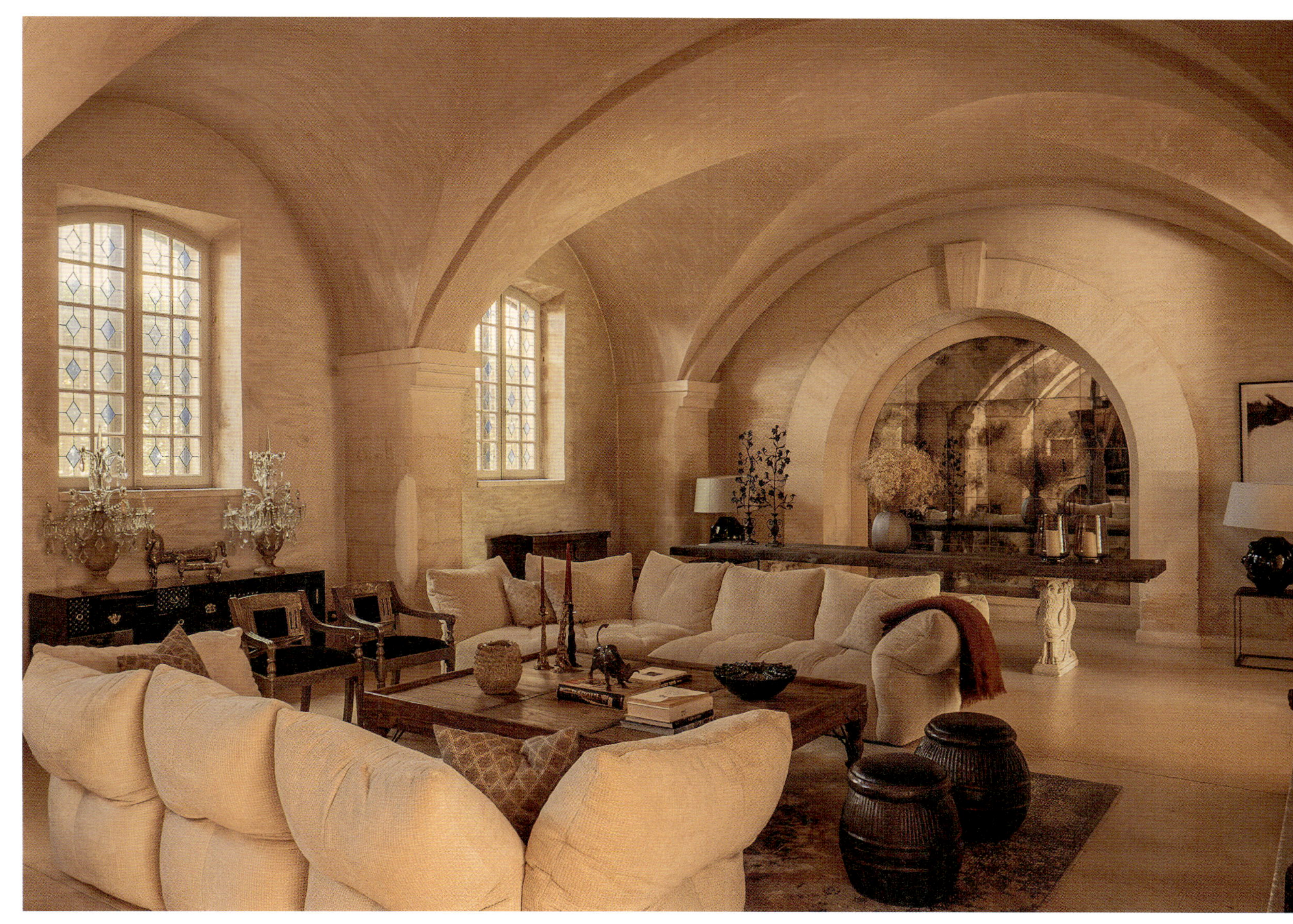

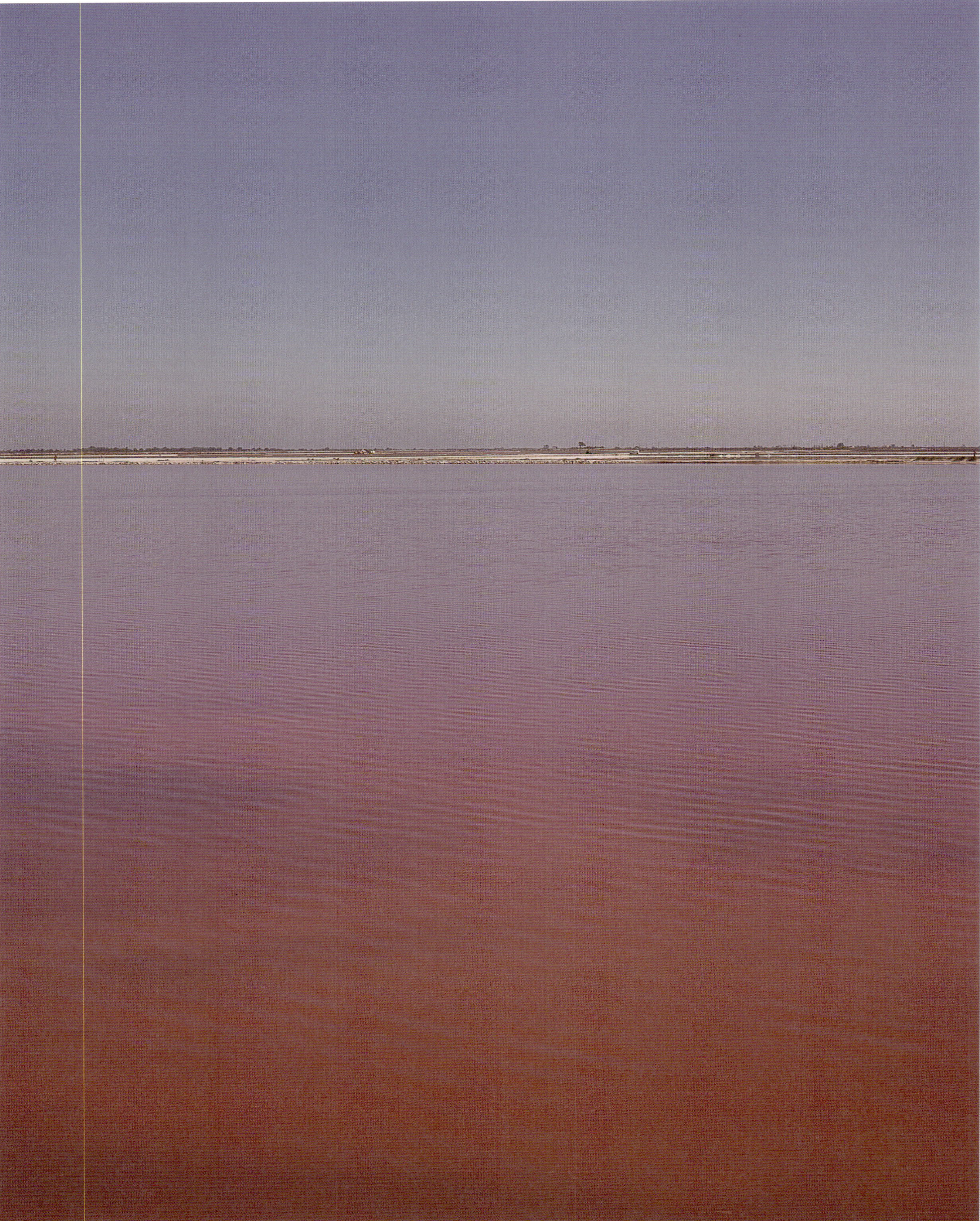

CAMARGUE

BOUCHES-DU-RHÔNE

SKIN OF SALT

Our day begins with an exquisite breakfast at Mas de Chabran, served beneath a rose-covered arch with an immediate view of the horse paddock. We're on our way to the Camargue for the day. For the full-bore Provençal fantasy, we could saddle up the estate's two horses and ride the 30 kilometers to the Camargue. But our riding experience is, shall we say, limited, and soon we'll have plenty of white horses to look at, and so we opt for electrical horsepower. As we pass the last remnants of the Alpilles, the landscape suddenly flattens out, becoming so flat, in fact, that the view stretches endlessly ahead—nothing but broad marshland, a tangle of irrigation canals, and impenetrable stands of reeds. We've reached the *bouches*—the mouths of the Rhône. The Camargue spans the delta for miles between Port-Saint-Louis-du-Rhône and Aigues-Mortes. Regular floods over thousands of years have shaped this landscape into a natural refuge of saline wetlands, a rich biotope for rare species like red flamingos, great white egrets, and the wild Camargue horses with whom they live in romantic symbiosis.

It's the flamingos we're after. The air shimmers in the heat, mosquitoes whirr, the greenery pulls back, and vast salt ponds begin to dominate the landscape. On the horizon, we spot the first pink speck in the murky, salty mud. As we draw nearer, that one single dot turns into a whole flock of pink flamingos, wading in unison, performing a choreography to the silence as they hunt for tiny crabs. The west wind is gusting in salty blasts that draw us toward the great salterns where the famous *fleur de sel* is harvested. White mounds of salt pile up beside broad basins where algae tint the brine red and cranes are poised to scrape off the dried skin when it's harvest time in a few months. The Camargue has a surreal, almost dystopian beauty—rugged, raw, and as full of diversions as anywhere in the south of France.

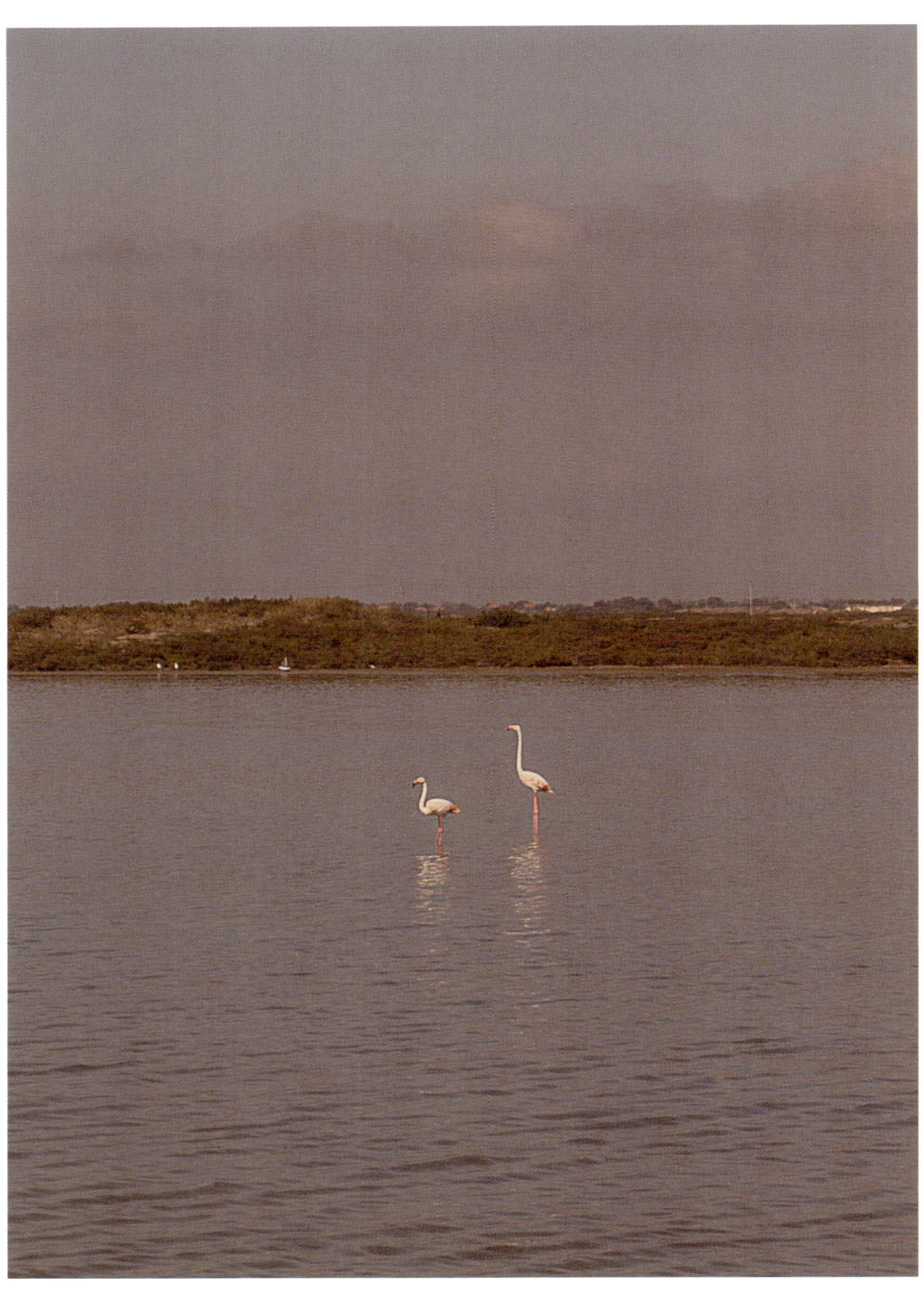

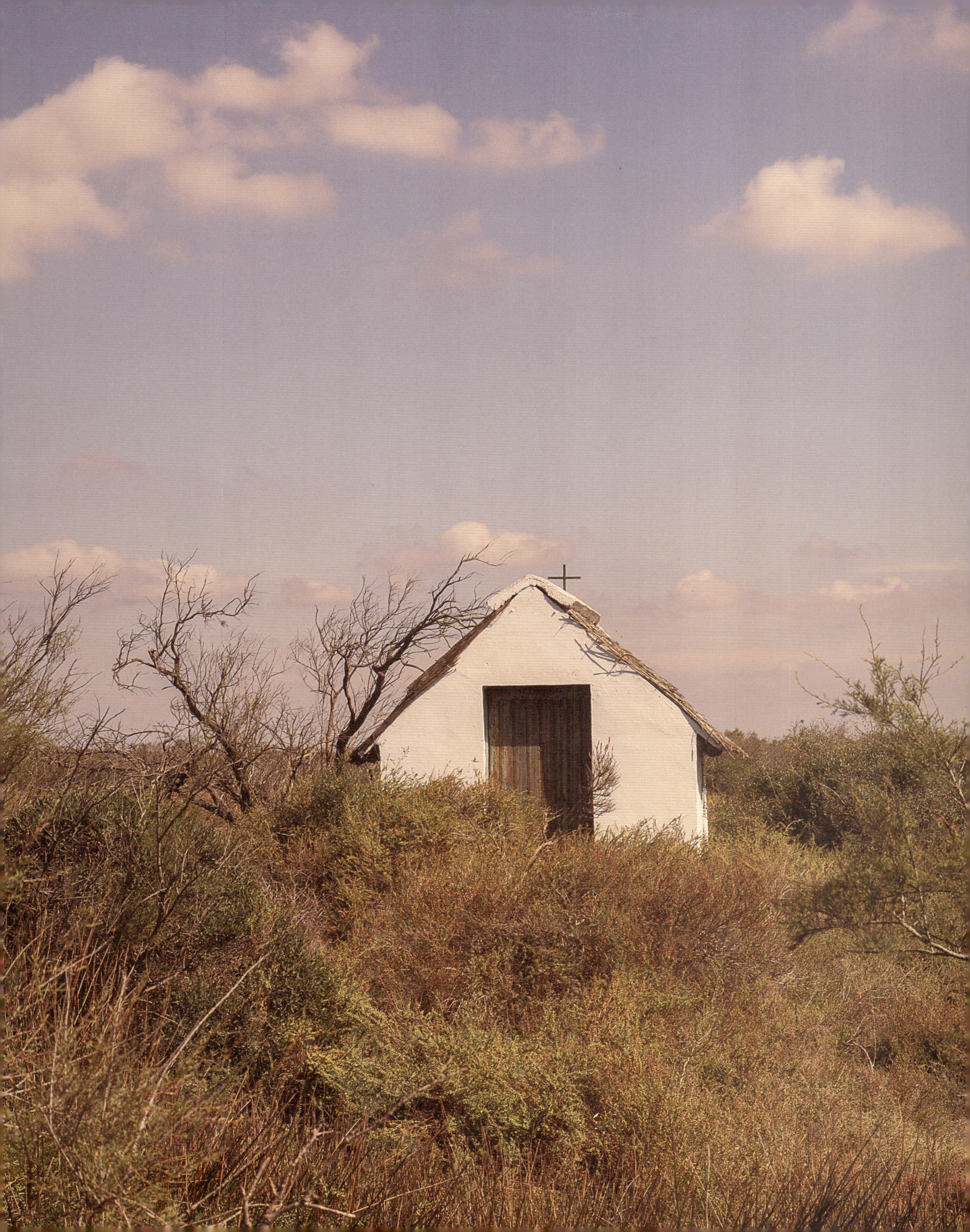

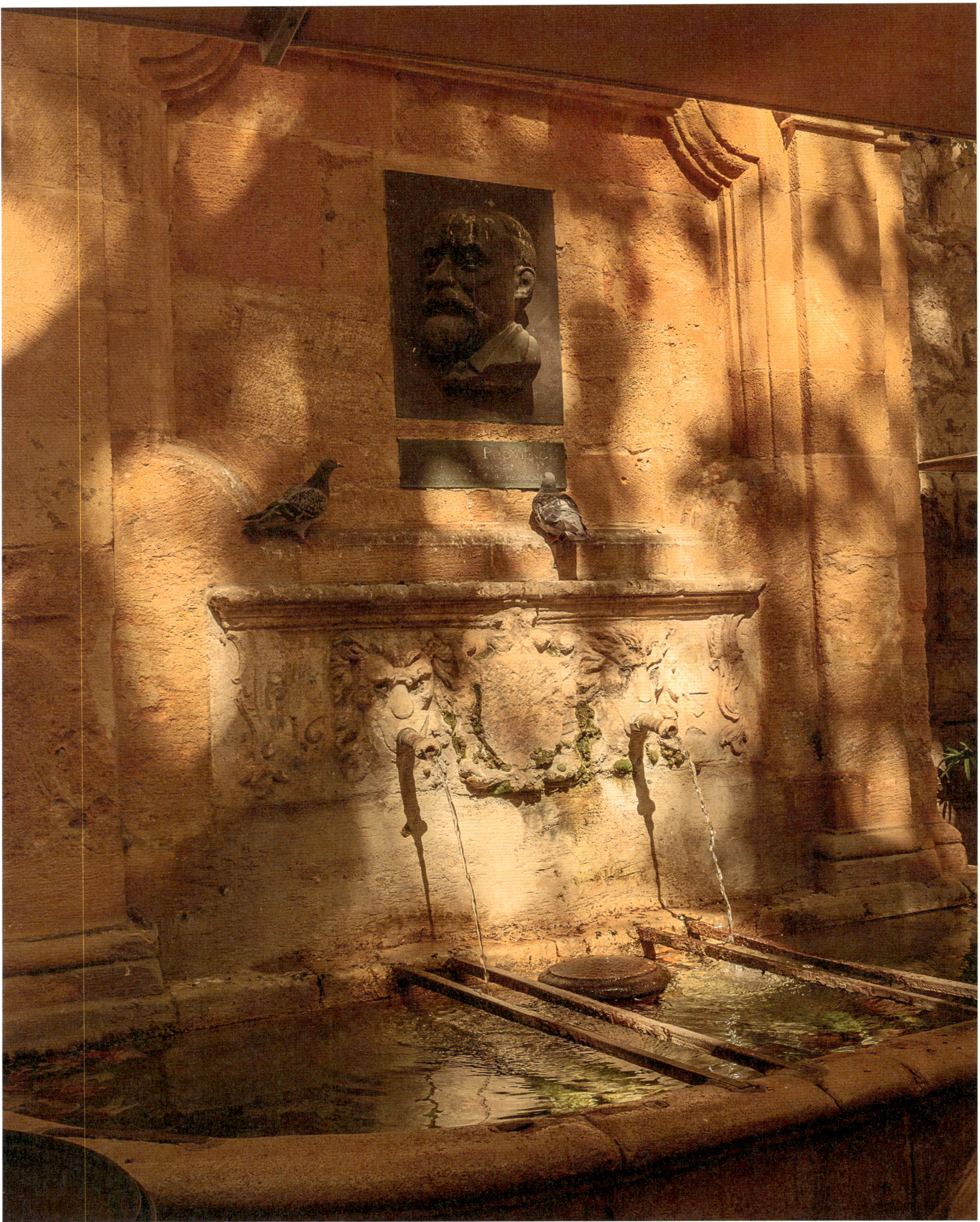

AIX-EN-PROVENCE

BOUCHES-DU-RHÔNE

SATURDAY IN THE CITY

We can't leave the Bouches-du-Rhône without a final detour to Aix-en-Provence, a city that, more than any other, embodies the prototypical beauty of Provence. We don't quite know why, but we always go to Aix on Saturdays. Maybe it's because of the lively hum of the markets and cafés, or maybe it's the day's easy-going, harmonious rhythm, which seems to echo across town. We've made it to the city center and are already wandering through the antiques market on Cours Mirabeau, the city's grand boulevard lined with plane trees.

Les Deux Garçons—favorite café of Cézanne and Cocteau—hasn't reopened after a fire a few years ago. So, we get breakfast to go, which in this case is coffee from a market stall and a bag of warm madeleines from Christophe. Aix is best explored at a slow pace anyway, snack in hand. Not that they last; it's more like new snacks keep popping into them as one market full of delicacies leads straight to the next. Greengrocers at Place de Verdun display heaps of fresh artichokes and yellow, green, and red tomatoes.

At Place de la Mairie, armfuls of lilies and bushy hydrangeas spill from the stalls. Bakers at Place Richelme sell crusty baguettes and pastries for an afternoon treat. But the squares suddenly fall quiet when the church bells chime in the afternoon. Now the market squares are swept clean, and the bustle relocates to bars and restaurants, of which there are so many in Aix that you can't keep track. It's a pulsating Where's-Waldo-esque scene beneath canvas

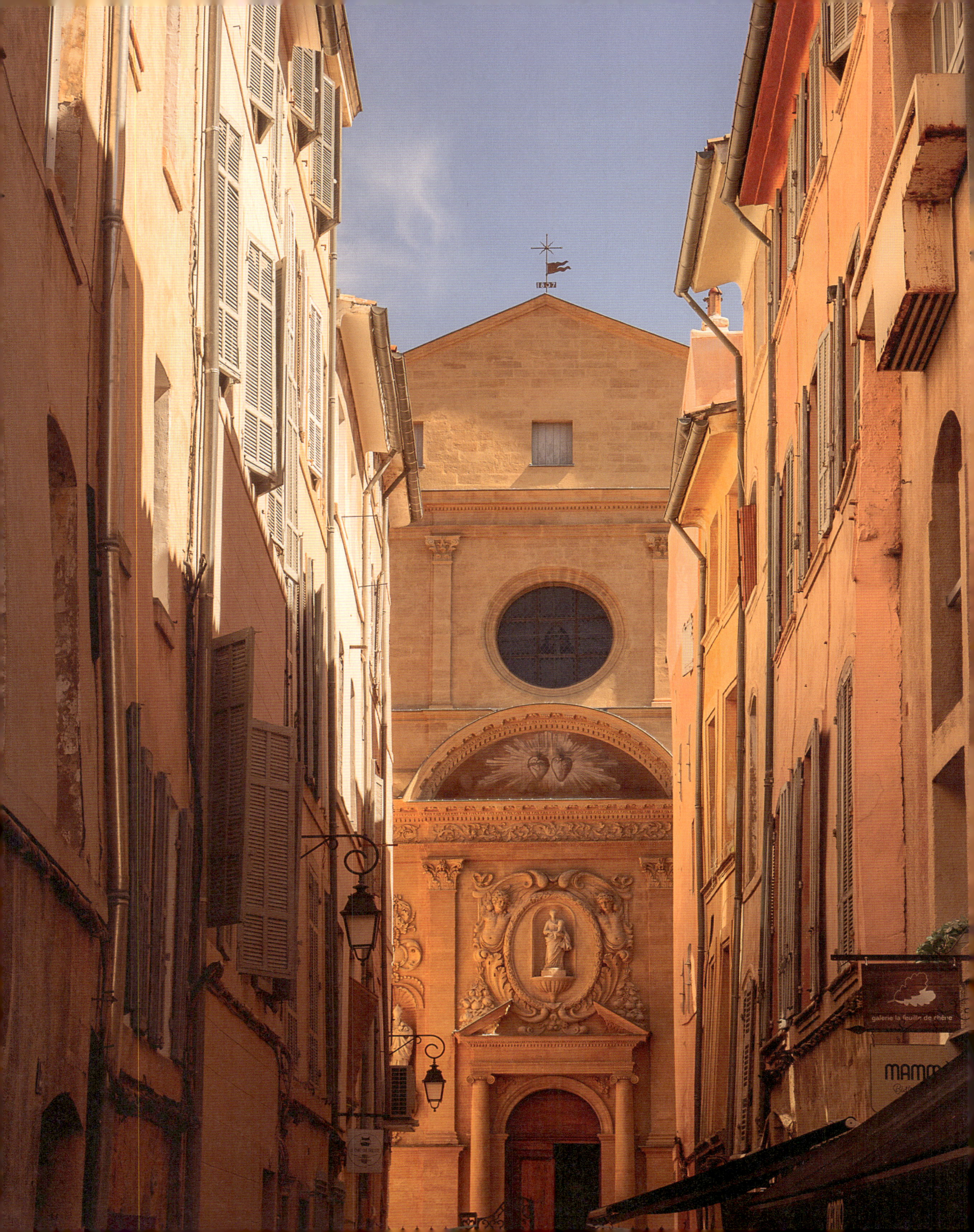
1857
galerie la feuille de chêne

awnings. There's no way to choose where to go, and we're still too sated to commit anyway, so instead the hour seems to have come for us to slip into the Musée Granet—one of France's most comprehensive art collections. A perfect Saturday in Aix.

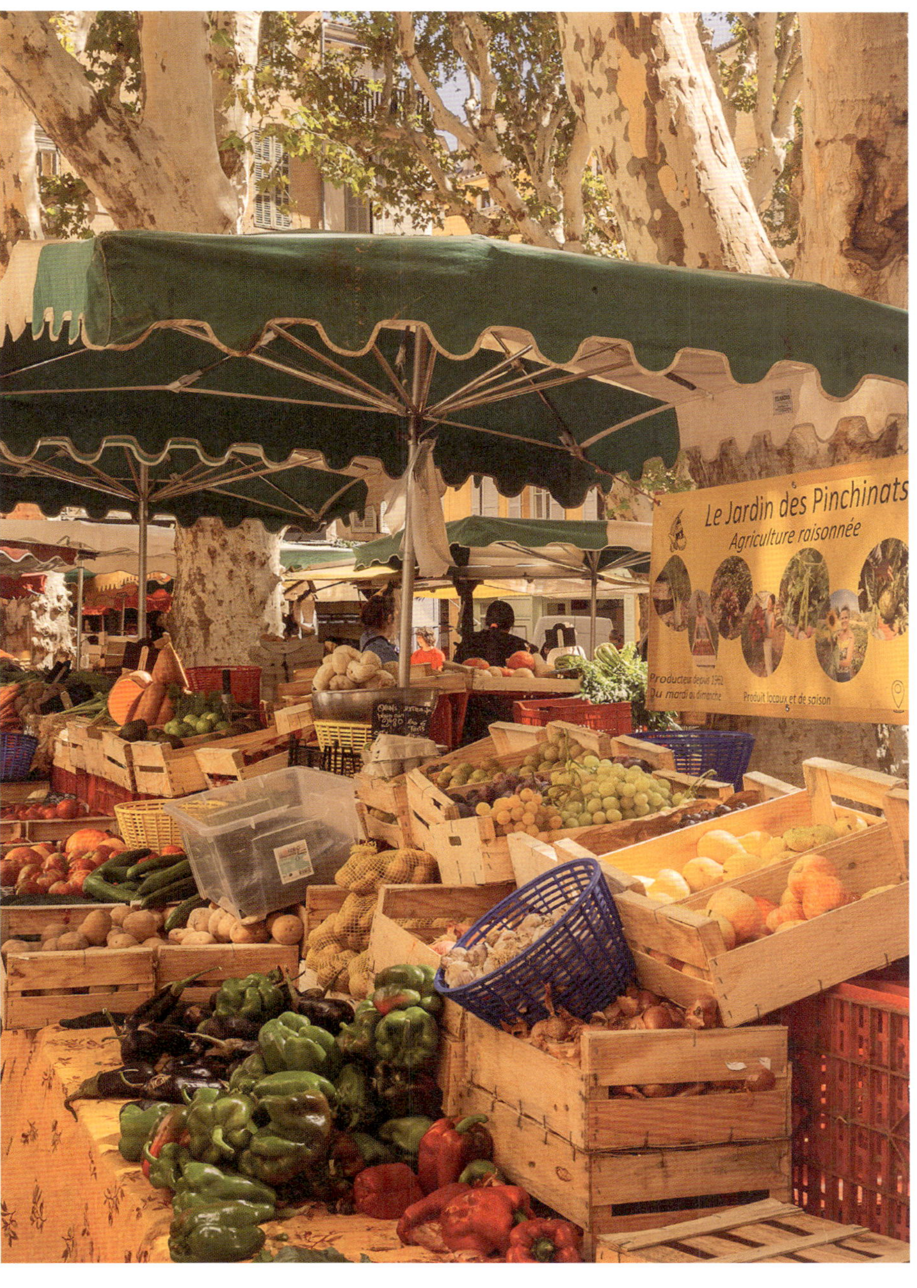

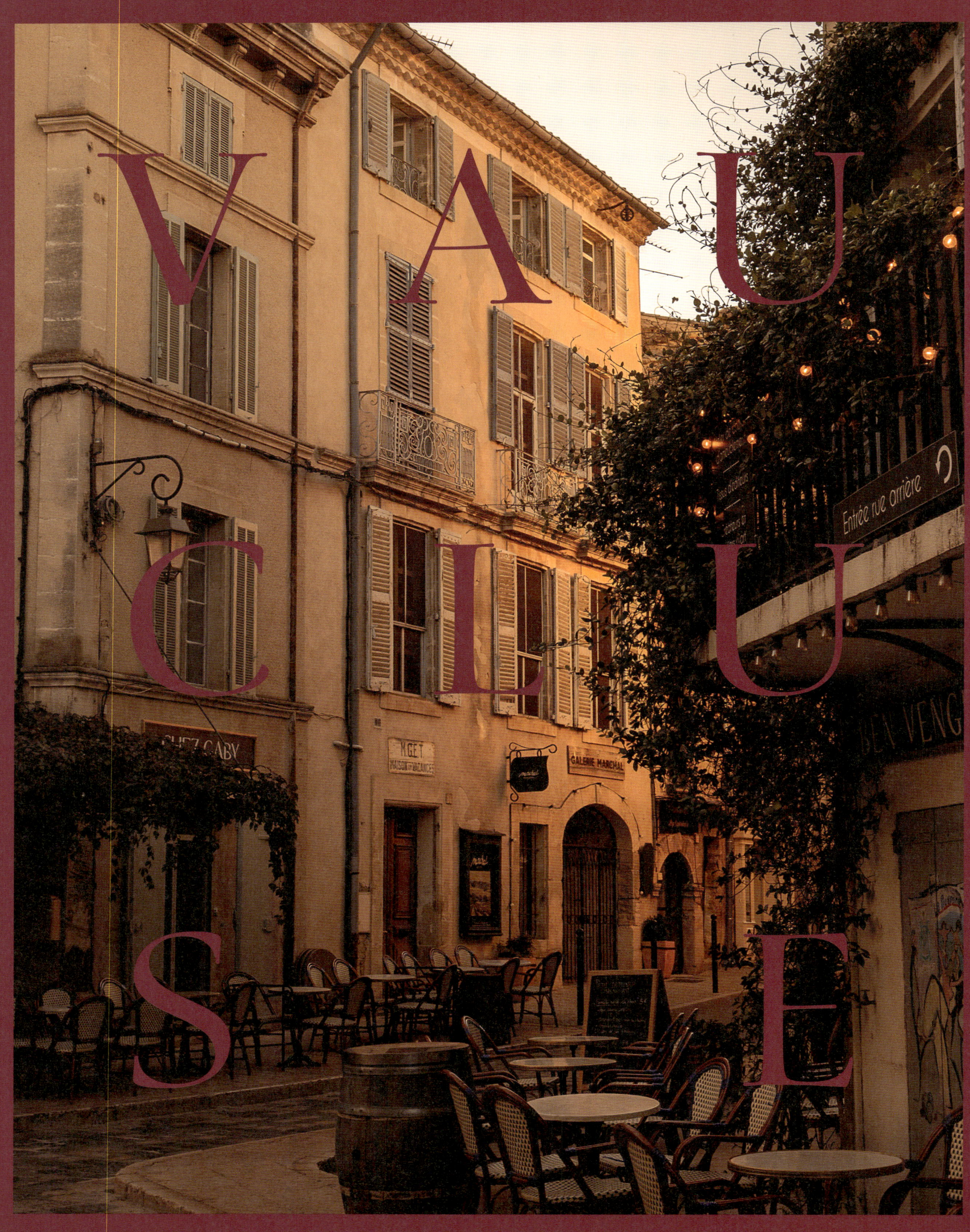
VAUCLUSE
CHEZ GABY
M.GET
GALERIE MARCHAL
Entrée rue arrière

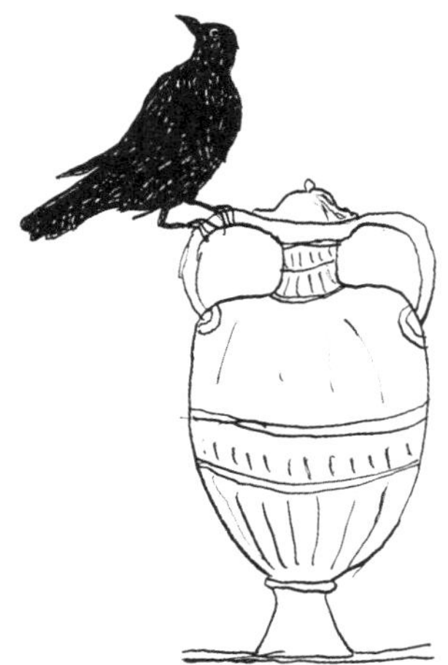

France keeps an official register of its most beautiful villages—*Les Plus Beaux Villages de France*—and Vaucluse is well represented. Whatever the list says, we think there's no other single département in Provence with such a concentration of hidden gems. Vaucluse is and will always be the département of beautiful villages. All along the gentle ridges of the Luberon massif and the valleys of the Sorgue and Coulon are villages like small jewels: sandstone, slate roofs, small forts and stone bell towers, framed by vineyards, the edges of lavender fields, and ochre cliffs. Vaucluse is where every postcard cliché and images and ideas about Provençal country life come vividly to life. Though the Côte d'Azur's polished luxury is only an hour away, Vaucluse feels worlds apart—more romantic, very rustic, and yet still unmistakably refined. Waiting for us in Vaucluse are noble châteaux, secluded monasteries and vintage curiosities next to sleek, contemporary retreats and family-run auberges along old fortifications of the Popes—a potpourri of rural Provence. To dial up the romance even more, go in late summer, when the leaves turn and when everything is enveloped in warm earth tones, the color of rust, and the green of old bottles. Summer *is* drawing to a close, so we're in Vaucluse at the best possible time of year.

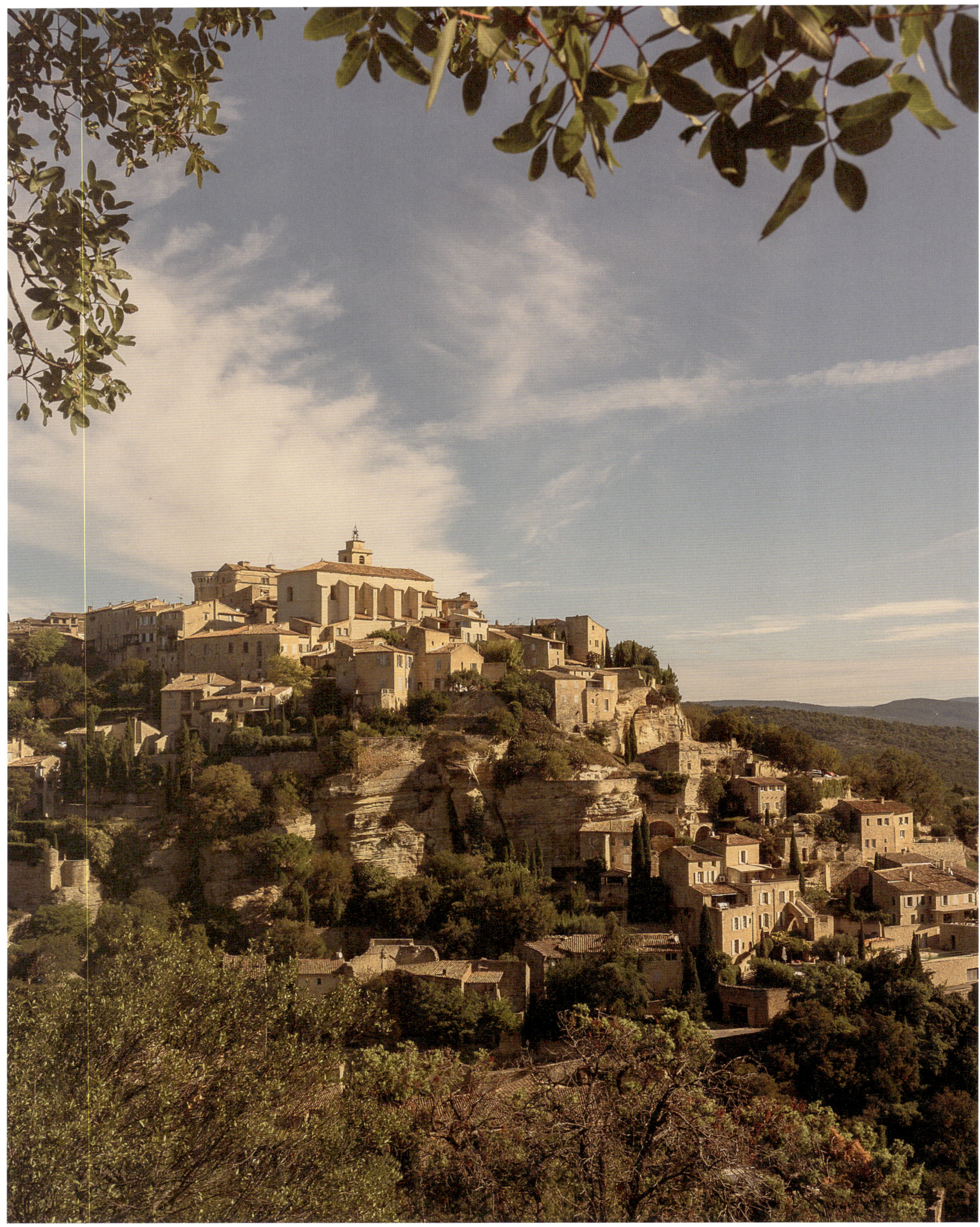

LA BASTIDE

VAUCLUSE

B O U N D L E S S

We start our tour of the villages along the Luberon massif in Gordes. Encircled by ancient ramparts, this postcard-perfect town overlooks the valley of the Coulon. As we climb the winding road toward the village center in the early morning, the last heavy wisps of fog still hover in the valley below. Gordes is tiny—you can stroll from its entrance gate to the far edge in just a few minutes—yet somehow (perhaps therefore) its narrow lanes are filled with the greatest beauty. Precisely here is where Airelles, in 2018, unveiled another in its string of fantastic hotels: La Bastide. It's a former gendarmerie station chiseled right into the stone walls across multiple levels, converted into an eighteenth-century–style French country château. Inside, Charles and Marianne—who manage and work at the La Bastide—greet us with open arms and golden smiles, ready to guide us through the interwoven corridors and staircases.

Every detail channels a refined French country aesthetic: carefully curated antiques and paintings, rustic fabric wallpaper, Empire-style and boudoir lighting with burled wood accents on each of the six floors, spanning 36 rooms and six suites. The château seems boundless, as is the quality of the accommodation. After coffee at the bar, with its red decor, we walk around the sun-drenched terraces, swim in the pool overlooking the valley, browse the library, and savor an early dinner in the conservatory at La Table de La Bastide before finally settling into our room. The old brass indicator dings as we step onto the third floor and enter our suite, which is decorated with rose-patterned textile wallpaper, antique rugs, and a featherbed on a wooden frame in a seamless extension of the country-estate theme. We fall into bed, exhausted. But then a bell rings. There's someone at the door.

After consuming excessively, we had decided to skip dessert. Well, La Bastide was having none of it: They have sent us madeleines to snack on before bed. With our first evening here now winding down, we've barely scratched the surface of this hotel's offerings. There's too much in tiny Gordes and this enormous hotel to explore in a single day—or in a short write-up.

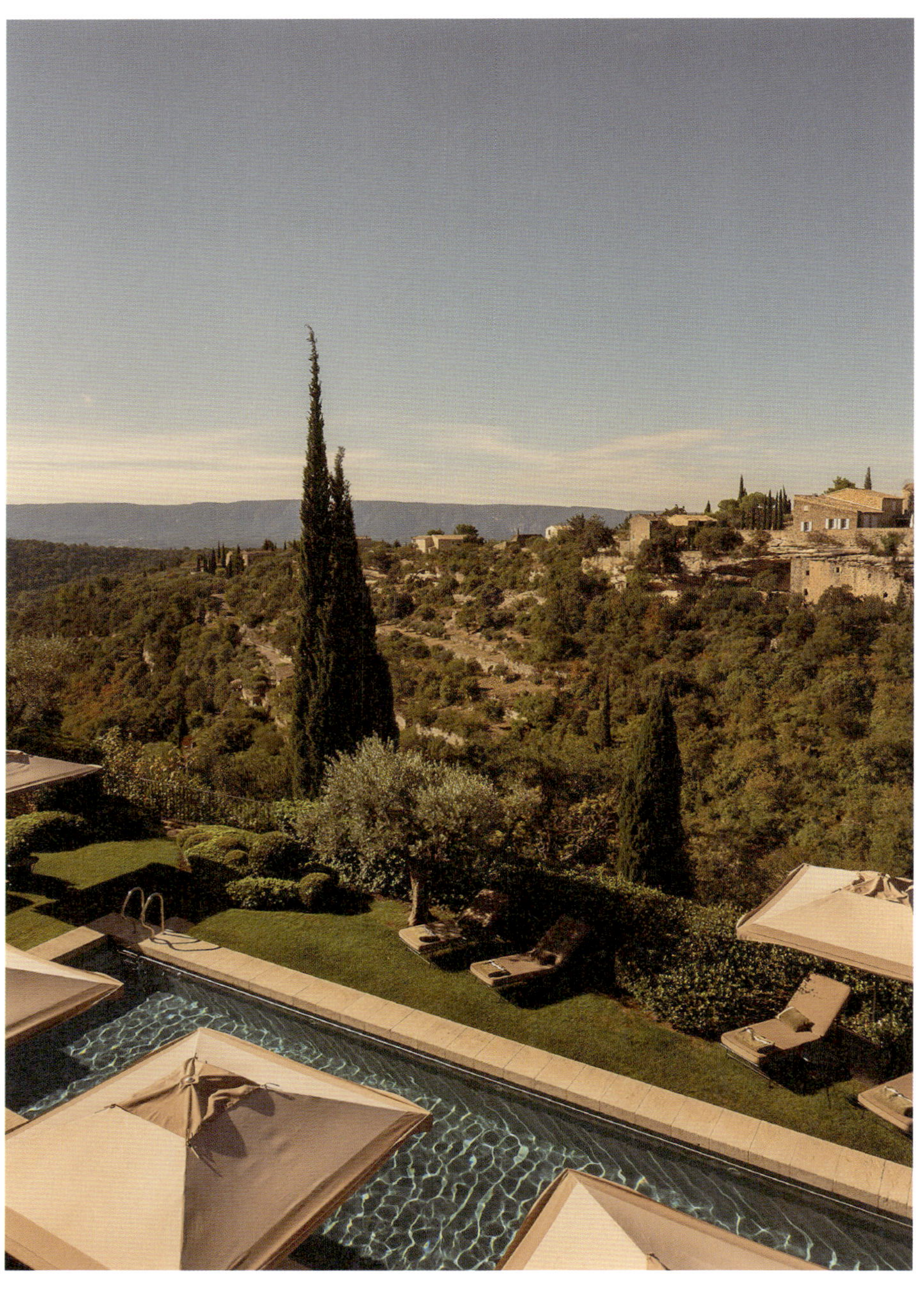

The outdoor pool on one of La Bastide's many terraces. Charles, who always has an open ear for his guests, invites them to a get-together here once a week with champagne flutes. Feel-good management par excellence.

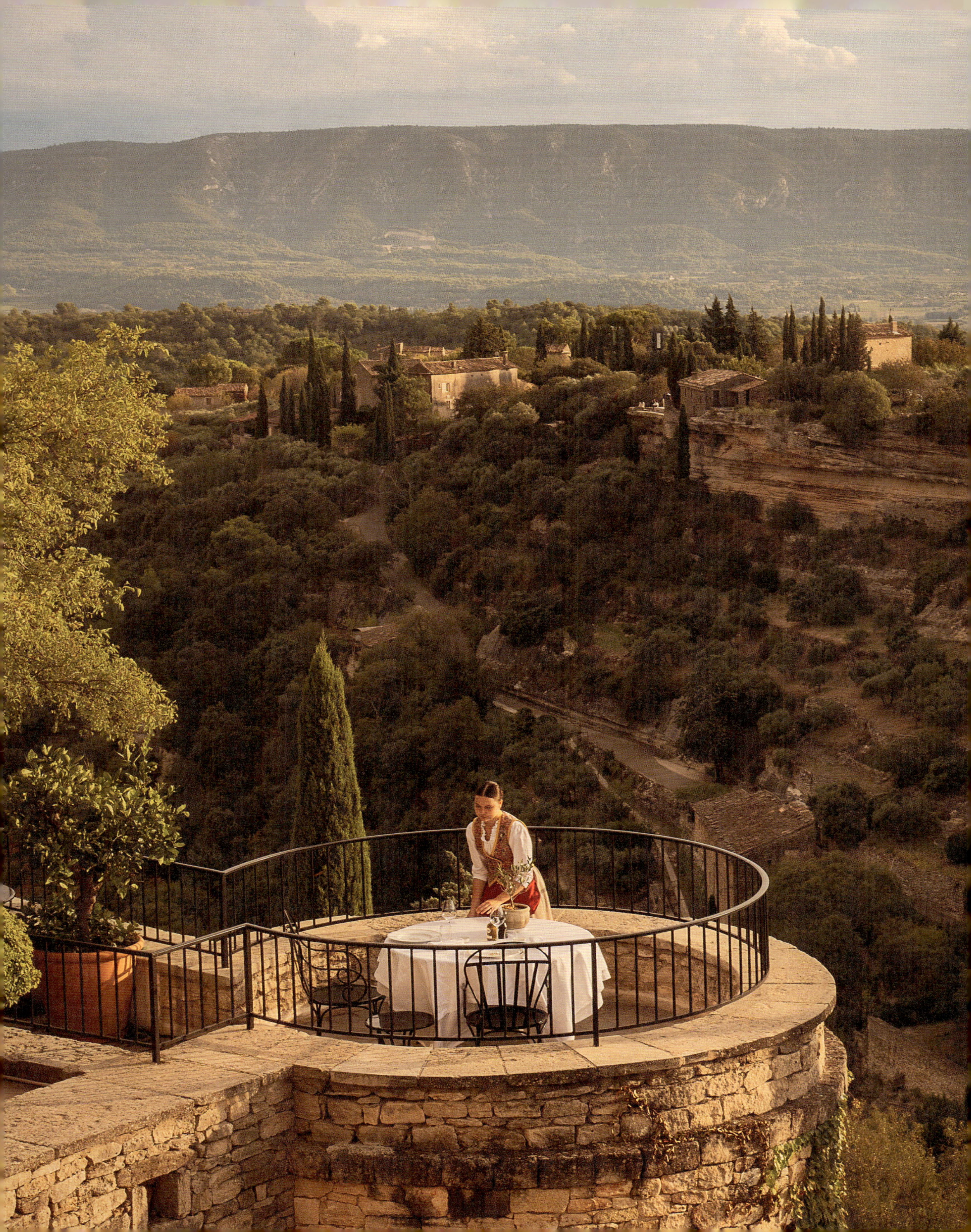

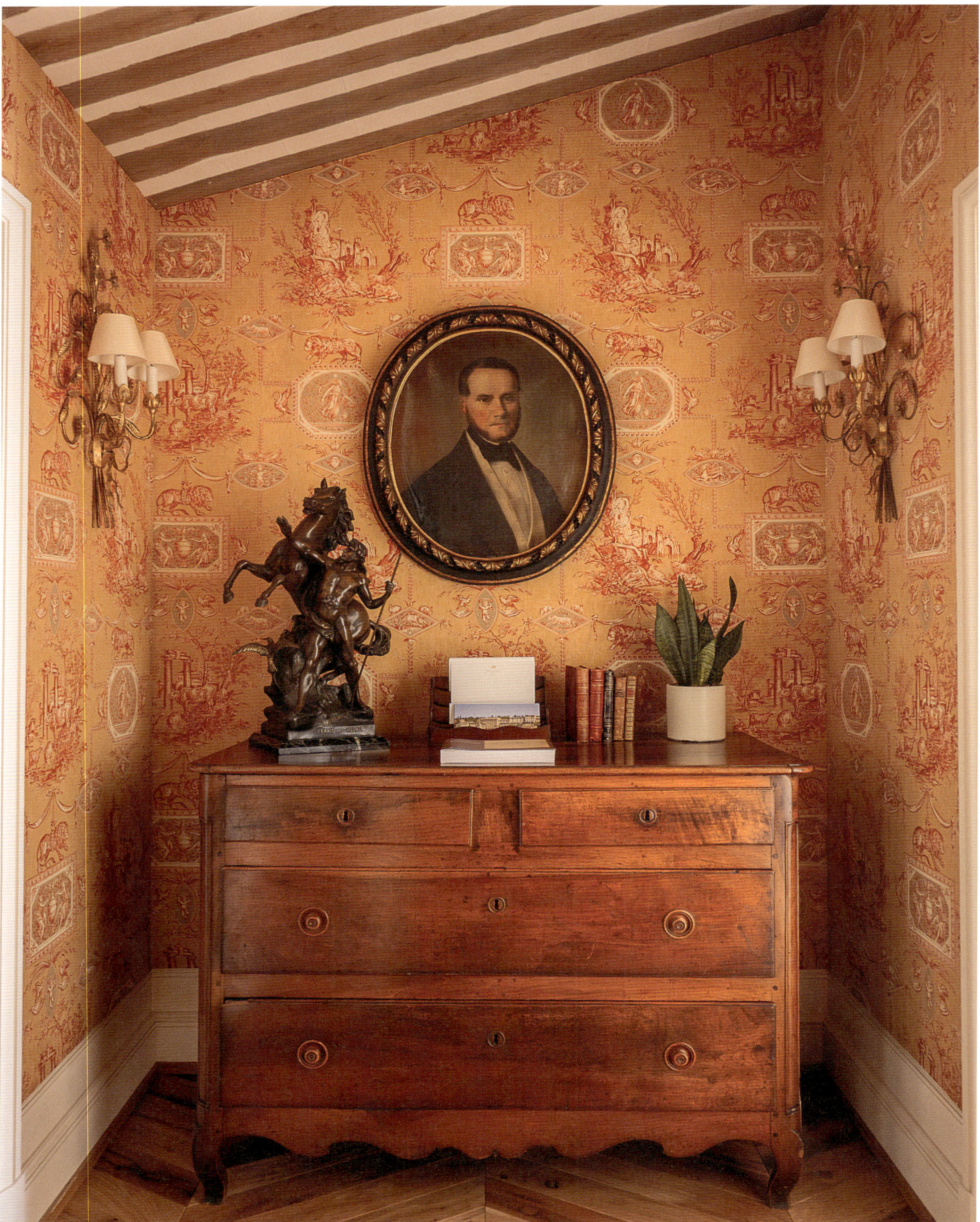

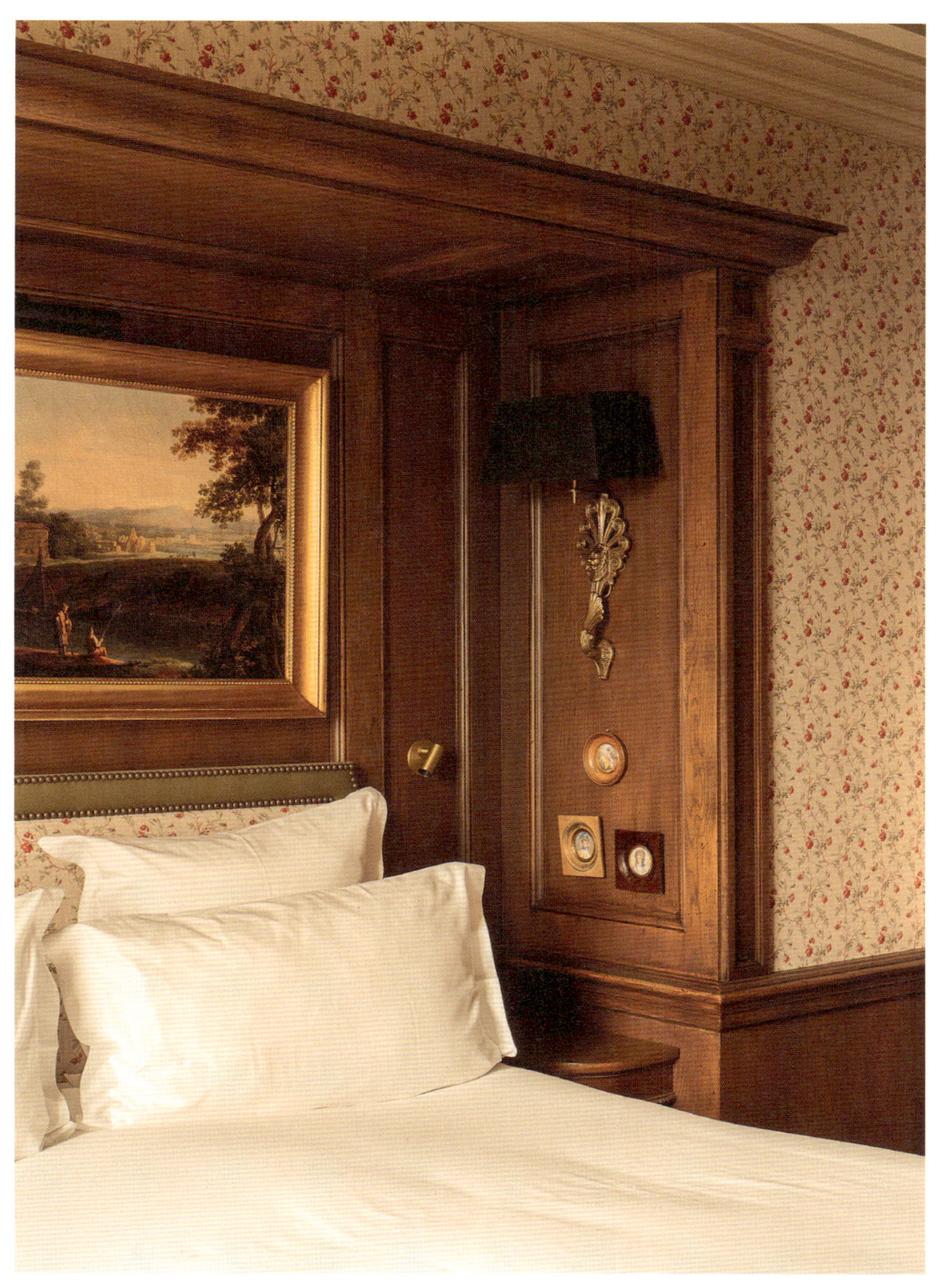

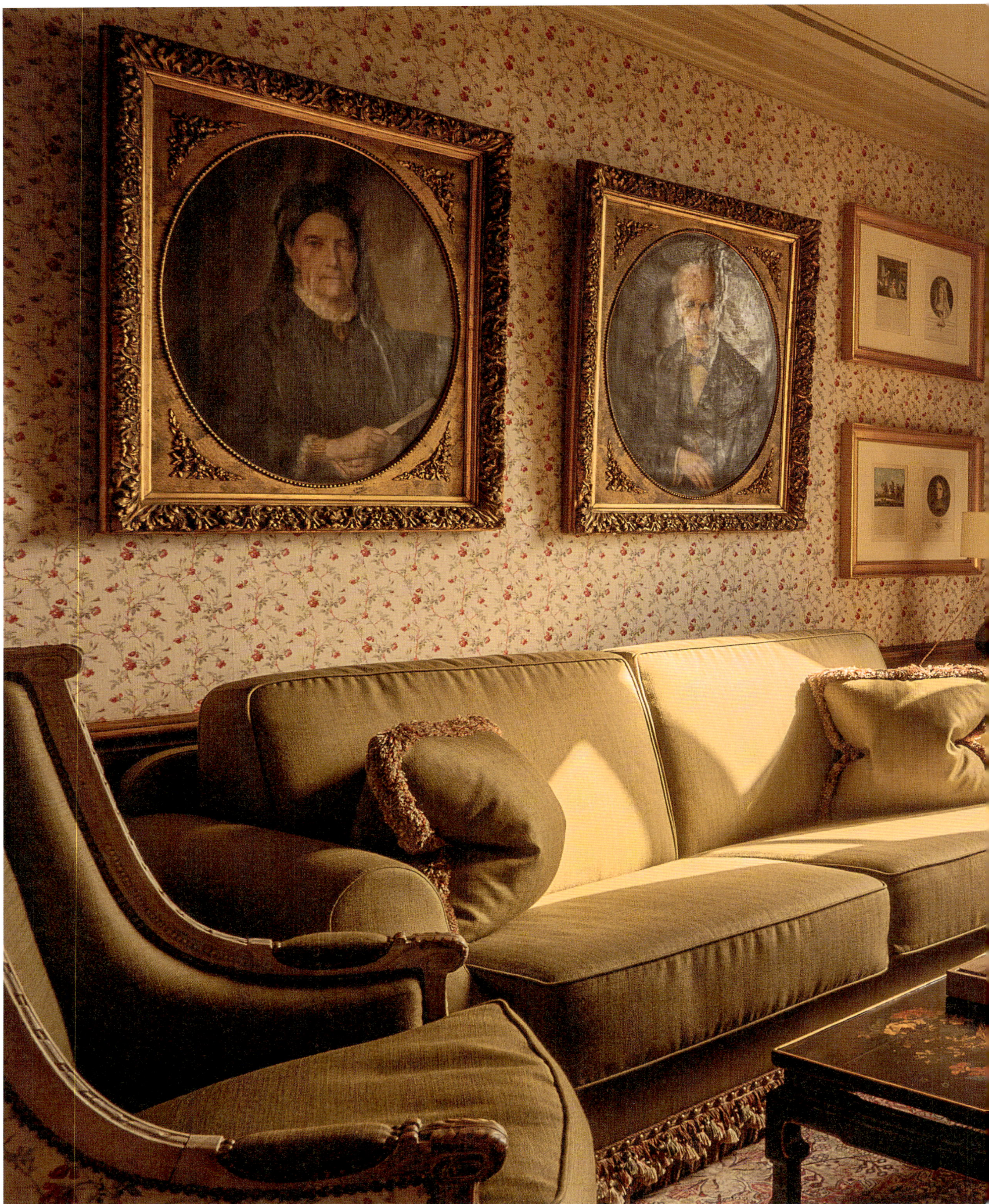

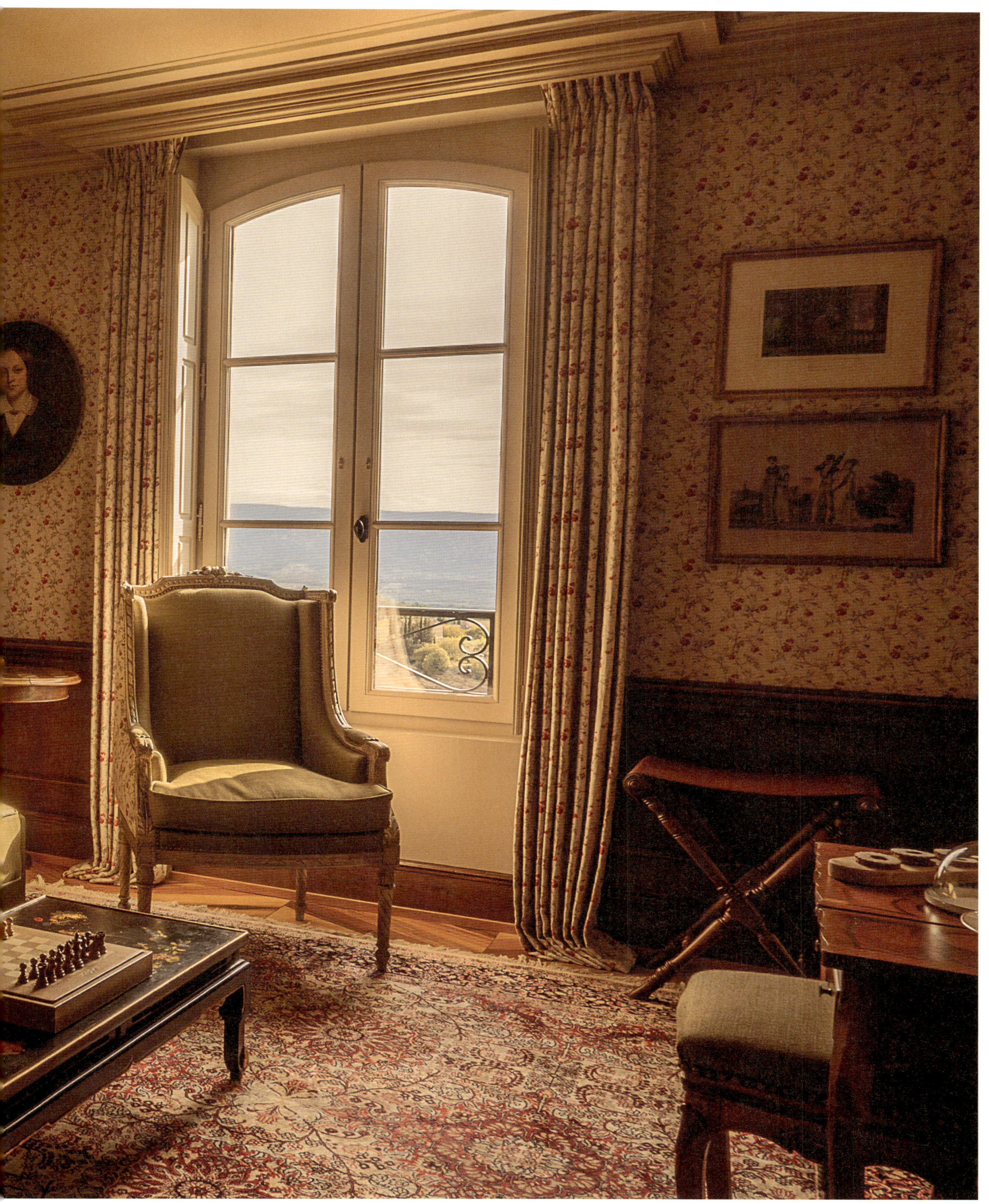

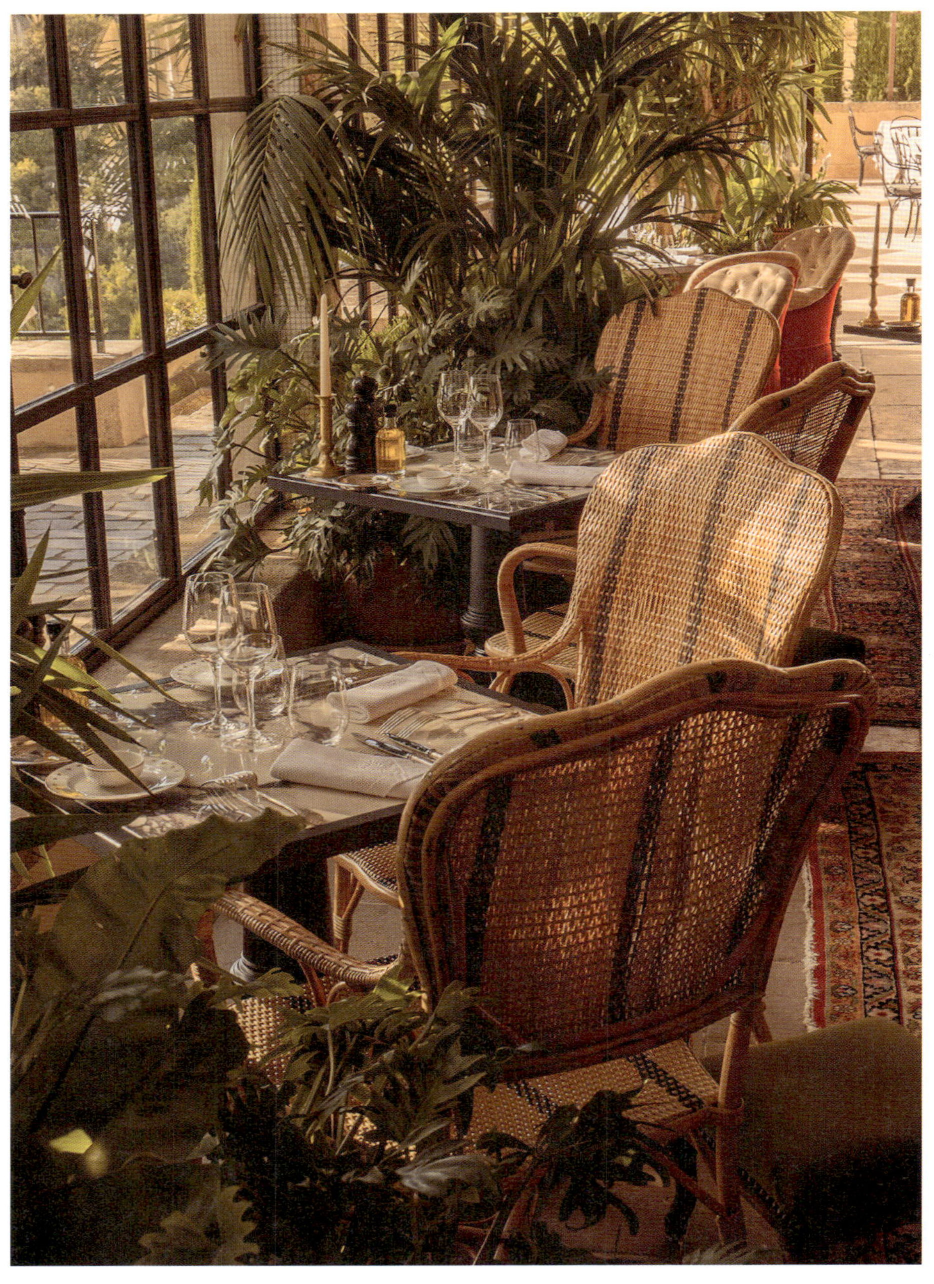

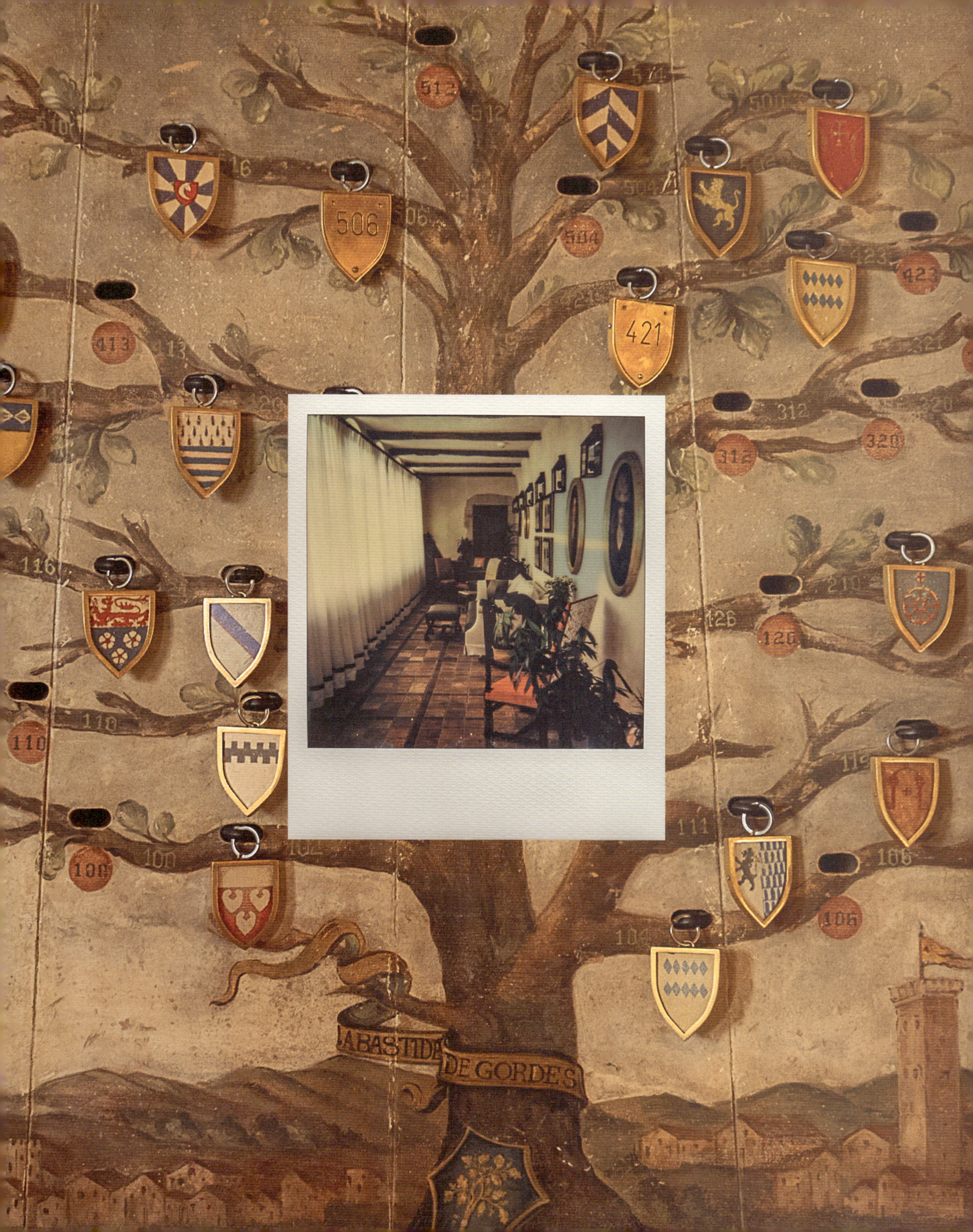
506
421
LABASTIDE
DE GORDES

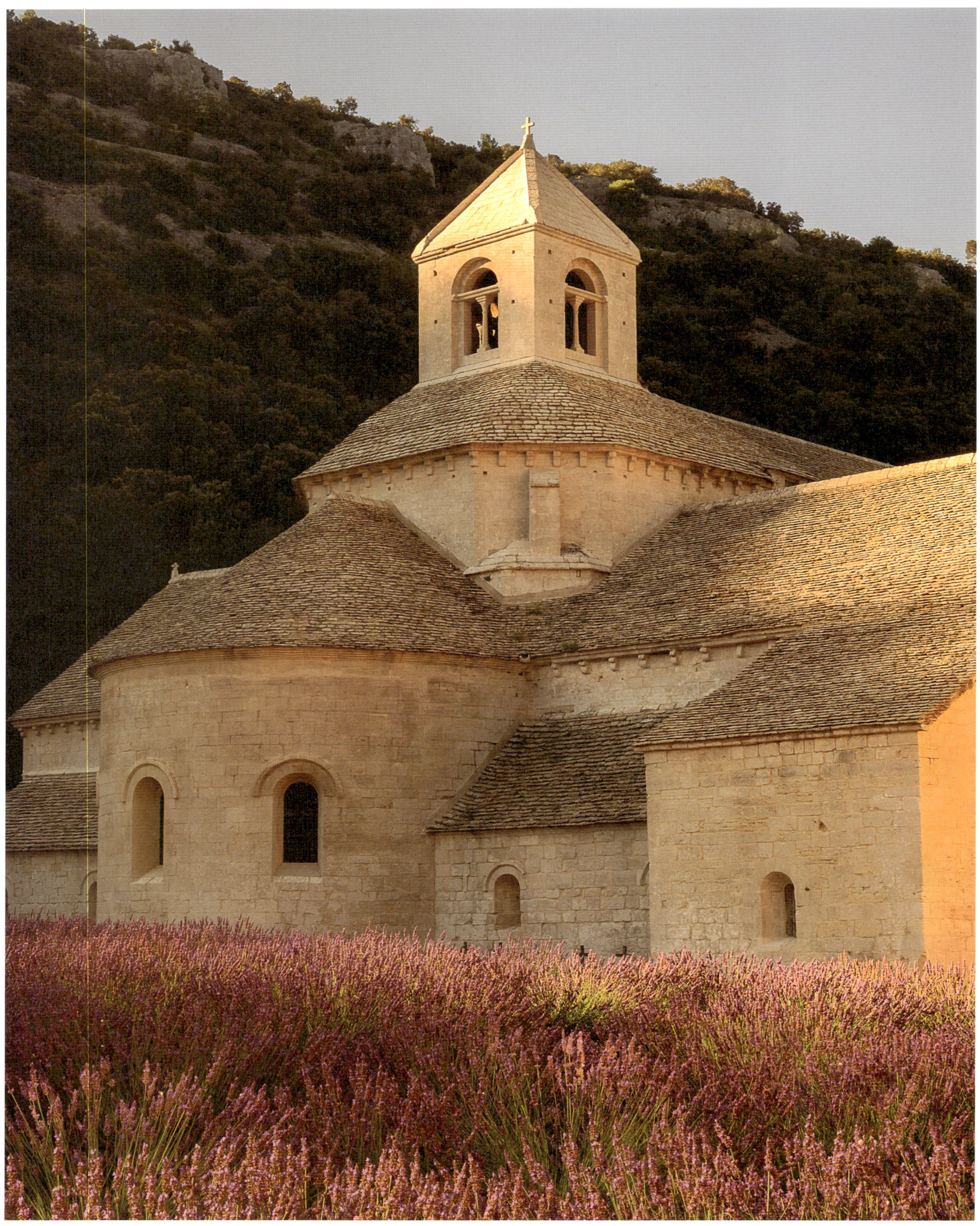

NOTRE-DAME DE SÉNANQUE

VAUCLUSE

QUIET RETREAT

It takes a lot to get us out of the plush featherbed at La Bastide at 5 o'clock in the morning. Or does it? Getting up at this hour certainly feels like no small feat. But sunrise is the most enchanting time of day to take in today's destination. Not a soul stirs, not in the hotel and not in the village. It's total solitude in the orange glow of the street lamps as we walk along the gently curving Rue de la Combe.

We walk to the very edge of this hilltop town, going down steep streets to a small wooded area in the valley. Dawn begins to chase away the night and the sky goes from black to blue-grey as we come to a stone arch with a copper cross that marks the entrance to the abbey of Notre-Dame de Sénanque. This abbey has been operated by the Order of Cistercians since the twelfth century. Its members live here in silence, removed from the world's troubles and renouncing worldly possessions. Visitors in search of peace and quiet can rent space for a retreat here if they like. Cars and telephones are out of bounds; meals are taken in silence. It's an absolute return to the self in a sheltered vale. As we continue walking past large vegetable gardens, we hear the ethereal choral sounds of early Mass drifting across the grounds before the abbey finally comes into view. It's a relatively simple structure, built of mossy sandstone and framed by fields of lavender and protected by the forested slopes of the rocky massif. Today we're the first tourists to arrive; here and there, we see monks in brown habit, quietly murmuring in prayer. Now the sun has risen but has not cleared the hills to illuminate the abbey.

It's a magical, almost mystical scene pervaded by a rare and contemplative quiet. Our retreat (this time) consists of the three hours we spend together in silence outside the walls of the monastery before the hordes of tourists arrive. Sometimes, it doesn't take much to get us out of bed early. Quite the opposite, in fact.

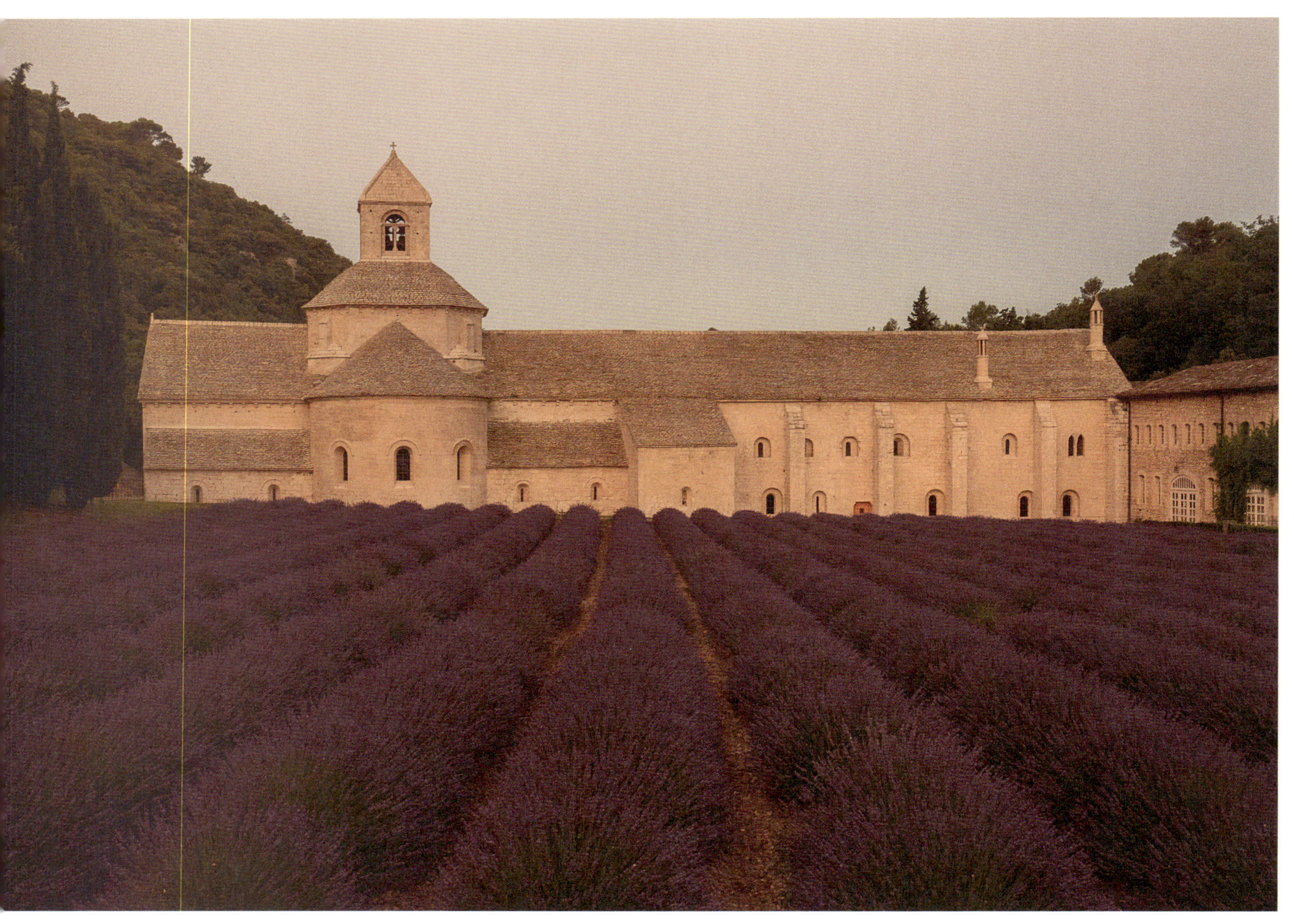

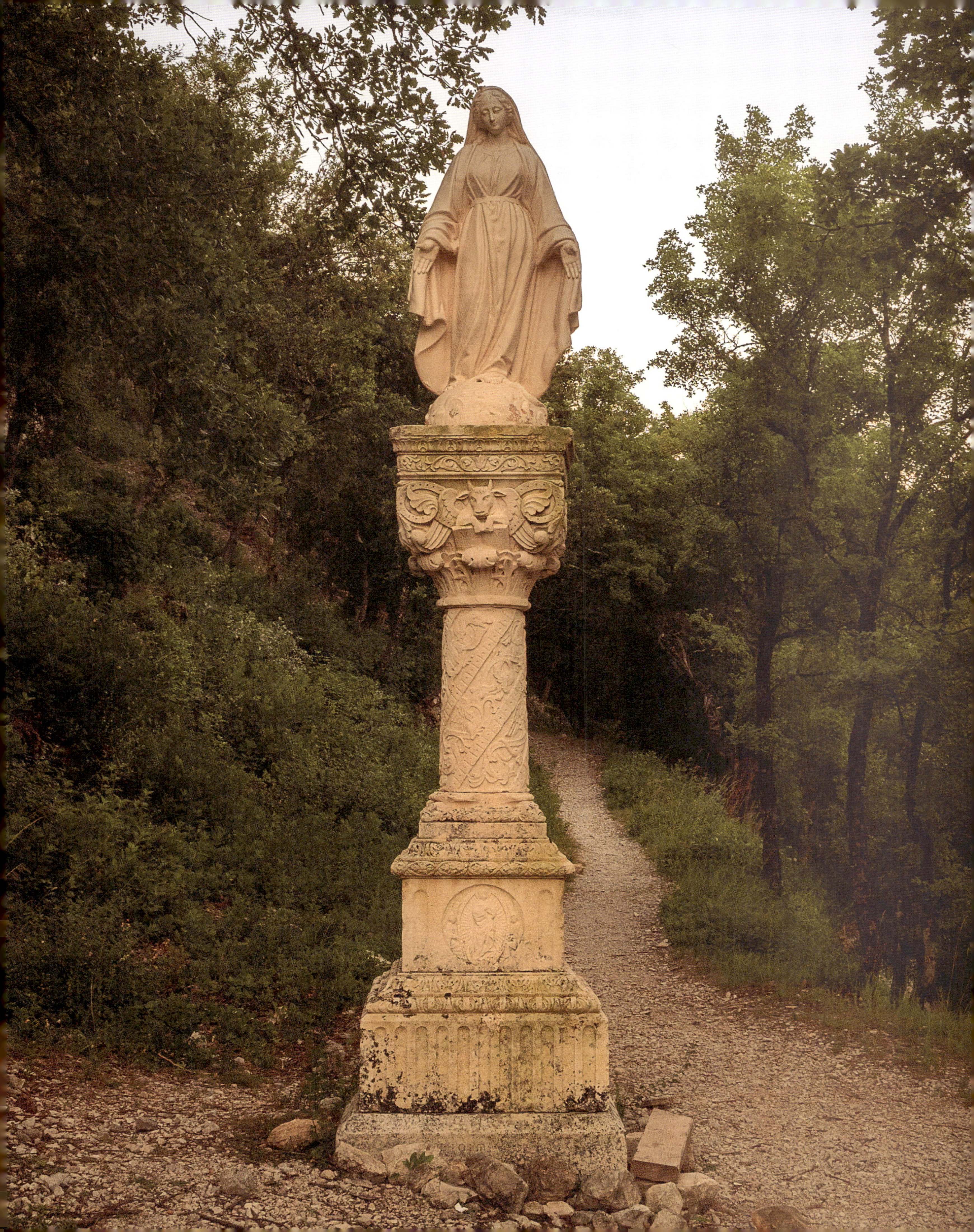

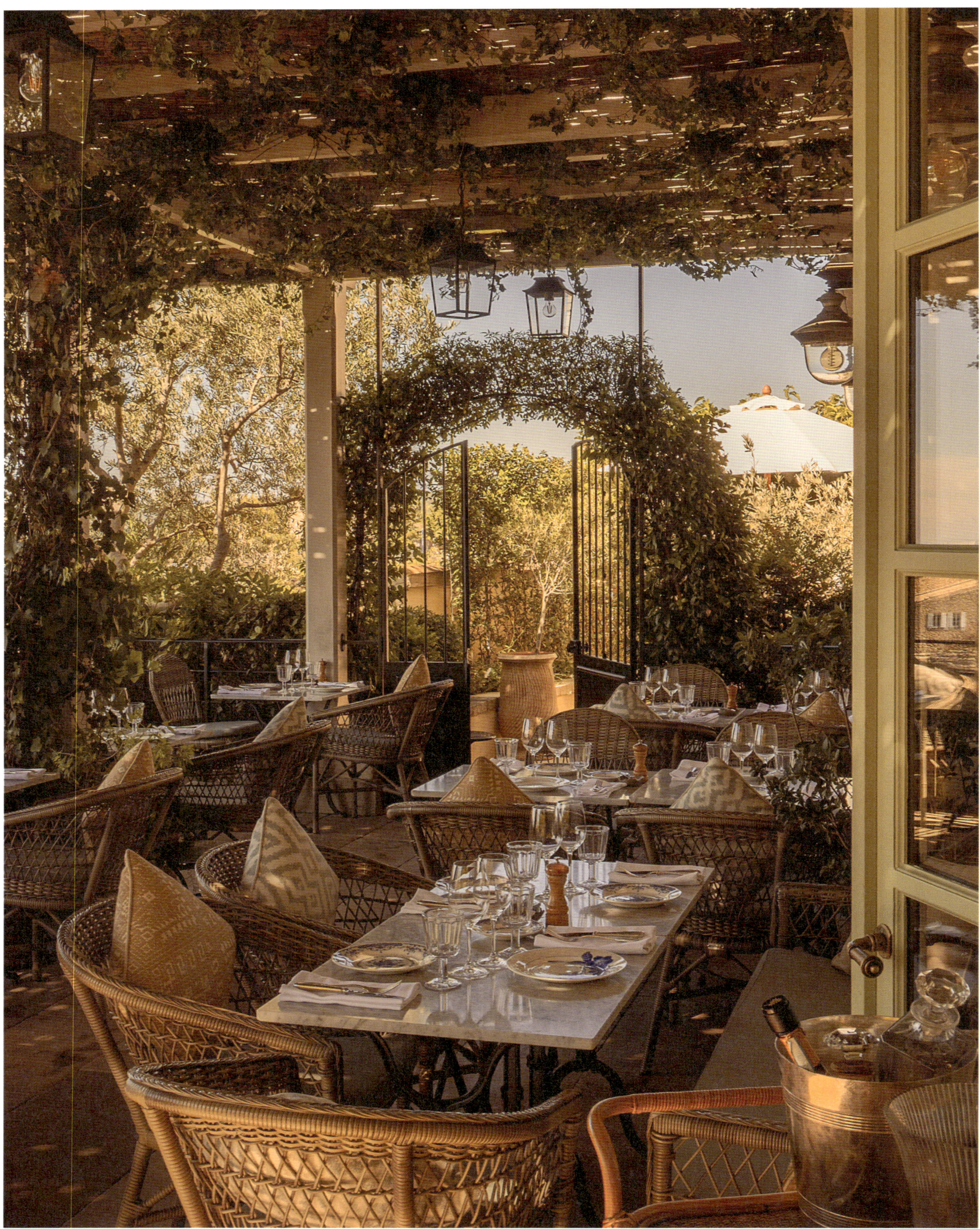

CLOVER GORDES

VAUCLUSE

GARDEN TABLE AT EMILY'S

The day is still young as we hike back to Gordes after our visit to the abbey. A warm midday breeze comes up from the valley. There's not a cloud in the sky. Before us lies a panorama best enjoyed over a light lunch and a glass of rosé, at no less suitable a place than Clover Gordes, one of four restaurants operated by Airelles and the latest *expérience culinaire* by Jean-François Piège. The multi-starred chef has been wowing Parisian epicureans for years at his Clover restaurants. Here in Gordes, he has returned to his Provençal roots. The heavy green wooden door opens at half past twelve. Hotel guests and external visitors are welcome. The room inside has the welcoming atmosphere of a brasserie, with pale-blue wood paneling, orange leather banquettes, and bistro chairs. But it's the terrace that holds our gaze. Beneath cascades of ivy and lantern light, white marble tables are set with blue-and-white pottery and crystal glassware, framed by the sweeping valley beneath Gordes. We feel as if we're sitting down at a carefully laid garden table at the house of our friends in Provence. It's also a table where a certain Emily from Paris once sat; she always knows best.

The first passage of our lunch is an olive oil tasting—four distinct presses, from fiery and peppery to grassy and mellow—with focaccia still warm from the oven. Next comes caramelized eggplant over mustard ice cream. Stuffed, garden-fresh zucchini blossoms materialize for our entrée. At Clover, Piège champions the integrity of Provençal cooking as well as his unabashed love of vegetables. It's the best of life's simplest pleasures, not to mention pure heaven for vegetarians. Condensation beads off our glasses of rosé onto the linen tablecloth in the midday heat. Lunch ends with a rich chocolate gratin served sizzling from a cast-iron pan. It almost lays us out for the afternoon. Our minds wander off to where we're having a nightcap on one of the brasserie's cool leather couches. But before you can stick a fork in us, Charles whisks us off to the weekly get-together in the hotel's garden, for champagne at sunset and a stunning finale to this garden party at our friend's house.

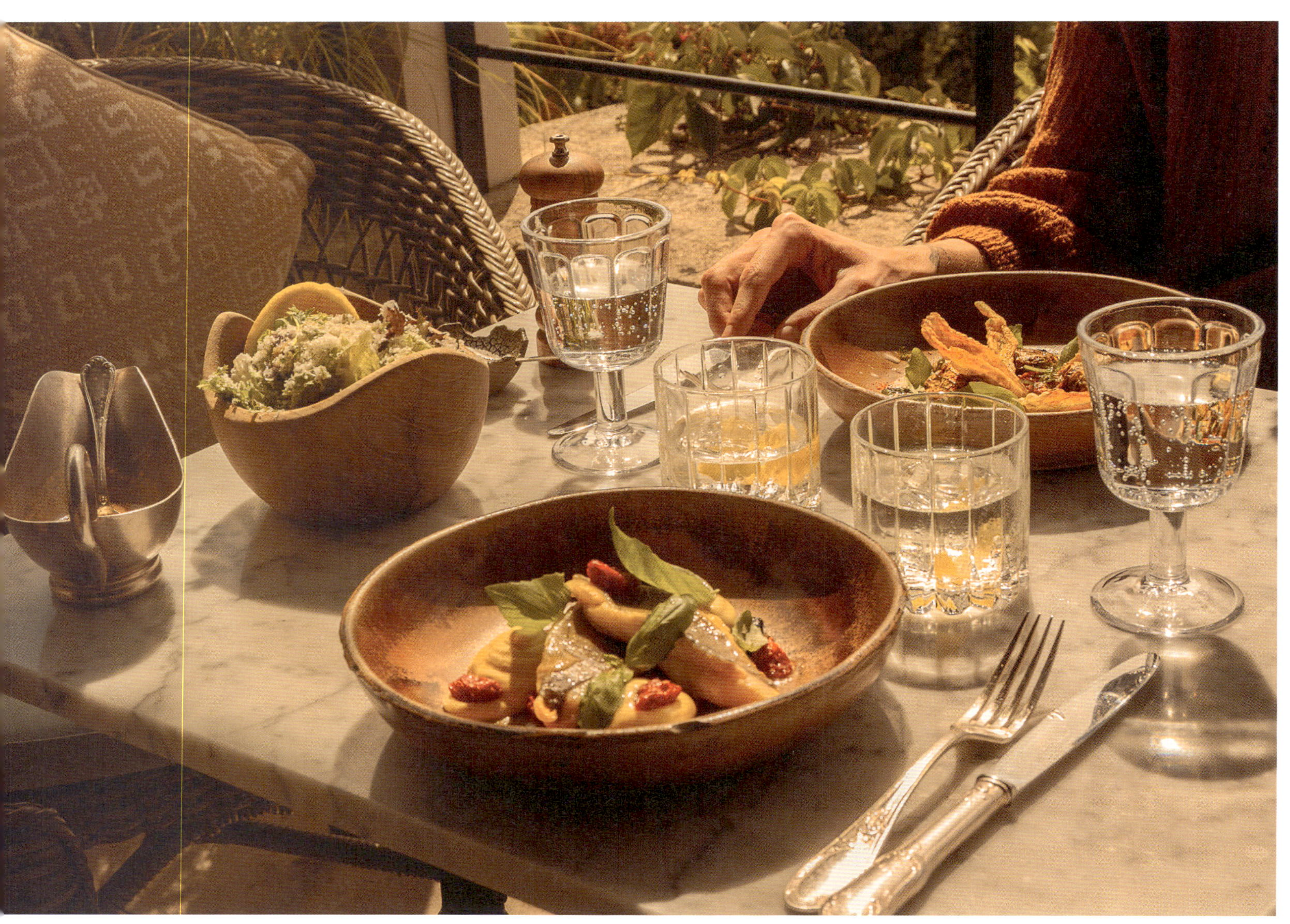

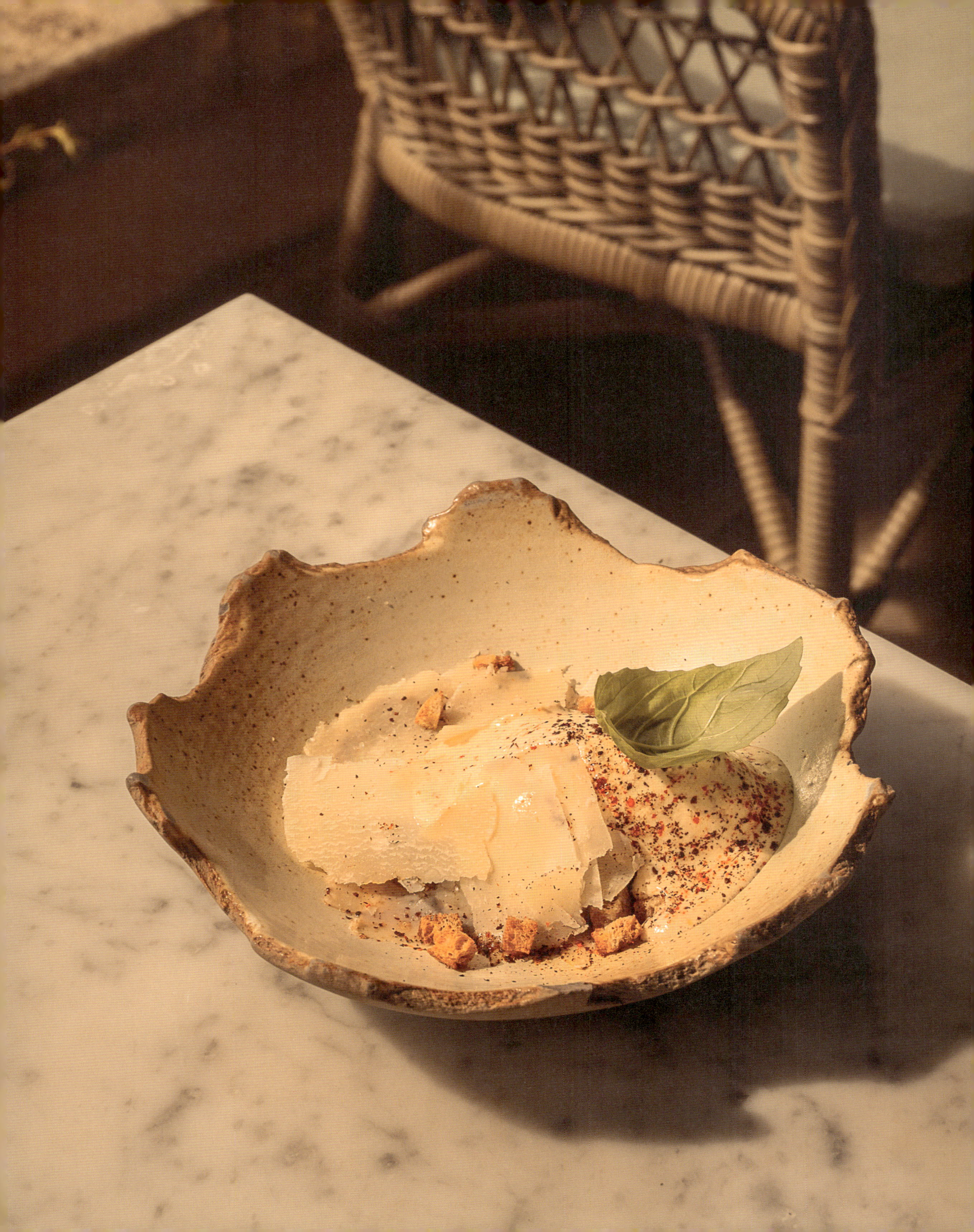

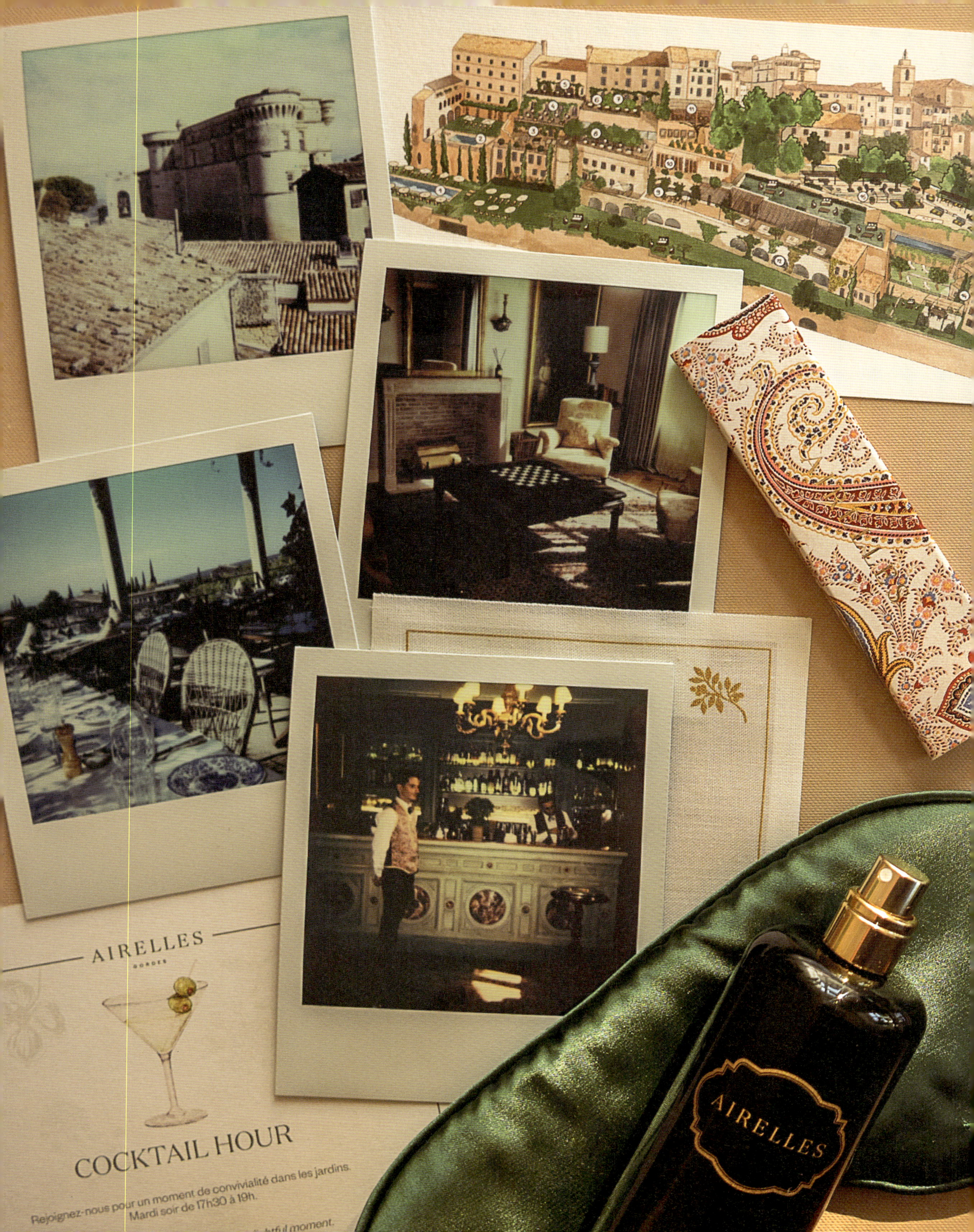
AIRELLES
GORDES
COCKTAIL HOUR
Rejoignez-nous pour un moment de convivialité dans les jardins.
Mardi soir de 17h30 à 19h.
AIRELLES

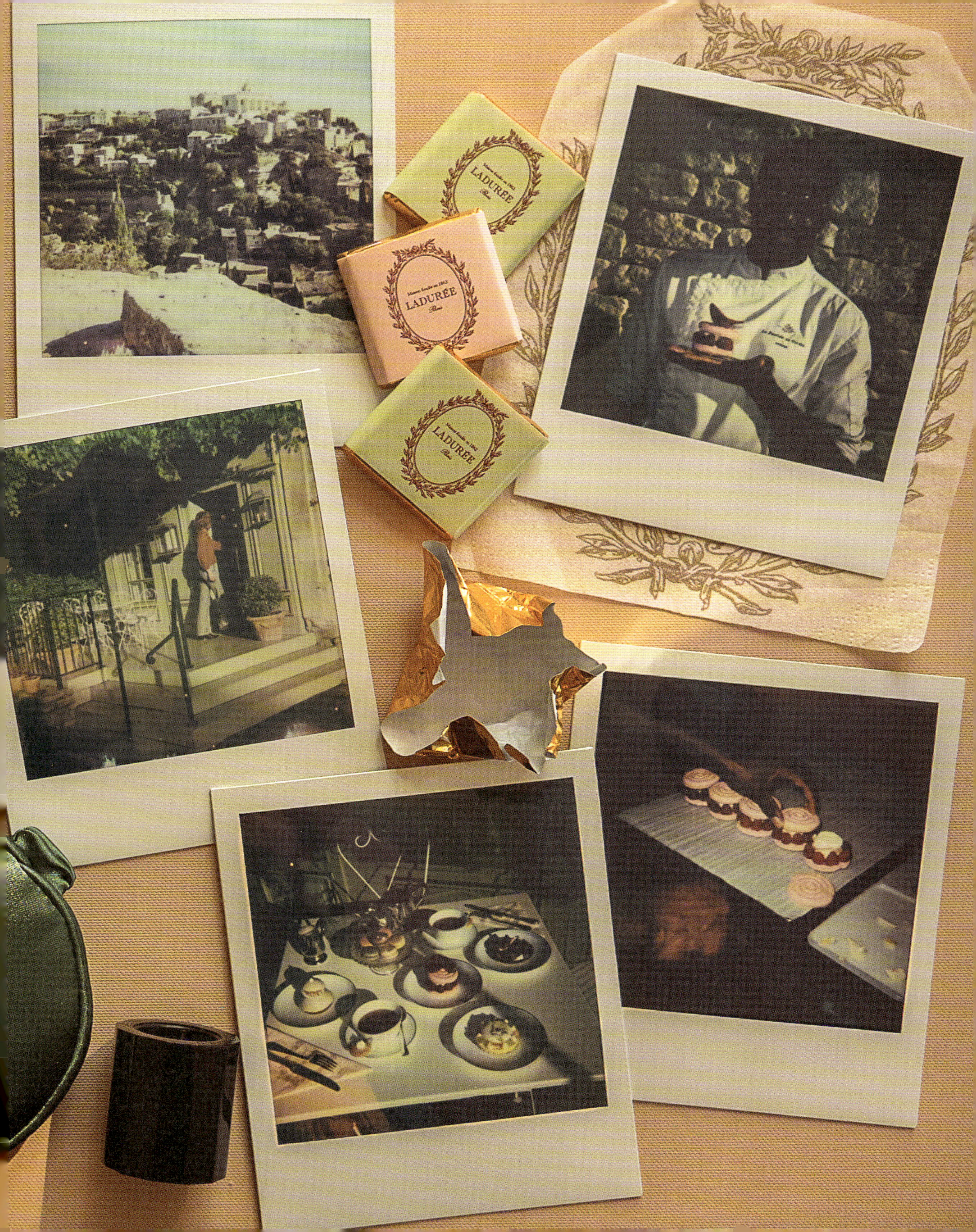
LADURÉE
LADURÉE
LADURÉE

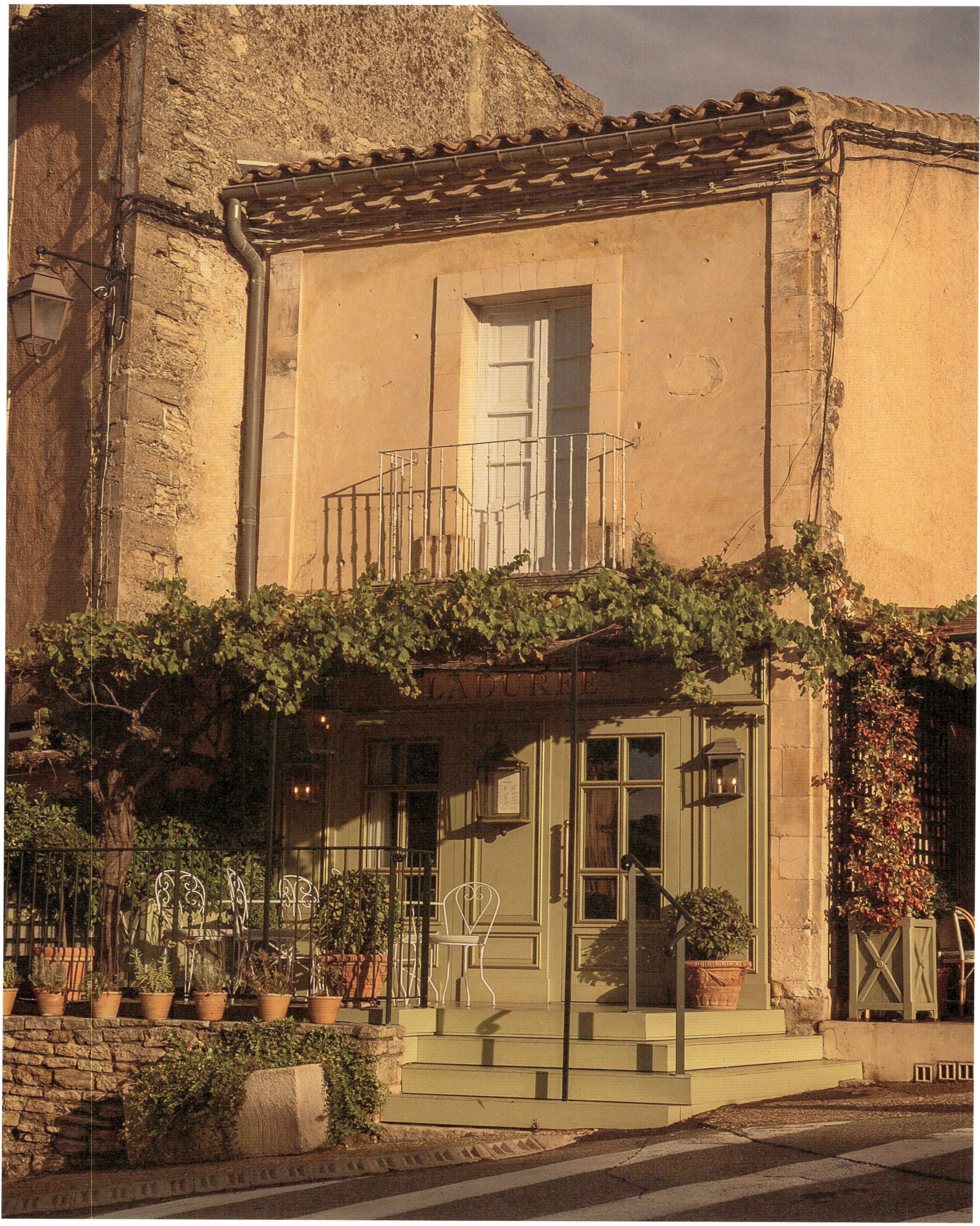
LADUREE

LADURÉE

VAUCLUSE

LA BELLE ET LA BÊTE

"Beauty and the Beast" takes place in a fairy-tale French village—no one knows which one, but Gordes certainly fits the bill. Picture a petite central square with a fountain, tin lanterns, and rustic sandstone houses with slate roofs and pale-blue shutters over wavy old casement glass. La Bastide seamlessly blends into the scene. But the hotel has gone beyond the château and brought its own café to the village. And it's not just any café: Airelles, tirelessly pursuing the most luxurious and the most desirable of all things, has teamed up with world-renowned macaron manufacture Ladurée—to open a shop on Gordes's central square. We naturally head there at tea time. Beneath a vine-draped, pastel-green veranda in the front of a charming two-story house, we find the entrance. Even sweeter and more romantic than the location and scenery is the pile of wares on display: rows of every color of macaron, exquisite tartelettes, éclairs, and all the other enchanting deliciousness of a French pâtisserie, all baked on the premises.

Before tea service begins, we are nabbed by *chef* Emanuel and shown to the kitchen. In a gleaming copper bowl, he whips up Chantilly cream, selects individual rose petals, raspberries, and lychees, and lines up large, ruby-red macaron biscuits, which he then assembles into the house's legendary Ispahan macaron, a true pinnacle of creation. Now seated on the veranda, overlooking the market square, floral jasmine tea in hand, we indulge in at least two of these masterpieces, followed by a white-coifed *religieuse* and a swarm of macarons.

Sure, you can find these treats in Paris, Berlin, or London—but against a backdrop this romantic? She probably had her reasons, but to us, it's baffling why fair Belle should have wanted to leave her village at all costs.

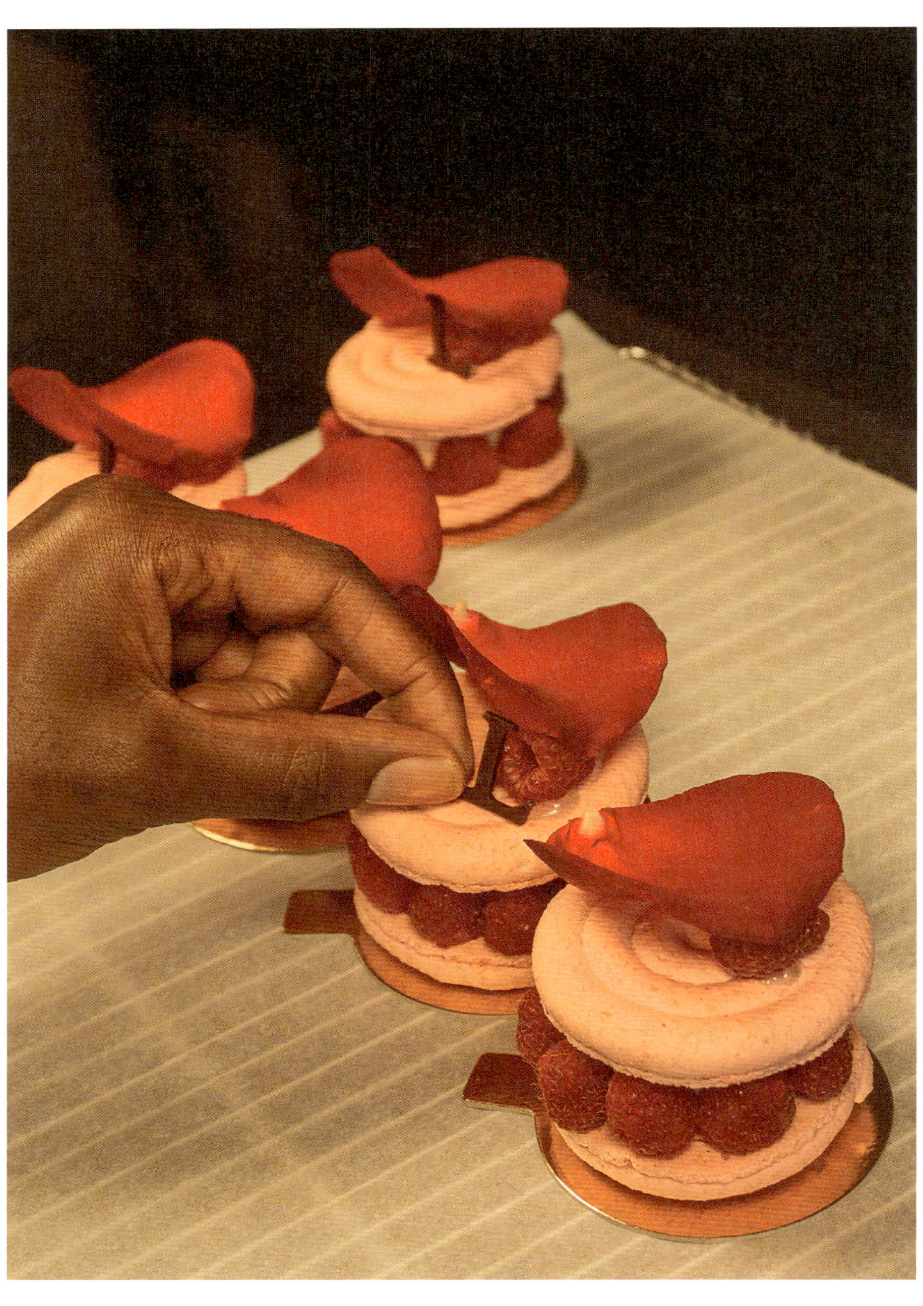

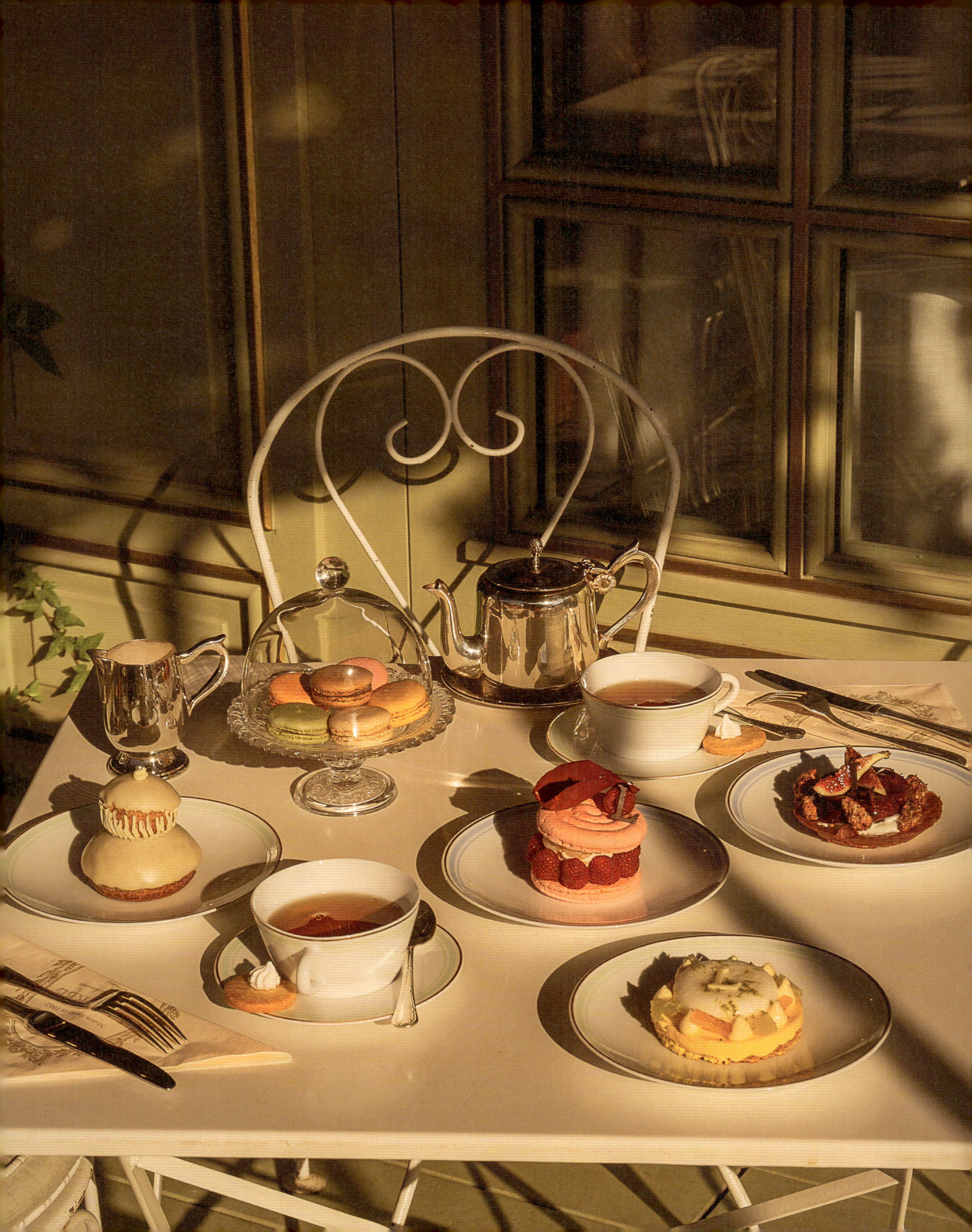

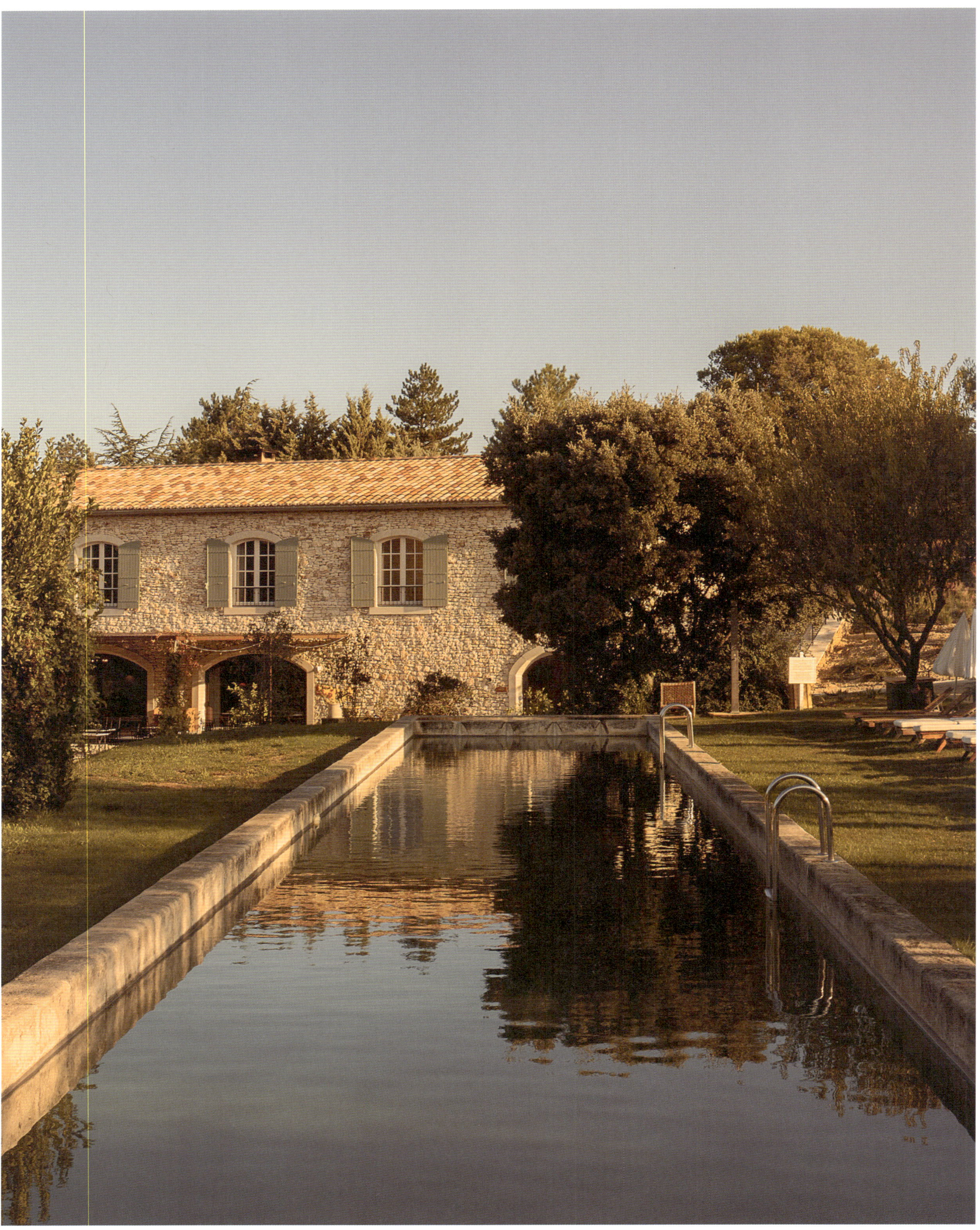

CAPELONGUE

VAUCLUSE

MILLENNIALS DREAMIN'

We leave the hills of Gordes, cross the Coulon, and slowly ascend the first rises of the Lesser Luberon. Abrupt white limestone outcroppings punctuate the forests of cedar, but the landscape retains gentleness and hints at romance in the way handsome hilltop towns such as Goult, Lacoste, and Bonnieux are strung across it. Amid olive groves in the backcountry near Bonnieux lies the entrance to Capelongue, which is where we're headed next. The Beaumier group, whose holdings also include Le Roche Rouges and Le Moulin, has taken this traditional hotel complex, situated on a plateau amid the hills, under its wing and infused it with a unique idea about how to style a vacation. Each Beaumier property celebrates and essentializes the character of the place it inhabits, fuses the work of local artists and interior designers into one, and tops it all off with Michelin-starred fine dining. They offer a trendy refuge that checks all the boxes, appealing to the millennial dream and cool kids from all places.. Capelongue is right on theme.

The whole of the spacious estate feels exuberant, but also calm and reserved. Guests are hanging out in the courtyard beneath olive trees, sipping on coffee from the bar and leafing through coffee table books from the library. On the left side of the layout, people are relaxing poolside on wicker chaise lounges and gazing upon the tranquil hills of Bonnieux. We get a room in a long stone building with our own terrace and a view of the pool facilities. The walls are finished in a traditional lime plaster, the tiles are red stone with a rustic glaze, there is pottery and vessels woven from dried lavender by local

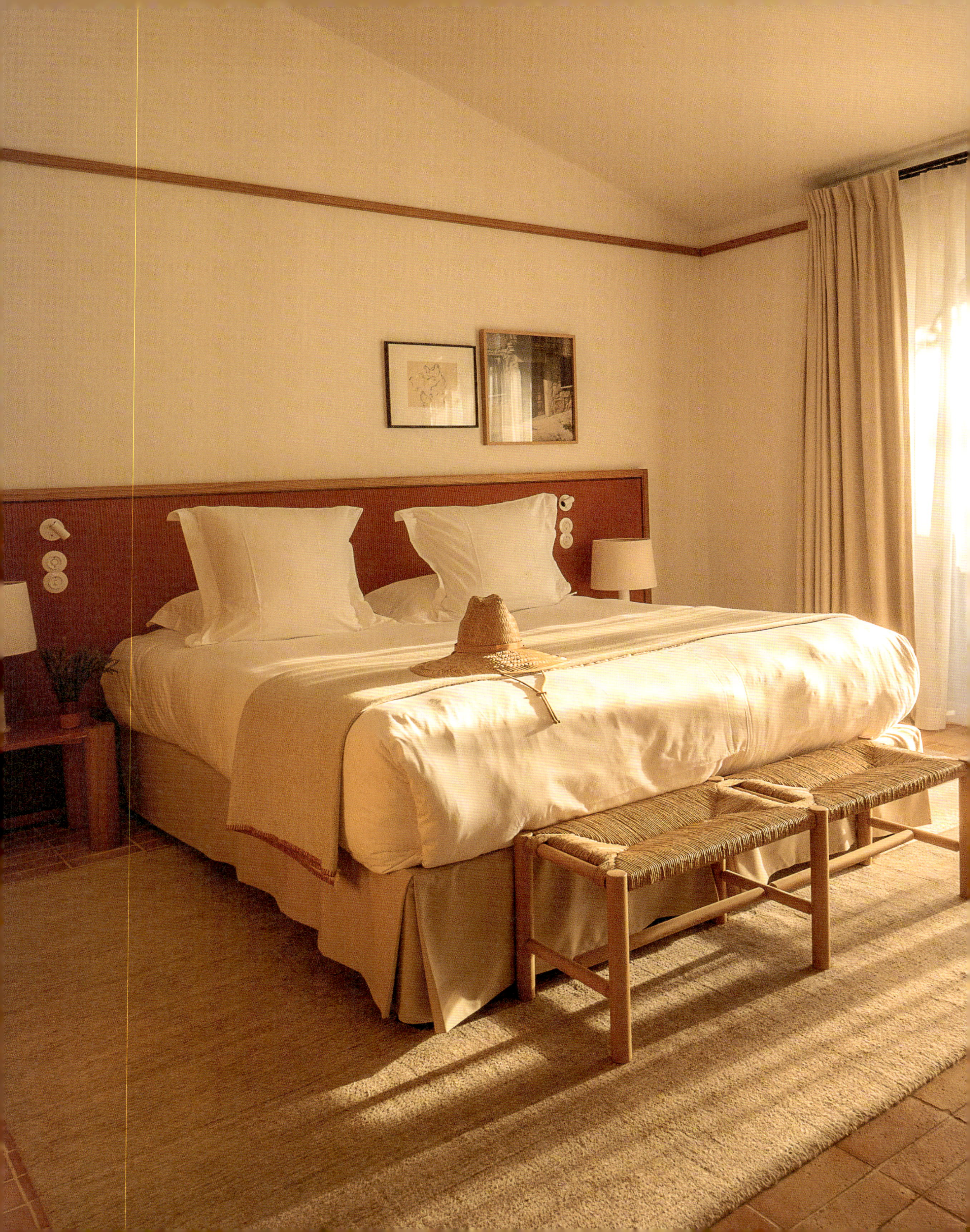

artists: Not only our room but the entire interior of Capelongue are a tangible vision of summer in Provence. We take an old edition of Monopoly from the library out to the pool. Three hours later, all the real estate is tied up, I am broke, and a ribbon of smoke is rising from the chimney of the stone building across the space. That means it's time for dinner: grilled veggies and Provençal truffle pizza baked over an open fire at La Bergerie. Capelongue is all you want in a vacation, which is regeneration, letting go, not observing the time, but still up with the zeitgeist.

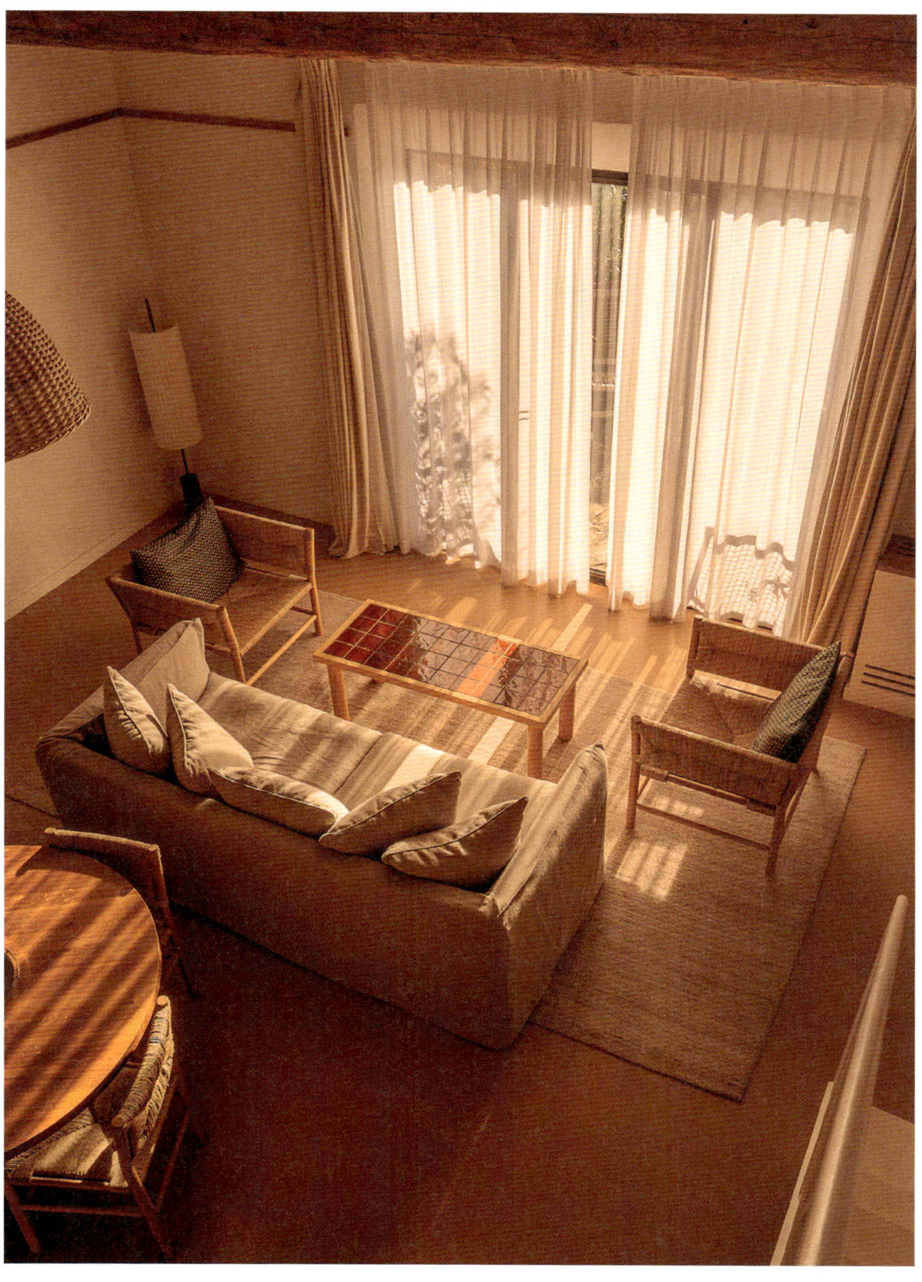

The interior of the Capelongue, by the architecture duo JAUNE, is fit to set the millennial heart aflutter: sisal rugs, glazed brick, wicker, and a wistful vision of summer in Provence.

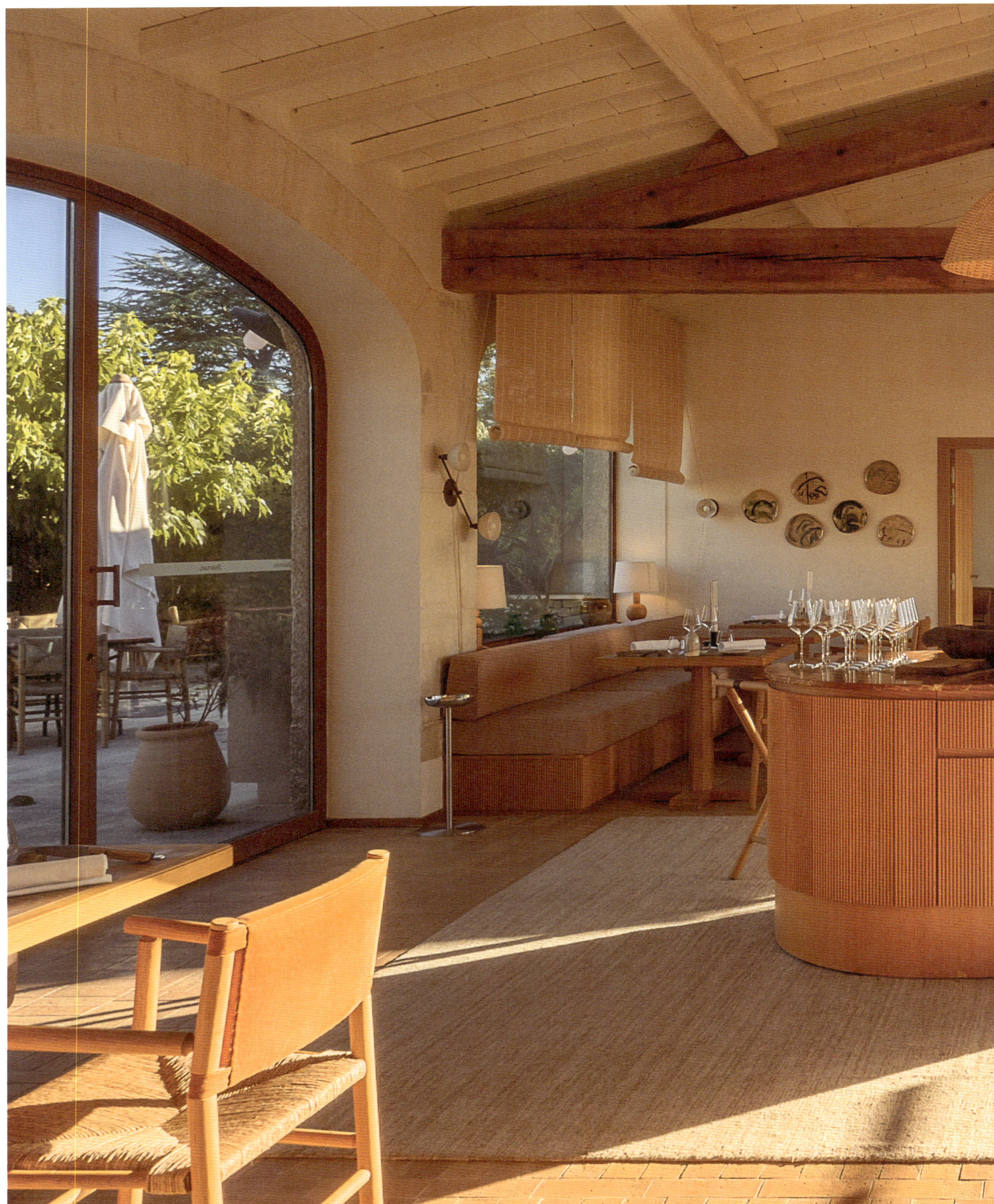

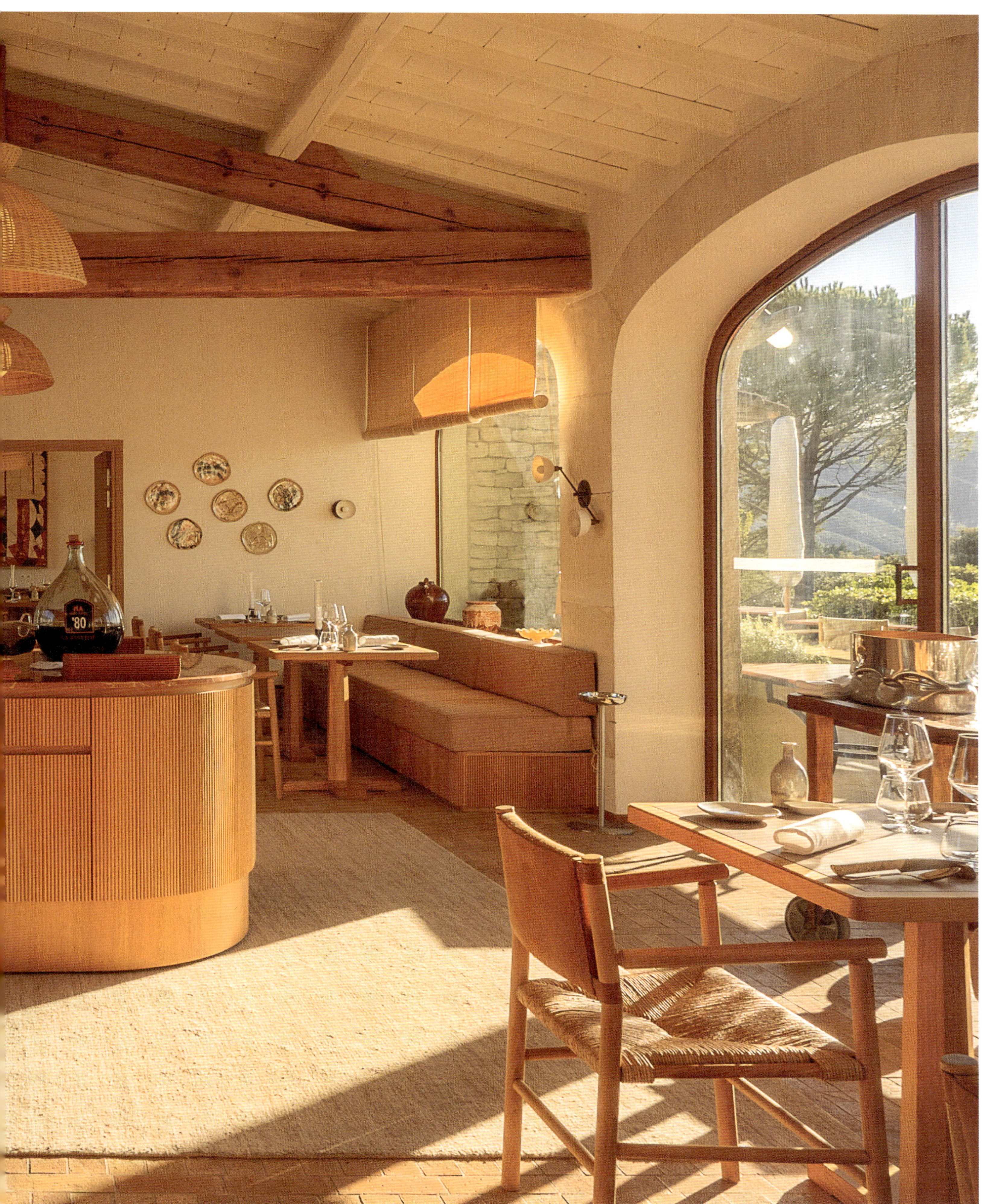

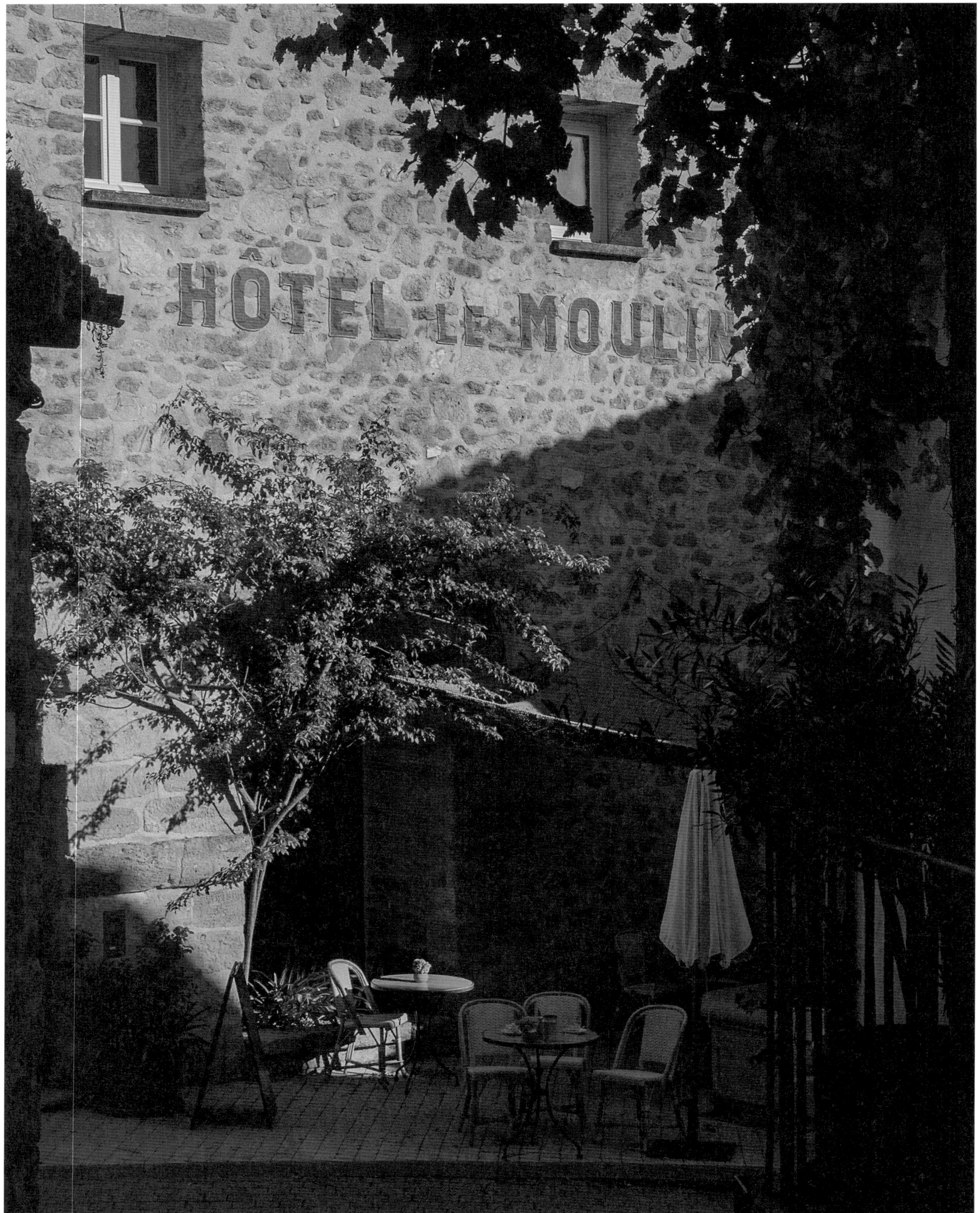
HÔTEL LE MOULIN

LE MOULIN

VAUCLUSE

THE INN

There are seven villages on the list of *Les Plus Beaux Villages de France* in the département of Vaucluse. One of these is Lourmarin. At the edge of this picturesque, snail-shaped sandstone village, directly across from the Renaissance-era château, stands an old mill that houses this region's second Beaumier residence, which is only fifteen minutes from Capelongue, across the crest of the Luberon: Le Moulin. The hotel was designed by JAUNE, a Paris architecture studio with Provençal roots. The country fantasy of Summer in Provence continues uninterrupted, only this time the notion of the village inn is also in play. Lime-plastered walls and ceilings, woodwork and raffia accessories, straw hats on the wall. The concept is open, accessible from all sides. Everyone—each hotel guest, visitor to town, or local—is welcome. Everyone can get a pastis at the bar or *un café* beneath the shade sails on Rue de Temple or a room in the old mill complex. The complex is spread across several buildings in the old town, as are we—at least until we find the right door, which is across from Le Commissions, the village wine store and deli, which is also owned by Le Moulin. Our room extends into every corner of the old water mill. We walk barefoot across the old sisal flooring, put up the roller shutters, and open the doors onto the terrace. We can hear the babble of the fountain-like pool in the garden and watch the goings-ons in the village from our window. To stay at Le Moulin is not to be a hotel guest but rather a resident of Lourmarin. After hiking around the village, which is so attractive it seems it must have been staged, the time has come for dinner at Bacheto, in the main hall of the old mill. With millstones all around beneath

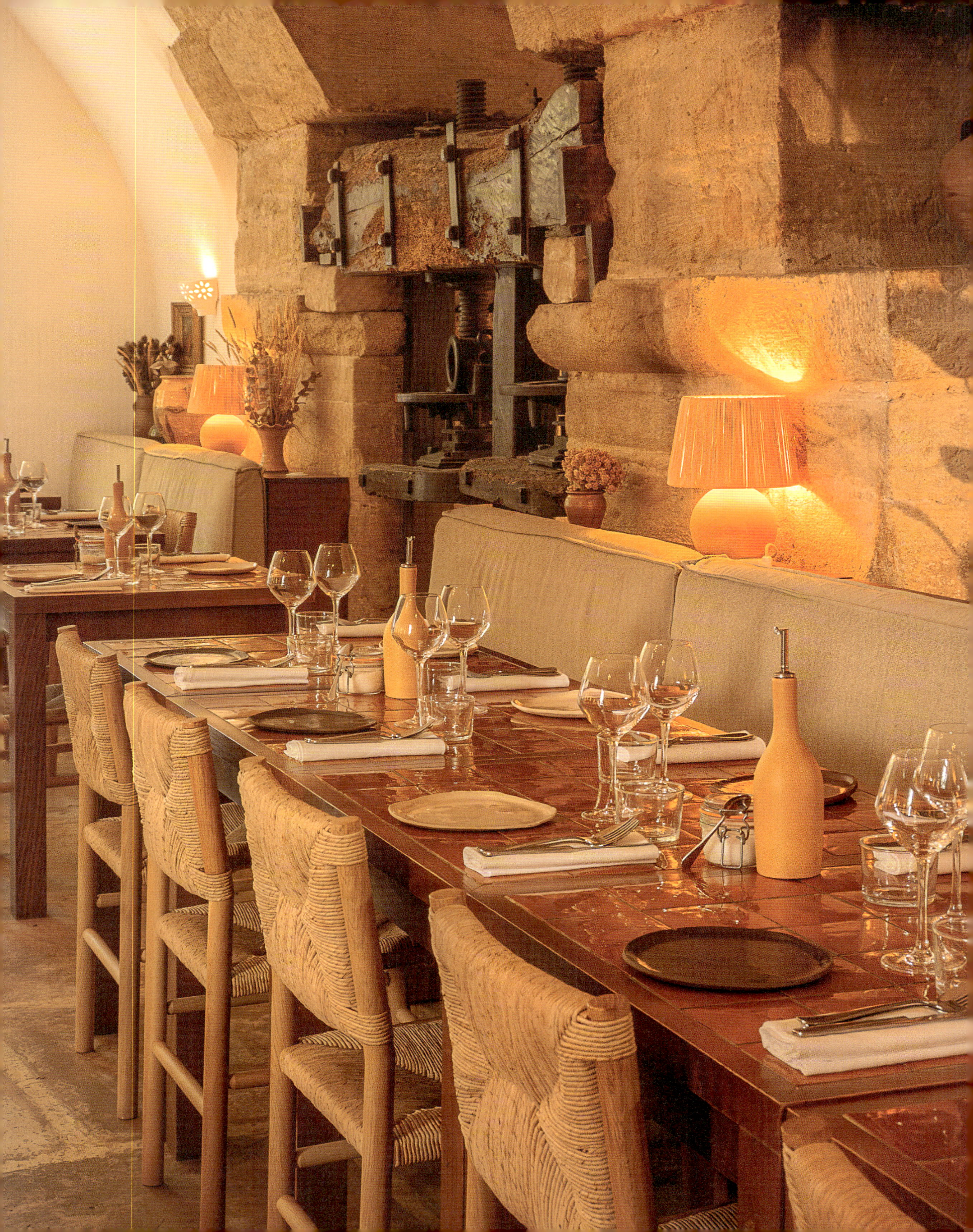

the organic arc of the lime-plastered ceiling and stylized wooden chandeliers, they serve tapas: grilled truffled chèvre, traditional farro risotto, and catch-of-the-day. The Beaumier feel has survived our change of location, and the vacation bubble is still immaculate, having only relocated across the crest of the Lesser Luberon.

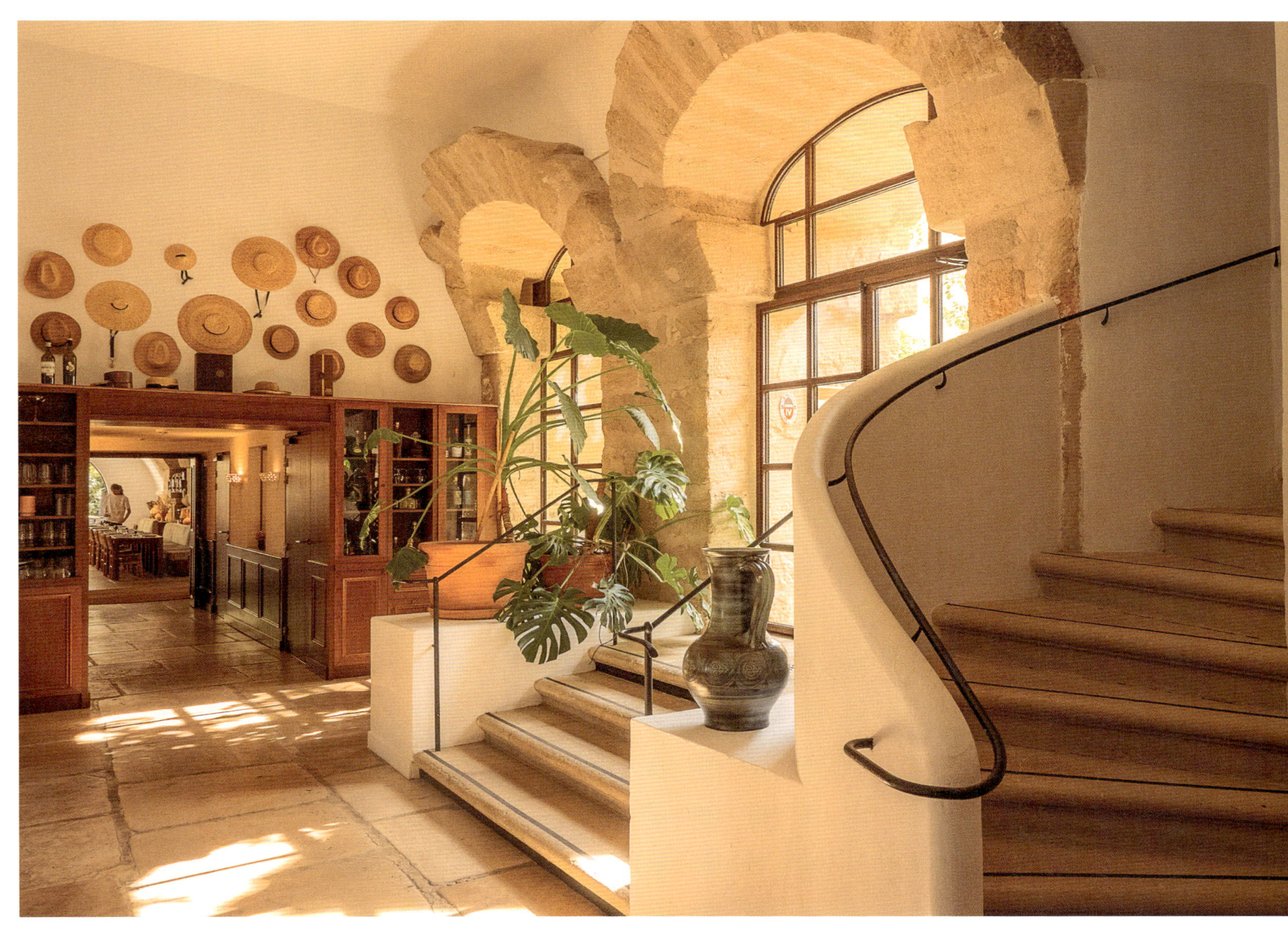

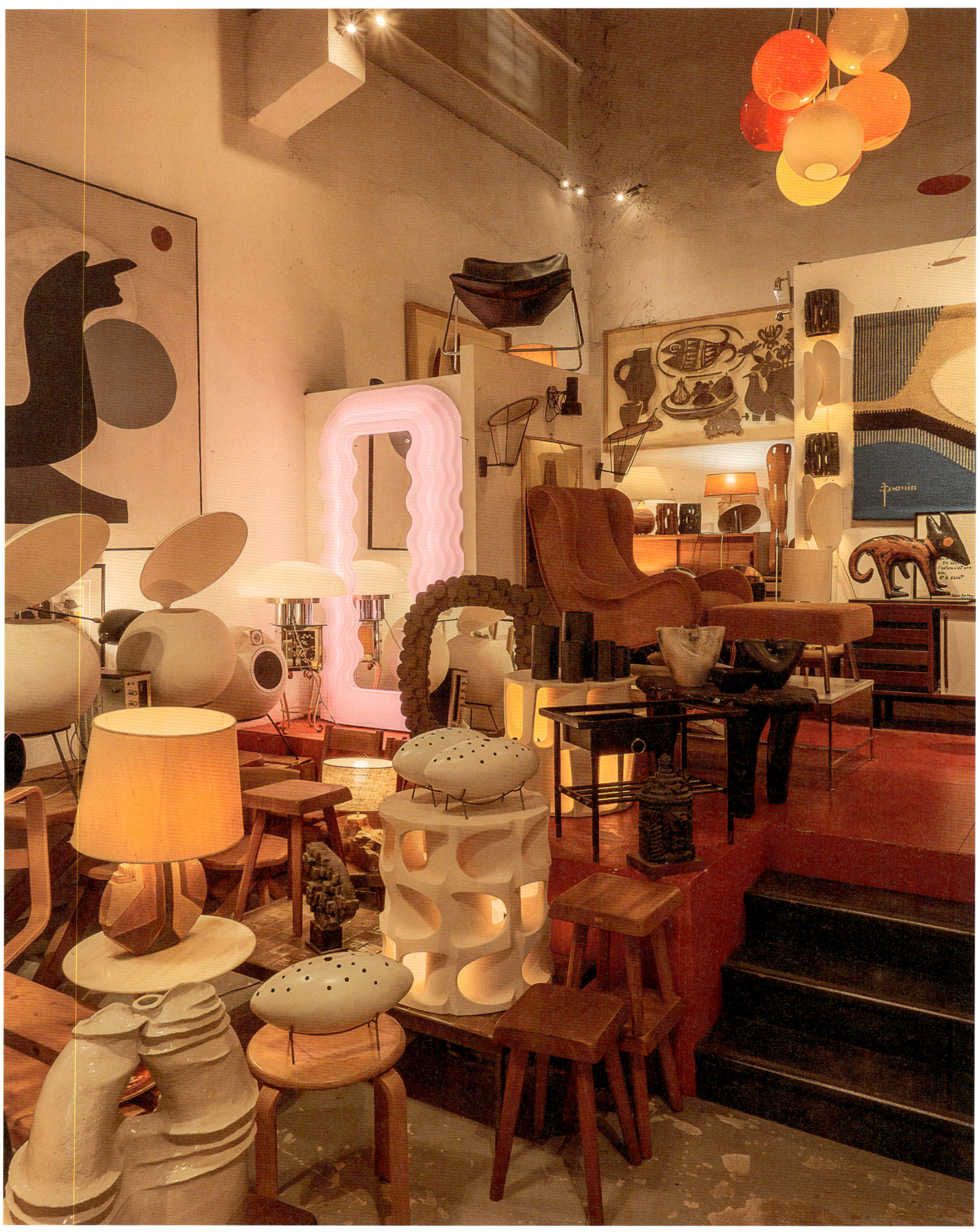

L'ISLE-SUR-LA-SORGUE

VAUCLUSE

MONSTER OF VINTAGE

Tim and I have a foible for antiques and vintage finds—furniture, clothing, jewelry, and miscellaneous doodads. Wherever we are, our eyes are always scanning. Is there a better way to get into the soul of a time, a culture, a place than through left-behind objects? So, when we're travelling through Provence, we never skip L'Isle-sur-la-Sorgue. This idyllic town, its center straddled by a river like an island, is a mecca for lovers of vintage stuff, and some serious dealers operate here. We've seen our share over the years, but nothing quite compares to what goes on here. The sheer concentration of vendors, troves of treasure, and one-of-a-kind items is so staggering that every time we visit, we play a game: Each of us is assigned an object he must find, and whoever fails to find his, loses. There are roughly 300 dealers, so...we're both undefeated. My mission for the day is to find a Vico Magistretti bench. There are plenty of Magistretti chairs, but a bench?—never seen one. Tim's task is even tougher: find the largest edition of the legendary Serge Mouille lamp, which has six arms. Only five of these lamps were produced. Game on! Just one word to the wise: Don't be fooled by the shops in the town center. Just because something looks vintage doesn't mean it is. The real action is in the southern part of town, along the crystal-clear river, where aquatic plants ripple in the stream and there are quadrangles and cavernous warehouses where dealer after dealer, smoking, snoozing, and haggling, does business. It's all there: baroque extravagance, medieval altar statuary, Memphis-style kitsch. And then there are your encounters with the dealers themselves, with their impassioned tales about the goods. I locate my quarry first. Karl and

Tina have one in their red warehouse in an overgrown courtyard. It takes Tim a little longer to track his down, but he does. It's at a place called 50 CINQUANTE. The monster lamp by Mouille is hanging there, spanning the entire west side of the store. The price has to be inquired about, and the person who asks had better have a wallet as fat as the lamp is wide. Whatever you find in L'Isle-sur-la-Sorgue, it's not going to be a steal. But you will probably find everything and anything that's ever had a previous owner.

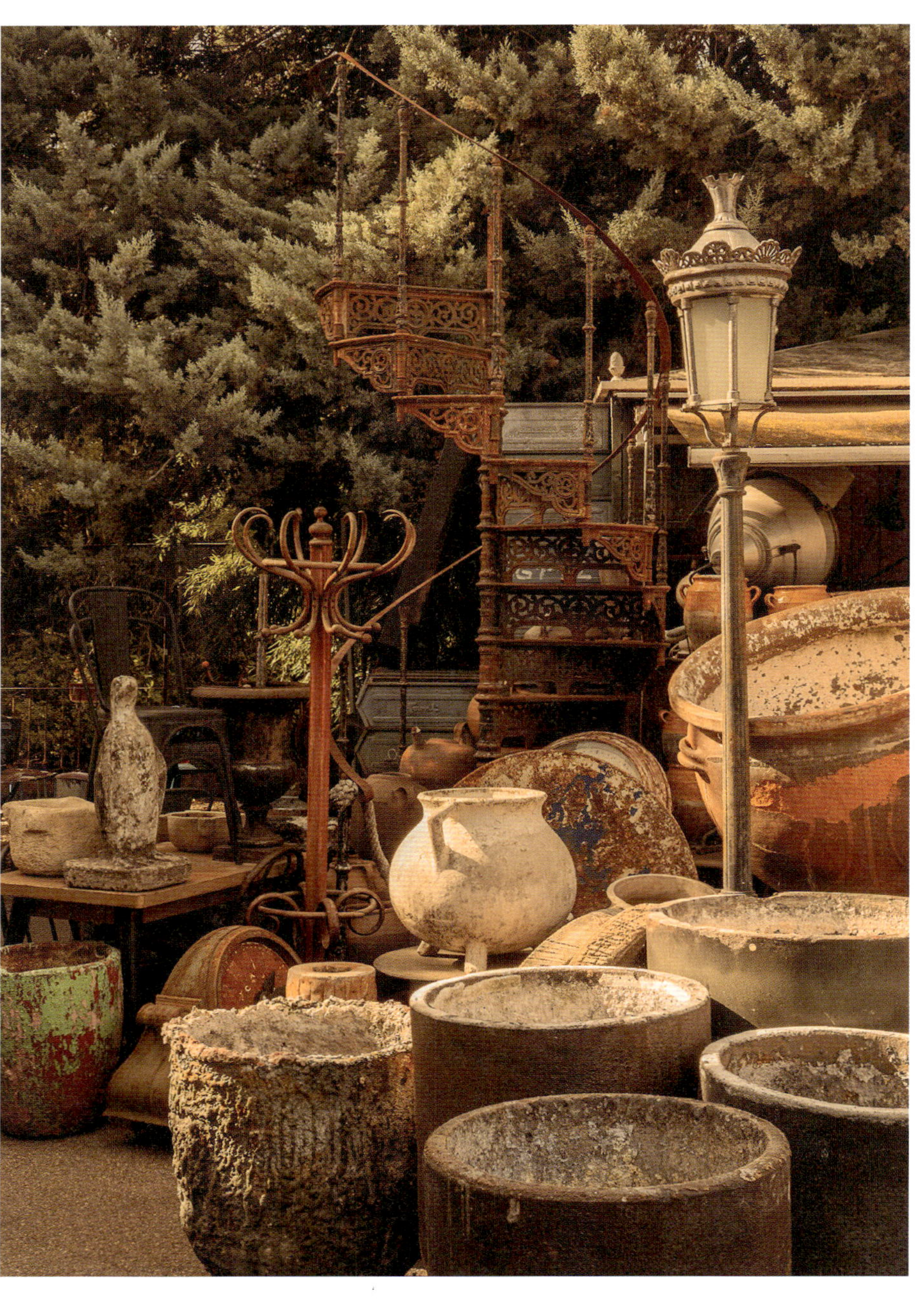

If you haven't found what you're looking for amid the innumerable stalls, or if none of the antiques and vintage truck in L'Isle-sur-la-Sorgue has quite struck your fancy, then 50 Cinquante is a sure bet. Specializing in fifties-thru-seventies classics, they display Ultrafragola next to Guzzini lamps next to Elda chairs next to Calder mobiles.

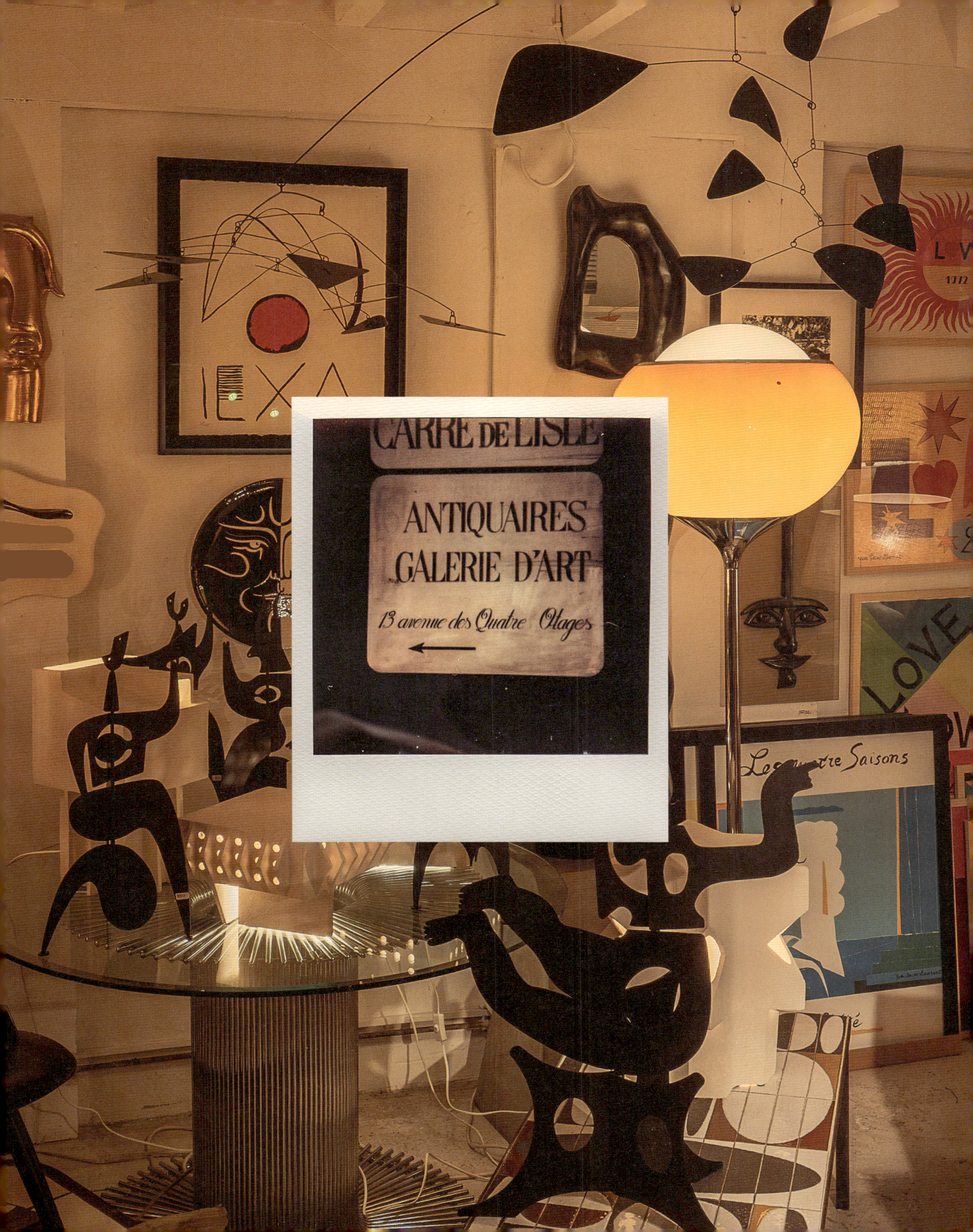
CARRE DE LISLE
ANTIQUAIRES
GALERIE D'ART
13 avenue des Quatre Otages
LOVE

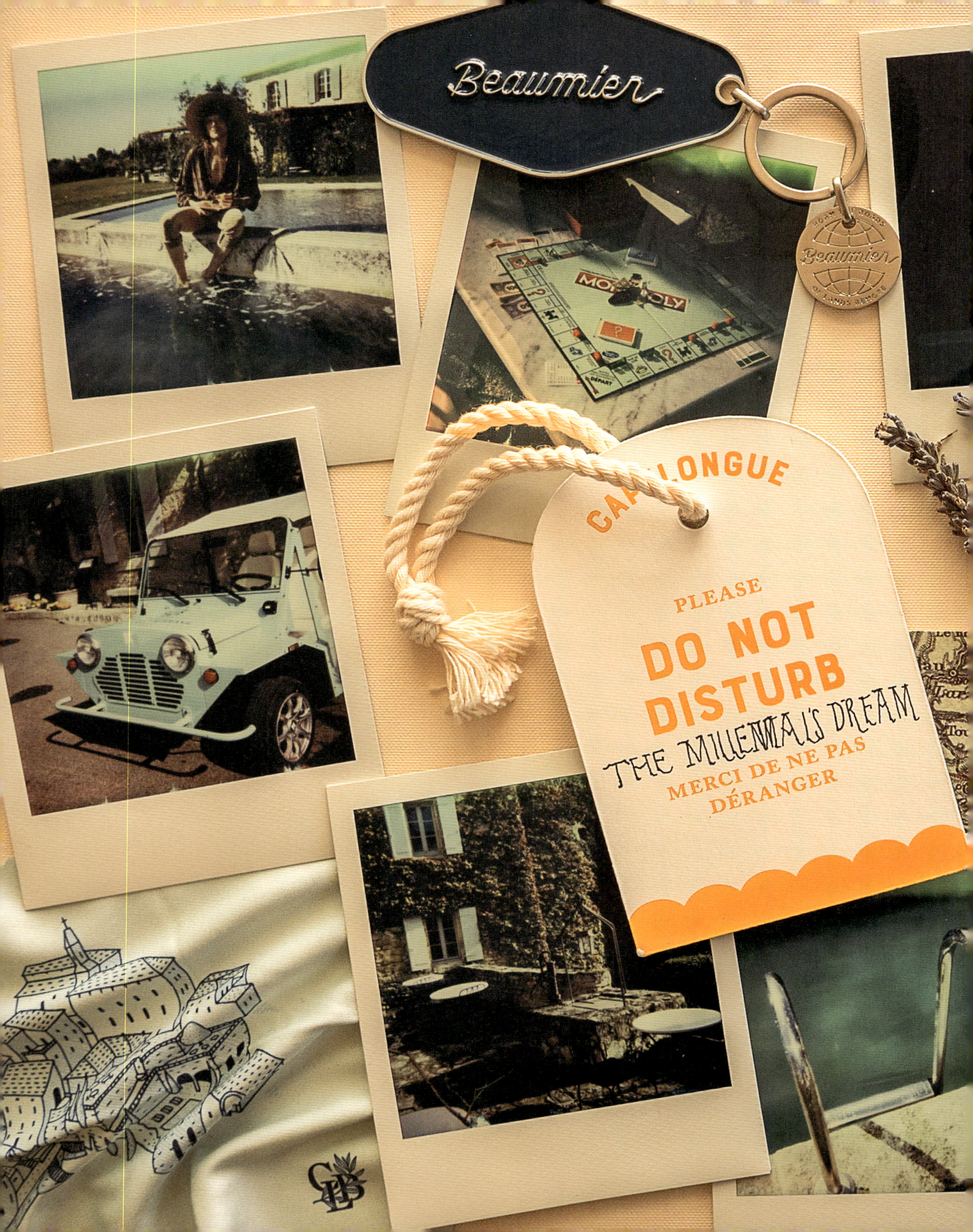

Beaumier
Beaumier
PLEASE
DO NOT
DISTURB
THE MILLENNIAL'S DREAM
MERCI DE NE PAS
DÉRANGER

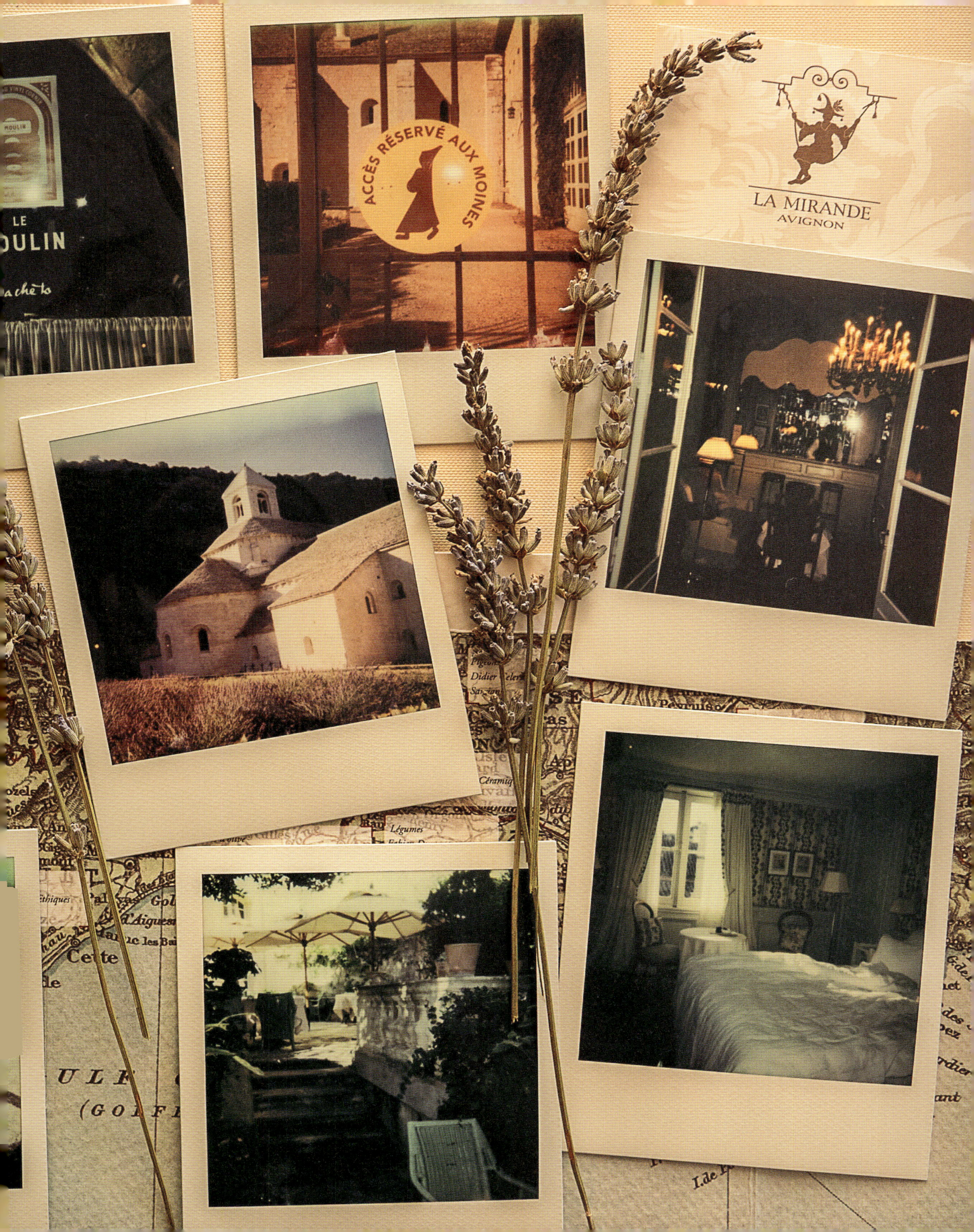
ACCÈS RÉSERVÉ AUX MOINES
LA MIRANDE
AVIGNON
Cette

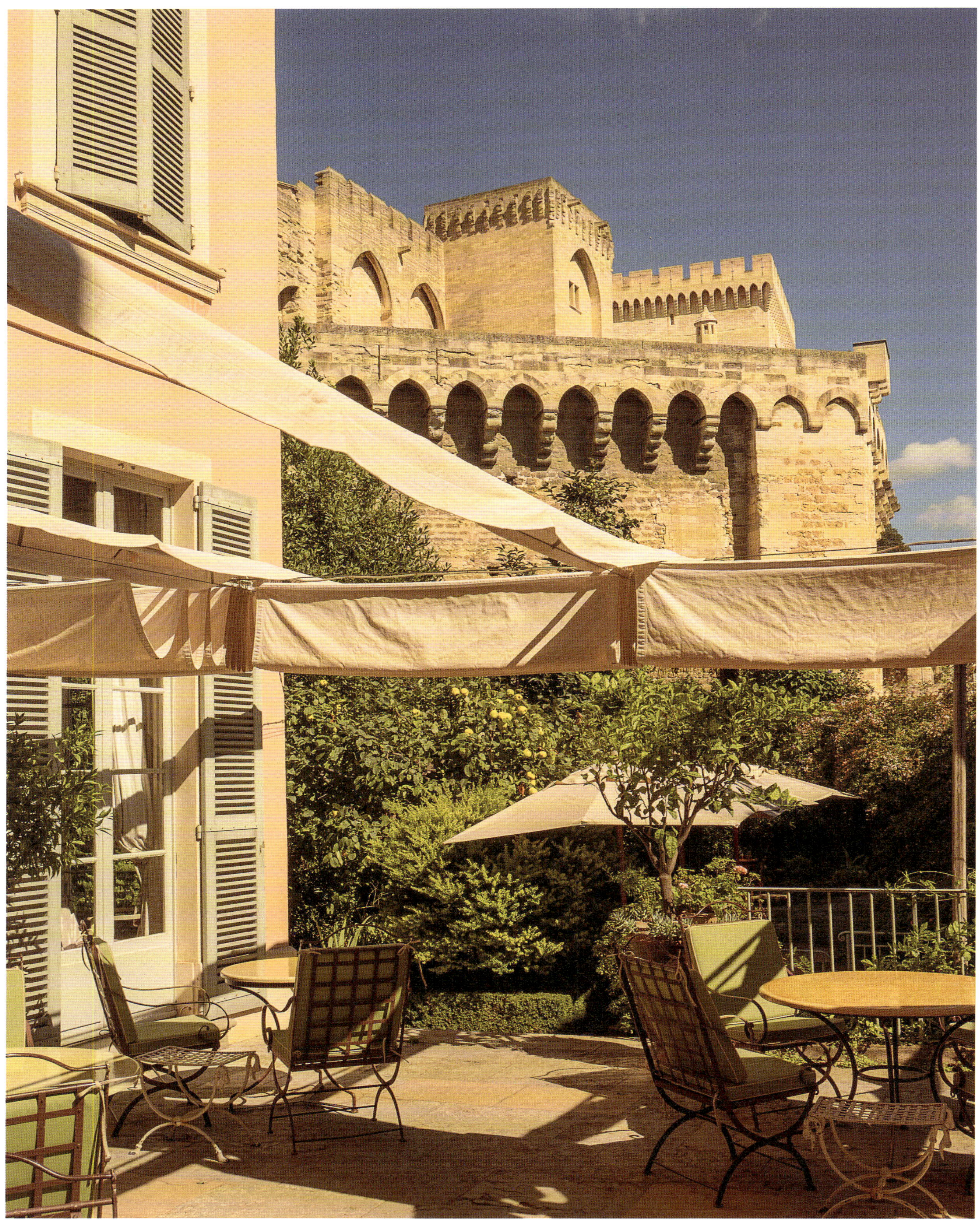

LA MIRANDE

VAUCLUSE

RESTORATION

We drive away from the Luberon massif and head for Avignon. Not only is this noble city the administrative center of Vaucluse, known to all for its great bridge, half of which is now submerged in the Rhône, but it's also where the Holy See was in the fourteenth century. The Pope brought wealth to Avignon, commissioned the Gothic Palais des Papes, and generally transformed the city into the epitome of a fortified town. We enter the old town through the northern gate. The streets narrow and the historic network of alleys, façades and parks draws in around us. Near the massive walls of the palais, just as we think the way is shut, a gate swings wide, and there we are: La Mirande.

In 1987, it occurred to a German family that they should awaken an old palazzo in the shadows of the palais from its long slumber, breathe new life into the rooms and chambers in a mix of Baroque, Rococo, and Gothic décor, and open an enchanted family hotel. Only a few minutes later, we are enthralled by the same magic. Carolin Stein, who took over the hotel from her father, gives us a warm welcome. She leads us across the Gothic atrium and with a sparkle in her eye tells us about her father's ambition and struggles to wipe hundreds of years' worth of dust off of this historic beauty of an object, to preserve all the details while also imbuing it with the modernity it would have to have, including a first-class restaurant crowned by a Michelin star. She takes us up a stone staircase to the second floor and shows us a few of the rooms. Each is a microcosm, a little cabinet of curiosities. The idiosyncratic, detail-obsessed charm of the rooms is the golden thread that brings

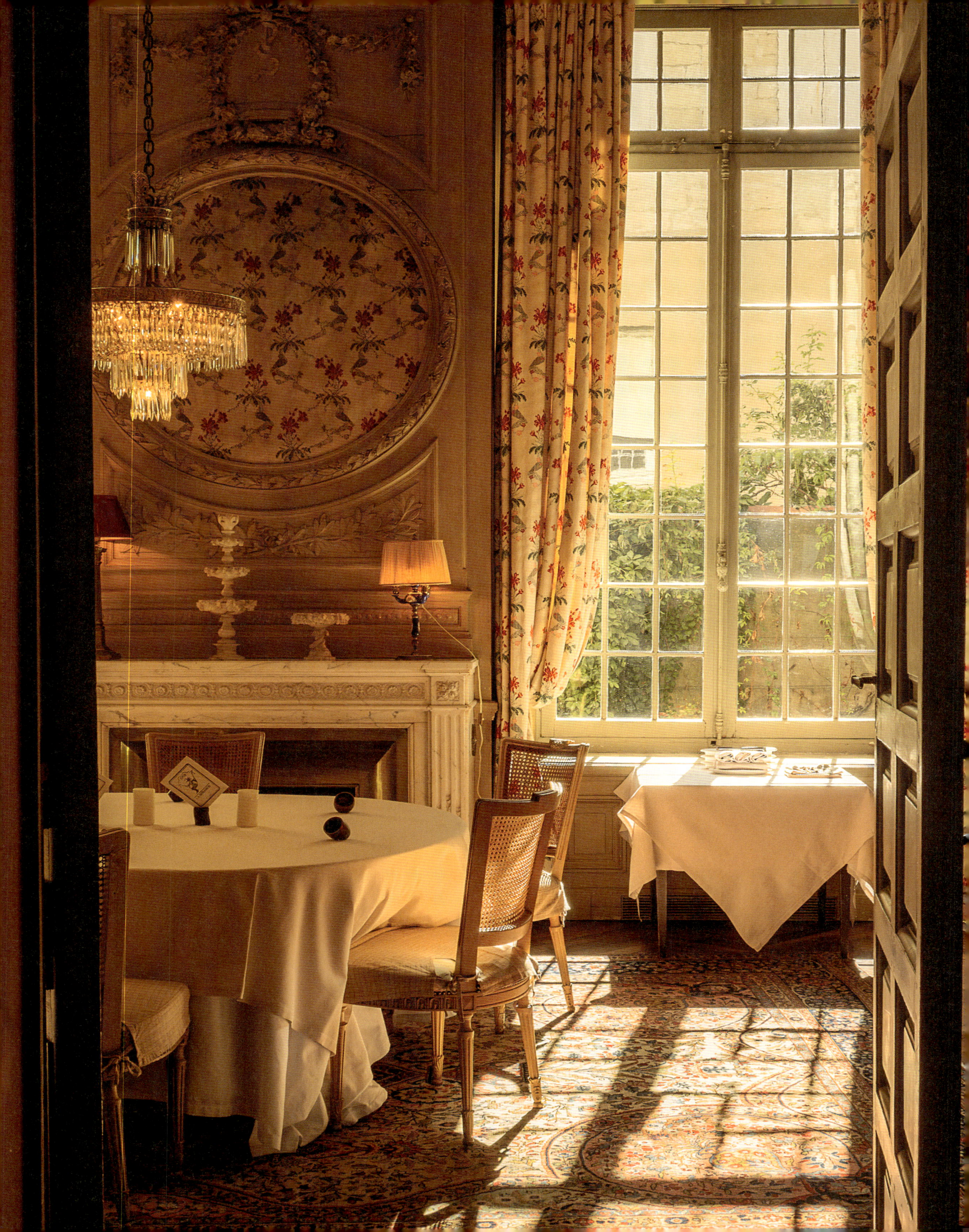

the hotel together. There are hidden spiral staircases along warped corridors, dim tea and reading rooms decorated with carmine floral paintings and sea-green plasterwork, convoluted gardens with beds of jasmine, and extensive china cabinets. The entire vibe is right up our alley. If you could peer into our minds, it would probably look kind of like La Mirande, and this is certainly one of the reasons we feel so at home here so soon. But another element of the magic is that it's family-run. It's something only the family touch can provide: warm, obsessed with the details, and probably a bit odd. But it's actually the perfect recipe for true hotel magic.

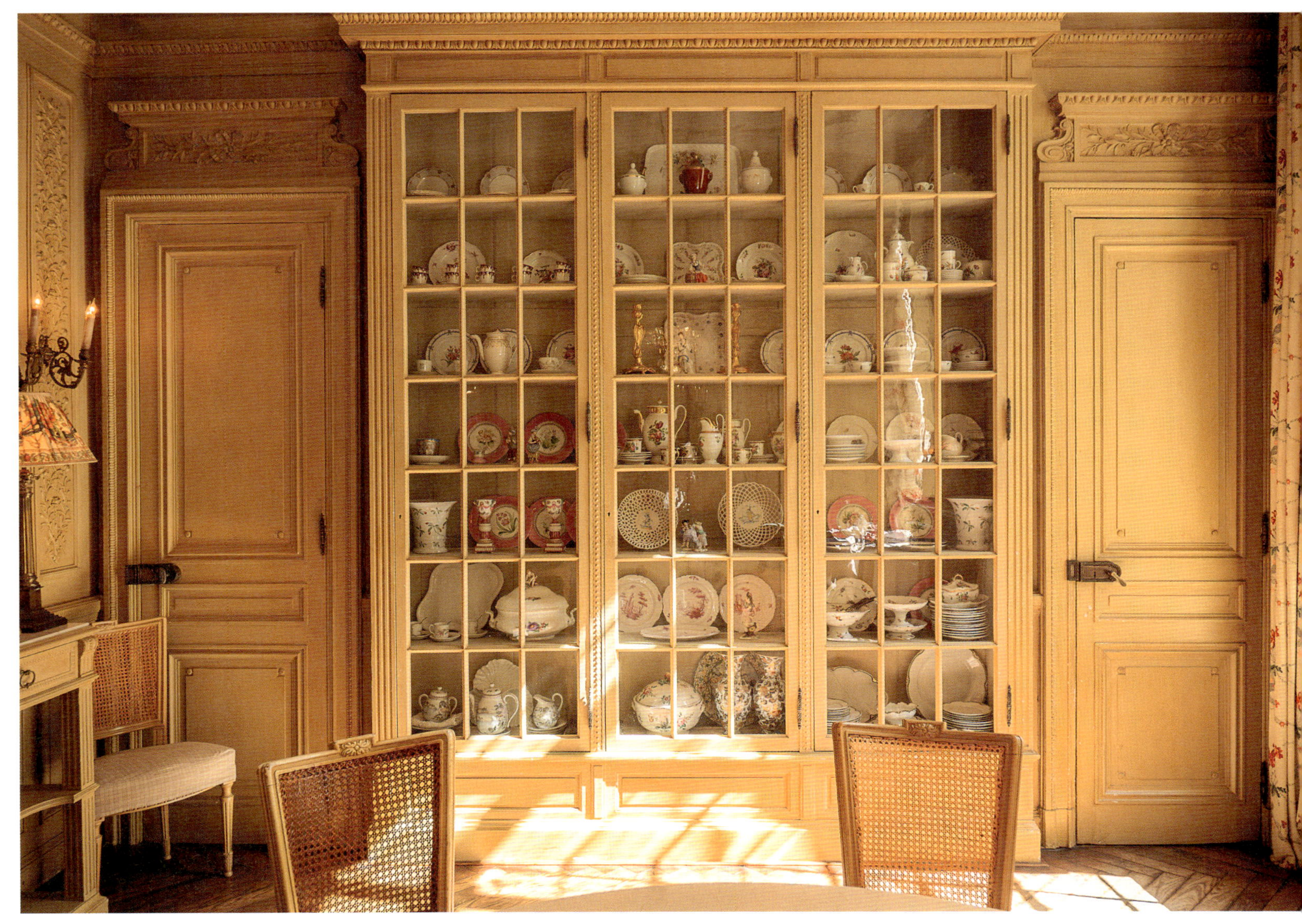

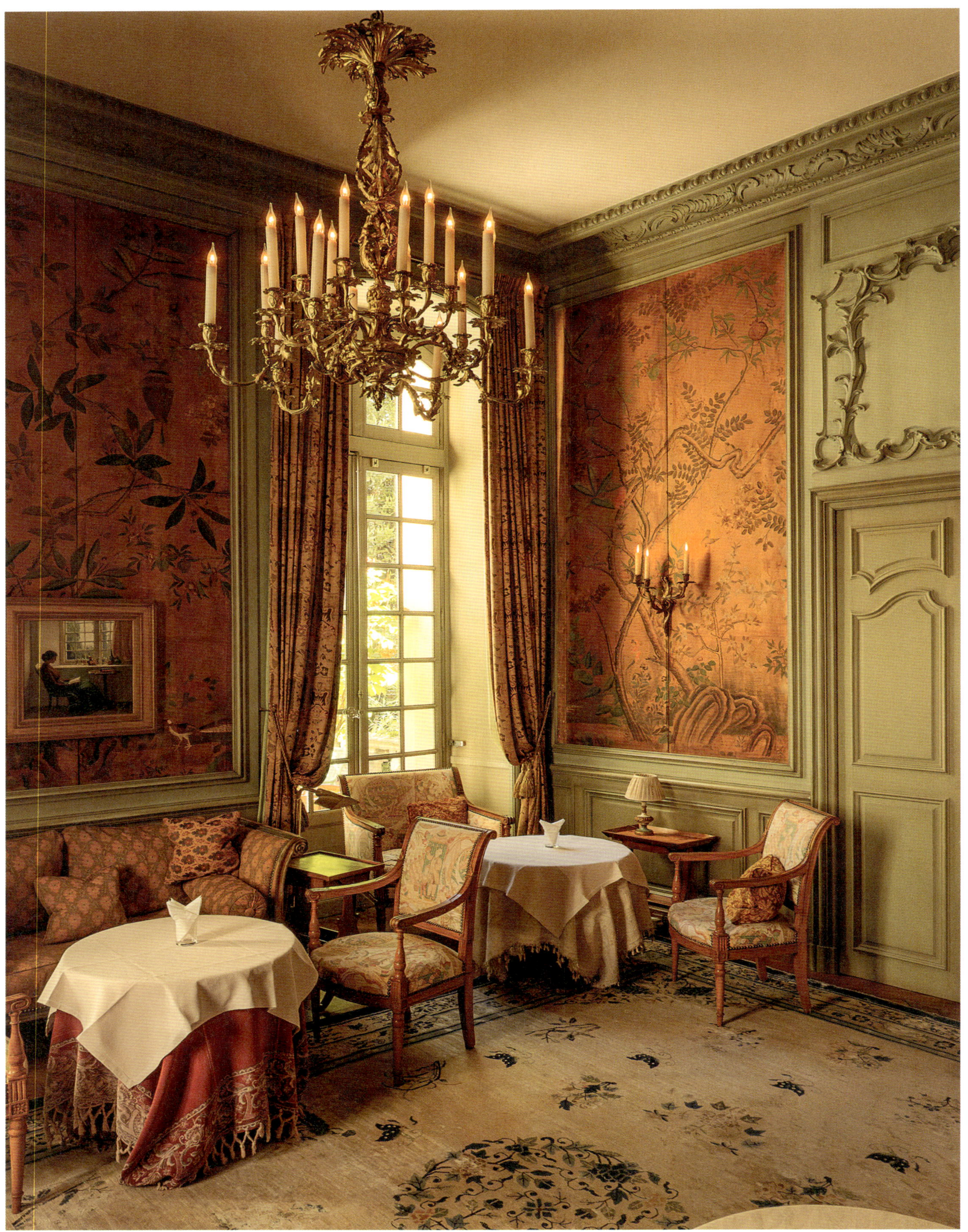

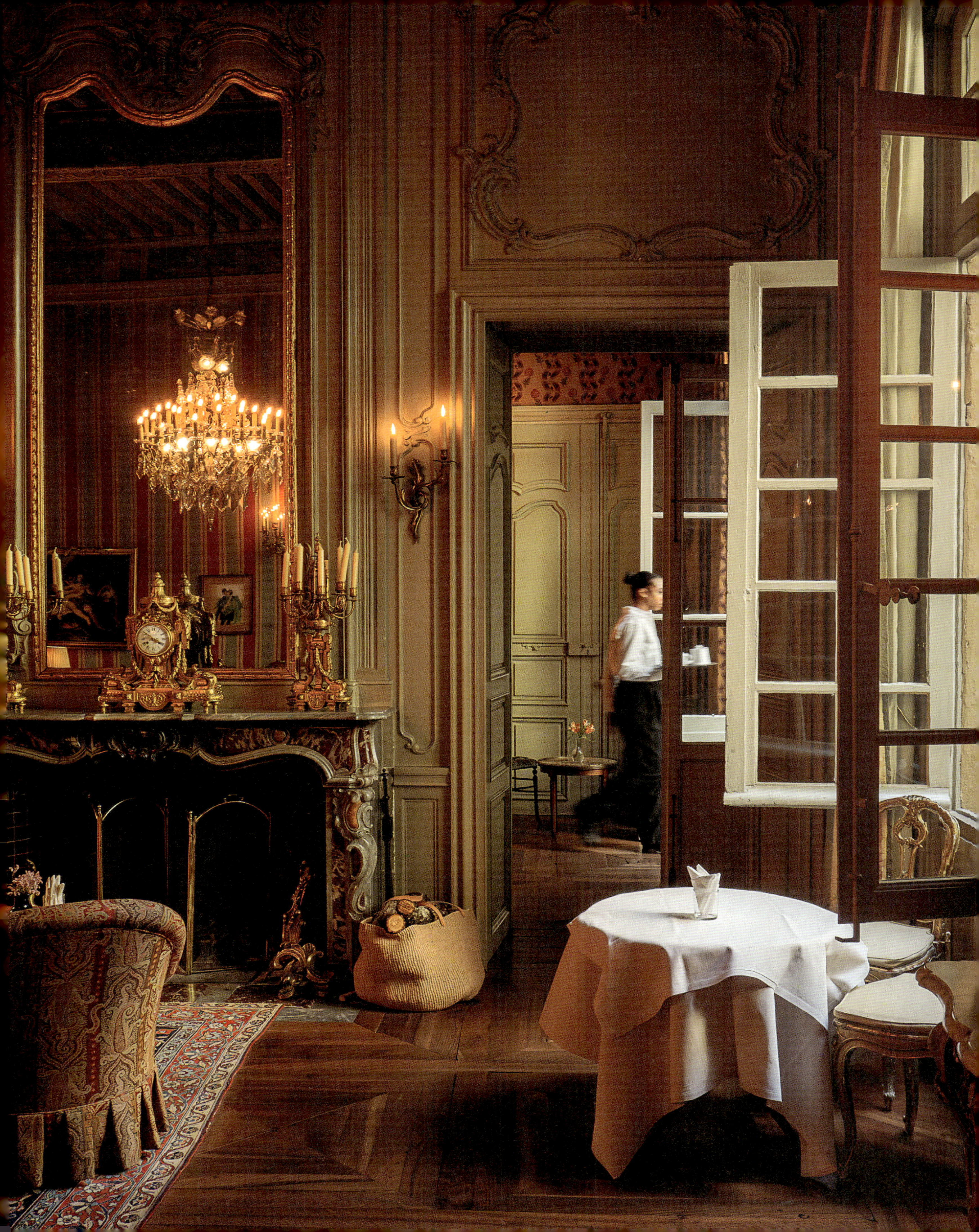

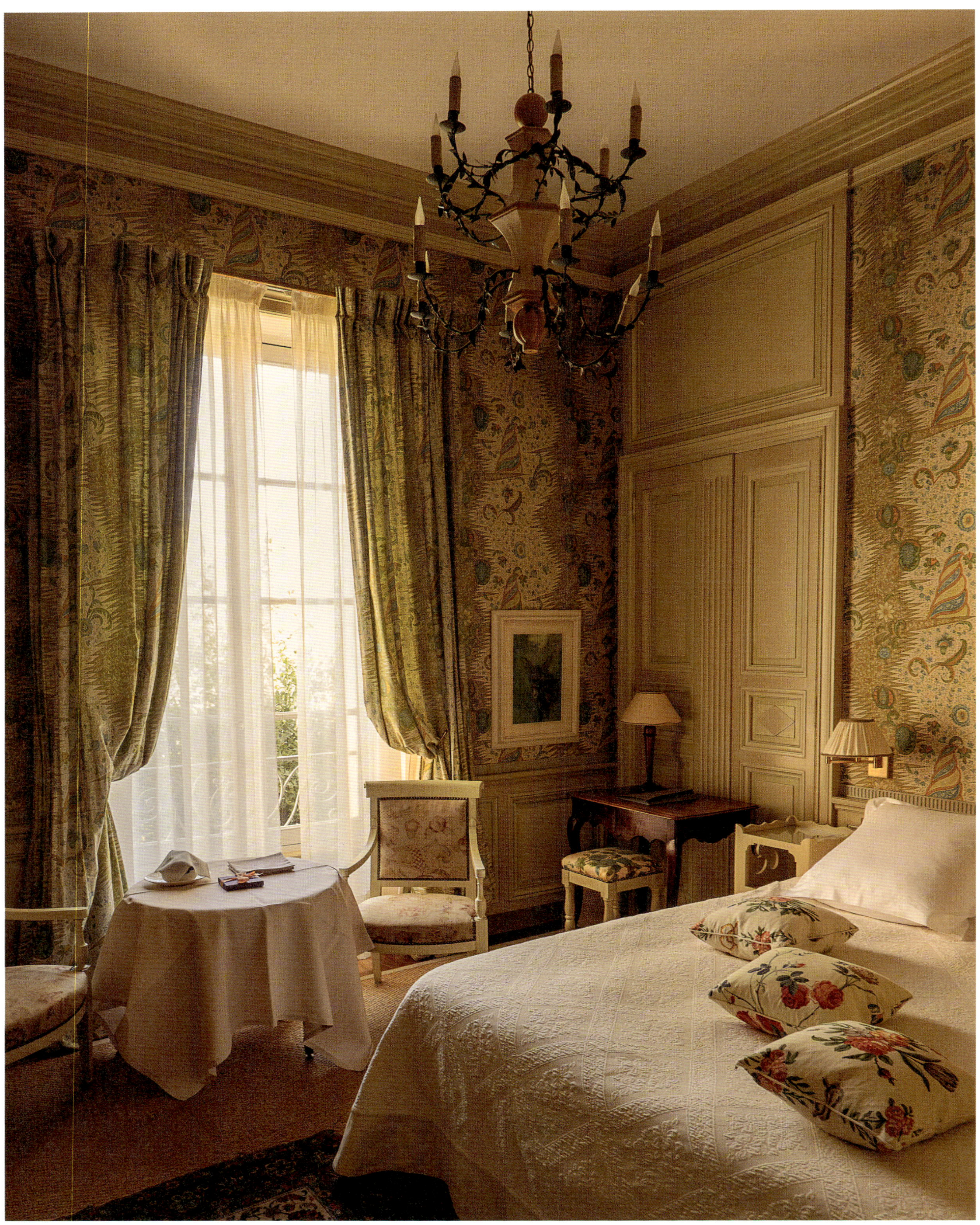

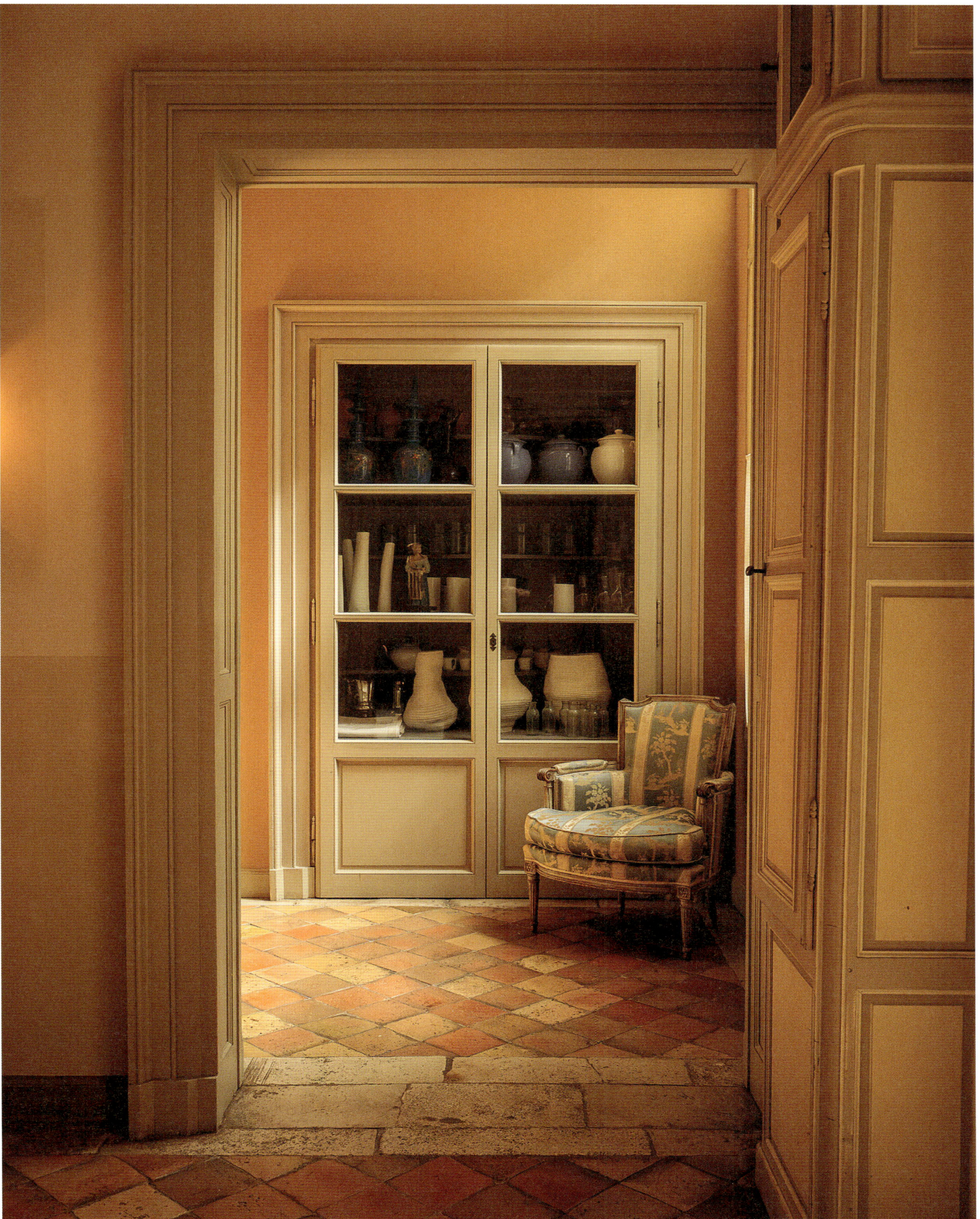

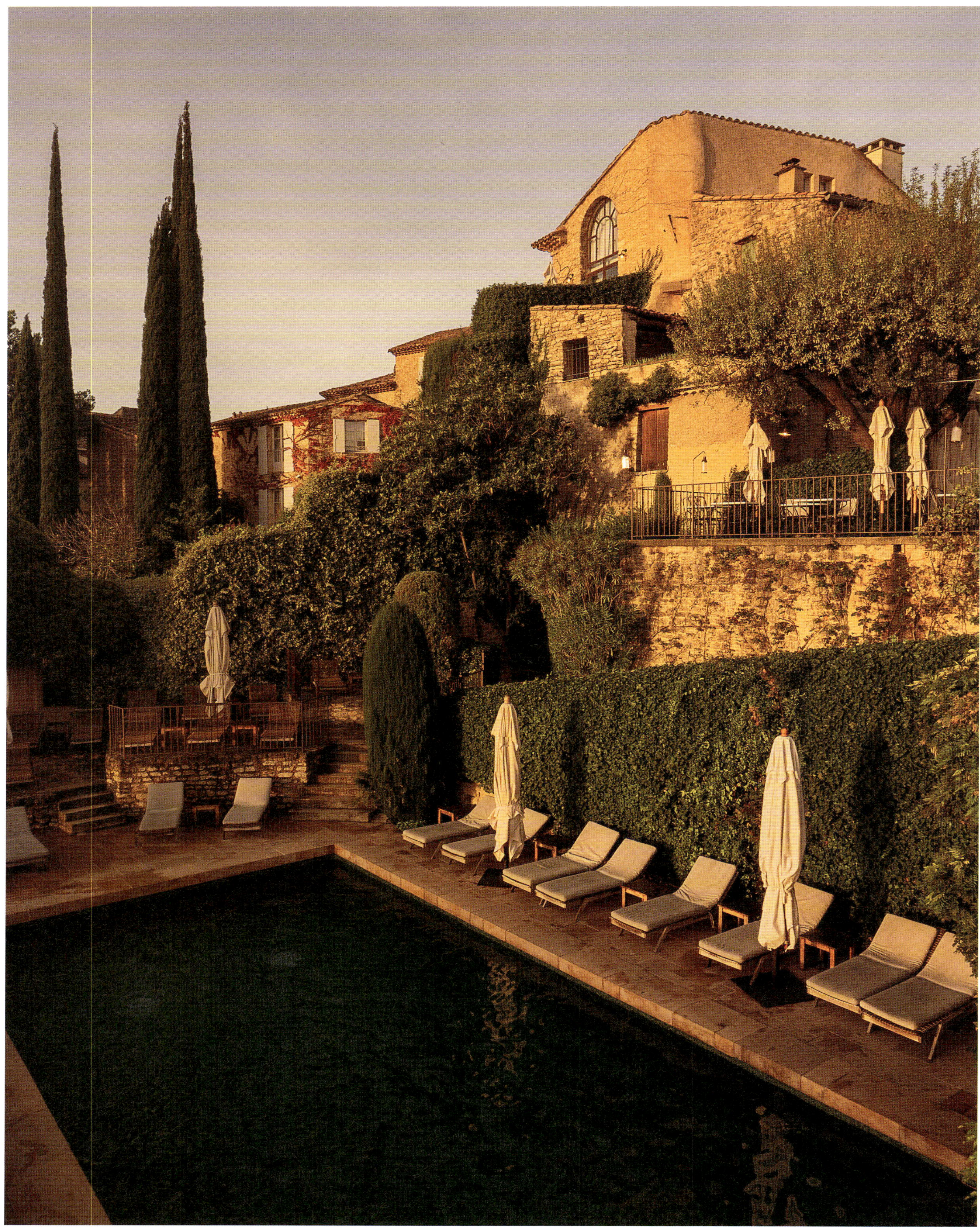

CRILLON LE BRAVE

VAUCLUSE

ONE WITH THE VILLAGE

The wind has cooled by the time we leave Avignon for the hills again, near Mont Ventoux, to the final destination on our tour, the tiny village of Crillon-le-Brave and its eponymous hotel. There's a good reason why the hotel and the village have the same name. We've seen a few hotels that blend in perfectly with their surroundings. But this one makes me think I've resorted to a platitude if I ever said so before. The hotel occupies so much of this idyllic village that it's hard to distinguish between the two. The one is the other in Crillon-le-Brave. We find the entrance to the hotel lobby near the church and are received there with a mug of steaming punch. Dagmar, the director, walks casually with us out onto the first of the hotel's verandas. As though it were part of a compact, intimate neighborhood, little stone stairways and archways lead around to several old stone buildings covered in vines. All of them have faded shutters and all of them have a view of Mont Ventoux. It's impossible to say where the boundary between hotel and village actually lies. We walk up another set of stone stairs and arrive at the pool. Loungers are lined up along a balustrade, and looking out across it we see a breathtaking panorama of the vineyards dotting the flanks of the mountain. Just as we're contemplating a dip in the pool, the bell tower tolls the arrival of afternoon. Maybe we should get settled in our room first. The entrance to our suite is from the church plaza. The hotel's interior couldn't be better integrated into the overall concept: carefully curated, charmingly rustic, and fused together over the years, from room to room and building to building, just like a village. Crillon-le-Brave feels like a warm embrace, like having found shelter at the end of a long journey—just the right kind of place to pause and let the impressions—all the different moments we've had during the last few weeks of our trip—sink in. The leaves on the grapevines are turning red, and temperatures on the day of our departure have plummeted. There is no denying that fall has descended on the south of France.

Our Grand Tour, our summer in Provence, is drawing to a close.

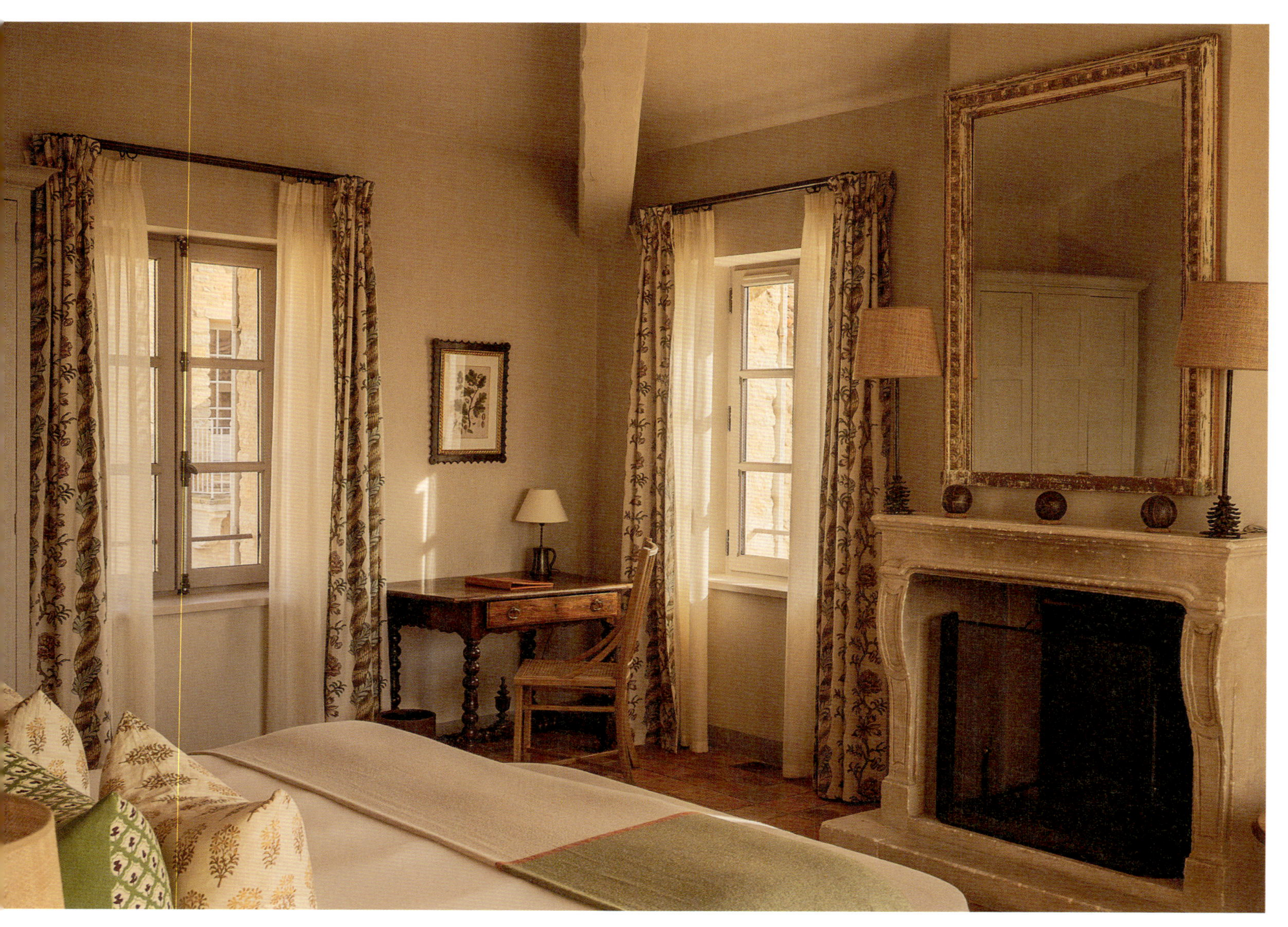

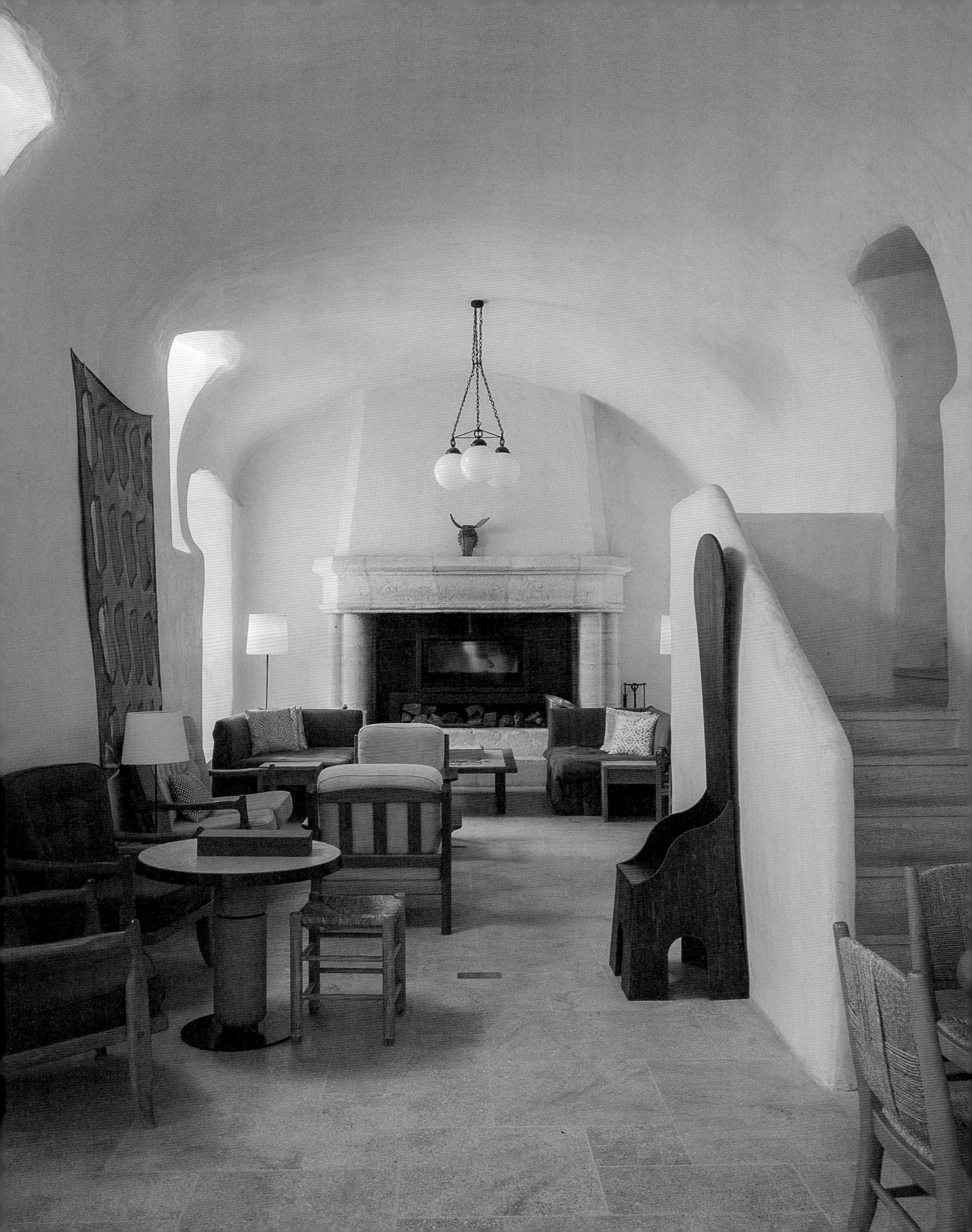

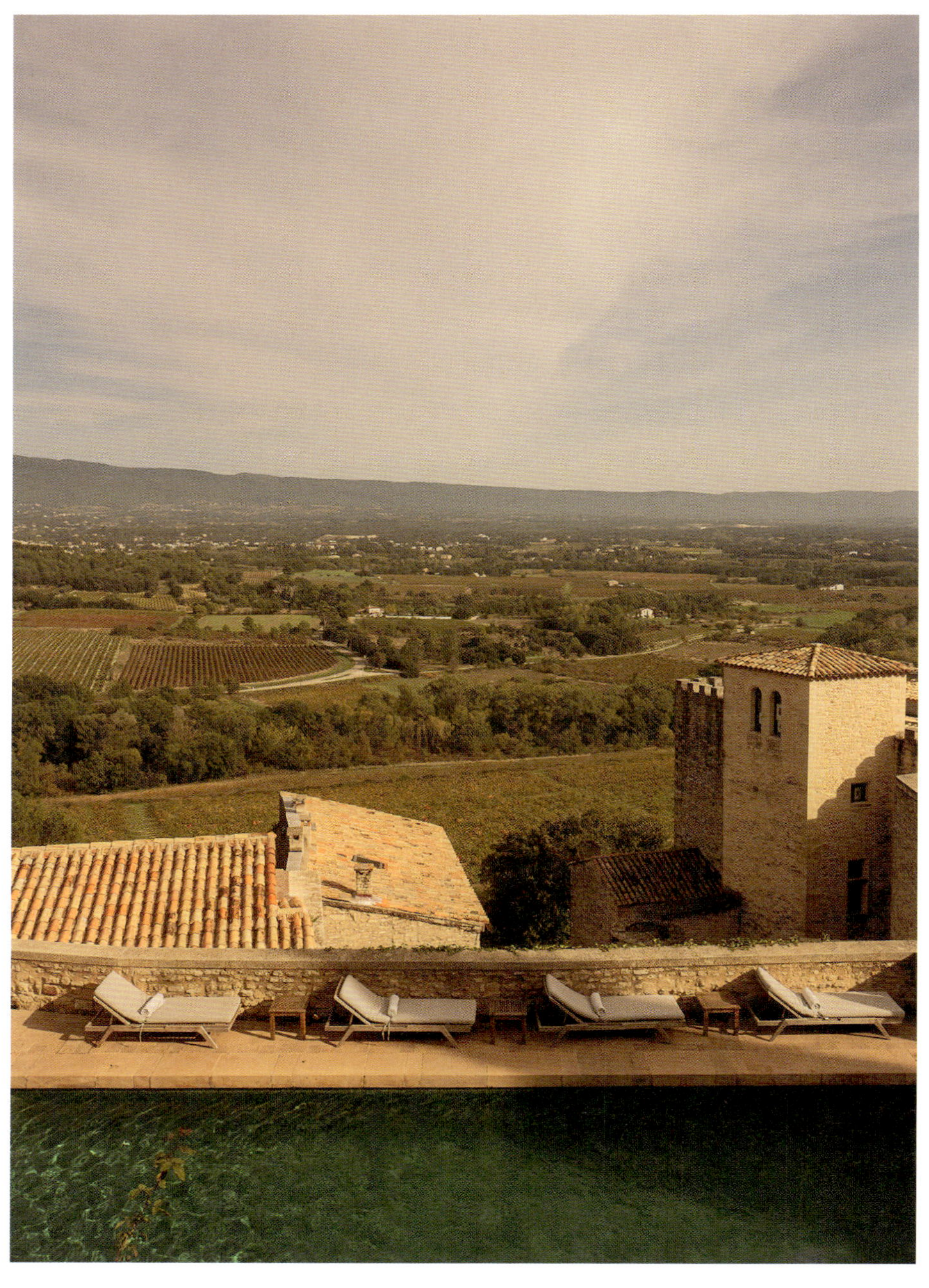

The view from a lounger by the pool at the Crillon le Brave is of the foothills around Mont Ventoux. In early autumn, you'll sometimes see tractors hauling a load of freshly harvested grapes to the nearest winery, or morning mists over the valleys that stubbornly refuse to dissipate as the day goes on.

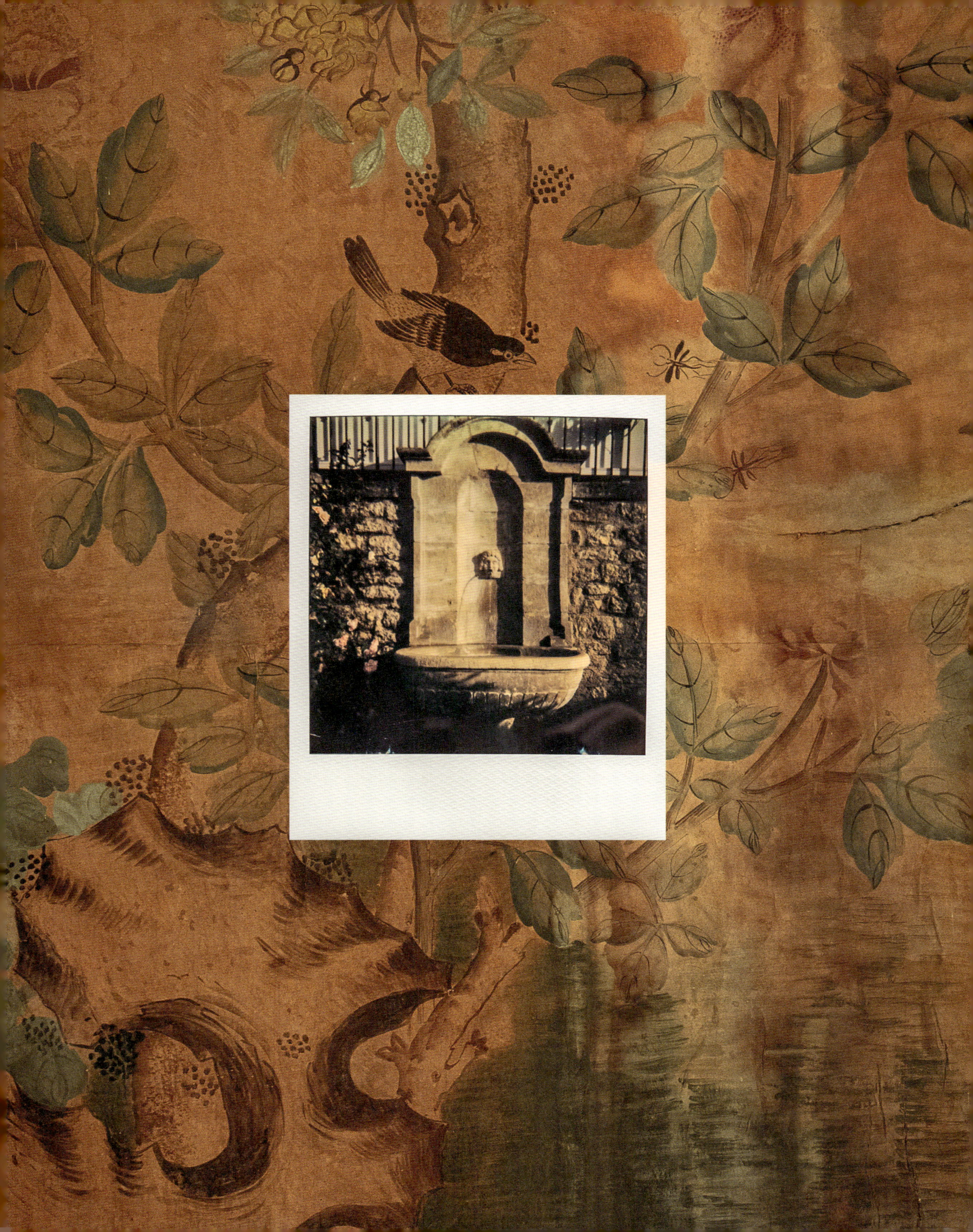

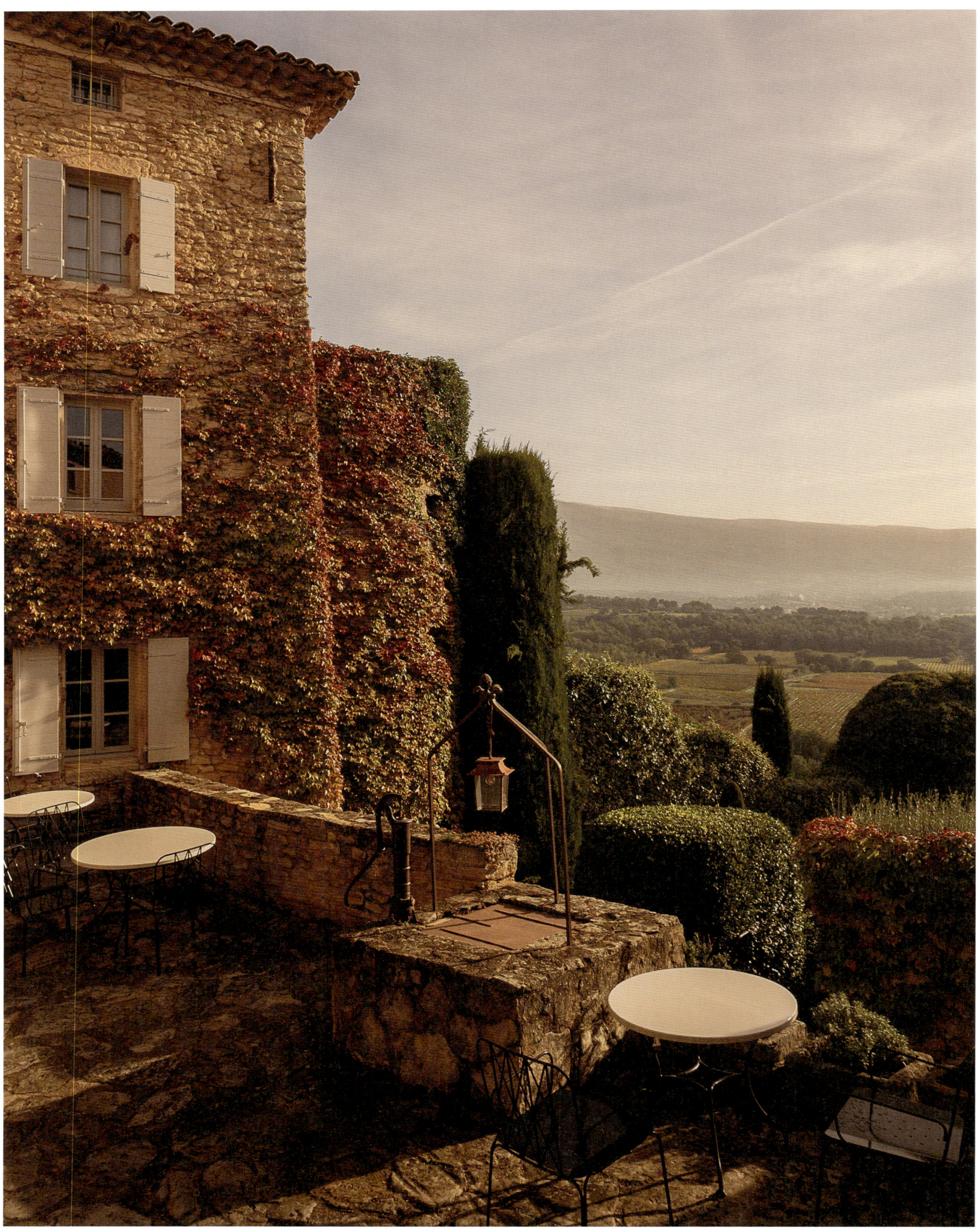

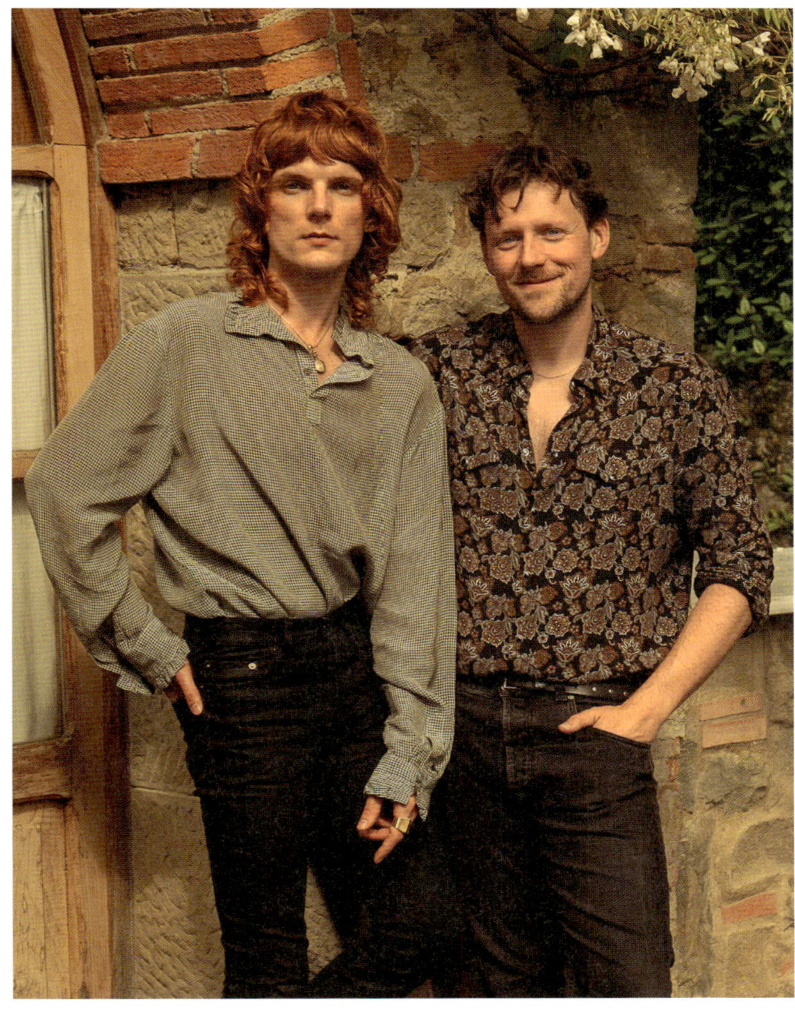

Tim Labenda and Hannes-Vincent Krause are a creative content creator duo based in Berlin. Tim Labenda is a fashion designer who previously ran his eponymous label and served as a consultant for fashion houses like Missoni before turning his focus to interior design and photography. Dr. Hannes-Vincent Krause works as a model, is a full-time psychologist, and is involved in research at a prestigious Berlin-based institute.

Together, they travel the world in search of the extraordinary, unconventional beauty, and hidden craftsmanship. Along the way, they bring their thousands of social media followers along for the journey, offering insights into their eclectic lives.

This book would still be nothing more than a figment of our imagination if it were not for our editor Johannes Abdullahi, who from the beginning was the biggest supporter of our concept and who shepherded us through the many phases, some of them quite daunting to us. We thank you from the bottom of our hearts. We would also like to thank Marcus Taeschner, who clothed our book in beautiful visual garb just as we had imagined, as well as our dear friend and favorite artist, Joseph Dupré, for such wonderful illustrations of our Tour. We also thank Sabine and Dieter Krause for their tireless support and for watching our poodle the whole time. Special thanks to Polestar for letting us borrow the Polestar II, which showed us how easily doable an all-electric road trip is—even a long one. Last but not least, there could not have been a Grand Tour at all if we hadn't had access to all the amazing places we've shown you in this book; thus we thank all those responsible, in particular the staff at all the hotels, restaurants and businesses, for your willingness to open your doors and receive us with open arms.

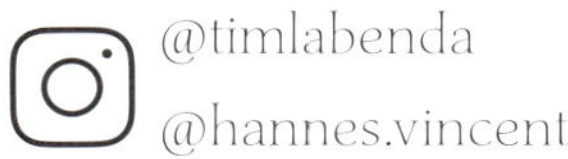

@timlabenda
@hannes.vincent

GRAND TOUR PROVENCE: THE RENAISSANCE
OF REFINED TRAVEL
TIM LABENDA / HANNES-VINCENT KRAUSE

This book was conceived, edited, and designed
by teNeues.
Edited by teNeues.

Photos by Tim Labenda
Texts by Hannes-Vincent Krause
Illustrations and Map by Joseph Dupré

Edited by Anne Paulsen
Translation by John Augustus Foulks

Editorial Management Benine Mayer,
Dr. Johannes Abdullahi, teNeues
Design by Marcus Taeschner
Layout by Marcus Taeschner
Proofread Susen Truffel-Reiff
Photo Editorial by Robert Kuhlendahl, teNeues
Production by Alwine Krebber, teNeues

Printed in Czech Republic by Finidr
Made in Europe

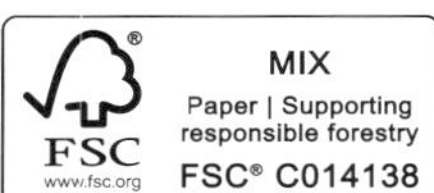

Published by gestalten, Berlin 2025
ISBN 978-3-96171-661-6

1st printing, 2025

The German edition is available under
ISBN 978-3-96171-662-3.

For more information, and to order books, please visit
www.teneues.com and www.gestalten.com

Die Gestalten Verlag GmbH & Co. KG
Mariannenstrasse 9–10
10999 Berlin, Germany
hello@gestalten.com

Düsseldorf Office
Waldenburger Straße 13
41564 Kaarst, Germany
verlag@teneues.com

teNeues Press Department
press@gestalten.com

Bibliographic information published by the Deutsche Nationalbibliothek. The Deutsche Nationalbibliothek lists this publication in the Deutsche Nationalbibliografie; detailed bibliographic data is available online at www.dnb.de

https://instagram.com/teneuespublishing

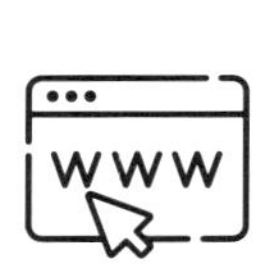

www.teneues.com

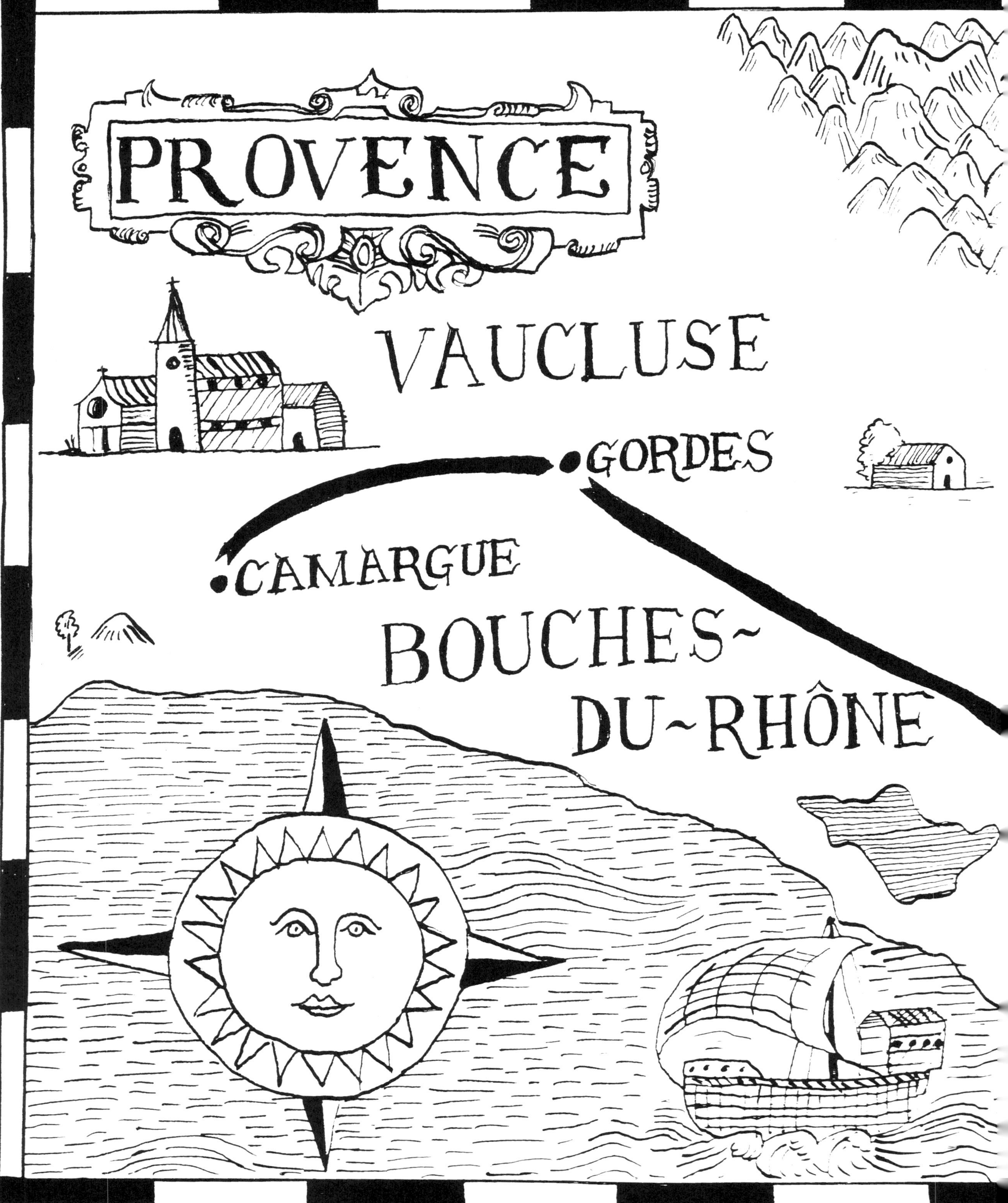
PROVENCE
VAUCLUSE
GORDES
CAMARGUE
BOUCHES-
DU-RHÔNE